The Strangled Traveler

The
Strangled

MARTINE VAN WOERKENS

Translated by Catherine Tihanyi

Traveler

COLONIAL IMAGININGS AND THE THUGS OF INDIA

The University of Chicago Press
Chicago and London

Originally published as *Le voyageur étranglé: L'Inde des Thugs, le colonialisme et l'imaginaire* © Éditions Albin Michel S.A., 1995.

Martine van Woerkens, an anthropologist and Indologist, is a researcher at the École Pratique des Hautes Études (EPHE), Sciences religieuses, La Sorbonne, Paris. She is the author of numerous articles on the status of women in India, on Indian cinema, and on colonial literature and anthropology. Catherine Tihanyi, an anthropologist and translator, is a research associate in the Department of Anthropology at Western Washington University. Among the books she has translated are Claude Lévi-Strauss's *The Story of Lynx* (1995) and Adam Biro's *Two Jews on a Train* (2001), both published by the University of Chicago Press.

The University of Chicago Press, Chicago 60637
The University of Chicago Press, Ltd., London
© 2002 by The University of Chicago
All rights reserved. Published 2002
Printed in the United States of America
11 10 09 08 07 06 05 04 03 02   1 2 3 4 5

ISBN: 0-226-85085-4 (cloth)
ISBN: 0-226-85086-2 (paper)

The University of Chicago Press gratefully acknowledges a subvention from the government of France, through the French Ministry of Culture, in support of the costs of translating this volume.

Library of Congress Cataloging-in-Publication Data

Woerkens, Martine van.
    [Voyageur étranglé. English]
    The strangled traveler : colonial imaginings and the Thugs of India / Martine van Woerkens ; translated by Catherine Tihanyi.
        p.   cm.
    Includes bibliographical references and index.
    ISBN 0-226-85085-4 (cloth : alk. paper)—ISBN 0-226-85086-2 (pkb. : alk. paper)
    1. Thugs.   I. Tihanyi, Catherine.   II. Title.

    DS422 .W6413 2002
    915.4—dc21
                                                                        2002007633

To Soifran, Risbo, and Véêr

Contents

CONTENTS

Illustrations

ILLUSTRATIONS

Following page 200:

Drawing of Shiva, the ascetic god, trampled by the goddess Kali

Drawing of Thugs strangling a traveler on horseback

Drawing of Thugs piercing dead travelers

Drawing of Thugs gouging out the eyes and piercing the bodies of dead travelers

Drawing of travelers' corpses being loaded up before burial

Drawing of murder technique used by the Thugs

Drawing of Thugs dismembering murdered travelers

Drawing of Thugs kneeling in a circle and performing the *kote* ceremony

Translator's Acknowledgments

There are numerous differences between this translated edition and the original French book as the author has made many changes, omitting some passages and rewriting a number of others.

I would like to express my heartfelt thanks to Martine van Woerkens for working closely with me on this translation, so generously answering my numerous questions, and engaging in an intellectual exchange that has opened my mind to new areas of knowledge. I thank T. David Brent for having entrusted me with this translation and for his kind encouragements, as well as Lee Siegel, the peer reviewer of this book for the University of Chicago Press, for his helpful suggestions. My thanks go also to Leslie Keros for so ably producing this book, and to Meg Cox for her outstanding copyediting.

Acknowledgments

This research was first made possible thanks to the Centre d'Études de l'Inde (Paris), which funded my first research trip to Delhi in 1989, and the École Pratique des Hautes Études, Section des Sciences Religieuses (Paris), which funded other research trips to Delhi and London. I greatly thank Marie-Louise Reiniche, professor at the École Pratique, and my friends and colleagues who have generously encouraged and helped me. My heartfelt gratitude goes as well to the librarians of the Indian National Archive (Delhi) and the Indian Office Library (London). I also wish to express my gratitude to Raymond Doktor, professor at the Ranade Institute (Pune); Jean-Luc Chambard, professor at INALCO (Paris); Catherine Clémentin-Ojha, researcher at the École Française d'Extreme-Orient; Jacques Pouchepadass, researcher at the CNRS; Alexis Tadié, professor at Paris X; Solange Thierry, professor at the École Pratique des Hautes Études; and Tzvetan Todorov, researcher at the CNRS. Their critiques helped me to clarify and deepen some of the aspects of my work. Finally, I thank my two *frères*, Lee Siegel and David Brent, for their confidence in me; and Catherine Tihanyi, who turned this translation into an intellectual experience that was collaborative, friendly, and exciting.

Note on Transcription

Most of the time I have kept the nineteenth-century English spellings of Indian words in the quotations. Place names (such as Jabalpur, Narmada, and so on) and important recurring words (such as *jamadar, zamindar,* and so on) have been written in their present-day spellings without the addition of any diacritical marks. I have kept Sleeman's spelling for certain words (such as *Ramasee, Thuggee,* and so on) so as to preserve their "colonial flavor." Retroflex and cerebral *s* and *c* have been transcribed as *sh* and *ch*.

Map of India drawn in 1832, when William Sleeman and Meadows Taylor were fighting against the Thugs. From Hugh Murray et al., *Historical and Descriptive Account of British India*, vol. 1 (Edinburgh: Oliver and Boyd, 1832).

Introduction

Three brothers come across a man who has lost a camel. They describe the animal without hesitation, this solely from clues of tufts of hair, broken twigs, lingering smells, footprints left in the mud. "It is white and blind," they say, "it carries two leather pouches on its back, one filled with wine, the other with oil." So they have seen it? No they haven't, yet the man accuses them of stealing it. But in the blink of an eye, they show how they were able to reconstruct the camel's appearance from insignificant clues even though they never laid eyes on it (Ginzburg 1989, 148).

According to the historian Carlo Ginzburg, this "oriental" fable is illustrative of a certain type of knowledge that came to flourish at the end of the nineteenth century. Just as the three brothers of the story had done, Morelli, Freud, and Conan Doyle based their investigations on undervalued traits so as to uncover secret and hidden things. The pages that follow also belong to this realm as their object partakes of both the oriental fable and the police investigation. I have made much use of a method of interpretation drawing from traces and clues. The action takes place in India; it seems incredible. The characters—judges and accused—follow this method. They reach their aim only by making use of discarded bits of information, a residue that is imperceptible to most people.

THE DISCOVERY OF THE THUGS

This is the case: on 3 October 1830, the readers of the *Calcutta Literary Gazette* discovered an amazing text in their magazine. It revealed that in India there were devotees who partook in a horrible cult of the goddess Kali, this under the benevolent gaze of the priests of the temple dedicated to her. Having come as pilgrims, these monstrous men regularly

1

offered their Goddess the fruits of the most reprehensible acts known to humankind: they murdered innocent travelers and then stole all of their belongings. They then set down a portion of this revolting haul at the feet of their Goddess. It was said that the priests promised a glorious future to these abominable pilgrims, these murderers oozing with devotion. Far from acting in an isolated manner, they depended on a powerful organization that prescribed their conduct. Already thousands of victims had died at their hands. This is how the author, who wished to remain anonymous, presented the facts:

> Kali's temple at Vindhyachal, a few miles west of Mirzapur on the Ganges, is constantly filled with murderers from every quarter of India who go there to offer up in person a share of the booty they have acquired from their victims strangled in their annual excursions. . . . The priests of this temple know perfectly well the source from which they derive their offerings and the motives from which they are made . . . and they promise the murderers in the name of their mistress immunity and wealth, provided a due share be offered up to their shrine, and none of the rites and ceremonies be neglected. . . . To pull down Kali's temple at Bindachul and hang their priests would no doubt be the wish of every honest Christian, but it would answer no useful purpose. Others would soon be found to answer the same purpose. . . . It is an organized system of religious and civil polity prepared to receive converts from all religions and sects and to urge them to the murder of their fellow creatures under the assurance of high rewards in this world and the other. . . . It is the imperious duty of the Supreme Government of this country to put an end in some way or other to this dreadful system of murder, by which thousands of human beings are now annually sacrificed upon every great road throughout India.

The article warned of a danger that was all the more concrete because it wasn't limited to distant and inaccessible areas of the country. The Thugs, it claimed, were camping undisturbed at the door of the British.

> In the territories of the native chiefs of Bundelkhand, as of Scindia and Holkar, a Thug feels just as independent and free as an Englishman in his tavern and will probably begin to feel themselves so in those of Nagpur now that European superintendency has been withdrawn. *But they are not confined to the territories of these native chiefs;* they are becoming numerous in our own. And, as hares are often found to choose their burrows in the immediate vicinity of the kennels, so may these men be found often most securely established in the very seats of our principal judicial establishments.[1]

This anonymous letter aroused "universal notice."[2] The government was called upon to act and ran the risk of being suspected of complicity if it did not. So it committed itself to take necessary measures. George Swinton, secretary to the Governor General of India, asked the magistrate Curven Smith to immediately recommend a detailed plan of action. He also entrusted him with the task of reassuring the secret author "who appears to possess extensive knowledge of the character and habits of the Thugs" (Bruce 1968, 84). The official campaign to eradicate the Thugs was launched the day following the publication of this anonymous letter. Up to that time, the assassins had only been pursued intermittently, with enormous difficulties and without any lasting results. Curven Smith brought this up in his report of 1832:

> In 1812 or 1813, the Government deputed that active and intelligent officer Mr. N. I. Halhead to attack their headquarters in the *pargana*[3] of Sindhouse which being situated on the right bank of the Jumna opposite to Etawah and consisting entirely of ravines and inaccessible fastnesses formed a suitable . . . retreat to the gangs to leave their families during their periodical expeditions. . . . The extent to which they carried their depredations may be appreciated by a perusal of Sayeed Ameer Alee's narrative transmitted to the Government on the 29th May 1832. He was present at 150 cases of murder wherein 719 people were killed and robbed of 67,000 Rs in hard cash and property estimated at 150,000 Rs. . . . That officer carried fire and sword into this small *pargana* and entirely drove away its predatory inhabitants. . . . It is to me extremely doubtful whether by this dispersion of the Thug headquarters we performed any real benefit to India. . . . The Nepaul, the Pindaree and the Mahratta wars of 1814, 1815, 1816 and 1817 ensued immediately after their dispersion into foreign lands and these formidable gangs, the more formidable from the secrecy of their acts, and the general ignorance almost of their existence by the public at large, gradually recovered strength.[4]

Not only did the Thugs come out stronger from their trials, but they couldn't be caught. Everyone insisted on this point. They left no clue after having committed their crimes. Thus it was always impossible to prove their guilt. And very often skeptical judges even let them go without any trial. On several occasions it was thought they had been eliminated. Warren Hastings,[5] the first governor of India at the end of the eighteenth century, let himself be fooled. In his report on the administration of the government, he evoked a "particular class denominated Thugs" and stated, "There is reason to believe that by this time the pest in question has been rooted out" (cited in Sleeman 1836, 18–19). In 1810, some *cipayes*—native soldiers—never came back from visiting their families while on leave. British authorities again became concerned. Major General Saint Leger wrote a pamphlet in which he warned his soldiers of the Thugs' "atrocious deeds" and advised them "to be strictly on their guard against all persons whom they fall in on the road . . . not to receive *pawn*,[6] tobacco, sweetmeats, etc. from such persons . . . and travel as much as possible with large bodies of people" (cited in Sleeman 1836, 15–16). The first arrests and sentences occurred only much later: Captain Wardlow in 1826 and the judge Boyd in 1828 experienced some successes. The first major blow to the Thugs occurred in 1829: Major Borthwick captured seventy-eight of them in Bundelkhand; thirty-nine were condemned to death by Colonel Steward, resident in charge of Indore.

But this terrifying information only circulated in the restricted circles of the upper echelons of the administration, and until the end of 1829 "the only modes adopted to check their audacity were of a local and precautionary nature."[7] The government, which had been aware for some time of the existence of the assassins, had lacked the resolve to take "general and comprehensive measures, which alone could have broken up a confederacy so extensive and of such a long standing"[8] Curven Smith's critique of the government appeared to share the somewhat naive attitude of the anonymous author of the letter about the Thugs. During the preceding decades his government had been busy taking over the subcontinent, and the Thugs were not at the forefront of its concerns. So we can well understand why there was barely a ripple in public opinion in 1812 when a certain Doctor Sherwood published in the fortieth issue of another literary gazette, this one at Madras, a long article titled: "Of the Murderers called Phansigars." And yet the Phansigars described by Sherwood were in the south of India, while the Thugs, described by the unknown author, were in the north. These professional murderers used the same horrific manner to strangle travelers with a noose called *phansi* in the south and *roomal* in the north; they always assassinated their victims when robbing them, they hid their corpses after dismembering them and cutting them open to speed up decomposition, and they insured the complicity of local chiefs (called *polygar*[9] in the south and *zamindar* in the north) by sharing their loot with them. They appeared to be peacefully settled in villages with their families, they pretended to be involved with agriculture to hide their true activity, they spoke a secret language, and so on (Bruce 1968, 13–26).

The anonymous letter was thus a revelation neither to the members of the government nor to ordinary Britishers, as they had already been informed in various ways; and yet, it did have an impact. Fourteen years separated it from Sherwood's article: the tumult of battlefields had died down, public attitude had changed.

There was yet another reason for this change. Both the tone and the content of the famous letter were different from those of the earlier article. There was a greater amount of information; it was more specific and the images were more gripping. Even though it was generally held that Thugs never killed Europeans, they were known to have been "for centuries living and exercising their horrid avocation in every part of India from the Sutledge to Cape Comorin."[10] But mostly it threw a new light on the motives for their crimes. The Phansigars' "superstitions" only held a minimal place in Sherwood's exposé. In contrast, in 1830, in the *Calcutta Gazette*, they were unalterably part of the murders. Symbolic practices and murdering practices coincided; they mutually explained and justified each other. According to the author, the link between the assassins and their Goddess was much deeper, more intense, and more compromising:

> There is not among them one who doubts the divine origin of the system of Thuggee —not one who doubts that he and all who have followed the trade of murder with the prescribed rites and observances were acting under the immediate orders and auspices of the goddess Devee, Durga, Kalee or Bhawanee, as she is indifferently called. (Sleeman 1836, 7–8)

We can better grasp the subtlety of the difference between the two observers' viewpoints if we think of the Latin differentiation between two meanings of the sacred. One of these meanings is that of *sanctum* and designates that which is submitted to divine approval, while the other, *sacer*, designates that which is devoted to the gods. The Phansigars, like the Thugs, put their crimes under the protection of the Goddess and, according to Sherwood, this was the sole extent of her role. But for the later mysterious author, the Goddess's impact was present all the way to the moment when the assassins dispatched their victims from the world of the living, when the strangler consecrated the victim and rendered him or her holy.[11] As Sleeman explained: "A Thug considers the persons murdered precisely in the light of victims offered up to the Goddess; and he remembers them, as a Priest of Jupiter remembered the oxen, and a Priest of Saturn the children sacrificed upon their altars" (Sleeman 1836, 7–8).

This paradigm of religious murder that provoked panic in colonial society also linked the Thugs to the barbarian spectacles of India. Every British colonizer had heard about them, had read descriptions of them, had contemplated representations of them in drawings or watercolor paintings, had even at times witnessed them in person. Here, devotees swirled in the air as their bodies hung on hooks (see, for instance, Oddie 1986). There, hysterical devotees threw themselves under the wheels of the god Jagannath's chariot during the great festival at the temple at Puri. And then, as described by a disgusted commentator, there was the spectacle of dying on the shores of the Ganges with death helped along by-well intentioned relatives:

> They are performing the last fatal rite. It consists in pouring a large quantity of water down his throat; filling his mouth and nostrils with mud; repeating the names of the gods, and shouting: "O Mother Ganges, receive his soul!" . . . The sick, instead of receiving medical treatment, kind nursing, and appropriate nourishment, are, in many cases, hurried away to the Ganges, to be purified from their sins, by dying on its banks or in its waters. (Wright 1854, 94)

In the name of the awesome Goddess, devotees threw themselves from cliffs in Birkhala, or they went to have their heads chopped off in the famous temple in the region of Goalpara, in Assam;[12] women, at times so young as to be still children, threw themselves onto their husbands' funerary pyres so as to die next to them.[13] Renouard de Sainte Croix witnessed a *sati* in 1804:

> At the moment she threw herself into the fire, the assistants let out terrifying yells and the musicians heightened their noises . . . to prevent the victim's cries from being heard. When she was reduced to ashes, the people present went to pay their respects to the fire and each brought away a piece of coal to preserve as relic. (Deleury 1991, 646)

Everywhere the Hindu gods, and particularly the Goddess in her terrible form, fed on human death. Far from revolting against these abominable ordeals and horrific deaths, people transformed the victims into objects of piety. Among this panoply of revolting cruelties, the Thugs were seen as the most horrible because their sacrificial folly was aimed at other people's lives. The Goddess's assassins were not like those unfortunate devotees who gave their own selves as offering and whom the British authorities were to soon try to save from their fate. Instead, they were the Goddess's soldiers, her army, her purveyors of death.

The author of this new viewpoint was to finally allow his friend Curven Smith to reveal his identity: he turned out to be the man whose name, whose life itself, was to remain the most closely linked with the Thugs. He was William Sleeman, and as he was noted for possessing such a "profound" knowledge of the character and mores of the Thugs, he was thus put in charge of their eradication. But contrary to the three brothers of the tale, the presumed assassins were not able to prove their innocence. Their judges triumphed as trials and executions multiplied.

HISTORIANS AND THUGS

This strange sect, this caste, this fraternity, according to the confused terminology of the time, is even more mysterious than it appears. Anyone interested in it is stymied by an unexpected obstacle. The only sources available are the texts written by William Sleeman himself and by his collaborators in their struggle against the Thugs. The imperial lion trampled on the traces left by the camel! Seemingly, no document in the vernacular enables us to confirm, invalidate, or balance the colonizers' accounts. So what of this improbable horde of sacrificers pitched against humankind? Could these merciless trials, those horrifying descriptions be explained not by their real existence but by the no less real needs of the British themselves? Were the Thugs an invention of the colonizers?

According to some historians, Thuggism (the name given to the phenomenon) is a myth invented by the British in order to extend their control over a mobile population, or to seize criminal jurisdiction in areas that had until then been in the hands of the Moghul rulers, and so forth. Colonialist historians such as George Bruce and Sir Francis Tuker propounded the opposite stance. For them, the facts conformed with the rumor: India is a land that shelters the most revolting beliefs, the Thugs were the enemies of humankind, and the English accomplished a civilizing mission by exterminating them.

According to others, official history is not a dogma and colonial sources cannot be reduced to a toxic project. During the last four decades of the twentieth century, historians have read these sources critically and restored one of the best known affairs of the beginning of last century to its various contexts.

Stewart Gordon (1969) analyzes indigenous political conditions in northern India at the end of the eighteenth century and explains the extent to which the legitimacy of power was based on violence. According to him, paralleling the way the colonizers constructed other concepts, *Thug* was the appropriation of an Indian word to give a meaning to a badly understood social institution. He refers here to roving bands on the prowl that at the time were systematically helping ruling rajahs as well as those that were harboring the ambition to create their own kingdoms. Jacques Pouchepadass (1979) looks at the Thugs from a sociological viewpoint. He places them into the context of the colonial process of criminalization of certain groups that led, by the end of the century, to a discriminatory category of "criminal castes and tribes". To the colonizers' judgment of exclusion, he contrasts the inclusive, holistic character of Indian society, which absorbs the norms of these deviant groups and does give them a place, albeit one at the bottom of the social hierarchy. A viewpoint close to the preceding ones is that of Sandria B. Freitag who shows that the British used the concept of "criminal castes and tribes" because their own notion of authority encompassed at once governmental power and moral influence. For the British, "collective criminal acts were perceived to be either directed against, or resulted in the weakening of, the authority of the State" (Freitag 1985, 142). Finally, Radhika Singha (1993, 1998) is particularly concerned with the "despotism of law," that is, the establishment by the British of criminal laws inspired by the discovery of the existence of the Thugs, and then by the "discovery" of other groups and communities alleged to be criminal. Through politics, sociology, and ideology, all four of these authors place Thuggism into an all encompassing framework that includes both Indian and colonial societies. They show that the powerful colonizers' distorting perceptions were at once the causes and the effects of the success of the strategies they imposed on the colonized.

THE "STRANGLED TRAVELER"

None of these works really explain what the word *Thug* stands for. Already inhabiting the boundaries between myth and reality, the word is made even more opaque by creators of fiction who took hold of the colonial rumor from its inception and have not let go of it since. *Indiana Jones and the Temple of Doom* (1984) triumphantly reminds the West of the assassins' terrifying existence. Spielberg's vision, like that of his peers, thickens the mystery of the Thugs even while pretending to resolve it.

In spite of historians' prudence and the certitudes of popular fiction, the question remains: who were the Thugs? And through them, what were the fluctuations, what were the depths of this meeting between East and West?

I have chosen to answer in two ways. The first focuses on a specific target. The Thugs had a secret language—in fact, a lexicon of six hundred words, thought to be of unknown origin at the time, along with translations and glosses. These words were the object of the greatest of suspicions prior to being studied. Now that their etymologies have been partially uncovered, they inscribe the Thugs into a concrete reality, one that is dense and convincing as the words complete and confirm what the documents revealed before, during, and after the colonial era. The mystery of the Thugs is not completely elucidated, but this ensemble of materials makes it possible to look at them from a new perspective that allows us to make out a history and a coherence different from those we have known.

In contrast, the second way I respond to this question is extensive. I am hypothesizing that the Thug phenomenon lies in the totality of the places, of the roads traveled by the assassins in the past and the present. It lies also in the facts of history that called for their extermination, in the conceptual imaginings underlying their "tradition" internally to their own society as well as in that of their observers within colonial society. And finally, it lies in imaginings bringing them back to life in fictional works that use them to assign antagonistic positions to East and West.

This extensive approach has led me to organize the present inquiry into two parts. The first brings together data from observation, the second analyzes discourses. They form a whole: conflicts between all sorts of criminals with the British, the campaign waged against the assassins, the assassins' murdering activities and sociological and religious identities—all these were constructed and reverberated at the level of the colonial state and its representatives. By claiming to accomplish a civilizing mission, the colonial state defined its right to monopolize legitimate physical violence through its laws. Its representatives adhered to this dominant ideology. They organized prosecutions and trials, they condemned the Thugs by inscribing their exceptional experience and knowledge into a discourse determined not only by truth, but by career and glory, by social relations and the desire for power.

Perusal of two different types of literature was required in order to construct these two parts and establish their specificity and their linkages. The first includes studies in Indian anthropology and local history, along with texts in Sanskrit as well as from the popular tradition, including epics, sacred texts, and tales. Along the way, I explain certain Indian notions, the caste system among others, that are indispensable to my purpose. I also draw from the histories of law, anthropology, ideologies, and the nineteenth-century imagination in order to analyze the framework of intellectual references and the practices of colonial society. The magnitude of the material led me to focus on exemplary individual cases. Thus rather than discussing all the Thug trials, I cover two of them during the year when their repression was at its harshest and the gap between the individual rights officially propounded by the state and their disregard under the guise of exceptional judicial processes was particularly striking. I focus not so much on the colonizers as on the rational William Sleeman and the romantic Meadows Taylor, whose writings, *Ramaseeana* and *The Confessions of a Thug*, respectively, placed the assassins into two contiguous but distinct niches that corresponded to nascent Western modes of exploration and sensitivity. We can follow the development of these modes through the figure of the idolatrous assassins.

The fable of the three brothers was taken up by Voltaire in *Zadig*, and in the twentieth century the philosopher Huxley called their method "Zadig's method." The Thugs too have traveled two parallel roads: one is that of the human sciences, opened by Sleeman and on which my own inquiry is located as well; the other is that of the imaginary in which, by way of conclusion, I analyze fictional writings and films. I thus give an account of the Thug phenomenon in its multiple dimensions, first between myth and reality, then between science and the imaginary.

Part I
British India

and Crime

THE THUGS BETWEEN MYTH AND REALITY

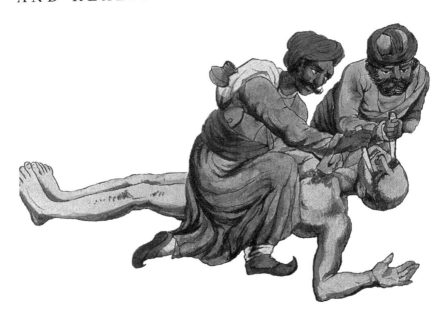

ONE

Colonizers and Bandits

In the eyes of William Sleeman, Curven Smith, James Hutton and others, the Thugs were the only criminals worthy of interest. And yet, in the course of the several decades surrounding the Thug extermination campaign, the British fought against all sorts of "bandits" who were no less threatening. There were rebellious mountain people; peasants held up in forts; recalcitrant tribal people; marauding caravanners; roving bands of mercenaries; and armed, ash-covered, naked ascetics wandering the highways. Altogether they exhibited a varied and large assortment of worrisome behaviors, and it proved difficult to distinguish between rebellion and crime, rightful cause and entrenched malevolence. Their patterns of behavior were perceived as forms of resistance and as provoking disorder that threatened the colonizers' authority and interests, and they were generally criminalized and even demonized. And yet the colonizers' discourse was more stereotyped than the various strategies they directed against this broad spectrum of behaviors they perceived as threatening.

In order to understand these various criminal behaviors and the ways they were treated and perceived by the British, I first need to discuss India's political situation during the period of conquest and focus on one of its most interesting aspects: the alliance between kings and robbers.

A BIT OF CONTEXT

To Conquer

Colonial ideology took on a particularly offensive hue in India, linked as it was to the idea that the English were the heirs and builders of a new Christian Roman Empire. Using this historical precedent as justification,

Governor General Wellesley claimed the right to conquest and took on the mission of giving back to peoples their civil and religious rights. In the course of his tenure (1798–1805) the British colony, though still threatened by the ambition of major native chiefs, took on the dimensions of an empire. The kingdoms of Mysore (1799), Benares, and Arcot (1800); large parts of the kingdom of Awadh (1801–1802); and the holdings of the Scindia and Bhonsla families were taken over. In 1818, British rule became hegemonic under the leadership of Hastings, who after having repelled the Gurkhas to the north (an expedition in which William Sleeman took part) defeated the Maratha confederation and dispersed the Pindaris in central India. England had seized almost the whole of the subcontinent. It could now impose itself as its dominant state.

This was evidenced a few decades later in a letter dated 1832, in which Governor General Bentinck gave instructions for the military defense of the colony. He stated the principle of British superiority, and aggressively advised his readers to keep in mind, along an implacable downward regression:

> 1st. That the whole of India from the Himalayas to Cape Comorin acknowledges the British supremacy.
>
> 2nd. That within these limits there is not a native prince capable of making the least resistance to the British power.
>
> 3rd. That the Madras Presidency has no frontiers to defend.
>
> 4th. That the Bombay Presidency is similarly circumstanced with the exception of that part of its territory which borders upon Sind. . . .
>
> 5th. That the Bengal Presidency alone has an assailable frontier.
>
> 6th. Considering the whole of India as one British kingdom, and the armies of the three presidencies as one army, it is necessary to know the amount of force that may be required for the mere preservation of order.[1]

From the beginning of their stay in India, William Sleeman, Meadows Taylor, and the sahibs[2] as a whole were the propagators and defenders of the directive to "simply" preserve this order. Along external boundaries as well as internal ones in the annexed territories, in the territories under treaties, and in those not belonging to any of these categories, the situation didn't match the resolutely optimistic one described by the governor general. Even though around the years 1830 English hegemony had become on the whole a reality, or at least a process well on its way, there still were loci of resistance and protest needing to be put down and criminal enterprises needing to be thwarted, at times at the point of the sword, at times through persuasion, or again through political action and law. This was only the tip of a very secular wave in the course of which the colonizers were to attempt, albeit with difficulty, to impose on the colonized their own political, economic, and social norms. As Sir John Malcolm noted in the conclusion of his book *A Memoir of Central India*, the conquest was the easy part in comparison with what remained to be accomplished: the preservation of the newly acquired empire (Malcolm 1972).[3]

Moghul Society
EVERYONE IS KING OF THE WORLD

From the end of the seventeenth century to the beginning of the eighteenth, Moghul society underwent a process of enrichment and profound change. A new, powerful class of merchants, bankers, moneylenders, large landowners, and scholars became increasingly autonomous from the emperor's central power (Bayly 1983, 1990 a and b). The high-ranking officers, the *mansabdar* who traditionally raised troops for the emperor and received lands, *jagir*, in exchange, gradually ceased to pay him tribute and retired to their domains. Thus between 1720 and 1750, the Muslim chiefs of Awadh, Hyderabad, and Bengal took over fiscal, military, and judicial powers; transformed the positions they receive from the emperor into hereditary ones; became patrons; and distributed honors and riches to the great landowners, the *zamindars*, and to their Hindu and Muslim partisans and clients, who played the role of intermediaries between them and the peasant masses. But the same process was repeated by these unruly big landowners: with their own networks of partisans and clients, they too tended to become independent. While the British conceived of themselves as a nation by drawing on the symbols of monarchy, in India everybody wanted to be king of the world.[4]

The map of India in the mid-eighteenth century is illuminating in this regard. The loci of power were proliferating. There were Muslim provincial kingdoms: Awadh, Hyderabad, Bengal. There were Afghan kingdoms: Rohilkhand near Delhi, the principalities of Bhopal and Mandu in central India, those of Gingi and Nellore in the south. There were also non-Muslim warrior kingdoms of the Sikhs in the Punjab and the Jats around Delhi, and finally the immense "Brahman" Hindu kingdom of the Marathas in the west, within which the great warrior chiefs, Sindhia, Holkar, Bhonsla and Gaekwar had carved their own kingdoms. There were also, from the shore of the Gujarat all the way to Awadh, a myriad of small Rajput kingdoms that had come into being in the eighteenth century thanks to the migration of "shifting bands of professional soldiers who attracted followers by marrying women from lower castes Hindu or even Muslim families" (Bayly 1990a, 23). And finally, there were the European trading posts, among which were those of the Honorable Company, settled in Madras, Bombay, and then Calcutta.

COU[

Drawing of the Moghul court. The original caption read, "There is basically only one master in Hindustan. The rest of the inhabitants are more slaves than sub-

jects." From M. De La Harpe, *Abrégé de l'Histoire générale des Voyages*, vol. 5 (Paris: Hôtel de Thou, rue des Poitevins, 1780).

One of the characteristics of all these loci of power is that they reproduced, each according to its means and ambition, the main figures at the center. As Shulman (1981) has noted, each monarch was a universal one; each royal court was the assembly of Indra, each altar a Kailasha. "There were many sharers in the dignity and power of kingship with overlapping rights and obligations" (Bayly 1990a, 13). This included the British, major intruders on this eventful map fraught with thorny questions.[5] Like increasingly smaller but identical matrioshka dolls fitting into each other, each of these kingdoms expanded or shrank by fragmenting, thus giving rise to fiefs of various sizes, which in turn generated yet other ones. Within this segmentary configuration, there was enduring allegiance to the emperor Muhammad Shah, whose eldest son succeeded him in 1748. His official recognition of new units was still sought even though his military power was reduced and his real authority had been taken away from him.

THE EXAMPLE OF MALWA

Here is the life itinerary of the two great military chiefs, Mahaji Sindhia and Rao Holkar. They fought for the *peshwa* of Pune, head of the Maratha Brahman kingdom. They enlarged his territory considerably and, even while remaining under his nominal authority, they carved themselves personal kingdoms out of the conquered territories and gave them their own names. This first level of segmentation was not the only one. Toward the end of the eighteenth century there were a number of other entities within and on the peripheries of their kingdoms. "East and West of Chumbul River, below the Marathas stood some fifteen major and many minor Rajput clans. . . . The military contingent might range from under 1000 for a small state like Banwara to 15,000 for Kotah, the largest independent Rajput state close to the Maratha dominions" (Gordon 1969, 421).

The historian Stewart N. Gordon proposes the following scenario to account for this fragmentation. In the course of the eighteenth century, the *peshwa* gave a young military chief the mission of conquering or pacifying a region, for instance the Malwa; the young chief succeeded, and the *peshwa* or his general, Sindhia, rewarded him with portions of the conquered or pacified territories. In order to feed his troops, the young ambitious chief struck a deal with local landowners who collected tax on the land, from which he expected to receive a substantial share. If this couldn't be done, he plundered the uncooperative landowners or raided adjacent territories. In order to acquire maximum gains and political control, he entrusted his men, soldiers and brigands, with this task. After the consolidation of the conquest and the setting up of an infrastructure, theft became a regular and legal tax. The young chief had become Sindhia's confirmed representative.

He kept up his alliance with brigands in order to fend off attackers, add to his income, and commit aggressions against his neighbors. This "plunder dynamics."[6] which appeared to be a preliminary step to the establishment of his independence from states whose ties with the central government had themselves become very loose, was never outgrown; brigandage became institutionalized so as to preserve or expand the power it helped create.

DID YOU SAY "BRIGAND"?

Who were these brigands who were systematically present at the points where power was seized and lost? The answer is not simple because their identity was neither defined nor definitive. The works of the historian Dirk H. A. Kolff on the military employment market of the fifteenth to the nineteenth centuries show that the peasant mass was armed; peasants were able, of course, to defend themselves against animal attacks, but also against military aggression and tax collectors. For instance, around 1650 the Rajputs[7] of the Agra region were represented "as a numerous industrious and brave race. Every village had a small fort. They never pay revenue to the *hakim*[8] without a fight. The peasants who drive the plough keep a musket slung over the neck, and a powder-pouch at the waist" (Habib 1980, cited by Kolff 1990, 6–7). We can thus see that the emperor and his subjects, armed even in their fields, had a shaky relationship. Writing about the "challenge of an armed peasantry," Kolff notes:

> I suggest, in conclusion, that not only the rebellious zamindars of the countryside or the hill rajahs with their pernicious war-bands were jealous rivals of central government in North India. More fundamental to the state was the problem of how to deal with the peasantry at large, how to subject to some manner of control and collect revenue from those almost ungovernable tens of millions of people protected by mud forts, jungles and ravines all over the plains of Hindustan and above all by the weapons they were familiar with. (Kolff 1990, 9)

At any moment, all seemed to feel they could decide to defend themselves against the central government's prerogatives, contract new alliances, become rebels, or simply engage in banditry to survive. This applied to the whole of the population, but more particularly to the peasants who were in the majority. "Often, men were not only familiar with the use of arms, but served as part-time rebels and seasoned soldiers. According to a Dutch observer writing in August 1636, plundering ceased on the roads of Gujarat soon after the onset of the monsoon that year. This was partly because the rains made the peasants devote their time to agriculture again" (Kolff 1990, 16).

In this society, the norm seemed to be to resort to conflict to establish an always precarious equilibrium; the emperor was only the first among his peers, the center was everywhere and nowhere (see Stein 1980; Dirks 1986).

GODS, KINGS, AND THIEVES

The roots of this aberrant "normal" state of affairs went back far in time. The famous treatise on the art of governing, the *Arthashastra*[9] (first century of our era?), viewed politics as an activity submitted solely to its own laws much like Machiavelli did. It noted that kings can use brigands in order to enlarge their territories. There are established rules governing this: one sixth of the goods they loot in a hostile area must be turned over to the sovereign. Tales, ballads, and epics often depicted this alliance which, in addition, often had a sacred aspect. David Shulman (1980) makes a useful survey of this issue in an article titled "On South-Asian Bandits and Kings" (283–306) in which he tells the following temple legend:

There was once a robber called Kaladushaka, who lived with his band in a wild area near a temple. Most of the time, he was spending half of his ill gotten money in gambling and with prostitutes; the other half he gave to the god of the temple. One day, the king was chasing the bandit and the latter found refuge with the god, who took him under his protection. The god disguised himself as a robber and appeared in front of the king. He advised him and scolded him: "things not given as *dharma*[10] will perish; kings seize them and robbers steal them" (Shulman 1980, 285). Then the king forgave Kaladushaka and begged the god to remain in the temple; he was to be thenceforth worshiped under the name Coranatha, Lord of Thieves. Since then, each year king and robber collaborate in decorating the town and in giving magnificent presents, particularly to the Brahmans.

This tale sheds light on the fragile boundaries separating the two characters. There are a host of other narratives showing their relationship to be at once opposite, identical, and complementary (Shulman 1980, 301–2).

The king and the robber are opposite in that the king, at the top of the ladder of power, embodies order, while the robber, at the bottom of this same ladder, embodies disorder.

They are identical because, as the god tells the king in the tale, "Kings and bandits share the use and misuse of power." The king is, of course, in theory and because of his status, on the side of legitimate violence, and his specific duty, his *svadharma*, is inscribed in the general *dharma*, the order of the world; but, as the god points out, the difference between seizing and taking does not rest upon the facts in themselves but on the position one occupies in the world and one's corresponding ethical judgment.

Finally, on the symbolic plane, they are complementary. The robber is at the periphery of the inhabited and cultivated world, while the king is its central axis. One is excluded even while being integrated; the other embodies the whole of the community. The outer limits of their behavior are totally opposite: kings are often tempted by asceticism, the Brahmanic model of renunciation, while "in general the bandit represents the transcendence associated with disorder and impurity. His true home is the dangerous wilderness that threatens to engulf the settled world of city and village but that also imparts vitality to that world" (Shulman 1980, 302); yet, paradoxically, they both find themselves in the same wilderness, the forest or the jungle. The tale resolves the conflict that sets them in opposition by showing the two personages linked in their devotion to the Lord of Thieves. In the eyes of the gods, the distance between the liminal figure of the robber saved by his devotion and the central figure of the king is abolished.

The colonizers find the multiple complicities linking kings and bandits scandalous, but Indian literature has been fascinated by them because they enable reflection on the ambiguous nature of the divine ("If God is a bandit, to rob is divine—especially if one robs in the name or interests of the deity") and of the royal *dharma,* and on the paradox of legitimate violence, of its closeness to criminal violence. But this doesn't mean that robbers and criminals are absolved of their actual actions: it is just that the boundaries separating them from the norm are not as sharp as in the West.

DARK AGE OR GOLDEN AGE?

The Colonizers

Sleeman wrote that there were certain circumstances peculiar to the whole of India that facilitated the Thugs' crimes (Sleeman 1836, iv–v). These included perennial factors such as the state of the roads, the slowness of transport, and the more specific one of the greed fanned by the enormous amount of liquid currency transported from the west coast of Rajasthan as result of the new opium monopoly in Malwa. But he blamed mostly the political and social organization of the subcontinent, which he saw as characterized by the absence of ties between rulers and ruled, and the absence of common interests between individuals not belonging to the same family or clan. He noted that the interests linking kings and robbers straddled this political aberration and social mosaic as their complicity transcended divisions between the categories and boundaries observed elsewhere.

For instance, the Muslim state of Awadh had since 1773 been in a "subsidiary alliance" with the British Company. The trading company collected a part of the taxes for the state and in exchange maintained troops and guaranteed the protection of the state's borders. Like Malwa, where the young, ambitious chief we encountered above has set up camp, this state had the reputation of harboring many Thugs and robbers; however, it was no longer the kings or warlords who hired the services of these criminals, but rather small landowners. In 1849, Sleeman made a three-month journey through this state (called Oude or Oudh at the time), and he wrote an account of it titled *A Journey through the Kingdom of Oude, 1849–1850.* He discussed the "baronial proprietors," the *talukdar,* [11] of the Dundalee district. "Government officers are afraid to measure their lands or to make any inquiries on the estates into their value, lest they should turn robbers and plunder the country, as they are always prepared to. They have always a number of armed and brave retainers to support them in any enterprise." This description could be applied to almost the whole of the kingdom, plunged as it was into a constant state of disorder where "plunder and murder" seemed to be all landowners' favorite pastimes (Sleeman 1858, 2:92–93).

Sleeman reported an exchange between Colonel Low, "then Resident," and Rajah Bukhtawar Singh:

> Low said with a sigh:—In this country of Oudh, what darkness prevails! No one seems to respect the right of another!
> —True Sir, said the Rajah. But do you not see that this is the necessary order of things? . . . Is not your Government going on taking country after country and benefitting all it takes? . . . Sovereigns cannot stand still, Sir; the moment their bellies are full they and the countries they govern retrograde. No Sovereign in India, Sir, that has any regard for himself or his country can with safety sit down and say his belly is full: he must go on to the last. (Sleeman 1858, 2:92–93)

Like many observers of the time, Sleeman interpreted this race for power, this *bhumiavat* as he called it—that is, the desire to possess holdings and enlarge them—as a regrettable confusion of categories. "In India, the difference between the army of a prince and the gang of a robber was, in the general estimation of the people, only in degree—they were both driving an imperial trade, a *padshahee kam* (emperor's work)" (Sleeman 1915, 396).

The traditional historiography written by India's dominators (Stein 1985, 387) described this period of general militarization as a dark age. Today's historians analyze the dilapidated state of the Awadh, so notorious in colonial history, not only in the light of native mores but as well in the light of the rivalries between the two major political powers confronting each other (see Frykenberg 1969, 123–41, 143–62; Metcalf

1964; Reeves 1971; and Bayly 1990a and 1990b)—the English resident had effectively become the co-administrator of the kingdom along with the nabob. We know that the Company never felt that "its belly was full." In order to aggrandize its territory and add to its profits, it too took advantage of the very disorder and the conflicts it stigmatized.

This is confirmed in Sleeman's account of the reply by "Mr. Seaton, the Governor General's representative at the court of Delhi" to the difficult question put to him by a "Muhammadan gentleman of high rank." . . . "'Pray, Sir, which of the things you have seen in India you liked the best?' . . . 'You have a small species of melon called *phut* (disunion); this is the thing we like best in your land.'" Sleeman commented: "Mr. Seaton was a very good and a very wise man" (Sleeman 1915, 485). But he didn't come to the conclusions drawn by present-day historians.

Present-Day Historians

Recent historiography emphasizes the positive aspects of this tumult through which England opened a path for itself within the general process of rearrangement of the political landscape that was occurring at the time. Christopher Bayly, following this turnaround in perspective, substitutes for the colonizers' Dark Age a Golden Age for native and English entrepreneurs, with their new and complex forms of trade and alliances, their business sense, and their acquisition of wealth. The consequences were of major import for the Company:

> The very flexibility and sophistication of these networks for making money inexorably drew the Company and its servants into politics. Politics, warfare and land management all delicately interpenetrated each other. And since the British inherited the expansive but fragile system of Mughal revenue management, the Company soon found itself in conflict also with the Hindu warrior lords of the countryside. The need "to pacify" this second key element of Indian society forced the European merchant adventurers to construct a larger and larger army, and the framework of an administration which could sustain trade and bring in ever-growing quantities of tribute and revenue. (Bayly 1990a, 46)

Undeniably, the states of North India were then "fluid, even ephemeral realities," this though the system of states that came to replace them was characterized by "an overall stability and a tendency to strengthen its local bases." In the course of this period of transition lasting from 1800 to 1830, the Company was not the direct successor of the Moghul as was usually thought at the time; rather, it effectively succeeded to "these regional states that themselves had succeeded to the Moghul empire" (Markovitz 1991, 198).

"The Company was able . . . to offer its own formidable services in the all India military bazaar" (Bayly 1990a, 48) that was flourishing, and thus to grab hold of the subcontinent, this not because it was drained and crumpling on all sides, but on the contrary, because the motivations (money, status, power) and the means of action of its agents were identical to those of native political centers (often war, and in times of peace the maintenance or creation of monopolies, the protection of trade, the dispersion of wandering armies, stabilization so as to be able to collect taxes regularly, and so on). It found in those centers the men, the support, the means, and the opportunities necessary to its economic expansion; these centers were not the victims but rather the active agents of the process of colonization. The troubles that affected India at the end of the eighteenth and beginning of the nineteenth centuries are no longer today labeled as caused exclusively by unfit and guilty restless natives, but are seen as the product of complex interaction at every level between the existing powers confronting each other.

NATIVE VIOLENCE, BRITISH REACTION

Dangerous Classes

Like Arsène Lupin or Fantômas, the Thugs constantly changed their appearance. The variety was infinite. According to Sir John Malcolm, "they assume . . . every disguise" (Malcolm 1972, 188). Colonial discourse asserted, as a matter of principle, that it was difficult to get to know anything about the Thugs as they systematically took on identities alien to their own. But there is a trail of clues that we can use to reflect on the social groupings of the persons from whom the Thugs more often borrowed their disguises: caravanners, soldiers, and holy men.

Some professional categories made up geographically mobile criminal groupings: the whole of India was their field of action. Among them were "people without fixed domicile, itinerant peddlers or transporters of goods," such as Banjaras caravanners; and also warrior communities, such as Pindari mercenaries;[12] or again, the fighter-ascetic Nagas. These three classes, labeled dangerous by the colonizers, made their living in part or in whole from the state of war prevalent at the turn of the century. British pacification was thus to seal their disappearance or at least their more or less successful absorption into sedentary society. What kind of violence did they engage in? How were the British able to control them? Did these dangerous classes have ties with the Thugs, and if so what were they?

FROM MERCENARIES TO SAVAGES

The Pindari[13] savages were mercenaries who played a determining role in the expansion of the Maratha Hindu kingdom in the eighteenth and nineteenth centuries. They "were a curious assortment of diverse races, castes and communities. They mostly belonged to the two religious communities—Hindus and Muslims" (Roy 1973, 23). Like the Thugs, the Hindus worshiped the Goddess, while the Muslims worshiped Muslim saints, the *pirs*. There were about twenty to thirty thousand Pindaris at the beginning of the nineteenth century. The British hated them. Sir John Malcolm described them as "a swarm of locusts, acting from instinct, they destroyed and left waste whatever province they visited. Their chiefs had, from grants or by usurpation, obtained small territorial possessions; but the revenues of their land were never equal to the maintenance of one-tenth part of their numbers, and they could, therefore, only be supported by plunder" (Malcolm 1972, 2:187).

They acquired a solid military organization in the wake of the Maratha army during the second half of the eighteenth century. As the *peshwa's* kingdom of Pune gradually fragmented into several centers of power, they ceased rallying under a single flag. Under the leadership of their own chiefs, Chitu, Amir Khan ("one of the most atrocious villains that India ever produced" [Sleeman 1915, 130 n. 1]), Wasil Mahamad, Kauder Baksh, Rajun, and so on, they formed autonomous bands that sold their services to the highest bidders.

At the height of his career, Chitu had an army of five to six thousand men, six elephants and twelve cannons. His banner, orange with a small white snake in the middle, had been given to him by the Bhonslas of Nagpur, one of the great families whose territories extended all the way to Orissa and that had seceded from the central government of Pune. The fearless Chitu harbored violent anti-British feelings and threatened to take over their territories around Calcutta to distribute to his men. He positioned his troops in the hills and wild areas of Narmada and of Vind-hyachal mountains. "Mangi Ram and Dhakun Seth were the bankers . . . advancing funds, either for the purchase of horses or for meeting their daily needs. These loans were promptly repaid after a plundering ex-cursion." Daulat Rao Sindhia gave Chitu the title of *nabob*, but Chitu remained effectively independent: though he claimed allegiance to the Maratha chief, this didn't prevent him from raiding him. They finally concluded a treaty whereby the Pindari would stop Chitu's depredations and provide a contingent of soldiers to Sindhia who, in exchange, was to give Chitu lands. "This was the first occasion on which he [Chitu] was recognized as a chief exercising legitimate rule."[14]

BRITISH REPRESSION. At the beginning of the nineteenth century, large portions of territories passed into British hands, while at the same time Pindari ranks swelled with demobilized soldiers, rebels, and suddenly impoverished adventurers. From the center of India, the Malwa and their hiding places in the Narmada valley, they multiplied their raids and attacks. In 1817 Governor General Hastings decided to intervene. The Maratha confederacy having been dislocated, he used his new dependents to finish off the Pindaris, who had issued "from within, like wild dogs from between the feet of their nominal masters . . . to slay, to burn, to plunder, and to disappear" (Vincent Smith 1987, 567). Dispersed in the regions of Bhopal, Gorakhpur, and so on, and captured one after the other, their leaders, "criminals and enemies of public peace" (Malcolm 1972, 1: 445), were given lands and pensions so as to engage in "more peaceful occupations." As to the anti-British Chitu, he didn't benefit from such clemency. In 1816, after having found refuge with a Gond chief, Kooshal Singh, who ended up betraying him, he was tracked by the British "like a hunted animal, through the jungles, by the prints of his hoofs," and finally eaten by a tiger. "The head," reported Sir John Malcolm, "was brought to me by Nanah, a Brahmin zemindar of Kantapoor, the district in which Chitu was killed" (Malcolm 1972, 1:447–48).

Some of his peers were still free continued their depredations, this particularly with the secret support of Daulat Rao Sindhia, who gave them shelter. Thus the terror of the peasants. Sheikh Dulla, who was "supposed to never have dismounted from his black mare even at night" (Roy 1973, 306), was only captured in 1828 after also having been betrayed by one of his companions. But by the second decade of the century, the death bell had definitively tolled. "As a body, the Pindaris are so effectually destroyed, that their name is already forgotten, though not five years are passed since it spread terror and dismay over all India," wrote Sir John Malcolm (1972, 1:462) in the conclusion of the chapter he devoted to them.

THUGS AND PINDARIS. In terms of space, the Pindari and Thug phenomena were adjacent to each other. The anti-Thug campaign organized from Sagar and Jabalpur covered a region, quite near the shores of the Narmada, where a concentration of mercenaries who sought refuge. In terms of practice the two groups again were close. They met and lived side by side, sometimes to cooperate and occasionally to destroy each other, as illustrated by the following story:

The Pindari Dulloo, for whom the Thug Ram Singh worked, refused to pay for the beautiful horse this latter had sold him. Ram Singh cut off Dulloo's head and brought it to Colonel Seyer, who had put a price on it. This latter sent Ram Singh to collect his award from Dhunraj Set. But this Dhunraj knew that Ram Sigh had killed his treasure-bearers and arrested him. The assassin succeeded in escaping and continued his activities elsewhere. The Thug telling this story sadly concluded: "He never got paid for his horse, nor for the murder of Sheikh Dulloo!"[15]

Drawing of a merchant *(left)* and a Byragee *(right)*. The caption in the original source explains that the figure on the left is a Thug in disguise but does not specify whether this is also the case for the figure on the right. From Caleb Wright, *Life in India* (1854).

They could also take on, as circumstances might call for, either one of the two identities, as in Meadows Taylor's novel. This might have been the novelist's invention, but social fluidity did go hand in hand with the shady opportunities offered by the crime market of the time.

Another, perhaps more determining element, helps us link Pindaris and Thugs. Like many soldiers at the time, the Pindaris were given as "wages" the official "right" to pillage. In exchange for this "right," their employers, the great Maratha chiefs, demanded they pay a special tax (*palpatti*) of more than one-fourth of their loot. This form of contract, in which a patron authorizes his "client" to pillage, also existed among the Thugs. It was often by paying a fixed tax to a village head or to the rajah that they were allowed to reside in the villages and pursue their murderous activities.

The British preferred to report their victories over the two confraternities of criminals as successive and definitive, and insisted on the differences between the two. In terms of collective psychology, this distinction was depicted in black and white. According to Sir John Malcolm, writing about the Pindaris, "courage and entreprise were often the qualities of their leaders, and no doubt of many of their followers; . . . all appear to have shared in the ignorance, the meanness, the rapacity and unfeeling cruelty, by which they were as a body, distinguished. . . . They had neither the tie of religious nor of national feeling. They were men of all lands and all religions" (Malcolm 1972, 1:431 and 434). The Thugs, in contrast, were described as opposite to every part of this description: weak, lazy, smooth, boastful, killing without cruelty, devotees of a single goddess, and in love with their villages. All accounts agreed that the mercenaries practiced a violence that was as uncontrolled as it was open. The British were repelled by the Pindaris' bloodthirsty behavior, but they nonetheless considered them as an enemy army against whom they must fight and with whom they must negotiate, even committing themselves to treat with "generosity and compassion" any of their chiefs who chose to surrender.

FROM ASCETICS TO MERCENARIES

THE NAGAS. One of the most surprising social facts of the eighteenth century was the presence of sometimes enormous bands of ascetics called Nagas on the roads, in temples and monasteries during the great feasts and pilgrimages of *kumbha mela*,[16] and particularly on battlefields. They were armed, naked, and covered with ashes. Their standards, their musicians, the marks on their faces, the position of their hair buns, the small black cords tied to either their left or right foot, all explicitly indicated the sect to which they belonged (Bouillier 1994, 238 n. 14).

Their obscure genealogy, patiently reconstructed by David N. Lorenzen, reveals the facts that led to their military organization. According to legendary hagiography, their warlike behavior originated in the eight and ninth centuries when King Sudhanvan, protector of the wise man Shankara, offended a *kapalika*[17] ascetic named Krakacha. "'I am not Krakacha,' he thundered 'if I do not cut off your heads.' He sent out crowds of angry kapalins whose cries were as terrifying as the clouds

28

of the deluge" (Lorenzen 1991, 41). The frightened Brahmans sought the protection of the wise man, who then reduced the king's enemies to ashes thanks to his magical powers. The legend tells that in the course of tours of conquest (*digvijaya*) to spread his doctrine, Shankara and his disciples often confronted "heretics" such as Jains, or Buddhists, or again the Tantrists, whose behavior, focused on pleasure and sexuality, horrified orthodox Brahmans. Oratorical jousts often degenerated into physical confrontations, and the name of Shankara remains linked to the origins of the fighting ascetics called Nagas. These followers of the god Shiva, one of the three great divinities of the Hindu pantheon along with Vishnu and the Goddess, had as their explicit mission the protection of the Brahmans and their monasteries.

Later facts explain the perennial presence of these hordes of holy men in arms. We know from written sources that during the pre-Moghul period some sovereigns,[18] motivated by greed or impoverishment, were persecuting wealthy religious institutions. Brahmans then defended themselves with their magical powers, their anathemas, the passive resistance of fasting, or any other form of ritual suicide in which moral responsibility falls on the aggressor. But the militarization of Hindu ascetics constituted a much better adapted response to a militant anti-Hindu attitude such as that held later by armed bands of Muslim fakirs (Farquhar 1925, 483).

At the beginning of the eighteenth century, the Bairagis, Vishnu's devotees, in their turn organized into fighting units. Like the parallel organizations of Shiva's followers, they organized into regiments (*akhara*) dependent on monasteries and divided into itinerant bands (*jhundi*). "Having a unified command structure and representing a considerable force, these Nagas never aimed to impose Vishnuism on everyone. But, organized to counter the influence of already existing similar groupings devoted to Shiva and to defend their coreligionists against the Muslims, they well illustrate this group morality according to which violence is justified as long as it is disinterested, that is 'at the service of the community'" (Clémentin-Ojha 1994, 150).

In 1760 eighteen hundred ascetics died as the two orders renewed the link with Shankara's legend and engaged in an armed confrontation in the course of a *kumbha mela* at Hardhwar. Thus, even while wearing the signs of their sectarian identities that required them to respect their pledge of nonviolence, which was the most important of the oaths they had to take at the end of their novitiate, these paradoxical ascetics did engage in violence in the name of duty.

A MERCENARY CAREER. The careers of two brothers, Anup Giri and Umrao Bahadur (Bouillier 1994, 224–26), provide an illustration of the vocation taking on a clearly mercenary hue over time. They were Shivaite Hindus of the Giri sect, and they offered their services to the nabob of Awadh, the Muslim Shuja-ud-daula, and soon Anup Giri became the chief of his army. In 1761, at Panipat, with his brother Umrao Bahadur, Anup Giri led twelve thousand men against Maratha invaders and defeated them. At the battle of Baksar again four to six thousand of them fought on the side of the troops of the nabob of Awadh; of Mir Kasim, nabob of Bengal; and of Shah Alam, emperor of the Moghul. This time they fought against the British, who were victorious. The Awadh lost its independence, and Anup Giri offered his services to the Jats. Then he came back to Awadh, where Shuja-ud-daula died. The regent of Delhi, Mirza Najaf Khan, hired him. Again in the service of the Moghuls, he fought with his Nagas against the Jats, themselves helped by other ascetics, the Bairagis, commanded by Nawal Singh. When the Delhi regent died in turn, Anup Giri supported the Marathas in the person of Mahaji Sindhia, whose main adviser he became. Then Mahaji expelled him from his court. He mistrusted him and, it turned out, with good reason, as his favorite adviser immediately engaged him in battle after having passed to the side of the Rajputs. To conclude this decidedly opportunistic career, the ascetic then allied himself with the British, who convinced him to lay down his arms. In 1803 the British gave him a *jagir* in the amount of twenty-two *lakhs* (*lakh*: 100,000) of rupees. By the time of his death in 1804 he headed a large territory that was a British protectorate. All along the stages of his career with the different rajahs, nabobs, regents, and colonizers, he received lands and honors in large numbers. His itinerary belongs directly in the line of the alliances between British, kings, and bandits that oddly ends up with his sacred nakedness.

THUGS AND HOLY MEN. The Thugs who "killed out of devotion" apparently shared a trait with these Nagas: the alliance of crime and religion. They also engaged in some of the same shady practices of other ascetics, though less spectacular than those of the Nagas. Because the Thugs took on the disguise of religious beggars to seduce their victims, they made use of their sacred appearance to get the upper hand in transactions and to extort information. "Some of them . . . settled in Bengal where they started money lending and river trade. In Rangpur they came to live in hermitages which they fortified and where they combined the trade of money lending with that of dacoity. Some were stationed by zamindars on the borders of zamindaris for protection" (Kolff 1971, 214).

At the end of the eighteenth century Jhansi and Mirzapur, the city with the temple of Vindhyachal where the Thugs came to worship Kali, were prosperous centers of commerce and banking led by some of the most prosperous ascetics. The Jhansi Gosains "formed a religio-commercial sect, militarized to some degree, and organized according to the *guru-chela* principle. . . . At fixed periods [others] went on religious pilgrimages, were seen armed with swords and matchlocks, occasionally also robbing people, and engaged in treasure carrying and trade, particularly trans-Himalayan trade 'in diamonds, coral, and other articles of great price and small compass'" (Gosh 1923, 22–23, cited in Kolff 1971, 216). These holy men, whom the colonizers called *sannyasi* or *gosain*,[19] thus practiced robbery and crime.

This confusion between crime and holiness not only makes up a fact to be observed, but is also a preferred theme in some Indian tales. Bloomfield (1924) collected an impressive number of these narratives, in which false ascetics and beggars use their holiness as a ploy to achieve their aims.[20] These crooks, who have names such as "Sweet Talker" or "Crooked Mind," worship Shiva and his spouse Kali. "In accordance with the character and needs of these Gods, their ascetic devotees are engaged in cruel practices, especially human sacrifices." and they seek to become masters of extraordinary magical powers, *siddhi*, such as flying, making gold, and even "shaking up the world."

> They carry a garland of skulls and a rosary, are smeared with the ashes of dead bodies. . . . Shiva himself is an ascetic. He, as well as his horrible consort, require human sacrifice, wear garlands of skulls and drink wine from these skulls. Hence both Shiva and his ascetic followers are designated as Kapalin 'Skull-carrier,' the latter also as Kapalika (Worshiper of Kapalin, Shiva, the Skull-carrier). . . . The story finds the Kapalikas as a rule looking for a victim which they intend to sacrifice in a cemetery or a Durga temple. . . . They use their holy calling as a mantle with which to cloak their design. (Bloomfield 1924, 202–203)

In the tales, this sort of abuse "broadens out a good deal by introducing people who are not ascetics at all but sham the get-up and behavior of ascetics for all sorts of nefarious purposes" (Bloomfield 1924, 205). In another article on "The Art of Stealing in Hindu Fiction," Bloomfield (1923) notes that the lost "Thieves Manual," the *Steya-Shastra*, probably recommends thieves to operate in the guise of assorted holy personages.

Colonizers' observations fit in a whole range of representations that included the fighting Nagas or the business-oriented ascetics described above; as well as popular narrative, always funny and biting, whose target was shady and dangerous religious characters; and finally some forms of the quest for salvation practiced by certain heterodox Shivaite sects with "resolutely aggressive traditions" (Padoux 1992, 63). I will come back to this last point later on.

A third group brought together, like the other two, people of all social origins, and the Thugs also borrowed their appearances from them, and fairly often, it was claimed. But this time we are crossing a decisive step in the order of closeness; these are no longer hypothetical conversions or partial superimpositions, but an almost perfect match between the groups in question.

FROM WAR PLUNDER TO CRIME

"Hundreds of 'tribes' with varying origins, customs, religions and caste status have come under the umbrella of the term 'Banjaras' but despite the consensus that Banjaras are gypsies, delineations of their identity have remained imprecise" (Varady 1979, 1). The accepted etymology of their name, *banijya-kara*, that is "merchant," is vague. We encounter them in India for approximately the past seven centuries, that is since the Muslims' claim to political hegemony over the subcontinent. Like the Pindaris and the Thugs, they include Hindus and Muslims. The British administrators attempted to understand their identity by drawing complicated graphs of their clanic subdivisions and subsections, and as usual they mixed value judgments with their observations: in the "Banjaras on the whole, and taken rightly in their clanish nature, their virtues preponderate over their vices" (Russell 1969, 2:191). Later on anthropologists, impressed by the legends of origins their storytellers told, were to "inundate them in a sea of *gotras*" (Varady 1979, 2). Robert Gabriel Varady finds several common traits among them: they are nomads; their language is close to Marwari, an idiom of the Jodhpur region; their ancestors are of Rajput origin; their subsistence is linked to cattle (in the seventeenth century Tavernier describes herds of ten to fourteen thousand animals); and they transport merchandise and lead pack bullocks.

THE BANJARAS AND COLONIZATION. The Banjaras' story is not unusual: the British caused them to lose their traditional occupations, and some of them were later to reminisce nostalgically about their picturesque caravans. Providers of food for the armies, they played a key role in the military campaigns of the invading Muslims; they seemed to have had a quasi-monopoly on this trade from the time of the Ghuri Sultanate to the collapse of Marathi power. They were then enjoying substantial privileges: "They are regarded as neutral in all wars; they enjoy a right of transit through all countries; and the armies, which spare nothing else, act under a species of obligation, seldom violated, of respecting the property of the Brinjarries" (Mill 1826, 5:333). Around 1820, with the north of India pacified, British armies used their own supply services in the South so the Banjaras were "spoiled of their former calling by the cessation of the continual wars which distracted India under Native rule" (Russell 1969, 2:191). Up to around 1830, observers wrote that the

Banjaras' large convoys (*qafilas*) could still be seen transporting salt, grain, and sweets. In 1907 Crooke noted that "their caravans of pack bullocks guarded by savage dogs, their women with free gait, wearing richly embroidered robes and abundant jewelry, are now seldom seen" (Crooke 1907, 117). From the middle of the nineteenth century on other means of transportation, linked to the creation of a road network, then later to the advent of railroads, brought the last blow to their way of life.

THEIR TRANSFORMATIONS. The Banjaras reacted in various ways to these changes. Some became sedentary agriculturists; others became cattle dealers, thus continuing their nomadic life; while yet others became bandits. "The need to protect their shipments had nourished aggressive behaviour and some 'tribes' took advantage of their fearsome image. . . . Subjected only to 'tribal' jurisdiction, individuals, usually united in gangs, made use of their independence by taking what was not theirs" (Varady 1979, 7). Abbé Dubois referred to them as "professional brigands." This reputation, in part justified but based on the incorrect assumption that this was the main occupation of the whole group, hardened in the nineteenth century.

THUGS AND BANJARAS. William Sleeman distinguished several Thug clans, some of which were called *Lodahas* (from the word *lodh* meaning "load") and others *Bangureeas*, a word in which we can recognize *Banjaras*. According to Malcolm, *Lodahas* and *Brinjarries* referred to the same people:

> Brinjarries and Lodanahs, or grain-carriers, are of the Rajpoot caste: these are of various tribes, Rhattore, Jalore, Puar, etc. They live in tents and can hardly be termed inhabitants of any particular province, as every place where they pitch is their home, and that of their families. They come and go to different countries, as their services are required to supply armies and to carry on commerce. . . . They live in a society of their own, and preserve, both in dress and usages, a marked separation and independence. . . . They are deemed honest in their dealings, though very ignorant and barbarous. (Malcolm 1972, 2:152)

One of Sleeman's Thug informants confirmed that the grain-carriers also engaged in the same "commerce" as he and his peers.

> We made sure of securing the five travellers at Hirora, and remained where we were to dine. We reached Hirora about nine at night, and searched all the village in vain for the travellers. . . . I recollected that about three miles from Hirora we had passed a Brinjara encampment. In the morning I went back with a few followers, and

there found a horse and a pony that we had seen with the five travellers. "What have you done with the five travellers, my good friends. You have taken from us the merchandise?" . . . They apologized for what they had done, said they did not know we were after them, and offered to share the booty with us. (Sleeman 1836, 154)

Was this rivalry, or did the two groups partake of a single identity? Murdering travelers was not exclusive to the Thugs. Moreover, it seemed to be the rule for these assassins of such diverse origins to amiably share the fruits of their misdeeds among them.

DANGEROUS CLASSES AND THE THUGS

The example of the Banjaras, like those of the Pindaris and the Nagas, shows that Thuggism was not the unique and isolated phenomenon described by the colonizers. These bands could be seen in the whole of the subcontinent; they were from many castes; they traveled and acted under the leadership of chiefs; they could be nomads or semi-nomads, perpetrating their "crimes" far from their homes in the form of raids, expeditions, or pilgrimages. Certain specific facts or traits justify linking the Thugs to them. These include geographical and historical proximity to the Pindari, religious motivations evoking that of the many and various classes of ascetics, and finally, like the Banjaras the Thugs favored highways for their crimes and travelers for their victims.

The British conquest forced these three groups to change occupations. Pindari mercenaries or ascetics were dispersed; they put down their arms and became sedentary. Certain caravanners, perhaps also some warriors not interested in working the land or who didn't have enough land to live off of, took the crooked road of crime. The formula according to which the Thugs disguised themselves into everyone's appearance should be inverted. Pindaris, Banjaras, and ascetics were in all likelihood able to join their bands after having lost their means of subsistence. Could the word *Thug* designate all those the conquest had left out?

Regional Rebels

In strong contrast to these forms of violence, there were yet other ones solidly rooted in specific regions. Most often, these were clearly articulated rebellions against the British, who responded in various ways. The complexity of Indian society, with its major regional differences, posed a difficult challenge for the colonizers, a challenge they resolved at times tentatively and at others expeditiously.

Since the 1980s historians in the current movement of subaltern studies founded by Ranajit Guha have been interested in the testimonies and the trajectories of people on the lower rungs of society as opposed to the role and the opinion of the colonial and Indian nationalist elites thought for a long time to be determining in the movement of revolt in India. Their research reveals the partiality of the colonizers' judgment on the individuals and on professional and ethnic groupings they considered outlaws. Deeds that were at the time perceived as criminal turn out to be acts of protest against the colonial authorities' interference and authority—the type of action usually referred to a social banditry.[21] What form did social banditry take in India? Can we include in it the practices of the classes said to be dangerous, which I just described? What was the Thugs' relation with those deeds?

RAMUSI NAIK UMIAJI IN MAHARASHTRA

A FAMILIAR SITUATION. Like elsewhere in India, armed bands were an integral part of the social, economic, and political landscape of the Maharashtra in the eighteenth and nineteenth centuries (Bruce 1985). Their services were bought by landowners to pillage their enemies' lands, by village chiefs to terrify tax collectors and moneylenders, or again to steal merchandise from travelers' caravans going between Pune, Satara, Nasik, and Bombay. In the mountains of the Western Ghats, forts had been built on all substantial heights overlooking "the impressive defiles with their wood covered slopes."[22] These forts were manned by troops under the authority of the *peshwa* of Pune and put under the command of a chief, a *naik*,[23] whose mission was to control the movements of these armed bands and keep the roads open.

The word *naik* referred to the chiefs of the mountains and distant valleys of the Ghats as well as those in command of the troops posted in the forts charged with keeping watch over the peasant warriors of these mountains and valleys. The majority of the *naiks* came from the "tribes" the British claimed to be predatory. They were mainly the Mahadev Kolis who lived in this area's steep eastern landscape. The Kolis were excellent warriors of great physical endurance and were in the habit of supplementing their resources by stealing from travelers and by raiding the more prosperous peasants of the plains. Umiaji was the chief of the "tribe" of the Ramusi (a word from the Maratha *ranavasi*, meaning "jungle dweller"), who were mostly living in the region stretching from Pune to Kolhapurand and were known as much for their daring and courage as for their robbing habits (Mackintosh 1833 in Yule and Burnell 1968, 756).

When the British came at the beginning of the nineteenth century, they decided to destroy most of the forts on the heights of the Ghats and to send back the official troops defending them. Convinced that "the best bandits make the best police," they entrusted the job of maintaining order to the *naiks* spread out in the mountains and valleys; the British perceived them as a traditional native police system.

In 1824 Ramusi Naik Umiaji, deposed by the *peshwa* of Pune, was left without a position in the new British order. He rebelled. He was the former chief of the fort of Purandhar. He gathered one hundred men, then stole, pillaged, even organized a raid aimed at Pune and the *peshwa's* treasure, and he let peasants know through resounding proclamations that taxes were to be paid directly to his men rather than to the government.

In Meadows Taylor's autobiography, Umiaji is a nasty brigand, and the reasons for his banditry, for his rebellion, are not mentioned. The British, defied by the inhabitants who protect and admire him, capture him only after "pursuing him fruitlessly for many years":

> [Umiaji] seemed to be ubiquitous, and we had many a weary, fruitless search for this noted and most mischievous brigand, whose robberies, often attended with violence, cattle-lifting, and all manner of villainy, had become the terror of the country. Umiaji had a spite against all authority, hated both priestly and secular Brahmins, and enjoyed nothing more, if he could catch one, than cutting off his nose and ears. . . . He led us on many a dance through the country, and often we were mislaid on false information. (Taylor 1986b, 52)

THE REBEL'S GOD STANDS AT HIS SIDE. Ramusi Naik Umiaji's surrender took the form of a ceremony. Dressed in royal regalia borrowed from the temple of Jejuri, Kandhoba's pilgrimage city, he presented himself along with his companions to the British, who were supposed to grant him a pardon, this to the sound of cymbals (Bruce 1985, 53).

What was he trying to accomplish by putting on this show for the colonizers? The effect, it seems, was a surreptitious inversion of roles. The rebel who offered himself to the British gaze not as a penitent but as a "king," a hero, was not the one receiving the pardon but the one granting it, thus probably righting the injustice, the ill deed of which he had been the victim. But mostly, it made his former enemies solemnly acknowledge their protection, their new patronage, while he was giving up neither his own social integrity (he is a chief, a *naik*) nor his regional and religious integrity (Kandhoba is a Maratha god). The royal and divine dignity thus conferred to Ramusi put a seal of respect, power, and material reward on the surrender agreement.

BRITISH CLEMENCY. The solemn pardon given to Ramusi came with the British appointing him to the post of police chief for the districts of Purandhar and Bhimthadi. He was also given a certain amount of land and a monthly pension of thirty rupees. Immediately other bands formed. They were the Bheels of Khandesh, the Mags of Satara, and the Kolis of the Deccan, and they took to the hills following Umiaji's example in the hope of obtaining concessions, titles, rewards and lands and also of claiming rights to the positions they had lost. But these rebel imitators were repressed, pursued, and defeated by the British policemen, who finally replaced the *naiks* of the deep valleys and inaccessible mountains.

After 1844–1845 rebellion definitely ceased to be a practical tool in the service of political ambitions or the acquisition of concessions from the British. Ramusi Naik Umiaji was thus the beneficiary of a moderate colonial policy that became markedly more aggressive in the face of this unexpected spate of copycat rebellions.

A few years later, in another mountain region but this time in the eastern end of India, the British dealt with similar movements of rebellion issued from populations said to be tribal and living on the margins of the Hindu world. There the British attitude was from the start more authoritarian and aggressive, but the colonizers were forced to make concessions in the face of the geographical and human obstacles they encountered. There too, the rebels crossed to the other side of the boundaries that had separated them from the norm and became the police. The result took on the appearances of the past, yet the content had changed. In both the Western and the Eastern Ghats, the colonizers were thenceforth to be vigilant partners in the new order they were bringing.

THE REBELS OF GUDEM AND RAMPA

THE CONTEXT. At the other end of the subcontinent, in the Eastern Ghats,[24] there is an area of hills, Gudem and Rampa, near the Godavari River in Andhra Pradesh:

> The contrast is stark. Below, the ghats' fertile soils, irrigation and centuries of settled agriculture have contributed to making the lowlands one of the most densely populated areas of southern India. . . . Above the ghat, at altitude from 1,500 to nearly 5,000 feet . . . a jumble of hills and plateaus merging distantly into Bastar and the northern Deccan. Dispersed in settlements along the river valleys and in jungle clearings lives a small population. There are few towns and metalled roads; until relatively recently shifting cultivation was the dominant form of agriculture. (Arnold 1986: 91)

At the end of the eighteenth century the India Company acquired Gudem and Rampa from the Moghuls, and in the course of the nineteenth century the region was divided into several administrative units.[25] There were three important groupings among the mountain dwellers of Gudem and Rampa: the Bagatas, having come from the plains in a distant past, form the majority *muttadar* of the local elite; the Koyas, who spoke Kui, the language of the Gonds,[26] from whom they issued; and finally the Kondas Doras, "lords of the hills," of the same origin as the Koyas but speak-

37

ing Telugu. Some other, smaller, groupings also lived there. This diversified, highly dispersed population nonetheless formed one social entity. Its
members entered into alliances with each other and held many cultural
traits in common. Their means of subsistence were identical (slash and
burn agriculture and gathering), and often so were their beliefs and their
places of pilgrimage. Like the northeastern Gonds they offered bloody
sacrifices[27] to their goddess Malveli, or Mamili Devata, whose personality is reminiscent of the goddess honored in the plains under various
names, such as Mariamma, Ellama, Angaramma, and so on. Their hostility to all foreign interference, be it British or native, was strong. Their
communities were united by the institutional structure of the *muttadari*
system. These *muttadars* were heirs to areas of land called *mutta*. They
didn't own them, but inherited the right of guardianship over them; they
were entrusted with delivering brigands and thieves to their superiors,
the zamindar of Golconde or the *mansabdar* of Rampa, as well as with
collecting taxes for them from the population, this often in kind or in
corvée labor.

BRITISH AGGRESSIVENESS AND AUTHORITARIANISM. In 1836, in the
Gudem region, the British administration removed Anata Bhupati, the
seventeenth zamindar of Golconde, who paid tribute directly to the Company, and appointed a woman, Jamma Devata, in his stead. This was an
insult to the *muttadars* of Gudem, who were not consulted and who had
never been led by a woman. They captured and killed her. In reprisal the
British took over the area and refused to honor their promise to give the
title of zamindar back to the family of Anata Bhupati, whom they put
in prison. In 1845 the mountain people proclaimed Anata's son, Chinna,
rajah and the hostilities resumed. Finally, the British gave three villages
to Chinna Bhupati and his brothers to compensate them for the loss of
the *zamindari* the colonizers had appropriated for themselves. In 1857
Chinna's nephew, Sannyasi, took up the torch again; the rebellion (*fituri*)
was yet again crushed, but the villages were given back to him.

There was a similar scenario in Rampa: first a woman, the daughter of the defunct *mansabdar,* and then his adopted son were appointed
by the British to replace him. For eighteen years the disgruntled *muttadars* instigated growing numbers of armed conflicts and highway rob-
beries (Arnold 1986, 101–2), this until 1848, when the British government
decided to give Rampa back to the *mansabdari* family they had taken
it from. The government then claimed that "tracts such as that under
consideration—wild and unproductive—and which from the character
of the country and climate must be difficult in management by the Officers of the Government, are always best confided to the administration
of their native chiefs" (Arnold 1986, 104).

The *muttadars*, whose interests were identical to those of the reigning families, again took up their traditional policing role. It was mostly those who dominated the scene of the confrontations with rebels who were to become famous, such as Taman Dora of Rampa, considered a hero by his peers but a "desperate man" by the British, who offered a reward for his capture. He and his ally Paulapu Peddi Reddi set daring traps and won substantial victories over the muttadars (Arnold 1986, 106–7).

PAX BRITANNICA

The colonizers' presence precipitated and intensified change, and they were thus confronted with a diverse and fluctuating internal situation in which the notion of crime was fluid. This was the more so in that through many aspects specific to native culture the lines of demarcation between legality and illegality were difficult to establish; the very principle of a caste system that discriminates, creates hierarchies, and links castes with each other (including those it excludes) leads to the acceptance of a multiplicity of norms. In spite of disagreements involving specific parts of the field, the research in new sources and the change in perspective in colonialism studies have shown three things. First, the process of judgment makes the delinquent: the colonizers apply their own criteria to define and condemn him. Second, the behaviors said to be criminal are banal in a general context in which the nonviolence of the population is actually a state of latent violence, a calm between two storms. Finally, the immense diversity in behavior is masked by the colonizers' dramatizing and homogenizing rhetoric. And yet two great forms of delinquency come out of the above. The first is disorder stemming from a revolt, a protest, and is rooted in the particular region that is the locus of action. The main activities of the actors are linked to the land they either cultivate or guard. They are full members of a specific social milieu, and their gods are honored by that milieu. In contrast, but keeping in mind that it is possible to pass from one form to another, the second form of delinquency is that of pan-Indian communities living on the margins of society, who follow rules, a system of justice and interests specific to them, and who draw their livelihood from crime, which is sometimes their principal occupation. They are recruited from many castes and they can be organized into sects like that of the Nagas. This hypothesis is that of the historian D. H. A. Kolff (1971, 215), whom I have already cited in regard to the Thugs.

In English eyes all forms of disorder could be attributed to the dangerous classes, regardless of whether these forms were customary or exceptional. And yet the British reacted in various ways and improvised as they went along: we have encountered statuses that were ignored (Ramusi Naik), or scoffed at (the Kallar guardians of the Vellala lands, described by Stuart Blackburn [1978] then restored [the *muttadars* of the Gudem and Rampa region]), or again created (the Naga Anup Giri). Some rebel fighters were decapitated (Chitu). The Kallars were treated ferociously, though it is true that in the course of the conflict ten of the British were assassinated. The colonizers' reprisal involved the killing of thousands of "rapacious and savage Colleries." The excessive vengeance of the victim-colonizers was linked to the cliché used to label the natives. In contrast, Ramusi Naik's violence was perceived as limited, apt to be controlled and corrected—and even though the concept of the "social bandit" was not given explicit expression, the idea was present. So compared to these graduated reactions, determined by specific circumstances and guided by political imperatives leaning toward prudence and negotiation, what are we to make of the massive irrevocable condemnation of the Thugs? Why were they the target of a noisy and relentless campaign of extermination?

BRITISH IDEAS AND COLONIAL PRACTICES

The Anglican church, like the British state, held negative views of the people of Hindustan. In 1792, upon the request of Henry Dundas, president of the Parliamentary Office of Control supervised by the government of the Company, Charles Grant wrote in his report:

> The generality . . . of those who have written concerning Hindostan appear to have concurred in affirming what foreign residents have generally thought, nay, what the natives themselves freely acknowledge of each other, that they are a people exceedingly depraved. In proportion as we became better acquainted with them, we have found this description applicable, in a sense beyond the conception even of former travellers. The writer of this paper . . . is obliged to add his testimony to all preceding evidence, and to avow that they exhibit human nature in a very degraded humiliating state, and are at once objects of disesteem and commiseration. (Grant 1812–1813 and 1831–1832, 43)[28]

Charles Grant, director of the Company for many years, went to India. Upon his return he settled in Capham, the place of residence of a number of evangelical priests and of intellectual and militant Christians, such as Zachary Macaulay, S. Wilberforce, and others. According to the latter, the most urgent "goal" was to send missions to the colony. He got his way. In 1813 he described the Hindu gods as "absolute monsters of lust, injustice, wickedness and cruelty. In short, their religious system is one of grand abomination" (Stokes 1959, 31). They were to finally have an antidote: "Great Britain unquestionably holds the place now, which Rome formerly had, in regard to the *power* and *means* of promoting Christian knowledge. . . . By the decay of the Romish church, an opportunity is offered of inviting the members of that church to receive the

Bible and to contemplate the purity of the protestant faith," trumpets Claudius Buchanan, the Company's chaplain, who reminds his readers of the "Bishop of Oxford's appeal to Britain in 1762: to send the gospel wherever she sends her sword" (Buchanan 1813b, 11–12).

England was swamped by a torrent of information about India. Books such as *An Account of the Writings, Religions, and Manners of the Hindus,* by W. Ward, published in 1811; *India's Cries to British Humanity,* by J. Peggs, published in 1828 with a third edition published in 1832; and newspapers such as *Missionary Papers* and *Missionary Register* sounded the alarm. These simple and direct texts with abundant illustrations denounced the cruelty, debasement, and depravation of the natives in the colonies (Ingham 1956) and led to passionate debates.

In 1823 the second bishop of Calcutta, the Reverend Reginald Heber, took actions to eliminate those rites judged to be the most inhumane, such as the immolation of widows on the funerary pyres of their husbands (sati), infanticide, idolatrous celebrations, and so on. In England as in India, the religious renewal mobilized opinion. This renewal was visionary and idealist and affected mainly the new progressive middle classes resolved to shake up the sacrosanct alliance of the church and the aristocracy (Bayly 1990b, chapter 5).[29] Wilberforce, Grant, and the archbishop of London, Beilby Porteus, refused to be parties to practices judged inhuman. The "British connection" with idolatry was no longer acceptable. The Office of the Directors asked Lord Bentinck to dissociate the government from any religious rite that might be contrary to the Christian spirit (Potts 1967). Though the governor general was personally receptive to the evangelists' crusades, "these enthusiasms were tempered by a spirit of gradualism" (Bayly 1990a, 121).

In fact, Christian fulminations were muted in India itself. It was thought that the natives should be impressed with pomp, with grand performances, but that one should be careful not to convert them in mass, which would result in tumult and protest. The model for the required prudence was Saint Paul, who first preached the good word to the Romans and the Greeks and not to the Barbarians. The famous theory of the ladder of civilizations that was dominant at the time and according to which mankind develops through progressive historical stages, going from nomadism to the sophisticated forms of industrial society, conformed with the measured imperatives of evangelization. The missionary focused on those close to the most accomplished stage of civilization: corrupted Christian communities, as for instance the Catholics, or the mixed-blood offspring of British men and native women, or again the servants living in the orbit of the colonial household. Likewise, intervening in native affairs relating to personal law (inheritance, property, marriage, and so on) that would have called for as much, if not more, attention from the authorities on account of their mass and often oppressive character, were "tempered [by] a fear of the consequences of sudden change—and an appreciation of the vulnerability of Britain's position in India which was almost as profound as that of the great conservatives, Malcolm and Munro." The measures taken by Bentinck were of great symbolic import, concludes Christopher Bayly, but their impact on society remained very limited (Bayly 1990a, 121–22).

The spokesperson of the strong reform current nonetheless assigned himself "a great moral task" in India. On 4 December 1829 he had the rite of sati forbidden. In 1830 the campaign of repression against the Thugs was officially initiated. By attacking the most visibly iniquitous religious practices, governmental action took on the ethical aspect of a crusade and fostered the illusion that all could bring their own remedy to an India in decline: evangelists by exporting their missionaries; utilitarian philosophers, of who Jeremy Bentham was the main doctrinarian, by changing the laws; the police of the empire by making sure these laws were applied.

As in colonial France during the Third Republic, the disagreements between the different currents of thoughts agitating the home country dissolved abroad. Everyone agreed on the deep discontinuity between "over there" and "here" and claimed the superiority of Europe, the center from whence the rays of civilization shined, shedding light in all directions (Stocking 1987). Imperial ideology—the coalition of the Crown, the church, and of law and business—was remarkably coherent in its field of action. To freely evangelize and trade, and as Bentham advocated, to tax lightly and make good laws, were all part of the program of consolidation of the young empire, inspired by the Christian renewal and Utilitarian philosophy. It was under these circumstances that the crusade against the Thugs began.

T W O   # The Anti-Thug Campaign

IN THE HEART OF DARKNESS

William Sleeman was the initiator and architect of the anti-Thug campaign. By 1819 the war against the Marathas had been won; the Pindaris had been demobilized and pacified; and the territories of Sagar and Jabalpur, reattached to the Northwestern Provinces,[1] had been taken over by the British. As his regiment settled in Jabalpur, Sleeman, thirty years old at the time, requested a position in the civil service. His request was granted. In 1821, at the age of thirty-three, he was named junior assistant to Molony, the governor general's agent, to help him map and register land holdings. In 1822 he was entrusted with administering alone the district of Narsimhapur in the Narmada valley.[2] This was a period when he had to perform the functions of both collector and policeman, a time he was to remember as one during which he accomplished "a herculean task" that couldn't be compared to any other. He evoked the most surprising aspect of this past in *Ramaseeana*:

> While I was in the Civil charge of the district of Nursingpore, in the valley of the Nurbuddah [Narmada], in the years 1822, 23 and 24, no ordinary robbery or theft could be committed without my becoming acquainted with it; nor was there a robber or a thief of the ordinary kind in the district, with whose character I had not become acquainted in the discharge of my duty as Magistrate; and if any man had then told me, that a gang of assassins by profession resided in the village Kundelle, not four hundred yards from my court, and that the extensive groves of the village of Mundesur, only one stage from me . . . was one of the greatest *Beles*, or places

of murder in all India; and that large gangs from Hindustan and the Duckun used to rendezvous in these groves . . . I should have thought him a fool or a mad man; and yet nothing could have been more true. (Sleeman 1836, "Introduction," 32–33)[3]

According to Sir Francis Tuker, Sleeman's biographer, a certain Kalyan Singh one day discretely talked to him at Narsimhapur and drew his attention to a band of travelers who had just left town. Kalyan Singh appeared to be frightened; he was under the sway of intense emotion as he whispered, "They are evil men. Their leader, Durga, is a cruel and unjust man." Then he added: "They are Thugs, sahib." Sleeman got excited. "What wonderful news and what an opportunity, at last. 'I know that,' said he calmly. 'Come with me. . . . I shall put you in jail now. It's the only safe place for you" (Tuker 1961, 39–40). He had his horse saddled and requested his troops to rejoin him as fast as possible, and he started out in pursuit of the travelers. They had not gotten very far on the road to Sagar when he caught up with them. He passed them and signaled them to stop. The soldiers surrounded them. Sleeman made them sit under a tree and settled down next to them. They spoke a language he didn't understand, but eventually bits and pieces of the Phansigar language that had been written down by the doctor Sherwood came back to him and gave him the key to this very professional conversation dealing with omens, treasures, and wealthy travelers. The band was accused of banditry and thrown in jail. That very night, its leader, Moti, betrayed the group. He led Sleeman to a mango bush and showed him the remains of four persons recently strangled. "Beneath my feet as he trod were men and women and even infants smothered through the years, calling him for the extirpation of a great wickedness" (Tuker 1961, 42). Sleeman had finally uncovered the evidence that had been lacking up to then.

Sleeman's biographer did not make up the casualness with which he threw the band of travelers in prison on the sole basis of Kalyan Singh's denunciation. Many suspects were arrested in this way and rotted in the prisons of the Empire waiting for their day in court, or for a kind soul to put up bail for them, or for their "good reputation" to be established. The prisons were full and justice was very slow due to the lack of manpower. Sleeman was free to interrogate the travelers at leisure. And if Moti betrayed his accomplices that very night, it was because his interrogator resorted to another widespread practice entailing the promise of a pardon in exchange of substantial information. The judiciary campaign against the assassins was to make systematic use of this. So this was the way Sleeman's investigations begin. He knew nothing in 1822, he knew everything in 1829. During that time, he collected many more

Thugs' confidences, he also became familiar with their secret language, *Ramasee*, and he gradually came to measure the spread of their networks and the gravity of their crimes.

And yet, "the diversity of customs and usages of the people brought under the scope of the East India Company, the confused and contradictory regulations which governed proceedings of the law courts in the different British Indian territories . . . created an atmosphere wholly uncongenial to impartial and equitable administration of justice" (Srivastava 1971, 143). The power of the Muslim courts that were the legacy of the Moghul empire had been decreasing since the beginning of the century. Thus even when the Muslim officers of the court rendered a *fatwa*[4] whereby the accused was only presumed guilty, the British judge had the authority to condemn him anyway. From 1817 on, the criminal courts of appeal of the Company, the *sadar nizamat adalat*, became all powerful: they could disregard or overrule *fatwas*. However, the legislation in use barred taking into account denunciations and accomplices' testimonies, and many judges thus let go accused Thugs because of insufficient proof. This was one of the main reasons why the reports Sleeman sent to Calcutta had no effect: the evidence he collected was not yet admissible at that time.

An important step was taken in 1829. The government authorized Borthwick to condemn to death a band of Thugs denounced by one of their members, a certain Amanullah. George Swinton, chief secretary of the government writes:

> These murders having been perpetrated in territories belonging to various Native Chiefs, and the perpetrators being inhabitants of various districts belonging to different authorities, there is no chief in particular to whom we could deliver them up for punishment, as their Sovereign, or as the Prince of the territory in which the crime has been committed. The hands of these inhuman monsters being against everyone, and their being no country within the range of their annual excursion from Bundelkhand to Guzerat in which they have not committed murder, it appears that they may be considered like Pirates, to be placed without the pale of social law, and be subjected to condign punishment by whatever authority they may be seized and convicted.[5]

Sleeman took advantage of the situation by publishing his famous anonymous letter on 3 October 1830, in the *Calcutta Literary Gazette*. His sounded the alarm with his demands: "It is the imperious duty of the Supreme Government of this country to put an end in some way or other to this dreadful system of murder." Lord Bentinck became concerned and asked for more information. Sleeman presented his previously prepared plan for the Thugs' eradication. Governor General Bentinck finally reacted somewhat vigorously with the support of the Board of Directors in London:

> We are by no means satisfied with the proceedings of the public officers in regard to offences of this class. Their exertions have been but too plainly unsuccessful yet we know no reason why some effective measures might not be adopted by an able and zealous magistracy with a sufficient police establishment, so that many of the offenders might be detected and the crime in a great degree put down in places where it was most prevalent. We trust that you will endeavour to have the reports of the cases of Thugs classed as accurately as possible in the statements, and that you will exact from the local officers a strict attention to their duties in regard to the discovery and apprehension of the offenders.[6]

Sleeman was thus put in charge of the anti-Thug campaign. He organized pursuits and arrests: he was given a troop of fifty cavalrymen and forty *cipayes*. He had the right to offer rewards as high as one thousand rupees to those helping him capture criminals; he was authorized to pursue these latter in the independent princely states and to bring them back to Sagar to be judged by his collaborator, Curven Smith, who had been given equally broad judiciary powers: he held not only trials of Thugs captured on the Sagar and Narmada territories, but also the power to try "those charged with murders perpetrated in any other territory, and beyond the limits of districts in which our Regulations are in force. . . . [This power] was made over to the Governor General's Agent in the Saugor and Nerbudda territories, who has since been entrusted . . . with the trial of those charged with the murders in the Hyderabad territories also" (Sleeman 1836, "Introduction," 56). Within the districts where these "Regulations" were in force—that is, on the whole of the annexed territories submitted to common "rules" and laws—Thugs were judged by the regular tribunal of the criminal courts of Calcutta and Allahabad.

Already in 1829 a first gang of Thugs captured on the territories of Bhopal and the Narmada was put on trial with the letter George Swinton had addressed to Borthwick used as if it were law. Sleeman convinced the authorities of the migratory character of the Thugs and the ease with which they could disappear given their many accomplices, the difficulties in identifying them, and their cleverness, which all made it very difficult to establish evidence (Bruce 1968: 47). Sleeman also took advantage of the particular nature of the juridical status of the territories in which he was posted: he answered directly to the governor general's secretary. This made it possible to bypass the opinion of the supreme criminal court, which was usually required in the annexed territories. Swinton's recommendations were thus accepted and applied[7] by the British residents, and this also in the states under subsidiary allegiance. The accused were branded and were given the following sentences:

> The death penalty when there was proof that the culprit had strangled or had helped or assisted a strangler, or if he had been *jamadar,* that is Thug chief.
>
> Deportation for life of the culprit if it was proven that he had been known to be a Thug, but when only one witness accused him of having been a strangler in the course of a single incident.
>
> Deportation for life for Thugs who performed important tasks such as digging graves, convincing victims, helping to make the bodies disappear.
>
> Fourteen years in prison for those who performed lesser tasks such as standing guard.
>
> Seven years in prison for those accused of having been present as the gang perpetrated its crimes but who did not actively participate in them.
>
> Release on bail for young boys taken prisoner.

Sleeman and Curven Smith demanded that special courts be set up in the annexed territories so that the supreme criminal courts could be kept outside the trials against the Thugs. Curven Smith wrote in 1830: "the Thugs are citizens of India and not of any particular division."[8] This supranationality called for a suprajustice. Curven Smith even proposed that all the trials should be centralized at Sagar so that he could make the best use of "the extraordinary fact, illustrative of the strength of memory of the Thug leaders as well as the extent of their information, that they are acquainted with the principal Thug leaders and Thugs all over India and can recognize them though they are not always familiar with their persons" (Bruce 1968, 161).

These were thus the powers, beliefs, and wishes of the two men who organized the trials in Sagar from 1830 on. Their tenacity and their power of persuasion were to win out, and in spite of their use of means embarrassing to the supreme government, their cause was to triumph, as shown by trials and the special anti-Thug laws finally promulgated in 1836.

But before discussing these laws that were to generate other ones heavy with consequence for the story of crime in the empire, we need to look at how justice was rendered in this newly acquired region of India, which shared borders with independent, and of course turbulent, native kingdoms.

ARRESTS

The Thugs' Mobility

To arrest Thugs was a complicated matter. They were extremely dispersed, as shown in the list of their arrests between 1826 and 1845. The campaign conducted against them began first in the center of India (from 1826 to 1832 at Jabalpur, Sagar, and Indore); it then spread into the Deccan (the *nizam's* states of Hyderabad, Pune, and Solapur in 1836, and so on); then to the provinces located to the north and east (in 1837 at Lucknow, Bareilly, the present day state of Uttar Pradesh, and Chapra in Bengal); and finally, the same year and following ones, in the south of the peninsula (Mysore, Dharwad, and Bangalore).

To this geographical explosion of the places Thugs inhabited was added the fact that they traveled far and wide in the course of their expeditions. For instance, Amir Ali, who confessed having committed close to eight hundred crimes in the course of his career, resided in the state of Rampur. In the course of his seventh expedition, which lasted six months, he was on the road for twenty days before perpetrating his first murders in the Gwalior region. He then crisscrossed the regions of Nagpur, Jabalpur, and Lucknow. Feringheea, who lived in Jalaun, in the state of Jhansi, also covered the whole of the center of India and in addition made incursions into the Deccan.

Except for two cases (Ksinath Jadu, one of the ascetic Thugs questioned by Lieutenant Burrows at Hardhwar in 1837, admits having killed a traveler five *kos* [one kos equals approximately two miles] away from his village; in an even more surprising case, a traveler was killed while crossing a Thug village), the murderers always killed far away from their homes, usually at a distance of several days of travel by foot. The arrests thus sometimes occurred in their homes (when they couldn't get the Thugs, the soldiers arrested their families to force their surrender), but more often on the road.

Their dispersal was also due to the circumstances prevailing at the time: the loss of customary protection and the growing number of police raids. Bheelam Barre Khan resided in seven different places in the course of his life; his case was common. Another accused told that he was imprisoned at Chinchole (one of the *nizam's* territories) by Gopal Rao, who took his oxen, his mare, and his colt and chased his family out of the village. His family then settled in a village in the same district, called Chilgurra. Three months later the freed prisoner came to join them, but after nine months the village head chased them away again. They settled in Hudulgee, where he was finally arrested by the British.[9] The start of the campaign triggered mass flights by the Thugs from the northwest, Bundelkhand, Gwalior, Malwa, and Doab, who fled toward Rajasthan,

Gujarat, and Marwar, while the Thugs from Arcot "have fled and settled in the *zillah* of Shorapur (Karnataka) which belongs to the nizam. . . . When Mr. Munro, the magistrate, arrested them, they fled again under the leadership of Sheikh Ahmed and settled towards Muslipatam, about fifteen days journey, where they stayed eight to ten years; then they settled in the district of Chuddupa."[10]

The difficulties encountered in trying to catch the murderers became yet more complicated when they found refuge in kingdoms that were independent or under treaty. As Meadows Taylor wrote,

> My district was much cut up by private estates, whose owners or managers defied or evaded the orders of the Nizam's executive government, and would only obey their own masters, some of whom were powerful nobles of Hyderabad, who jealously resented any interference by the executive minister, while their agents were well-known protectors of thieves and robbers, whose booty they shared. (Taylor 1986b, 53)

The British thus bent the law and justified this by arguing the infamy of the Thugs. Curven Smith dealt with these issues in a letter to George Swinton:

> I am aware that the use of general warrants, is disapproved of generally by Government and is liable to great abuse, and to lead to serious oppression. It must however be recollected, and the fact deserves the highest consideration, that the hands of these miscreants are raised against mankind, in general, of all descriptions, sparing neither Hindoos nor Musulmans. . . . The liberty of the subject must bend to a temporary suspension as the lesser evil of the two, and therefore though the use of spies and general warrants, will doubtless, occasionally create great evils and much distress to individuals, it must be submitted to, as the least of the evils attending such a depraved state of society, as at present obtains . . . in general throughout the whole continent of India.[11]

In the independent territories, this exceptional measure could only be applied after asking for permission or expressing threats in order to obtain aid and assistance. In general, chiefs and native kings complied because the colonial authorities interpreted lack of cooperation as rebellion or complicity with the criminals.

Simultaneously Sleeman drew on the colonial network: the residents of the allied kingdoms of Gwalior, Hyderabad, Awadh, and so on were given directives to arrest Thugs and had the duty to try them. The British officers recruited "locally" were asked to help. This was the case of Meadows Taylor:

[In 1833] those famous discoveries in regard to the practice of Thuggee had recently been made at Jubbulpore and Saugor by [then] Captain Sleeman, which made a sensation in India never to be forgotten. . . . I volunteered my services in the labour of collecting evidence, and they were accepted. Day after day I recorded tales of murder which, though horribly monotonous, possessed an intense interest; and as fast as new approvers came in, new mysteries were unravelled and new crimes confessed. . . . The reader will remember my intense anxiety on this subject in 1829, and my conviction that deadly crime existed and was only awaiting discovery; now it was all cleared, but I felt sore that it had not fallen to my lot to win the fame of the affair. (Taylor 1986b, 53)

"Sleeman's organization covers the whole of India," exclaimed enthusiastically Sir Francis Tuker. More specifically it included the former Marathas territories, the independent states, and the treaty states of Bundelkhand, Marwar, Awadh, Rajasthan, and Hyderabad, as shown on the following list in *Ramaseeana* in which the superintendent in 1836 thanks his most illustrious collaborators:

Colonel Low and Captain Paton in Awadh; Major Borthwick in Western Malwa, Delhi, Gujarat; Major Halves, Mr. Wilkinson, agents in Bhopal; Colonel Spiers, agent in Rajasthan; Captain Reynolds, in the territories of the Nizam; R. Cavendish, Resident at Gwalior; Mr. Graeme and Colonel Briggs, Residents at the Nagpur Court; Captains Robinson and Johnstone, Assistant and Resident at the Court of Holcar; Mr. Williams and Colonel Balfour at Baroda; Major Ross, Agent at Kota; Mr. Aisnlie and Mr. Begbie, Agents of the Governor General of Bundelkhand.

His hopes were thwarted in Bihar, Bengal, and Orissa (Sleeman 1836, "Introduction," 40–41 n. 51), but soon Sleeman, having been named general superintendent of the Thug repression, was to be able to catch assassins in these regions as well.

How to Catch a Thug

The pursuers were given specific lists of alleged culprits as well as letters requesting the collaboration of native and British officials in the regions they were visiting. Numerous letters persistently and sternly reminded the Thug hunters of the rules they are supposed to follow.

The instructions given to every party who goes out in pursuit of Thugs are: 1. That they shall arrest such men only as are named, in the lists furnished by them; 2. That they shall release such man

whom they have once arrested till they have taken him to the constituted local authority of the place where he is arrested; 3. That
they shall at all times when demanded show their lists to the local
authorities and act in concert with them; 4. The receipt of the local
authority for any prisoner is immediately forwarded to the European officer under whom the party is acting; 5. That no Approver
is to be allowed to go into any village unattended though it may be
often necessary that he and the persons who attend him, shall go
in disguise, and so on.[12]

There were, of course, slips among the members of these special
commandos as evidenced in the rest of this letter to Captain Reynolds.
The letter writer suggested the adoption of "the best measures to check
the abuses to which such authority might give rise." But optimism was
the rule: "The checks we adopted have had the desired effect and though
complaints are still occasionally made they are rarely of a serious nature
when our rules are rigidly enforced." However, one year later in 1836,
William Sleeman repeated the same recommendations in a note that included "18 rules for the guidance of Indian Officers sent in command of
parties for the Arrest of Thugs." He added instructions that are telling of
the treatment of Thug collaborators: "That no Approver shall be relieved
from the irons without orders from Headquarters and when to any place
under a charge of misconduct he must have fetters on both legs. . . . To
punish any Approver for misconduct by additional irons and cuffs and
cutting of his daily allowance one-anna per diem." The native officers
who accompanied them were as well under scrutiny: they were required
to provide receipts for all their expenses actually incurred because it
came out that some of them attempted to receive free help, or goods
from the inhabitants.[13]

Bounty Hunters

The reward for bringing in a Thug, this "necessary incentive," as Sleeman
put it, possibly appealed to people who knew a lot about the criminals and
who denounced them the more readily when they were then compensated
for their loss of "income." The method was an old one; Chitu, the Pindari
chief, was its victim in the past.

The rewards for Thugs' convictions were thus substantial. Two hundred rupees were paid for "the arrest of Zolfukar, son of Thugs, whose
father has just been captured with eight men of his gang in the *jagir* of
Pune by the cipayes troop of Jhansi assisted by the rajah's soldiers." "I
was authorized to offer a reward of five hundred Roopies for the apprehension of these leaders who had again taken the roads through Rajpootana,"[14] that is, the rebel area of Jodhpur. In 1830, in the framework

of the Thug repression, Curven Smith set the maximum reward at one thousand rupees: "Specific reward to be offered by the Superintendent with the sanction of the Agent to the Governor General not exceeding 1,000Rs for each leader of Thugs proved to be of that description by trial already concluded."[15]

The colonizers rewarded the bounty hunters and all those who distinguished themselves over the year with their good services just as they did former rebels. "In addition to pecuniary rewards small jaheeers burthened with a trifling *obaree* or quit-rent might be granted. . . . Honorary distinctions and titles might also be granted on special cases."[16]

Native Cooperation, Resistance, and Complicity
GIFTS AND RACKETS

It is true that the Thugs enjoyed complicities and support: *burgela* in their secret Ramasee language means "the one who knows Thug secrets and keeps them." *Tome* means the part reserved "to the village chief or any patron as gift." "Our chiefs give a part to our village chiefs before giving us our part," stated an accused. "All Thugs know this." "The handsomest horse, sword or ornament, that they got in an expedition was commonly reserved for the most powerful patron of the order," claims Sleeman (1836, "Substance," 224). His informants gave accounts of conversations that made this obvious: village chiefs, *zamindars*, officers of the state, nabobs, rajahs, and so on protected them for reasons both religious and economic.

They all worshiped the same Goddess, particularly "when the small pox or the cholera morbus rages. [They] worship at the temples, and prostate themselves and their children before the image of the goddess" (Sleeman 1836, "Substance," 151). They were convinced Kali protected and respected the Thugs, and they were thus afraid of meddling. None of the informants personally witnessed the divine, fantastic punishments that befell those who dared harm the Thugs:

> Has not Nanha, the Raja of Jhalone, made leprous by Davey for putting to death Bodhoo and his brother Kumolee. . . . He made them trampled under the feet of elephants but the leprosy broke out upon his body the very next day. . . . He did everything to appease her. Bodhoo had begun a well in Jhalone; the Raja built it up in a magnificent style; he had a tomb raised to their names, fed Brahmans, and consecrated it, had worship instituted upon it, but all in vain. . . . When Mahadjee Scindia caused seventy Thugs to be executed at Muthura, was he not warned in a dream by Davey that he should release them? And did he not the very day after

their execution begin to spit blood? And did he not die within three months? (Sleeman 1836, "Substance," 156)

The Dureear families of the Rathor clan of the Kuchwaha Rajputs were decimated after the death of thirty Thugs from whom they had extorted fourteen thousand rupees, and the *subadar* (prince or governor) who collected the money saw his son and his best horse die in front of his own eyes before dying himself.

> The Raja of Kundule arrested all the Thugs in his Raj for some murders they had committed. For three successive nights the voice of Davey was heard from the top of every temple in the capital, warning the Rajah to release them. . . . The third night the bed on which he and his Ranee were sleeping was taken up by Davey and dashed violently against the ground. . . . They were not killed but they were dreadfully bruised; and had they not released the Thugs, they would certainly have been killed the next night. (Sleeman 1836, "Substance," 156–58)[17]

Sleeman's informants were telling him that "Thugs everywhere made friends . . . among the land holders and other heads of villages; and without patrons they could not have thrived. They were obliged of course to give them a liberal share of booty" (Sleeman 1836, "Substance," 153). But this "friendship" was less than cordial. Many *zamindars* rented out land to the Thugs for five times the usual rate. Some helped them by posting large bails for them and taking on the responsibility for their future actions. In exchange, of course, they required their cut. The *subadar* of the Jabalpur district used a better tactic: he had Thugs arrested, and "after having been made to disgorge all their property, they were all suffered to escape" (Sleeman 1836, "Substance," 244). Some individuals specialized in this type of maneuver. Bearee Lal, Dhunraj Set's agent, sent the Thugs off on an expedition. "He got a great deal of money by procuring the release of all the noted Thugs in confinement at different places. . . . Lal had always half a dozen of the principal Thug leaders about his person, and used to attend all our marriages and festivals," claimed Sleeman's informants (Sleeman 1836, "Substance," 190–91). In 1835 Sheikh Sahabeen told Reynolds, the magistrate who was interrogating him, that when the Thugs of Arcot settled in Shorapur, the rajah demanded a rent of two thousand rupees per year. When he noticed that the murderers were collecting large sums of money, he assessed an extra fine on them.

Thus the Thugs fed the prince's treasure. And their legendary "solidarity" could crumble with the dark conflicts sometimes tearing them apart, as in this story, where yet again the tithe collected by the local potentate takes on the form of a fixed tax:

Hirroulee and Rae Singh were arguing about a diamond that the latter had kept hidden when the loot was shared. Rae Singh grievously insulted Hirroulee, who then ran his sword through him.

> His bowels burst out, but we got a silver platter applied to the wound and Rae Singh recovered. . . . He went to the *Rana* of Gohud, from whom he got the farm of the customs for one hundred and thirty thousand rupees a year, and the farm of the *purgunna* of Omree at sixty thousand. He induced the chief of Gohud to invade Sindhouse, which was burnt to the ground, and from that time the Thug families were made to pay every three years a tax of twenty-five rupees each. (Sleeman 1836, "Substance," 225)

In contrast, in Bundelkhand the Thugs were not lords of pillage and murder, but people who had been left out, poor folks used for the magnates' own benefit. The disappointed landowners had lost the "gifts" the Thugs used to bring them.

The complicity between Thugs and native authorities took on very diverse forms, ranging from "gifts" so they would be able to "thuggee" in peace to efficiently organized rackets; from graceful acceptance to demanding violence aimed at oppressing and exploiting the Thugs. These were not well-oiled complicities as Sleeman was claiming, but ruthless relations of force that at every moment were renegotiated and could swing in favor of one or the other of the parties.

Who controlled whom? The nabob Dollee Khan of Madura attempted to sever the tie linking him to the Thugs: he offered a major Thug chief "a high post with rent-free lands if he would leave off the trade. He would not." The nabob had to resign himself to keeping on receiving his criminal gifts (Sleeman 1836, "Substance," 151).

And yet the majority of the people appear to have wanted to get rid of the Thugs, as evidenced by the success of Sleeman's campaign. In their depositions peasants showed no qualms in pursuing Thugs, whom they called *dakou* (a variant of the word *dacoits*, meaning "bandits," or "thieves") when describing their misdeeds. Taylor gives us a description of the emotions of those who discovered the murdered corpses:

> Dead bodies, evidently strangled, and in no instance recognized, were found by the roadside, and no clue could be discovered as to the perpetrators of their death. In two places, jackals and hyenas had rooted up newly made graves, in one of which were found four bodies and in another two, much eaten and disfigured. The whole country was in alarm, and the villagers had constantly patrolled their roads, but as yet in vain. (Taylor 1986b, 61–62)

COOPERATION AND RESISTANCE IN RAJASTHAN

The Thugs were sometimes pawns in the confrontation pitting the colonial authority against independent chiefs demanding the right to have their own police and, the British claim, not missing the opportunity to enrich themselves through the usual scheme of complicity between kings and brigands.

The native chiefs cooperated as a rule, except for those of Jodhpur and Jhaipur, who were, of course, accused of profiting from the Thugs. But things were not that simple. In fact, these chiefs were motivated not so much by material interest as by the desire to establish a different type of relationship with the colonizers. By giving aid to both the Thugs and the British they showed they were in control of the situation and gained the power to negotiate.

In 1835 H. W. Trevelyan,[18] who was posted in Jodhpur, finally got the maharajah to promise to give his support to the troops coming to arrest Thugs. But Trevelyan doubted that they would be successful, this for several reasons. The first was the ignorance in which the maharajah "is kept [in Marwar] of what goes forward in this State both near and remote from his capital"; the second was "his own reluctance to infringe and trench upon what he conceives to be the established privileges of these religious classes from fear of bringing discredit upon himself." There were, wrote Trevelyan, "numerous villages belonging to Charuns, Jogis and other religious sects, who set the orders of the Government and its local officers at defiance and harbour all descriptions of Offenders (many of whom are guilty of the grossest crimes receiving a share of the profits of their atrocities)." Trevelyan had several meetings with the king, and he reported that in the course of the last one

> His Highness [Ram Singh] informed me that orders had been issued to the Principal *Thakoor* of Marwar, to the *Hakims* of Pergunnahs and other local officers to render every possible assistance which might be required by parties in the course of their proceedings and the only doubt which remains in his mind . . . was as regarded the Village inhabited by Charuns who were in the habit of resisting all authority and when coerced or pressed to act in a manner displeasing to them would threaten to resort to acts of violence upon themselves which always deterred the Government officers from interfering with them. To this I replied that when the Charuns discovered that threatening would no longer answer their purpose, they would in my opinion much prefer obeying orders. . . . Under any circumstances the maiming or self-destruction of one or more of these pertinacious people ought not to be allowed to have any

weight in impeding or frustrating the operations in progress to exterminate these murderers who are the enemies of Mankind.

The king agreed to cooperate with the British, but wanted bards' villages
to be handled carefully because

> Their chief power is derived from an impression, that it is certain
> ruin and destruction to shed his blood, or that of any of his family,
> or to be the cause of it being shed. . . . A Charun becomes the safe-
> guard of travellers and the security for merchants. . . . When he sees
> [robbers] approach, he warns them off by holding a dagger in his
> hand; and if they do not attend to him, he stabs himself in a place
> that is not mortal, and taking the blood from the wound, throws it
> at the assailants with imprecations of future woe and ruin. . . . The
> evil consequences of a Charun being driven to undergo a violent
> death, can be alone averted by grants of lands and costly gifts to
> surviving relations. (Malcolm 1972: 2, 134–37)

As could be expected, Trevelyan was irritated by the protection enjoyed
by these villages of sacred bards suspected of being Thug sanctuaries.
The king agreed with him even while claiming he couldn't touch their
privileges. Like the Jodhpur chiefs, he consented and resisted all at once.
Through the Thugs, colonial authority was thwarted and constrained.
Its abuses were resented not only by local chiefs, but as well by some
colonizers, who embraced and defended these latter's viewpoint.

English Protestations

The intrusion of Sleeman's troops in the princely states displeased some
of the British residents. Lord Cavendish at Gwalior and Lord Lushington
at Bharatpur were incensed by arrests made on the basis of simple denunciations as well as by the Company's interference in the internal affairs
of reigning kings. Lushington singled out Lieutenant Colonel A. Lockett,
representing the governor general at Ajmer:

> I beg to observe that in the instruction of the Government the pos-
> sibility of these persons being innocent is not so much alluded to
> nor is the slightest notice taken of the insult put upon the Bhurt-
> poor Rajah in arresting one of his Sepahees without his knowledge
> or consent. The Government may be of opinion that a humiliation
> of this sort is not felt by a native Prince but I can take upon me
> to assert that it was felt and deeply too, and that it is not by such
> measures as these that the Bhurtpoor (or any native authorities)
> will be induced to cooperate heartily in the suppression of Thugs.[19]

Lushington was asked to keep his scruples and political considerations to himself and to let Sleeman's men do their job. He complied. Lord

Cavendish, whose post at Gwalior was much more prestigious, was able to resist. He wrote Sleeman: "I am not, as you are, armed with judicial power. Whatever remonstrances are made, must be made in diplomatic language and not in judicial orders." He wrote as well to the Governor General and pointed out the unjust and dangerous nature of the procedures used: "Their apprehension, detention and confinement, if innocent, must be considered a great evil. The Gwalior territory has had several visits for this purpose since my arrival and having been a magistrate in former days I know of the difficulty of preventing extortion and oppression" (Bruce 1968, 151–52). He requested that arrests be overseen by a British officer and not be left to the discretion of native police who might be corrupt. He won the argument and MacLeod was appointed supervisor of the anti-Thug campaign in Gwalior, Malwa, and Rajasthan, while Paton was appointed in Awadh and adjacent territories. The affair of the Thugs, "citizens of India," led the colonizers to think in terms of an India that didn't exist yet; the vast territories the Thugs were supposed to cover were actually those the empire wanted to possess and rule. Thus the criminals provided an argument to put pressure on the independent states and reformulate the colonial power's relations with them.

The reason Sleeman and Curven Smith succeeded in having their opinions implemented was that the pan-Indian scourge of Thuggism could be imagined as matching the dimensions of the British Empire. The two leaders of the anti-Thug campaign were not met with long-term resistance anywhere, but they exaggerated the resistance they did encounter. At any rate, this resistance was extremely localized, as evidenced in the triumphant summary of the anti-Thug operations in 1834.

Spread and Success of the Arrests in 1834

Sleeman's report of 1834 shows the success of the campaign, the vastness of the territories over which it unfolds, and finally, the support of the local native and British authorities from which it benefits.

Of course, such a success was not permanent: "the *burkas*, or fully initiated Thugs, who have as yet escaped us, are capable of creating new gangs in any part of India that they may be permitted to inhabit; and that they will so create them if left for any time undisturbed in any place, no man who is well acquainted with the system will for a moment doubt." Yet success was undeniable. The colonizers moreover showed their gratefulness towards those who helped them. Native collaborators whose job consisted in bringing back the criminals and their loot intact to their British master were rewarded. For instance, Raslum Khan was given a palanquin and a pension; he must have respected the two rules of not brutalizing the population and not appropriating Thug possessions for himself.

However, as we have just seen, the rules of conduct were repeatedly restated and abuses denounced. Obviously, rules were broken. The respect of the right of persons was, in fact, officially suspended, but the British lawful state was not supposed to suffer from this; slippages were thus controlled and evaluated and met with reprimands when they went beyond certain limits.

The confiscation of goods found with Thugs as they were arrested was directly linked to the funding of the campaign against them. This provided the motivation for the British care to come into possession of the whole of this wealth.

The Economy of the Repression
THUG WEALTH

A detailed list of the "property having belonged to the Thugs and sold by order of Lieutenant Lumley, assistant to the superintendent general of Solapur (in Maharashtra), from 14th May 1836 to 1st April 1838"[20] allows us to get a look at Thug wealth.

In two years the total sum of the profit made from the sale of their possessions was 2,414 rupees. Almost half of this sum, 1,185 rupees, came from the sale of the goods that had belonged to a certain Manajee Sulgur, "Thug and hanged." The list includes clothing (saris, pajamas, turbans and several *roomals*), numerous kitchen utensils, jewelry, coins of various origins worth four hundred rupees, and finally, agricultural tools and livestock (nine large oxen, eight young ones, twelve cows with their calves, a mature bull and a young one, a horse and a pony) in sufficiently large quantities for us to speculate that Manajee Sulgur was involved in agriculture.

Of the other half of the profit made from the sale of Thugs' possessions, one-third came from the sale of goods belonging to "unknown owners" and the other two-thirds from the possessions of other Thugs, of whom two were deported and five were informers. For six of them the sale brought less than five rupees: Manick: a sari (one rupee); Shewa Dhungur: a pistol (four rupees two annas); Sher Khan: a sword (twelve annas), a cow and her calf (one rupee twelve annas), and a black-powder rifle (one rupee four annas); Anundha Dhungur, prisoner: six goats (two rupees twenty-nine annas); Sahiburna Kolee: a black-powder rifle (one rupee); Mowalla, informer: a knife (four annas), and a *roomal* (fifteen annas).

The profession of Thug didn't always bring "riches and fame." There were great inequalities. Manajee Sulgur swam in wealth, but it is clear that most of his peers were very poor, even indigent. Like the armed peasants D. H. A. Kolff writes about, their only possessions were some livestock and a few arms, among which the *roomal* was the least costly.

The details of this list are also precious on account of the information they give us on the prevailing price of things. We can thus appreciate the exorbitance of the reward for the capture of "Bhumee, *jamadar*": the reward of five hundred rupees represents five hundred saris or five hundred black-powder rifles, or again a herd of 250 oxen!

THE USES OF THIS WEALTH

In a letter addressed to Lieutenant Briggs in 1835,[21] William Sleeman requested that all the proceeds from the sale of Thugs' possessions be given to the government. The Board of Directors in London congratulated his department: "We are glad to learn that the plunder recovered from the Thugs and to which no claim can be established by individuals, is likely to afford a fund sufficient to cover the Extra expenses occasioned by your proceedings for the suppression of Thuggism."[22] We thus can see that the financing of the anti-Thug campaign was just as circular as the constructed image of their crimes. The greater fairness imposed on the arrests, the repression of corruption, and mostly the end of Thuggism brought, in Sleeman's words, a diminishing of this unholy loot.

The issue of compensation of the victims is nowhere brought up in the documents I consulted, though it is true that it was not possible to restitute victims' possessions because no one, or almost no one, filed complaints. The colonizers were thus the last stage in the fraudulent succession of appropriations of these goods (first by the Thugs and then by their pursuers). The British noted that no one asked for them, at least formally. This was a necessary clause that allowed them to become, in turn, their legitimate owners.

The loop was complete when Lieutenant Lumley wrote out in neat columns the dates of the sales, the name of the former owners (including the note "unknown"), the list of the prices of each item, from the humblest one, worth four *paisas*, to the most expensive, a horse worth eighty rupees. At that moment at last these goods reached an honorable destination; their value became that of the official market rather than that of the parallel market of the Thugs.

Thus substantial money stakes were involved. The British knew that the individuals entrusted with arresting Thugs were exposed to "temptations," temptations the colonizers preferred to keep for themselves. In this way, their campaign was almost completely self-financed. To exceptional murderers corresponded exceptional financial means.

TRIALS

The most pressing issue facing us is that of the truth of the accusations against the Thugs. This not from the perspective of the "guilty or not guilty" question asked of jurors, but rather from that of how the truth of their crimes was established.[23] I would like to reconstruct this process here.

For police authorities the first and essential step consisted in collecting detailed narratives of the murdering expeditions. These confessions were usually made by Thugs themselves who became informers in exchange for the promise that their lives would be spared.

Depositions: Interrogation and Memory

"The magistrate is, in the first instance, to place on record a faithful narrative of the prisoner's life of crimes, noting every thuggee in which he has been employed, the names of the Thugs," with whom he has been associated, and their respective actions in the course of the murders.[24] These were the general instructions given to the policemen-magistrates sent out in the whole of India, sometimes thousands of kilometers away, to interrogate Thugs.

There are clues that in addition to these general instructions there was also a specific questionnaire guiding their investigations. Its existence is apparent in the form of the depositions preserved in large bundles in the Delhi archives. They contain identical narrative sequences, regularly punctuated with an abundance of similar details accompanying the unfolding of the crimes. These accounts often deal with several expeditions resembling and following each other, and at times occurring dozens of years prior to the deposition. As Curven Smith and William Sleeman often pointed out, Thugs' memories were extraordinary.

An instance is Doorgha's exceptionally detailed narrative.[25] He was asked on 20 August 1833 to give an account of his fourteenth expedition, which lasted six months and in the course of which, as the crow flies, he covered 940 miles, that is an average of seven and a half miles a day.[26] In these six months, he participated in thirty-two murders, and at the end his total loot, like that of each of his accomplices, came to sixty rupees. The twists and turns of the story provide a break from the monotony characterizing the other accounts, though his does follow the same narrative logic, including simple and more complex sequences. The simple sequence, and the more profitable one from the point of view of the criminal, is made up of four major propositions:

1. First the victims must be found, contact with them made, and their trust acquired. Doorgha tells his interrogators that a Rajput traveler on his way from Agra to Deccan mistook them for travelers. Subhun *jamadar* gained his trust and he settled down next to the gang.

2. Then the passage to action, with the killing and the disposition of the remains: in the morning the gang leaves in the company of the traveler on the way to Esagurh, and when they arrive in the jungle, the Thugs strangle him and hide his body under some stones in a river.

3. Finally two levels of conclusions: The first pertains to the profit the criminal and his accomplices gain from the action. The total take is seventy rupees of Jhansi and some kitchen utensils and clothes. They get a rupee each and use the rest to pay for their common expenses. The second level highlights the judiciary framework in which Doorgha makes his deposition. He gives a detailed list of the members of the gang to which he belongs, a list that also contains information about the criminals' kinship relations to each other, their castes and their religions, as well as the specific roles they played in the murders: stranglers, gainers of the victims' trust, holders of arms or legs, and so on. The list also tells us whether they are dead or alive and their penal situation (arrested, free, in prison, and so on). The investigation's metanarrative infiltrates the narrative of the crime. The deposition thus encompasses both the infraction and its repression. It obeys a double temporality: a past without the British and a present with them in which the accused is or will be subject to their law.

This stable structure could contain a variety of circumstances. In Bheelam Barre Khan's account, the narrator's gang joins another band that finds and gains the trust of the victims:

> On our arrival at Bedar, Shib Kahn *jemadar* with his gang had put up at the Moosafur Khana before us. . . . The *jemadar* had with him three Travellers with four tattoo loads of goods. I and the said *jemadar* consulted together; the result was that I went on before and sat down at a *Baollee* called Begum. Sahib Khan *jemadar* followed with the Travellers, we found no opportunity of strangling them there, so we went on to Chilmurree and the next morning proceeded towards Sungun, we went on to Koss on the other side of Sungun, and at a convenient *nullah* strangled the Travellers. We were observed by a cowherd who was sitting on a tree and who gave the alarm.[27]

The presence of a witness forced them to temporarily split up and meet again later to share the loot. Two more victims who happened to be at the wrong place and time were added to others and met the same fate. The Thugs used the same strategy as they realized there were too many travelers to be assassinated all at once. They decided to send out a part of the gang with seven Hindu travelers while the remainder of the Thugs would follow with the fifteen others. Forty Thugs, led by Judae and Hura, thus departed with the seven Hindu travelers while the 135 remaining gang members, among whom was the narrator, took the fifteen other travelers.

The incidents punctuating the course of these repetitive sequences were few. Doorgha and his group crossed the Sirbungha, then a jungle, and seeing a small river by a monastery, they decided to stop "to wash themselves and answer the call of nature." At that point there was a confrontation between what we might call a recalcitrant victim and a heroic Thug, the narrator's brother.

A strangler was posted behind each traveler as they awaited the return of Ram Singh, a traveler who had wandered about fifty feet away from the small river. When he finally returned, one of his companions called out to him. The stranglers, thinking that this was the *jirnee*—that is, the secret signal given by their leader—fell on the fourteen travelers, whom they killed all at once. Seeing this, Ram Singh fled as fast as he could. The narrator's brother, Kurghoo, ran after him and yelled, "Where are you going, you're already caught!" Ram Singh pulled out his sword and gave a blow to Kurghoo, who was protected by his shield. He was getting ready to hit him again when Kurghoo threw him to the ground while others Thugs arrived at the scene. With their help, Kurghoo strangled him. They dragged his body to the other side of the river and buried it with the others.[28]

In the meanwhile, the other gang still had not killed the seven Hindu travelers. The narrator tells us the sinister sequel, in which the next morning his gang took the road to Chutterkote as the other group had done. They found the other gang camping under the trees outside of a village. Doorgha's group arrived around noon. Upon their arrival, the seven travelers inquired about the other travelers. The Thugs told them that they had stopped at a village where they had visited some of their kin, but that they were to meet them again in Chutterkote. The following night the whole group set out again, and after about one *kos* and a half Hura Lodhee gave the signal: *Pan lao!* The seven travelers were strangled. After spending the night together and sharing the loot, the two gangs split up.

Not all outcomes are happy for the Thugs. Doorgha tells that one day his group, made up of sixty Thugs, arrived at Koraee Bhowrassa in Sindhia's territory and settled in a grove. The two travelers accompanying them were destined to be killed that very night. The Thugs, however, heard two jackals fighting, a very bad omen. So they didn't kill the travelers, and in the morning the Thugs told them to leave as they had some business to settle. The travelers answered that they weren't in a hurry and stuck to them. They all finally arrived at Udaipur, five *kos* away from their previous camp. After they set up camp outside the village, a fight started between Doorgha's brother Kurghoo (the heroic Thug of the preceding narrative) and Loobhoo *jamadar*, as a result of which they split up. The spared victims had refused to leave their would-be assassins! They were now the ones persecuting the Thugs, of course in a much more benign manner, by keeping them from putting the bad omen behind them and neutralizing it.

The scarcity of such incidents make them all the more interesting. The least frequent ones were of a religious nature: a bad omen that stops the action, a rope that breaks when water is being drawn, the cry of the owl, the fowling of a mare; or on the contrary good omens calling for immediate action, as when, at three o'clock in the morning, Sayyid Amir Ali and his band were awakening travelers to start on their journey when one of the Thugs tripped and fell. This was interpreted as a good omen, and the travelers were killed on the spot.[29]

The uniformity of these depositions, which are made up mostly of nearly identical sequences, is partially counterbalanced by the many concrete details giving each narrative a unique, contextual, and authentic character. These details draw from two registers, that of names and that of numbers.

Names (the village where the Thugs rested is called Jalaun; the strangler is called Doorgha, and so on) give a strong aura of truth to the information. Numbers produce the same effect, whether they be vague (the loot was worth about one thousand rupees, the grave dug was at approximately three *kos* from the village) or specific ("my part was worth eight rupees and nine annas"). All of these human and topological data, these arithmetic markers, appear to answer the interrogator's questions, the needs of his inquiry. They also concord with the notion of what a convincing deposition should look like.

The memories of the suspect fulfills these expectations. The narrative unfolds in a numbered time ("three days and three nights went by this way," "I returned to the village and stayed eight months") where the names of towns and villages are as so many buoys marking the space where the Thug traveled. And yet the suspect seems to have suffered from memory lapses. Upon a closer look at the narratives it becomes apparent that the physical characteristics of the landscape are described with vague formulas: jungles, ravines, rivers, dirt paths. There are many omissions. For instance, the discussions between the two gangs are not described; the reasons for their frequent fusions and separations remain obscure most of the time. Internal conflicts are not explained. What was the disagreement pitting Kurghoo against Loobhoo? It is true that this fight erupted after a particularly stressful sequence, that of the spared victims refusing to leave their would-be aggressors, and perhaps this had an impact. But there is no clear indication of this.

Finally, while we have an idea of who did the killing, we know next to nothing about who was killed. Except for their number and occasionally their castes and religions, the victims remain anonymous. Since the murderers so often lived for a time with their victims, why was their memory so lacking in this regard? Though the victims' identities didn't seem to interest the investigators, their possessions certainly did. The Thugs' memory on this point was unbeatable. Each of the interrogation sessions was crowned by a dizzyingly specific inventory. This excessive precision

This painting by M. Schaeft, exhibited at the 1857 *Salon*, shows a peaceful encampment of Thugs away from any village or house and placed under the protection of the debonair god Ganesh. It depicts mothers tending to their children, musicians

playing their instruments, and some young people nonchalantly asleep. There are also two travelers lulled by the scene into trusting their hosts and obviously without a clue of the hosts' murderous intentions.

is troubling, and the more I contemplate the "five rupees and eight annas" collected twenty years previously in the course of an expedition that included more than a dozen equally precise takes, the less I believe it.

The many place names and the specific distances between given villages and groves where the band camped made me think that it would be easy to retrace their exact itinerary. I tried, but in vain: there are numerous elisions in their narratives and it is easy to loose the thread of their wanderings, the places they visited, the time spent in going from one to another. And yet the accumulation of details does produces the effect of reality. Moreover, the crimes described by Doorgha mesh perfectly with the narrative of another accused. The deposition is convincing because it appears that it can be validated (it is possible to verify the facts), it is not false (as proved by the corroborating account), and it is credible in the manner that scientific and conjectural explanations are. [30]

The depositions are shortcuts and dramatizations of the facts: no intermediary stage is provided, [31] the work of memory striving to remember is not noted, the questionnaire is erased. The details—that is, the quantities that can counted and the data that can be objectified—give the impression that they can be checked at any time, and that if at some point they were indeed checked, the result would undoubtedly be a positive one. As we will see later, when the investigation showed that these details could not be matched with the facts, judges used a reasoning based on synecdoche whereby the part stands for the whole. The bits of evidence that could be made to concord with each other were taken as a set of real proofs.

The diversity of the loot, the successes and the failures, the flights, the incidents, do not disturb the uniform facade of a criminality that has been made peculiar by the nature of its misdeeds along with the extreme depersonalization of its actors. According to the official written instructions the interrogator's aim should be to report only on "the prisoners' lives of crimes" and not on their lives as a whole. The investigation focused thus on "Thug crime," and it carried in itself a stereotypical stress between the general and the particular, between the invariant narrative morphology and the profusion of details. Doorgha was the spitting image of Bheelam Barre Khan, who was that of all the others. The typology of the group to which he belonged was preconstructed in the interrogation. Their "extraordinary" and faithful memory was given pride of place in it. These hundreds of identical inventories do indeed seem to demonstrate the existence of a group of individuals each made out of the same cloth.

Did Thugs' crimes inform these narratives or did the narratives themselves construct "Thug crime"? As I will show later on, the answer lies halfway between the misdeeds of the perpetrators and the visions the British have of them. Limited to place-time facts, the "objective narrative" so often used as the oppressor's weapon carries within itself the assumption that each suspect is a link in a hereditary chain of criminals and that he is motivated by material interests.

Denunciations and Informers
FROM SILENCE TO CONFESSION

"The witness, after being warned to speak the whole truth relative to the murders was duly sworn and deposed." Every suspect had to take an oath. Depending on his religion the authorities put in front of him water from the Ganges or the Koran. The suspect had to involve his faith so that his gods or God would punish him if he perjured himself. Divine justice and the threat of punishment in the afterlife was evoked. Sometimes terror was struck by bringing out the murder weapons. James Paton objected to "this custom in our Courts to make Thug approvers swear in addition to the Ganges water, or the Koran, by the cloth with which they strangle their victims! The knife with which they stab the corpse!"[32]

Once the oath taken, the findings as well as the degree of guilt could vary. While most of the depositions concord with my preceding general description, they altogether cover a more diversified continuum ranging from total refusal to speak to confession or avowal.

Many suspects, in the course of a trial, declared they had nothing to say about the matter at hand. Others gave a testimony that was of no use to the investigators, such as that of this young groom,[33] a "servant" whose job was to cut grass to feed the horse of his master Feringheea, and who each time a crime was perpetrated saw nothing, knew nothing, and at any rate did not collect a share of the take, as his employer was only giving him "food and clothing."

The colonizers often had recourse to the evidence of the neutral forms of testimony and depositions along with that of the less-used confession.[34] Their often imaginative use lacked systematic correspondence to the various contradictory modes of the narrative, such as its exhaustiveness or imprecision, or to the attitude of the witness, who spoke in a manner that was either restrained or unrestrained. In the instructions regarding cooperative suspects, they were expected to make a "full and ingenuous confession": The right honorable governor general wrote to the "Magistrates and Joint Magistrates of the North Western Provinces":

> You are hereby authorized to offer mercy in the name of the Government to any Thug from whom you may have reason to expect that useful information may be procured on condition that he'd make a full and ingenuous confession. The promise that you are authorized to make is not a promise of entire pardon. His Lordship in Council has before him such strong proofs that offenders

of this class are irreclaimable that he cannot consent to let any of them loose on society, however long the period of their confinement may have been, however unexceptionable their conduct during that confinement may have been or whatever may have been the value of the information given by them. The mercy which you are authorized to promise extends only to exemption of capital punishment and transportation.[35]

There are many implications to the use of the word "confession." It certainly implies that divine justice is linked to human justice, as indicated by the required oath on sacred objects. It also brings out the shame of the accused. And then, it underlines the peculiar nature of an informer's narrative. In the British judicial parlance of the time the informer was an "approver," and proof of guilt was usually referred to as "King's evidence," a term rarely used in the archives pertaining to the Thugs.

In order to fulfill the requirements of authenticity, there were strict directives aimed at preventing communication between informers:

> The approving Thugs who are all kept apart and not suffered to have intercourse with each other give narratives of their past proceedings in which of course their accomplices are named; the accomplices thus named are apprehended . . . and when brought to Saugor are immediately confronted with the Approvers, who are also kept separate and one after another examined as to their knowledge of the Prisoners before them.[36]

The legislator was convinced of the efficacy of his methods: "there is not much chance . . . of innocent people being injured by such cautious proceedings; but should any innocent individuals be brought to Saugor, their innocence at the trial can hardly fail to be made manifest."[37]

THE INFORMERS

Thugs' motives for denouncing their associates might be revenge, the lure of a few extra rupees, but mostly the hope of saving their lives. It seems that some of them came spontaneously, this so much so that Curven Smith had to sort them out: "The number of approvers already admitted I however judged to be ample and I felt no inclination to save from the due punishment of the law more of these wholesale murderers than were deemed sufficient for the condemnation of their accomplices."[38] The simple desire to become an informer was not enough. The colonizers laid down specific rules so as to obtain as much information as possible and to ensure the sincerity of the informer's testimony.

Exhaustiveness of information was ensured by targeting certain potential informers: Sleeman recommended that Thug leaders be used because "subordinate characters know little of the proceedings of the gangs they have followed." This manner of thinking was solidly implanted in the colonizers' minds: kings, chiefs, and leaders, be they rebels or criminals, were the privileged interlocutors of the British. In the present case, the guiltiest were spared hanging. The efficacy of the campaign was unambiguously linked to this elitism. "Our success in the pursuit is attributable almost entirely to my having as principle admitted leaders as Approvers in preference to their subordinates," wrote Sleeman in a letter addressed in 1833 to MacLeod. This principle revealed to be morally advantageous: the leader's superiority could be seen in that he understood both the power of the mighty and their aims: "[for] feelings of degradation which those who betray the secrets of their associates in crime commonly feel . . . [they] instead substitute a conscious pride of serving the State in its duty."[39]

In his apology of snitching, Sleeman rejoiced that even chiefs' sons[40] can manifest that enlightened reason their fathers sometimes lack. Sleeman's musings were speculative, for on the rare occasions when informers did speak of their betrayal, they stated very pragmatically that they obeyed the reality principle: the British were more powerful than they were. The informer was moreover often a man who had been betrayed, such as Kunhae by his two sons; or Feringheea, who surrendered to the British to free his family, whom they had imprisoned. So even if in Sleeman's eyes the benefits of the denunciation rebounded like a happy bouncing ball on the preceding generation in cases where, contrary to custom, the children acted for the good of their parents, or again he imagined the informer to be proud to serve the state, all these were the other side of a troubling coin. At that time, denunciation was not a judicial category, though it was used. It was so essential at trials that legislators planned a new law "providing that no person shall be incompetent to be a witness in any case by reason of a conviction of any offence. When this Act will be passed, a convicted Thug will be competent to give evidence against his accomplices."[41] In 1872 there was an attempt to give a moral justification to this condemnable practice: the confession of someone previously found guilty had to be made voluntarily and it could be used as evidence *"only if* the making of the confession appears to the Court not to have been caused by any inducement, threat or promise [*Indian Evidence Act*, 1872, Section 24]" (Amin 1987, 170).

Of course, the depositions hold no trace of the pain or physical harm that might have been inflicted on the Thugs to make them speak. But in the eyes of this law, the promise of sparing their lives invalidated their denunciations. In 1872 their trials would simply not have been possible. In practice, however, the apparatus of remorse that had been set up generally implied that the one who "tells all" is to get a lighter sentence as reward for helping the judicial system.

DENUNCIATION AS EVIDENCE

Denunciations become evidence to the extent their description of the fact can be verified. This was rarely the case in investigations of the criminals. The exhumation of the bodies was often useless as they were in most cases in advanced state of decomposition or torn apart by animals, rendering them unidentifiable. As to their stolen possessions, they had been sold, resold, given, abandoned; they had circulated so much that they couldn't be found. These two "collateral" proofs, the exhumation of the victims and the recovery of the stolen goods, were, of course, much sought after, but seldom found. As to the gathering of other testimonies, it met with great difficulty.

In numerous letters Sleeman's colleagues complained of the population's systematic refusal to testify. The proverbial slowness of British courts, the loss of time that would be disastrous for the harvest, the loss of income, and so on were the reasons the colonizers used to explain this general reluctance. The fear of falling into the grip of a frightening foreign power and its judicial system certainly played a role, but in general it was not recognized in the documents.

There were yet other causes for the obstacle to the validation of evidence; these were linked to the fact that the Thugs bribed those whose protection they sought, so that the secret of their dangerous creditors was well hidden. Between a reticent population and the complicity of some individuals, there remained few people to give substance to the prosecutors' cases.

From a judicial point of view, the situation was thus very peculiar. No one was filing grievances because the victims, travelers often far away from their homes, were dead. There were no witnesses because families and friends refused to testify. The accusations against the Thugs thus came from the Thugs themselves. Their trials rested almost entirely on denunciations instead of evidence.

In 1830, Curven Smith gave an account to H. P. Princep (Secretary to the Governor General) of the procedures that were applied to

> a number of persons confined in different jails under charge of Thuggee, ever since 1823 A.D. without having had any regular trial. They form three classes of approvers and have in turns caused the arrest of the friends and allies of the others and when their testimony is imputing guilt on any individual, I cannot imagine a stronger evidence on which to ground a conviction. I have for the sake of perspicuity marked the classes A, B, and C. Class A is bitterly opposed to class B; class B is bitterly opposed to class A; class C is bitterly opposed to both.

Informers constituted in different factions were denouncing each other, while according to the magistrate "the divided interests and deadly animosities of the witnesses towards each other, warrant the general fidelity and truth of their narrations."[42]

In this closed system, lacking all of the usual judicial mediation, the informer denounced his friends even as he was denouncing himself. The accusations were accepted because they concorded with each other. Through the British the Thugs engaged in an internal settling of accounts. The colonial belief that they formed a close-knit community was swept away. Bands that British pursuits had made disperse over several different regions, but that formerly had had regular contact with each other, were lacking in the most elementary solidarity.

THE ACCEPTABLE MARGIN OF ERROR

The colonizers meted out severe punishment on the approvers who made mistakes, even though the British were well aware that "they say the least possible out of fear that the smallest mistake would prove to be fatal to them." This comment seems odd given the wealth of details in Thug depositions. It leads me to sense a concern with an elusive equilibrium between too much and too little, and an uneasiness felt by all. From the isolated policeman in his distant district to the very important secretary of the governor general in Calcutta, the authorities suspiciously heaped praise on the virtues and efficacy of their method and heatedly denied the possibility of errors. And yet they did exist.

An example is that of Elwall, posted in the Bangalore district: he wrote in a letter that a certain Khadir Sahib had caused two innocent men to be arrested and do prison time. But he protested right away that "this is a unique case given the system of proof and counter proof at his disposal."[43] And yet that same year, in another letter, he informed his superior Clarke in Bangalore of an imbroglio involving contradictory testimonies. This provoked his superior's anger, but did not lead them to question the system: after all, it was the only one in existence.

Clarke answered that "I firmly believe our usual precautions are sufficient," but he went on to mention that

> the disparities between the original confessions and separate depositions . . . are easily to be accounted for from the difficulty of any person giving correctly and at once and without any assistance to his memory the details and names of parties to a number of murders committed during a series of years, more particularly when the gangs generally counted as in the present instance upward eighty men.

The investigators were confronted with "false and contradictory evidence" for a variety of reasons. The following is a typical example:

Question: Why did you cause by your deposition any persons to be arrested with whom you were not acquainted?

Answer: I thought it had been ordered that all persons living in the same villages with Thugs and connected, and friends with them all, should be seized.

Clarke noted that the danger lay not only in that the informers were the sole judges of how deep their answers must go, but also in the fact that the culprit did not respond to the explicit demand of truth, but to the secret expectations of the colonizers. This double tendency, of course, had to be discouraged. For Sleeman, "any Approver who denounces an innocent person as a Thug should be considered as having forfeited all claim to exemption from the punishment of death and brought to trial for his past crimes as soon as possible. Among the men lately executed at Jubulpore were three Approvers who had absconded while employed as such. These examples have a very salutary effect."[44]

Clarke's notion of the depth of answers is admirable: it is possible to be convinced of the truth of something we are told without therefore being able to measure its scope and extension, its "depth." These sorts of scruples were overshadowed by the dominant discourse according to which false accusations were based on the desire for revenge and the animosity between rival bands. When they were uncovered, they were severely punished, but the remedy consisted in denying the existence of error. In a letter addressed to William Sleeman, the agent of the governor general bestowed legitimacy on the system: "It is beyond the verge of credibility to suppose that five or six individuals at different times and without the possibility of any concert should concur in framing such a story to fix guilt on an innocent person."[45]

The Indictment

In the years 1832–1833, Thugs arrested at Hyderabad were not judged by the Resident as they should have been; instead, they were brought to Sagar. In a letter[46] addressed to Reynolds, who was posted at Hingolee, Curven Smith asked him to take care of a certain number of formalities aimed at establishing the prosecution's case before sending the prisoners.

When the prisoners arrived at Sagar, and before they appeared in front of the judge, William Sleeman proceeded to double check the work of his collaborators by using his own informers: "With the labour I take and the knowledge regarding these men and these proceedings it is unwholly possible that I should send before you for trial a man who has not been engaged on those murderous expeditions."[47]

Once all the checking and rechecking done, the main pieces of the prosecution's case were assembled. For the Jubra Patun and Goolgunje affairs[48] tried at Sagar during the 1832–1833 session, Curven Smith had the following at his disposal:

1. The informers' testimonies and the master narrative written by the police magistrate who conducted the interrogations.

2. Official reports on the exhumation of the victims' bodies (collateral evidence of the crimes).

3. Reports of the confrontation between the informers and the whole of the suspects.

4. For the suspects' defense, testimonies about their innocence and good reputations.

Now that I have laid down the overall framework, I can proceed to look at two cases that help us follow the unfolding of the trials. In the light of the documents at my disposal, and given the British penal traditions, an indictment must precede the trial of the crime itself along with the sentencing. Sleeman, the main assistant to the judge, was in charge of the indictment. After having proceeded with the verifications, he gathered all the evidence and laid out the reference narrative for the case.

The Reference Narrative

Sir,

I have the honor to forward proceedings of the case of Bunsee, son of Rambuksh, Brahmin, and others charged with the murder of five men at Patun and five men at Lakheree in the Kotah and Bundee territories in the latter end of year 1821.

FIRST SEQUENCE

From the evidence record in these proceedings it appears that a gang of fifty thugs under Fereengheea, *jemadar* from Alumpore in Holcar's Territories and another of forty under Mandheta and Sutar Kahn, in Scindeea's Territories, set out after the Rains of 1821 on an expedition to Oojein. In Oojein they fell in with seven horse dealers who were persuaded to accompany them to the village of Ghutteea, about eight *coss* north of the city, where they encamped with the gang in a mango grove near a *Bowlee,* and were at night strangled, and their bodies buried in the jungle a quarter of a *coss* distant.

SECOND SEQUENCE

After this affair the gang proceeded on Gungarawal three long stages from Ghutteea on the road to Kotah, where they fell in with a *Resaldar* and eight companions on the road from Aurungabad to their homes . . . Having been persuaded to travel for security in the Company of the gang, they went on together to Punjgahar in

Holcar's Territories where they encamped in a mango grove and at night the whole nine were strangled and their bodies buried in the grove between a temple and a Kuranda tree which is very near it. The gang got from the *Resaldar* and his party, two horses, a camel, and four ponies with about four thousand Rupees worth of other property in money, ornaments and other things of value.

After their murder they went on to Jubra Patun and sold, it is said, a horse, a mare and a colt, and a camel . . . to the Commandant of that place under Kotah, Munnoo Khan, for five hundred rupees.

THIRD SEQUENCE

The day after their arrival, three men carrying each a thousand rupees, passed on their way from Jhubre Patun to Kotah; and the gang perceiving immediately the value of their burthens, kept up with them, some going on before, some keeping behind, till they reached the bank of a Nalah within about four *coss* of Kotah with a jungle of Polas trees along its banks, when they rushed in upon them and two were strangled and the third was cut down with a sword by Phoolse, a Thug who has since died. The bodies concealed under some stones and dirt and the booty taken on to Omedpoor.

The troops of Zelim Singh, the Kotah Minister were at this time, it is said, encamped at Mungrole about 14 *coss* from Kotah, with some of the Honorable Company's; and Fereengheea took the five horses acquired from the horse dealers to the camp and sold them; and on their rejoining the gang at Omedpoor, the whole booty was divided. The different gangs under their respective leaders, now took different roads, and Zelim with his gang promised to rejoin Fereengheea at Patun.

FOURTH SEQUENCE

Fereengheea at the head of a gang of thirty, went to Kotah, where they encamped on the Bank of a tank outside the town to watch the travellers who might pass on their way to Agra. Here they were joined by Bhora, *jemadar* with a gang of ten Thugs. The next day Fereengheea left Kotah with his party and proceeded to Patun, a distance of four or five *coss* on the bank of the Chumbul, where they encamped under some Tamarin tree. The next day Bohra joined them with his party of ten, Oman Subadar with his gang of twenty-five, and Zelim, jemadar, with his party of sixteen from different quarters. Bhora went into the Bazar and brought back with him two travellers on their way from Kotah to the Doab, who took up their quarters with him and in the evening three other travellers were passing the encampment on their way from Kotah to Bhurtpore when Fereengheea entered into conversation and prevailed upon them to take up their quarters with the gang for the night, proposing that they should all set up together the next morning. They were soon after joined by Pucholee, *jemadar* of Thugs, at the head of a gang of 50 who encamped at a short distance from the rest.

All the arrangements for the purpose having been made, two hours after dark the two *gulundazes* were strangled by the fire at which they were warming themselves by Bohra *jemadar* and Bhowanee, who was hung at Jubulpore in 1830, Husanooa who is still at large and another. Their bodies were buried in the grove near some indigo vats, and have been lately pointed out by people sent up by me for the purpose, taken up and examined by the officiating Agent of the GG at Kotah, Doctor Corbet. The gang got from these five victims a gold Necklace and other property worth between three and four hundred Rupees.

FIFTH SEQUENCE

The next morning they left Patun for Lackheree and after going on a *coss* they were overpassed by two *chuprassees*[49] supposed to have been in the service of the Kotah minister on their way from Kotah to Doab. They are said to have been cousins and the name of one, Gholab, and that of the other, Nismut; going on two *coss* further, they were overtaken by a *monshee*[50] and two attendants on their way from Sitarah to the district of Mynporee in the Doab, they went on with the gang to the village of Nautara in the Boondee Territory, where the party encamped at different places.

The following day the gang proceeded on with five travellers; and on reaching the bank of a river three or four *coss* from Nautara they fell in with some shepherds and purchased from them a goat for the purpose of giving them a feast, and on reaching Lackeree they all took their quarters in some empty houses, which bear the name of a Byragee by whom they were built. Here they killed the goat and gave as much as they required of the meat to the travellers who however declined accepting the other articles of food which the gang offered them, and cooked and ate the flesh with their own flour *dal*. About an hour after dark while the *Moonshee* was sitting outside the door of the house in which he lodged . . . and the others were sitting engaged in conversation with the gang the whole were seized and strangled, their bodies were buried in a grave made in the floor of one of the houses.

They have been lately pointed out by people sent by me for the purpose, taken up and an inquest has been held upon them by the officers of the officiating Agent of the GG at Kotah. The gang got from them some hundred Rupees in money and about 200 Rupees worth of gold and other property. They got two ponies from these travellers. . . . A mare was taken by Lal Khan and the box containing the gold was burnt.

SIXTH SEQUENCE

After this affair, Aman and Pucholee, with their gangs, took the road to Bondee; Fereengheea, Bhora and Zelim with their gangs took that to ?[51] where they, a few days after that, murdered Akder Khan a *Sabadar* Major in the Hon. Service, his six bearers, one *Sepahee* and a personal attendant, as will be described in another case to come before you.

I should remark that these gangs of Thugs generally concentrated upon any point were troops were likely assembled for hostile purposes, in order that they might intercept the soldiers and camp followers on their way from camp with their pay, prize, money, etc.

The Approvers in this case are Fereengheea, Sutram, Moollo, Kurhara, Lal Mohamed alias Nanhee."[52]

This expedition was the object of five denunciations. Only one of these, that of Feringheea, is complete and detailed. Except for a few details, Sleeman's reference narrative is its exact copy; it includes the same facts though with perhaps a heightened dramatic dimension. In the third sequence, for instance, Sleeman draws attention to the brutality of the crime—the murderers rush to strangle their victims—and in the fifth sequence he emphasizes premeditation through the episode of the feast the Thugs gave their soon-to-be victims.

Feringheea's account is less dramatic: he admitted having bought a sheep (not a goat) and having roasted it and offered some to the travelers who, far from refusing the windfall, were glad to eat it. Moolloo, another informer, didn't deny this version when he declared in telegraphic style: "We came to a river where we all bathed. Bhowanee there purchased a sheep. We then all arrived at Lakheree. Here we slaughtered the sheep and feasted the travellers on a part of it. The Thugs ate the rest. At 8 p.m. we strangled all the travellers."

Sleeman oddly left aside some details that could have served his aim of indicting the accused. Feringheea's premeditation was evidenced not only during the short melodramatic moment when the trusting travelers are about to be killed, but also in the time he spent scouting the terrain and setting his traps. In his narrative the military camp was a hunting preserve that he frequented often enough to know the names of his future victims: those of the two *chaprasis* and the son of the camp commander, Zalim Singh. He also baited the travelers: he pointed out to the horse dealers that "they had just come from Kashmir without having been able to sell their merchandise" and that "Zalim Singh's troops are quartered in Mungrole and that their horses would easily find buyers there." This camp, so profitable on account of the numerous uses he made of it, finally also served as the place to sell his loot.

The reference narrative focuses on the crime scene rather than on the preparations anticipating it. This is not important, however, as the differences between the report and the criminals' depositions are minimal. Written in the form of a letter addressed to Curven Smith, the reference narrative, as I noted earlier, is the key part of the indictment.

COLLATERAL EVIDENCE

The following is an extract from S. Wilkinson's report of 4 March 1833 on the Jubra Patun case, a report signed by all the witnesses:

> On the ninth November 1832, in conjunction with the two Approvers above mentioned, Thakoor Persand Duffadar who is placed in charge of them; Nundram and ?, *Cotwals* of the town of Patun; Motee Nanga Khoostal *Potails* and Shunkur Patwaree I got the earth dug up by the *Bildars* as pointed out by two Approvers. At the distance of 300 paces from the city gate, their skulls with a number of bones complete and the teeth of a fourth person with the bones in a state of dissolution, were discovered under some indigo and some tamarind trees.
>
> Subsequently in ? with the *Duffadar*, the Approvers, etc., I proceeded to the town of Lakairee. On the 14th November 1832 at a distance of 160 paces from the town gate, at a spot now inhabited by a Bairagee and pointed out by the Approvers, the earth was dug up in the presence of the *Duffadar* etc., the authorities of the mentioned town. Two skulls with the bones of the body were discovered within the bastion. Three skulls with the body bones, and the bones of another body without the skull were found under the ? of the building at the very place pointed out by the Approver Feereengheea.
>
> To authenticate the fact I caused the authorities of both places to affix their signatures to this paper.[53]

In a letter dated 19 February 1833, William Sleeman requested Doctor Corbet, surgeon at the Political Agency, to write a report indicating that he was present when the bones of the victims in the Jubra Patun case were exhumed and whether after examining them he thought they were human remains. Doctor Corbet answered: "I was present at the disinterment of the skeletons at the Kasoree Patun, and feel quite satisfied that they were bones of human beings."[54] The exhumation of recently dead bodies was very rare, so judges had to be satisfied with just an opinion on the human origin of the bones. This piece of "collateral" evidence, the only one that could be really decisive, was never clearly established.

In 1832, in the course of another trial pertaining to the seven murders of Goolgunge, H. Wilson collected the testimonies of Jourukkhan Lala Suruk Ameen, forty years old, and Khooman Zamindeer, fifty years old.[55] This latter told that in 1829 soldiers were camping in his village:

> An elephant keeper had taken one of the camp elephants for the purpose of drink at a tank situated a quarter of a *coss* from the village and while the elephant was drinking it brought up a human corpse. The *Mahoot* on returning to the Camp and seeing that I was a *zumeendar* of the village apprehended me that I might give some account relative to the corpse. I acquainted Lalla Jewra Khanlaul of the circumstances. . . . Having collected together the people of the neighbourhood for purpose of bringing up the dead bodies . . . the five bodies that were brought up the aforesaid Lalla caused to be burnt. I also went and saw all with my own eyes. I could not recognize whether the bodies were those of Hindoos or Musulmans or whether they were young or old, because from the corpses being exceedingly swollen and in state of putrefaction the hair has fallen off their heads.
>
> Jawra Khanlaul Suruk Ameen declared: "to be agreeable to the aforesaid gentlemen I caused them to be burnt. . . . They appear to be Hindoos of the Sepahee caste and their Age I should say might be from 30 to 35 none were older by their having around their necks round melas or beads and the quality of the cloth of the *mirzy*.
>
> From the swollen state of the bodies they had become hard and every corpse had become exceedingly offensive so much so that none could bear to stand near them. There did not appear any signs of wounds or bruises about the bodies but it was evident that they had been strangled. Guensh Brahmin Jemadar also testified: "They were young for their hair was black."[56]

The murders of Goolgunge had occurred about five days before the bodies were discovered, but the testimonies were collected three years later in 1832. J. K. S. Aureen, apparently the man entrusted with having the corpses burnt or with burning them himself, gave the most precise description. The *zamindars*, probably remaining at a fair distance from their sight and smell, couldn't agree on the hair color (one claimed it was black, the other didn't see any hair) or the age of the victims. This disparity was not brought out because there was no doubt about the fact of human death. The informers played a crucial role in obtaining this sort of evidence as they made it possible to find the traces in the form of bones. In the narratives the eyewitnesses remembered having seen the bodies that were then burnt.

EVIDENCE: CONFRONTATION OF THE INFORMERS AND THE ACCUSED

After the testimony of an approver was gathered, the prisoners were then shown to the witness to be identified. Feringheea, face to face with the twenty suspects of the Jubra Patun case, answered a series of identical questions. He was asked to identify each of them by giving his name, the name of his father, and the band to which he belonged ("This is Pan Mohomud, nephew of Nutta of whose gang he is; his father Madaree was a noted Thug"). He was also asked to tell how long he had known each suspect, what the crimes were in which they were implicated, and finally the role they each had played in the case on trial "I have known him for seven years in an Affair in which he only shared. I did not see him in these two Affairs." Feringheea denounced ten of the suspects as being sons or adopted sons of notorious Thugs; he distinguished between the individuals charged with dividing up the loot,[57] the grave diggers,[58] the stranglers, and those charged with holding down the hands of the victims.[59] The other informers generally confirmed his statements.

Denunciations aimed to establish the exhaustive narrative of the crimes, their specific circumstances, and the list of participants. The confrontation of several witnesses' testimonies served to tighten the case against suspects; their past criminal lives were brought up in addition to their involvement in the case at hand.

THE PRISONERS' DEFENSE: THE LAW OF SILENCE

In the Jubra Patun case, involving twenty suspects, not one of the accused admitted guilt. In their defense, two of them briefly stated: "The Approvers accused me falsely. I have never thugged." As to the others, they gave the names of persons supposed to testify that they "never left [their] home" or that they had always been of "good behaviour and character." Only two suspects brought up their profession. Gunaish stated: "I have always been a cultivator, Sherpand and Shopersand of Manaackore can swear to my never leaving home." Darreo likewise claimed that "Kosree Chowdree of Nusingpore is a witness of my having been a regular tradesman and that I am not a Thug."

In the Goolgunge case tried during the same session, two-thirds of the suspects claimed to be cultivators. For instance Munsook stated: "Enquire in my village if I am not a cultivator." Others: "I never committed any crime except being a cultivator." Bhugga even called upon the rajah of Rushdan: "I am innocent. The Rajah of Rusdaun can swear that I have never been absent from him." Chotee used a standard formula: "I am guiltless of having committed Thuggee. The event is in your hands."[60]

The brevity of all these statements and the stereotypical forms of the answers are disconcerting; the suspects all claimed to be innocent, and the witnesses they called upon to vouch for them were never more than two, at most three, in number. In contrast, the ironclad prosecution takes up pages and pages in the archives. The informers' long and abominable descriptions written up by the magistrates are in striking contrast to these almost mute murderers' claims of innocence. The unbalance is so great we might be tempted to believe the latter. But that would be overlooking the law of silence. I now turn briefly to their alibis.

THE ALIBIS

Even though it seems obvious that the magistrates were already persuaded of the suspects' guilt, investigations were conducted to check their statements. Thus the majors Halves at Bhopal, MacLeod at Gwalior, and H. Wilson at Etawah were asked to "examine the individuals noted therein whose evidence the prisoners conceive to be necessary in their defense."[61]

The testimonies collected were damning. Major Halves did not find the suspects' village; he wrote in a first letter that "It will be necessary to have the locality of the village described, to distinguish it from others of the same name." In his second letter it seems that the sole witness he uncovered "has not come in to depose by reason of his entire ignorance of the characters of these persons." MacLeod had access to the testimony of a rajah: "The Rajah Lasla of Gopalpore respecting the character of Zalim prisoner denies all knowledge of such a person. The rajah states he has ascertained from the zumeedars of his village that he cultivated land for the last five years but they know nothing of him previous to that period." As to H. Wilson of Etawah, he let his own biases poison the positive testimonies he collected during this trial on behalf of a certain Bhugga:

> There are seven witnesses to his good character, and did I not know the loose manner in which all depositions are taken in almost every court. . . . I should be inclined to think him [Bhugga] an innocent man. There is also a letter from the rajah of Rushdan in his favor. On this I place no reliance whatever as I have a letter of his now in my possession in which he was guilty of knowingly writing a wilful falsehood.

The witnesses thus either couldn't be found, or they knew nothing, or at least not much; and when they did know something, it was considered false. The colonizers mistrusted not only witnesses, but also the native authorities gathering their testimonies!

Once all the documents for the prosecution's case were gathered, the trial could proceed. It was held in secrecy. There were no lawyers, no juries, and no opposing arguments. The magistrate alone rendered judgment on the basis of the evidence held in the file established by William Sleeman, who thus cumulated the distinct functions of police investigator and prosecutor. Those witnesses who were present were the Thug informers; as to witnesses for the defense, they were not even called to appear because the only way of obtaining their testimony was to promise that they would not be required to give it in person.

Sentencing

The summary of the trials of the 1832–1833 session[62] identifies the Thugs sentenced in a certain number of cases, among which are those of Jubra Patun and Lakheree, of which I wrote above.

The accusation and the sentencing for the first prisoner on the list is couched in the usual formula: "Bhunsee, son of Rambuksh, aged 35 years, noted Thug and Shumseeah":

Prisoner pleads not guilty of the murders in question. But, it is proved in evidence, that the gang, of which he formed one, strangled 5 men at Jubra Patun in the end of 1821; and five men at Lakheree, of whom the names of Jowadir Lale Moonshee and his two servants Himmut and Golab has been ascertained. It is also in evidence that the bodies of the murdered people have been disinterred and a knife, said to have been part of the property plundered at Lakheree, has been found upon the person of Man Khan.

The following evidence was recorded against the prisoner in this case (in the summary of evidence): "Fereengheea: swears that the prisoner was present at and shared in both affairs; and that he has known him for the last 18 years in 20 or 25 murders. He was not actively engaged." Suttram, Moollo, Khudoreh, Bhole, and Mehdo also testified that the suspect was present during the murders in question. Only Lal Muhumud "swears that he does not know the prisoner; but he saw him in company with the Thugs at Lakehree."

His defense : "I have nothing to say in this Affair."

Verdict of the Court: The prisoner, in this case, is proved to be a noted Thug; to have followed the profession of Thuggee for many years; to have been present at the murder of 10 persons; to have shared in the spoil; but not to have been a Bhurtote (strangler).

In this case (n. 19) the prisoner is proved to have been a noted Thug from his youth; and to have been present at the murder of 5 men at Pv·.na and 4 men in Jubulpor.

In this case (n. 20) the prisoner is proved to have followed the profession of Thuggee from his youth; to have been present at the murder of 5 men at Singhasun, 3 men at Setane, and 3 men at Jytpoor. Etc.

Sentence: Ordered, that the prisoner Bunsee son of Rambuksh be imprisoned in transportation beyond seas for the term of his natural life, and branded with the *Goodna* process[63] in the shoulder and forehead with the words Munshoor Thug in Hindi and Persian. Markhan, son of Duroo, aged 35 years, proved to be a jemadar of Thug and a hereditary Thug; to have followed his profession from his youth . . . and to be a Bhurtote, is ordered to be hanged by the neck till dead.

Three death sentences were given during this particular session. One of these sentences applied to "Bhowanee, alias Mendhata, son of Hursok alias Chimdubann, Brahmin," who repented, became an informer, and pleaded guilty. He was one of the defendants in the trial. Even though he wasn't a direct participant in the murders and thus deserved only deportation for life, the text of the sentence states that "as the prisoner is proved to have ran away while performing the duty of Approver; and to have been retaken with difficulty; it is therefore ordered that Bhowanee . . . be hanged by the neck till dead." If an informer failed to respect the agreement he entered into with the British authorities, he received a death sentence regardless of the nature of his crimes.

From 1831 the sentences became harsher and the informer who ran away was condemned to the same punishment as the strangler or the Thug chief.[64]

The sentences have been passed in concurrence with the views of Government as detailed in Mr Chief Secretary Swinton's despatch of the 2nd of April 1831, namely:

1. Every adult person convicted of being a Thug by profession and present at the perpetration of Murder by a gang, though not personally assisting, sentenced to transportation for life;

2. Every jemadar or leader of Thugs, every Runaway Approver who may have subsequently returned on his old course; every servant of Government, or who had formerly been such, have been sentenced to death;

3. All persons convicted of being professional Thugs or present as boys, or for the first time at a murder, sentenced to imprisonment for life, or for such period as it may be deemed unsafe to release them on security.[65]

The law no longer differentiated between "subordinate" and "superior" tasks. Defendants were condemned to prison terms regardless of their actions: "There are several prisoners upon whom I have passed sentences of imprisonment for life. . . . They are either youths or persons proved to be Thugs, but not to have been present at any particular murders,"[66] stated Curven Smith. It is obvious that if the fact of being absent was severely punished, that of being present was much more so! The judge alone decided between a death sentence and deportation. In those cases when the defendant had not been proven to be a professional Thug, the judge had full discretion in passing sentence.

> In the course of the 1832 and 1833 sessions, the most repressive in the history of those trials, Curven Smith condemned 145 Thugs to be hanged, 323 to deportation and 41 to life in prison. In his report on the 1830–1831 session to the secretary general in Calcutta, he concluded: It is probable such dreadful disclosures of the villainy and blood thirsty character of the people of India, for the Thugs are taken from all classes of the community, was never before submitted to the abhorrence of Government. In all my experience in the judicial line for upwards of twenty years I never heard of such atrocities, or presided over such trials, such cold blooded murders, such heart-rending scenes of distress, and misery; such base ingratitude; such a total abandonment of every principle, which binds man to man; which softens the heart and elevates mankind above the brute creation, were probably never before brought to the notice of a Court of justice. . . . Mercy to such wretches would be the extreme cruelty to mankind, and they must be met in their own ways, by a rigid adherence to the law, of *Lex Talionis*—blood for blood.[67]

Between 1826 and 1835, according to Sleeman, 398 Thugs were condemned to death, 999 to deportation for life, 77 to prison for life, 71 to prison for limited terms; 21 were acquitted for lack of proof, 11 ran away, 31 died before trial, 49 became informers. In his book *The Yellow Scarf* (1961),[68] Sir Francis Tuker gave the following figures for the whole of the trials until 1840: 3,869 hangings, 1,564 deportations, 933 imprisonments for life, 86 acquittals, 56 who became informers, 208 deaths before trial.

The Law Damaged

Srivastava (1971) writes a devastating description of British justice during the colonial era: there was the multiplication of forgeries and perjuries and delays, and costs were so high that people preferred to rely on their local judicial assemblies, the *panchayat*, rather than on the British courts, which they nicknamed "scorpions." The colonizers themselves virulently criticized the system, at least in its most basic aspect, that of communication between judge and defendant:

The European judge can never be so much a master of the language as to follow and detect the minute points by which truth and falsehood are often separated. The voice of a witness, the manner, the mode of expression, the use of words of a less positive though often similar sense, all these must be beyond the reach of an European whose knowledge of Indian language can never extend to such niceties.[69]

The people in charge of the repression of Thugs were conscious that they were using problematic means that compromised the dignity of justice. But instead of criticizing them, they attempted to justify them. Moreover, they never mentioned any language problem, even though the poverty of the language of the depositions evidences the interrogators' limited knowledge of the languages of the people they were questioning. Curven Smith used two sets of arguments in order to make up for the lack of collateral proof and to justify the system of denunciations. In the first set he claimed that the Thugs knew fully well how to manipulate the legal system. Thus, methods of accusation that were outside judicial rules were needed to ward off the criminals' ruses. In the second set he evoked a principle with which we are already familiar: in the absence of reliable, legally correct testimonies, the judges have to make do with the least objectionable among the defective testimonies.

The thesis he defended is that of compromise. The law was not besmirched; it was adapted to a situation described as being urgent and extreme, which fit with British legal practice, in which the law is interpreted and changes according to new circumstances.[70] At any rate, after 1830 the exceptional measures promulgated by the supreme colonial authorities at Calcutta to punish the Thugs backed the magistrates' actions even though it is clear to us that Curven Smith's convoluted argument came with a strong dose of his own imagination (for instance, Thugs are not specialists in British criminal law).

Government authorities who were checking each case file at times refused to approve the sentences passed by these special tribunals. According to the standard formula: "There being no direct evidence beyond that of the Approvers, His Lordship in Council has been pleased to commute the Sentence of Death to Imprisonment for Life."[71] It was explicitly recognized that in the end the validity of the accusations depended on the judge's and prosecutor's personal convictions, so doubt could occasionally lead members of the supreme government to lessen sentences. The judicial authorities thus enjoyed a substantial margin of maneuvers but it was nonetheless bounded by certain rather mysterious limits.

As we have seen, the repression met with hardly any obstacles, and

Sleeman was quite satisfied with his reliance on retrospective denunciations:

> Their conviction depending principally upon their own disclosures—and above all that their own maxim "once a Thug, always a Thug" is almost as true as their other maxim that "dead men tell no tales" for among about a hundred men who were arrested along the Nerbudda in 1820 and released . . . the greater has been since brought to trials and convicted of murders. Almost every one confesses his crimes declaring that murder being the trade to which he has been brought up he could follow no other.[72]

William Sleeman and Curven Smith's panegyric of their way of establishing the truth on the Thugs was generally accepted by their collaborators. And yet there was still a remnant of reticence and doubt behind this optimism. The British involved in this campaign were not all convinced that the good cause they defended freed them from ordinary laws: "in the event of an innocent being sentenced to death or other punishment the blame would rest entirely with the committing Officer of this Department," wrote J. C. Elwall, pleading for mercy for Abdool Khadir, who had given a false testimony.[73]

The truth on Thug crimes was for the most part the product of overlapping denunciations. Judicial authority came to tolerate a fairly large margin of error in its verdicts. Such a stance, along with the systematic recourse to informers and the uncertainties it entailed, makes us doubt the guilt of the condemned. It seems evident that some of them were hanged by mistake.

As evidenced by the depositions we have just read, and as corroborated by their secret language, the Thugs did not form a "system of civil and religious administration" in collusion with society, but rather bands, families of individuals loosely organized and plotting and putting their plans into execution. They were wont to pay dearly for their freedom of action and be abandoned by everyone when the law got hold of them. The Thugs had more enemies than friends. This is implicit in the way they were pursued and in their trials. The British obviously had interest in emphasizing the resistance of the population, but without its help they couldn't have enjoyed such a quick and radical victory over the assassins. This is evidenced by the contrast of their repeated failure to capture Ramusi Naik, the beloved bandit of the Marathas.

EXECUTION OF THE SENTENCES

The condemned Thugs thus traveled the whole or parts of the stages of imprisonment, branding, deportation, and hanging. The softening of penal practices in the West at the beginning of the nineteenth century that was aimed at "the disappearance of the spectacle and the elimination of pain" (Foucault 1979, 11) was not yet at play in the young empire of the Indies. This change in attitude was to happen only toward the 1840s, when halfway institutions, aimed at reinserting prisoners into society, were established and there were fewer executions. The British reformers of that time wanted punishment to be directed at the soul rather than the body, as G. de Mably had hoped in 1789. At this point I give front stage to the observers' discourse, as we can access events only through their interpretations and their reconstructions.

The Goodna *Process*

Adverting to the inveterate habits of the individuals brought up to the horrid profession of Thuggee and to the obvious expediency of setting a mark on those who have been convicted of this crime, His Lordship in Council is pleased to direct that in addition to the infliction of imprisonment, the Thugs now under sentence should be branded with the *Goodna* process on some part of their body not exposed to view, so that they may be recognized as old offenders should they again be apprehended in the pursuit of their inhuman calling after their liberation from jail. Their names and the words "convicted Thug" may be stamped on the back or shoulders of all sentenced to seven years imprisonment and upwards, a deviation from the Regulation fully warranted by the enormity of the crimes of Thuggee which firstly place those who practiced it beyond the pale of social law.[74]

Sleeman wrote in 1835 to Captain James Paton that the prisoners of Sagar and Jabalpur were tattooed by an old woman (was she a Thug elder? Perhaps!): "The Thugs sentenced at Saugor and Jubulpor have been marked with the *Goodna* process by an old woman whose profession it is to mark in this way, and I would recomand that the word THUG be marked in large English letters on the inside of one shoulder and in Persian letters inside the other."[75]

James Paton, in charge of the eradication of the Thugs in the kingdom of Oudh, is the author of a large illustrated manuscript kept at the British Library in London.[76] One drawing depicts four men with turbans. Along their lower eyelids and close to their eyelashes the word THUG is written in capital letters. In spite of this infamous mark visible to all onlookers, the expression on the face of the youngest man, on the right, in the foreground, is not that of someone beaten. The sinister tattoo near his eye seems rather to be the signature of an obstinate "vocation." Did the captain overinterpret the orders that were given or, on the contrary, did he

Drawing depicting Thugs branded on the face. According to the law, the Thugs were supposed to be branded on the shoulder, but were they branded on the face as well? Artist and date unknown. Reprinted by permission of the British Library (Paton's papers, Add. 41300, no. 58827).

draw an imaginary and dramatic representation of Thugs brought to the light of day and punished, but still remaining fearless and dangerous?

In Prison

Though we have little information about the Thugs in prison, we do know enough to understand that they were not all passively awaiting their fate. For instance, "three prisoners escaped from jail on the night of the 14th. . . . It appears that Makun cut through one of the bars of the iron grating about a foot and a half from the ground, with a string covered with a composition of powder glass and sand; and by the same means through his own iron and those of nine other prisoners."[77] I have not encountered examples of collusion between guards and prisoners, and according to the figures for different prisons, few Thugs actually succeeded in escaping. Thus in Awadh from 1835 to 1846 only one did so. But forty-six Thugs died before their sentences were executed. This high mortality raises questions. Sleeman writes:

It was found that the mortality prevailed most among the oldest and most noted offenders deprived of all hope of ever being released. They were therefore indifferent to the injunctions of the surgeon regarding the nature and quality of their food, and could scarcely be induced to come to the hospital exceptly in forceable means. It is I believe the opinion of all medical men at Saugor that the jail is badly situated as being within the range of a current malaria arising from the lake and flowing North East between the two hills. . . . I am strongly disposed that a new jail should be erected.[78]

Whether rebellious or resigned, the Thugs were surrounded with guards who repressed them and doctors who tried to keep them from dying before the time fixed by law. As in the West at the time, the doctor was the helper of the police. His expertise was required when bodies were exhumed, and he had to witness public hangings. The doctor's qualifications didn't quite pertain to the judicial or medical domains. Rather, his was an instance of the control of "abnormality" that at once described and produced the norms it required (Foucault 1999, 39).

Thugs' Deaths

In his book *Modern India* the doctor Henry Spry, stationed in Bengal, gives an account of a Thug's execution. The man of science was interested in the whole process: he wasn't content with just observing the last moments of the condemned; he observed them the day preceding the fatal dawn:

Sentence of death was pronounced in a very impressive manner, by Captain Sleeman, on different parties of Thugs, executed during my residence in Saugor. The criminals, drawn up in a semicircle round the bench on which the judge was seated, were surrounded by a strong guard of musketeers and dismounted cavalry. The warrants were placed before them, and each name, as called out by the court, was repeated by the *Sheristhadar*. At the conclusion of this ceremony, Captain Sleeman addressed them in the Hindustanee language, in a few sentences, which may be rendered thus: "You have all been convicted in the crime of blood; the order from the Calcutta Council therefore is, that, at to-morrow's dawn, you are all to be hung. If any of you desire to make any further communication, you may now speak." . . . Few answered; those who did reply merely requested, as a dying favour, that their bodies, on being taken down, might be burnt. One hardened villain, however, as he was turning round to leave the court, disturbed the solemnity of the scene, by muttering : "Ah, you have got it all your own way

now, but let me find you in Paradise, and then I will be revenged!"
(Spry 1837, 164–68)

This Doctor Spry, a cousin of William Sleeman, revealed yet another
of this latter's multiple functions in the anti-Thug campaign. He over-
saw the execution of the sentences, and the ceremonial with which he
surrounded himself was such that he was taken for a judge in the eyes
of all the onlookers; even the "hardened villain" was fooled. There is no
hint in his account that Thugs were respectful of the authority that was
executing them nor seized with fear at their punishment. The colonizers
perceived this attitude as both unnatural and false. To their last moment
the Thugs were perceived as lying :

> The night was passed by these men in displays of coarse and dis-
> gusting levity. . . . Stifling their alarm with boisterous revelling,
> they hoped to establish in the minds of their comrades . . . a reputa-
> tion for courage, by means, which, at once, proved their insincerity
> and belied their fortitude. Imagine such men on the last night of
> their existence on earth, not penitent for their individual errors, . . .
> not even rendered serious by the dismal ordeal which in a few hours
> was to usher them in the unknown; but, singing, in the condemned
> cell and repeating their unhallowed carols while jolting along in
> the carts that conveyed them to their gibbets! (Spry 1837, 164–68)

Meditation, mortification, remorse, silence, fear, all those things expected in the Christian West from those condemned to death are missing
in the rendezvous. At dawn the doctor who accompanied them finally
thought he saw what he expected (their "haggard" physiognomy) as po-
liteness suddenly replaced "boisterous reveling":

> The place appointed for the executions was on the north side of
> the town of Saugor, about a mile and a half from the goal. "*Rooksut
> Doctor Sahib, Salam Doctor Sahib,*" were the salutations which I
> received. . . . As each hackery load of malefactors arrived, it was
> taken to the foot of the respective ladders, and . . . [they] one by
> one got out [and] mounted to the plat-form or foot-board. Their
> irons were not removed. All this time the air was pierced with the
> hoarse and hollow shouting of these wretched men.
> Each man as he reached to the top of the ladder, stepped out on
> the platform and walked at once to a halter. Without loss of time
> he tried its strength by weighing his whole body on it. Every one
> having by this means proved the strength of his rope with his own
> hands (for none of them were handcuffed), introduced his head into
> the noose, drew the knot firmly home immediately behind the right

ear, and amid terrific cheers jumped off the board and launched himself into eternity. (Spry 1837, 164–68)

Fanny Parks, in her *Wanderings of a Pilgrim,* a book she intended to be light reading, adds a picturesque detail: "One of them who had leaped off the beam, and had been hanging for more than three seconds, put his hand up and pulled [his turban] over his face" (Parks 1850, 1:201). In executions in Britain, condemned persons stood on a moveable support that was suddenly opened under their feet "thus avoiding slow deaths and the altercations that occurred between victims and executioners. It was improved and finally adopted in 1783, the same year in which the traditional procession from Newgate to Tyburn was abolished, and in which the opportunity offered by the rebuilding of the prison . . . was used to set up the scaffolds in Newgate itself" (Foucault 1979, 12).

The condemned men of Sagar and Jabalpur died in public on gallows lacking movable trapdoors underfoot. Sleeman admits that they were submitting to Kali's will with "good spirit." In contrast, Doctor Spry reasons as a sociologist: "Thus in the moment of death we see a scrupulous attention paid to the preservation of caste. To wait to be hung by the hands of a *chumar* [a tanner], was a thought too revolting for endurance. The name would be disgraced for ever, and, therefore, rather than submit to its degradation every man hung himself!" (Spry 1837, 164–68).

All of the Western observers seemed to be in agreement: the Thugs' guilt was confirmed by their keeping calm at the moment of their death or in their invoking the Goddess. "This bravado of theirs served to make the bystanders feel satisfied by their guilt and indeed of their glorying it" (Parks 1850, 1:202). No eyewitness made the link between the voluntary suicide of the gymnosophists, the famous Indian philosophers who left a deep imprint in the West since antiquity;[79] the "devotional" sacrifices observed at the time in Puri, Banaras, and Goalpara; and Thugs' attitude in the face of death. The colonizers saw only gross impudence in their demeanor. And yet, when they rebelled in prisons, they claimed it was to regain their names. They did not consider themselves fallen men. Dignity, honor, gratefulness were their values, which their demeanor on the gallows reflected. Thugs' attitude toward death surprised Western witnesses, who nevertheless depicted them according to their preconceived expectations. The magistrate and the doctor thought they were uncovering the secret of Thugs' souls just as they had uncovered the mystery of their crimes. Even though the victims' laughter had the ring of defiance, their desire to die from their own hands was interpreted as fear of being sullied by contact with a "lowly tanner." Their deaths couldn't be heroic ones.

The population didn't protest the executions: "There was not the slightest disturbance nor did the natives betray the slightest emotion of any kind, except one Nujeeb who fainted." However, in contrast to the Thugs, who claimed not to be bothered by the spirits of their victims, ordinary people feared the spirits of the hanged Thugs.

> Some of the inhabitants of Saugor thought that the lives of the Brahmins ought to have been spared, but the General Superintendent's impression was decidedly in favor of the guilt of the convicts. . . . All feared however that the spirits of the dead would return to haunt the town . . . but their fears might be quieted namely by making a slip incision above the ankle bone after death which would effectually prevent the spirits' return to this sublunary world."[80]

"All the Hindoos have been burnt in the usual manner, and all the Muhumuduns after executed were buried."[81] Native funerary rites and "superstitions" were respected. Evil spirits were induced to exit. The neutralized remains of the assassins were returned to their culture of origin. "Somber punitive celebration," as Foucault writes. We need to add to this commentary the bravado and courage of the condemned. These might have been linked to their murdering practices, but it must have been as well to the image they wanted to leave of themselves, and also for some of them, to the feeling of having been unjustly victimized by the colonial power.

Thug Violence, Colonial Violence

The society in which the Thugs were perpetrating murder had been for quite a while in a state of political instability, rebellion, and war. At any rate, bands of Thugs included people from all sorts of background. "Mudee Khan . . . had a gang of fifty Thugs of all castes and descriptions. I asked him who they were; he told me that they were weavers, braziers, bracelet-makers, and all kinds of raggamuffins, whom he had scraped together about the new abode on the banks of the Herun and Nurbudda rivers" (Sleeman 1836, "Substance," 153). In his deposition, Sayyid Amir Ali, who did twelve years in prison before being freed, told of roaming the highways in search of a band. So the old saying, "Yesterday a weaver, today a Sheikh, and tomorrow, if the prices go up, I'll be a Sayyid!" took on a Thug form for similar economic reasons: "Yesterday a weaver, today Thug, tomorrow . . ." The alibis given by some of the defendants were undoubtedly true: cultivators pushed to Thuggism, or falsely accused, men reduced to extremities, migrants in search of some work. These conditions made it impossible to establish a reputation of long standing.

This being said, Thug violence seemed indeed real, and to extirpate it the colonizers responded with violence. The "ferocity" and the "cynicism" of the stranglers were matched by that of their judges. The *lex talionis,* the exaction of an eye for an eye invoked by Sleeman, clashed with nineteenth-century notions of justice. In the nineteenth century West, natural law, the main tool used to establish the unity of the social group, was conceived as a contract. In its framework law was the social acknowledgment of the power of the individual. Western law was defined by the principles of liberty and protection of human life and respect of private property, and it claimed a universal moral dimension. This contrasted with the principles of Indian society, where hierarchy and interdependence occupy the foreground and where the social system implies multiple and flexible norms. After conquest the empire laid claim to the monopoly on violence and defined itself as a state of law. The trials against the Thugs show how the colonizers progressively constructed a positive system of laws modeled on their own norms.

This law was that of jurisprudence, in the sense that it was based on precedent, in this case on that of the letter written by Secretary General Swinton following Borthwick's 1829 accusations against the Thugs. The measures enacted by Swinton progressed in the direction of greater harshness even as the judgments on the criminals' responsibility came to be based on increasingly looser criteria. These went from a crime actually committed to simply witnessing one, to, finally, being accused of belonging to a band that commits this sort of crimes. The notion of collective responsibility thus came to be substituted for that of individual responsibility. The sentences passed took on the force of law, and soon, in 1836, they became laws as they matched the outlook of most colonizers.

Did they fit Western criteria of justice? Yes, in that they referred to norms said to be universal; because the crimes were proven (in the judges' eyes); and finally, because the guilty were looked upon as having free will. The colonizers claimed that fanaticism and heredity drove the Thugs to kill, but they also saw them as responsible for their actions. Today we see this line of argument as paradoxical, but it wasn't thought to be so in the nineteenth century. The criminal was felt to be lacking proper socialization, "civilized habits" (Mayhew 1867, 386). "Crime was essentially seen as the expression of a fundamental character defect stemming from a refusal or an inability to deny wayward impulses or to make proper calculations of long-run self-interest" (Wiener 1990, 46). Criminals were thought to be free, to be able, regardless of external circumstances, to direct their wills in the proper direction. The legacy of the Enlightenment, the psychic unity of mankind, individualism, all likewise made them accountable for their faults, and this everywhere in the world. Colonial violence, based on objective practices and rational thinking, was fully unleashed to exterminate the Thugs, whose legitimacy was based on murderous practices and particularistic "beliefs." Colonial justice, rational and reasoned, drew its strength from a powerful state, while that of the assassins was linked, through bribes and at the cost of constant renegotiations, to native authorities under surveillance, which on the main did not really support them.

CORRECTION AND REHABILITATION

The Jabalpur School of Arts and Manufactures

The informers took a decisive step in espousing the cause of the colonizers. Traitors to their community of origin, they were no longer ordinary Thugs. Of course, they were never to be set free: "It was a condition necessary to our success that no accused Thug would ever be released," but, in contrast to the four tattooed men in the drawing, they could change. They were condemned to life in prison, and their existence had to be organized.

The overpopulated prisons were filled with a heterogeneous population that included major repented criminals and boys condemned to variable limited sentences. The prisoners were probably first made to labor at outside work, mainly on roads and earthworks, as was the custom of the time. But escapes and abuses were so numerous that the committee of discipline for the prisons recommended in 1838 the organization of a system of imprisonment in which the prisoners were made to perform tedious and monotonous indoor tasks.

The panopticon, this new principle of construction "applicable to all sorts of establishments where people must be kept under surveillance," saw the light of day at the end of the eighteenth century. Its author, Jeremy Bentham, listed its promised benefits as "morals reformed—health preserved—industry invigorated—instruction diffused—public burthens lightened—Economy seated, as it were, on a rock—the Gordian knot of the Poor-Laws not cut, but untied—all by a simple idea in architecture" (cited in Foucault 1979, 206). This moral, hygienic, economic, and architectural utopia was strongly propounded in some currents of thought in Britain at that time,[82] and it wound its way to India. But it raised a host of questions. If the repented could be made to reform, what was one to do with their sons? Thus this category of repented Thugs along with their descendants were the object of "techniques of transformation" aimed at their normalization (Foucault 1999, 18).

HEREDITY WITHOUT CHRISTIANITY: SLEEMAN'S PROJECT

The Thugs' fatal heredity had to be counteracted by preventing their children from following in their fathers' footsteps. In 1835 William Sleeman asked the secretary of the government of India for an allocation of four hundred rupees to built forty dwellings for the prisoners' families:

> It is my intention at a future period to propose the means of providing for the boys and their families. Their fathers have all followed

the trade of Thugge from their boyhood . . . and everyone of these fathers' admit that if any Thug is left within their reach when their sons grow up they will assuredly join it . . . rather than descend to manual labour for subsistence. They may with safety be placed in service public or private, on large manufactories in situations where they can hold no communication with the former associates of their fathers and where they may intermarry with honest and industrious families, and this is what I shall probably propose; but before they become fit for service or work it will be advisable to provide for them in some useful seminary of education at the Presidency.[83]

Three years later, in 1838, thanks to Sleeman's support, Captain Charles Brown, holder of the post of "Assistant to the General Superintendent" at Jabalpur had "the Jubbulpoor School of Industry" built. His architectural model was not the panopticon, but military barracks on a single row. The repented, their spouses, and their children were gathered there and a program of gradual reinsertion was established.

In a 1846 letter, that is seven years after the opening of the school, William Sleeman stated his aim to teach Thug children "professions they could practice all their life." In order to incite them to learning, their fathers, "old Thug informers, are themselves led to work hard and to learn trades." In 1848, the results were beyond all expectations:

I inspected this establishment only a few days ago, and nothing could be more gratifying than the state in which I found it, showing that the object, which Government had in view, had been carried out beyond my most sanguine hopes. A great number of the sons of Thugs are amongst the most expert of the members, and can earn a very handsome subsistence by their labour as such. These will, by degrees, become independent of instruction and aid in the factory; and instead of retaining them upon the establishment as journeymen or day-labourers, they will be allowed to set up for themselves in the town of Jubbulpore, and to sell their finished work privately, or to the factory, when of the approved quality which the factory turns out. A small capital will be advanced to the head men of all such establishments to set them up, to be refunded as their finished work is supplied or sold. Jubbulpore will thus become a manufacturing town; and as the fathers and other male relations of these boys, who spent the early part of their career in the murder of their fellow men, die off, as they are now fast doing, the recollection of their horrible trade will cease to excite any other feeling than such as that which converts to a new creed feel for the errors of their forefathers; and one of the best signs I saw at the School of Industry on this visit was, the dislike which all seemed to feel, on being questioned by the officers, who accompanied me, on any thing about the trade of Thuggee.[84]

Work, discipline, the value of the mutual example from one generation to the next, the murderers' natural death, made it possible to foresee the insertion of the Thugs' sons into the public life of the town they were helping transform. As new heads of enterprises they were already participating in a market in which the British held privileged positions. The right over their best products was already inscribed within this moral and economic agenda.

JAMES PATON'S UTOPIA: HEREDITY AND CHRISTIANITY

That same year, in 1837 at Lucknow, James Paton founded a small "thuggery," where, on the basis of the same principle, the prisoners and their families received room and board, work, and education. But in Paton's view, the problem of the hereditary nature of Thuggism could only be resolved by permanently separating parents from their children. "Evil is so ingrained in the human heart that they would transmit them the taste for their profession."[85]

Paton, worrying that "there will be some difficulty in getting the Thugs to part with their children," proposed the following agreement: "That Thug Approvers desiring to have their wives residing with them may have this indulgence but expressly on this condition, that after three years of age, all the children must be separated from them. . . . In such cases Approvers will receive one Roopie additional for the support of their wives." The artificial orphans were destined to serve the colonizers, "in the humbler branches of the Government's services." As to Thug daughters, they were expected to meet with great success on the marriage market: "In like manners the Female children should be kept separated from their parents . . . to be religiously educated and married to Applicants for Wives, who might be expected to be numerous, seeing that young female Thugs would probably be well trained useful housewives, superior from their education to the generality of their country women."

There remained the problem of financing the institution. "It is presumed a great and enlightened Government would not grudge the very trifling expense necessary for its accomplishment. And if the Government did not deem it expedient to undertake this work, Thank God, there is a public benevolence enough in India at once to come forward and undertake so pleasing a duty." Carried away by his vision of Thugs converted to Christianity, he imagined them trading their work clothes for a missionary vocation:

> It would appear after rescuing them from being murderers to give them anything short of a Christian education which alone can thoroughly with God's blessing eradicate from the minds of Thugs the curse of a seared conscience or correct a bewildered understanding, which has been used to hear of murders as of hunting fields. . . . That the children of darkness should be children of light! In due time they might go forth under God's blessing . . . as a noble little band to lead their countrymen into the path of virtue. . . . What a delightful termination would this be to Lord William Bentinck's energetic measures for the suppression of Thuggee! Not in eradicating but in preventing the evil by engrafting upon the evil stock of the fathers in the children the delightful fruits of Christian instruction and virtue! . . . That as their fathers trod the highway of India from East to West, from North to South, swift to shed the blood! So may the feet of their little ones hastening to instruction speedily treading the highways of India from the Ducckun valley of Nerbudda the Doab, from Oude, etc. Imagine them all assembled before you, with their little hands joined in supplication for your favor! . . . Your zeal is known! You have a noble Cause!"[86]

William Sleeman didn't seem to be affected by these entreaties and rejected this plan to dismember the families. But the utopia of the visionary Paton is an instructive caricature of the "techniques of transformation" of the rational Sleeman. Both men were driven by a similar optimism when they thought that the children of the Thugs were to make up the core of an almost alchemical transmutation between Evil and Good. Both saw them as a malleable, virgin land that education, example, even conversion, could make into superior colonial subjects, submitted to British interests. Thug children were doubly carriers of redemption: first for their murderous fathers and then for their colonizers and spiritual fathers, who finally could shed the judge's robe to don the radiant vestment of the social benefactor.

Being a Thug: A Mental or a Biological Legacy

Unfortunately, the rest of Paton's letter is unreadable, except for a short passage in which the notion emerges that the hereditary part of the Thug profession is not only mental but also biological. As I said before, he propounded the idea that wives should be separated from their Thug husbands so as to avoid propagating the Thug race. In *Thug or a Million Murders*, by James L. Sleeman, William's grandson, which was published at the beginning of the twentieth century, the thesis that Thuggism is propagated through sexual reproduction is presented as an "unquestionable fact" (J. L. Sleeman 1933).

At the beginning of the nineteenth century, in accord with the ideology of the time, determinism was linked to education and modes of life. This environmental scheme viewed the proper conditioning of Thugs' children as the most efficacious solution. By the end of the century the idea of biological heredity came along with that of the "forced celibacy" of the members of the group whose extinction was sought. The rigid classification of castes in colonial representations of Indian society intertwined with the racist theses propagated in the course of the century. From this British lawmakers constructed the sociological penal category of "criminal castes and tribes."

Ethics and Profits

The School of Manufactures, built with governmental moneys, gradually became a profit-making operation.[87] I have in my hands the table of expenses and profits for the years 1845–1865. Profit grew eightfold, from 4,049 rupees to 23,279.[88] The government had a close interest in this prison-school. Various officials reported on its developments, its success, its difficulties in the economic domain. The list of the school's accomplishments in 1866 mentions the presence of 320 informers, 113 prisoners, 54 women, 169 boys, 8 girls.

Spinning, carding, dyeing, sawing occupy the majority of the inmates as production is mainly oriented to the making of tents, rugs, blankets, table linen, clothing for the men and horses of the army. Purchases of linen thread, of cotton and wool are the main expenses (2,545 rupees), with a long section "miscellaneous" (2,342 rupees), which includes items for daily needs such as milk, wood for heating, coal, oil, salt, tools, and books in Hindi, along with the costs of funerals. The purchase of raw materials, mostly dyes, indigo, borax, and so on, came to 95 rupees, while 177 rupees were spent for the wood used to make tent poles. A variety of things were made within each specialty. For instance, the school could sell tents with one or two poles, mountain tents, tents in the style of "Swiss chalets," and so on. The largest tents offered were 8.7 by 4 meters, and there were even 1.2-meter wide "verandahs." M. Williams, in charge of the school from 1840 on, was even the inventor of a mountain tent bearing his name. The British colonizers had to move a lot in the course of their careers: inspection tours, migrations to the mountains during the hot season, and so on. Their caravans, carrying these very comfortable, enormous tents, probably rivaled those of the Banjaras for a while.

The school was just as energetically led in the human domain as it was in the economic one. In the letter with the list of profits and expenses I referred to earlier, M. Williams made the case for the need for expansion.

He argued that the growth of the prison population called for a transfer of technology, namely bringing to Jabalpur a young man from the town of Kidderminster in Worcester county:[89] "The factory will not only be able to bear the cost, but will benefit much by the acquisition in its out-turn; and be better able to bear the increased number of pupils which it has to expect in the professional Dacoits, who have been or are being seized, and their sons."

The products of the school received awards when exhibited: at Nagpur in 1866, first prize for carpets; second prize for rugs; first prize for cotton rope. Major R. Ranken planned to send "two carpets and four Rugs" to the Paris exhibition.[90] The school became so famous that Balfour's Encyclopedia claimed the best Indian rugs came from it. Queen Victoria even received one of them as gift. It weighed two tons, and each side measured twenty-five meters. Sir Francis Tuker wrote that he went to the castle of Windsor and saw it. It can still be admired today in the Waterloo Chamber. From the strangler's noose to the rug maker's knot, whether they were criminal or honest, the Thugs seemed fated to cope with tightening knots. This was again evidenced as the ever-productive and inventive colonial power forced them to finance their own repression and rehabilitation.

Justice in India and Britain

This episode in the Thugs' repression was typical of colonial mentality and attitudes: ethics, profits, progress all interwove to form a tight crown. The stain of heredity was expelled, nature was corrected; justice had become a do-gooder. The deep-rooted murderous compulsions of the criminals had become work values. This miracle happened in the course of a single generation.

However, not everything was accepting of the legal rules of exception that had been used to legitimize Thug repression. There was an attempt in England as well as in India to stabilize the rigor and the uniformity of the sentences so as to ward of the unpredictability making judicial decisions appear unjust. Gang leaders, stranglers, and later on renegade informers were sentenced to certain death. Active accomplices went to forced labor, boys to prison. The spectacular aspect of the punishments was not a colonial invention either. Until the 1870s[91] in Britain too, hangings, the parade of convicts on their way to deportation to Australia, brandings, and floggings were public spectacles.

Likewise, the foundation of the School of Arts and Manufactures and Paton's idea of his thuggery were the marks of a new dynamic of gradually making law serve as a guide to human beings. "Criminal policy was enlisted in the effort to advance the civilizing process by fostering personal discipline and foresight" (Wiener 1990, 49). The criminal in prison had to be corrected. But the home country lagged behind the colony, where the colonizers thought to lock up the sons and daughters of the assassins to keep the group from reproducing itself. In Britain, it was only in 1866 that "Adderley's . . . Industrial Schools Act . . . widened the definition of children eligible for commitment to include orphans, children of a surviving parent who was undergoing penal servitude or imprisonment and refractory children of criminal parents who were regarded as unsuitable to be kept in workhouses" (Wiener 1990, 147). Were the criminal "clans" and "tribes" the colonizers saw in the subcontinent the ancestors of the idea of a hereditary "dangerous class," which was then re-imported from England? Were they doing here what they didn't dare do over there? This second proposition seems to be confirmed by the extreme harshness of justice in India as evidenced by the criminal laws promulgated in the colony. Death was more readily imposed here. The reader might remember how Lieutenant Rumley gave the order to execute three thousand Kallars as reprisal for the murder of a handful of British settlers. Approximately the same number of Thugs were given the death penalty. At that same time in Britain itself there were about fifteen hangings a year. However, because the so-called dangerous classes concept was at play in the home country as well, there had to be additional rationales at play in India. Whether these be the crude "might makes right" or the legal right of reason, the maintenance of order and security in the colony foreshadowed in a more aggressive mode the new forms of repression that were in the process of being established in the West.

THE SCOURGE OF THUGGISM AND THE TENTACLES OF THE LAW

The Thugs were in the process of disappearing: they were hanged, corrected, transformed into citizens of the empire. They were on the wane. But as soon as they disappeared, other criminals, just as cruel, made their appearance. They resembled them so much that they could have been their cousins. This chapter concludes on this state in which nothing changes. Criminality cured in one place reinfects another. The distance between yesterday's and today's Thugs grows, but the link remains.

In 1836 *Ramaseeana*, Sleeman's monograph on the Thugs and the campaign against them was published. It contained this triumphant statement: "India's roads are finally safe," but also this warning:

> That the system has been suppressed in every part of India where it once prevailed (and I believe that it prevailed more or less in every part) is, however, a proposition that neither ought nor can be affirmed absolutely . . . as justly observed by the able Magistrate of Chittoor in 1812, Mr W. E. Wright. To affirm absolutely that it has been suppressed while any seeds of the system remain to germinate

and spread again over the land might soon render all that has been done unavailing, for there is in it a "principle of vitality" which can be found hardly in any other. (Sleeman1836, "Introduction," 21)

Eighteen thirty-six was also the year when the first anti-Thug law was promulgated. What was its content and what was this "principle of vitality" that, according to Sleeman, moved the Thugs?

The Anti-Thug Law
TEXTS

The Act of 1836 and its successive amendments gave a legal form to the practices with which we are already familiar:[92]

ACT NO. XXX OF 1836

1. It is hereby enacted that whatever shall be proved to have belonged, either before or after the passing of this Act, to any gang of Thugs, either within or without the territories of the East India Company, shall be punished with imprisonment for life, with hard labor.
2. And it is hereby enacted, that every person accused of the offense made punishable by this Act, may be tried by any court which would have been competent to try him, if his offense had been committed within the Zillah, where that court sits, anything to the contrary, in any Regulation contained, notwithstanding.
3. And it is hereby enacted that no court shall, on a trial of any person accused of the offense made punishable by this Act, require any Futwa from any Law Officer.

ACT NO. XVIII OF 1837

. . . Any person charged with murder by Thuggee, or with the offense of belonging to a gang of Thugs, made punishable by Act No. XXX of 1836, may be committed by any Magistrate or Joint Magistrate, within the Territories of the East Indian Company, for trial before any Criminal Court, competent to try such person on such charge.

ACT NO. XIX OF 1837

It is hereby enacted, that no person shall, by reason of any conviction for any offense whatever, be incompetent to be a witness in any stage of any cause, Civil or Criminal, before any Court, in the Territories of the East India Company.

ACT NO. XVIII OF 1839

It is hereby enacted, that any person accused of the offense of murder by Thuggee, or of the offense of unlawfully and knowingly receiving or buying property stolen or plundered by Thuggee, may be tried by any Court which would have been competent to try him, if his offense had been committed within the Zillah where the Court sits, anything contained in any Regulation or Regulations, to the contrary, notwithstanding.

Act No. XXIV of 1843 extended the anti-Thug law to professional bandits, dacoits, whose crimes, like that of "Thuggee," were not defined explicitly in the 1836 law. It applied to those "who belong to certain tribes, systematically employed in carrying out their lawless pursuits in different parts of the country" (Sleeman 1849, 354). Act No. XI of 1848 laid down a punishment "with imprisonment, with hard labor, for a term not exceeding seven years" for the offense of belonging "to any wandering gang of persons associated for the purposes of theft or robbery, not being a gang of Thugs of Dacoits" (Sleeman 1849, 357).

THE SPIRIT OF THE LAW

The death penalty was no longer compulsory. This did not mean that it was no longer exacted, but that it was up to the judge to make the decision on the basis of the seriousness of the crime, and up to the general government to either accept or reject his decision. Death sentences for the crime of Thuggee were gradually becoming scarcer, and in 1845 not one such sentence was given.

In contrast, while the harshness of the sentences had lessened, the target population was increasingly more numerous. This legal net had become very loose, the more so in that the system of informers was still used. The supreme government was opposed to these arbitrary banishments and preventive detention, but some magistrates had the tendency to bypass its orders. Thus, the Agra magistrate ordered "the banishment beyond the Yamuna of a whole tribe of Nats (acrobats); an act which [the second judge] described as 'of the same value as would be the order from a London Magistrate to put all Italian Opera dancers and foreign singers across the water'" (Singha 1993, 115). In 1837 J. R. Lumley, posted at Shorapur, related his latest exploits to the magistrate:

> I have seized lately 50 or 60 Jogees . . . among whom more than a dozen have confessed or recorded Thuggees against their accomplices. The Headquarter of the Jogees is at Sonaree . . . where there is a Jogee Temple, some fifteen or twenty Gooroos (the greater number being engaged during this period of the year in visiting the Jogee disciples throughout this Presidency) and three or four Muctiyar Jogee families I wish to seize.

Requesting the magistrate to provide assistance for this capture, and even though he didn't think the Gooroos had "any connection with Thuggee,"

Lumley suggested apprehending "a few of them to initiate us into arcana Jogeeana."[93]

The law wasn't directed at any specific group, but its definition was so fluid that it could give rise to all sorts of abuses. It targeted all migrant bands of persons decreed to be suspect. It filled a desire for police and political control, desire becoming compulsion in some employees of the Company. However, the shortage of material means and the presence of liberal ideology advocating the free circulation of goods and people dampened the excesses to which the law could lead.

The Principle of Vitality
THE HOLY MEN

The laws promulgated in 1836 could only have pleased Sleeman because they perfectly took into account his warning about the criminals' infinite ability to reproduce and multiply. As the Thugs became scarcer, Sleeman was convinced that all the *gosains* and the *bairagis* residing south of the Narmada river were Thugs.[94] Between the years 1836 and 1838, the lieutenants Burrows and Reynolds at Dharwad,[95] the captain J. Vallancy at Cuttack, and J. R. Lumley at Shorapur arrested certain bands of religious beggars and extracted confessions from them. Lumley states: "I have the very strongest ground of suspicion for believing all the twelve tribes of Jogees to be in truth Thugs but ostensibly Beggars and Peddlers who traffic in small wares."[96] Sleeman shared this conviction: "We have always had reason to believe that a great part of the Byragees, Gosains and other religious mendicants that infest all parts of India were assassins by profession." But in spite of "abundant proofs of their atrocious character" and the discovery of "the most horrible crimes," he had "begun to despair of being ever able to lift the veil from their crimes."[97]

The evidence was so slim that in 1838 Sleeman "earnestly recommended" to his collaborators "to direct the release of the whole unconditionally." Though he remained certain of his views, he gave up on this new target: "There are not anywhere worse characters than these Jogies, or greater pests to society—I believe, save the regular Thugs—we should leave them to be dealt with by the ordinary Police of the Country."[98]

The arrests of great numbers of holy men thus ceased. However, the suspicion in which they were held remained strong, as shown by the 1844 example of Captain Fulljames who wanted to have all the Banjaras and all the important priests of the various shrines arrested in the province of Gujarat. Judge Fawcett tempered this zeal and argued that the crimes were not perpetrated systematically by the members of a given social group, but by individuals under the sway of specific circumstances.

POISONERS AND KIDNAPPERS

Sleeman discovered the river Thugs who perpetrated their misdeeds mainly on the Ganges, or again those who poisoned travelers with *datura*.[99] In 1839 his list got longer with the "Meypunnaists" Thugs who "kidnap children to sell them." Finally, he discovered the "Tashmabazes Thugs," the product of an insane marriage between British and Indian crime. Fanny Parks paid tribute to the perspicacious Sleeman before invoking the extravagant discovery:

> Thuggee and Meypunnaism are no sooner suppressed that a new system of secret assassination and robbery is discovered. . . . At least one set of new actors are to be introduced to the public, and these are the Tashma-baz-Thugs. 'The Thugs formerly discovered went forth on their murderous expeditions under the protection of the Goddess; the Tashmabazes have for their genius a European! Who in England would be prepared to credit that the thimble-riggers of English fairs have in India given rise to an association that, in the towns bazaars and highways of these provinces, employs the game of *stick-and-garter* as the lure for victims be robbed or murdered? Yet this is the simple fact. The British had hardly gained possession of this territory before the seeds of the flourishing system of iniquity, brought to light almost half a century afterwards, were sowed in 1802 by a private soldier in one of his Majesty's regiments stationed at Cawnpore. The name of this man is Creagh. He initiated several natives into the mystery of the *stick-and-garter*, and these afterwards appeared as the leaders of as many gangs, who traversed the country, gambling with whomsoever they could entrap to try their luck at this game. . . . Indeed the gangs seem to have been of a more hardened character than any yet discovered, for their sole aim was gain, however it might be secured, without the plea of religious motive which regulated the proceedings of the other fraternities.[100]

These new Thugs were arrested and put on trial and became a hot topic in the press and for British travelers. And yet, the existence of these cousins of Thuggism, unfortunate people having lost along the way all religious aura and all power to frighten, evidenced for the British the intercontinental solidarity of the dangerous classes. This time, instead of India, their existence points to Britain as their place of origin. The prolific series of modes of Thuggism looped back to Britain: both countries were contaminated by the same evil.

In 1840 the Court of Directors, while praising the government of India and Sleeman for the results of the anti-Thug campaign, clearly put a stop to the harshness of the past:

> In the Provinces in which the operations were first commenced, it would appear that there are now few or no Thugs remaining at large. In Oude and in the South of India, to which your efforts have been recently directed, great numbers of these offenders have been apprehended and convicted and in Bengal the formidable confederacy of River Thugs has been almost entirely suppressed. The progress of your investigations has brought to light other fraternities of professional murderers closely allied to the Thugs in particular the Meetawallas or poisoners in Bengal, a class in the Upper Provinces who murder parents for the sake of obtaining possession of their children, a certain class of religious mendicants in the Deccan, some of whom are proved to practice assassination in the manner of the Thugs. We trust that the very efficient machinery which has been created for the suppression of Thugs will be found equally . . . able against the other classes of atrocious criminals. Very few capital sentences are reported to us and it is stated by Captain Reynolds (who as General Superintendent has succeeded Major Sleeman) that prisoners are now usually committed merely on the general charge of Thuggee under Act XXX of 1836, which limits the punishment to imprisonment for life. This is satisfactory.[101]

THE DACOITS

In 1837 the government was concerned with the growing number of acts of violent banditry, sometimes involving murder, in the north of India. The repression of dacoity (*dacoity* comes from the word *dacoit* meaning "brigand") was on the agenda, and a special post was created by Charles Metcalf. Hugh Fraser was the first to hold it, but he obtained few results. Two years later, in 1839, Sleeman, who had rid India of the scourge of Thuggism, replaced him. As new official in charge of the suppression of Thugs *and* dacoits, Sleeman settled at Moradabad (Sleeman 1849, 355).

In Sleeman's eyes, the dacoit group known as "Budhuk" shared numerous traits with the Thugs. The Budhuks were found in the same areas: the north of Awadh, Rajasthan, the valley of the river Chambal, the state of Gwalior, and their expeditions ranged as far as Bombay, Delhi, and Baroda. Bands of one hundred to one hundred fifty men led by a *jamadar* chief attacked at night, then dispersed dozens of kilometers away into the jungles or the forests. They too had a secret language, worshipped the Goddess, and disguised themselves as pilgrims, as Banjaras, and as ascetics. But this time the government reacted vigorously when Sleeman proposed to use the measures of judicial exceptions he had used against the Thugs:

> It must be remembered that the crime of Dacoity differs most essentially from that of Thuggee. The one is a secret crime; in which the murder of all the victims, systematically, is the first step—the search for booty the subsequent one—a crime rooted in the very heart of the country . . . throwing away its deadly rumours, scarcely to be distinguished from healthy products over the whole surface of the land. The other lies comparatively on the surface, it is "robbery by open violence." . . . Thuggee is a crime known to no other country in the world, and which could have existed nowhere but in India. . . . Gang robbery by open violence is an offence known to every nation, civilized or savage—for the suppression of which the laws commonly found in the statute books have proved sufficient.[102]

Assisted by the same troops and the same collaborators with whom he fought the Thugs, Sleeman followed familiar methods. He collected information by interrogating dacoits in prison and offered rewards and pardons for complete denunciations. He gathered some of them in a small colony he called Budhukpoora, "Budhuk bandits' town," near his house at Moradabad. His investigations led him to claim that the dacoits comprised twelve hundred families living in the princely states of Alwar, Karuali, and Jaipur. Others resided in Malwa and near Jodhpur under the protection of large landowners. As for the Thugs, his range of action swept all annexed, allied, and independent territories. In his report on "gang robbers by hereditary profession" (Sleeman 1849), the groups that are named include the Banjaras along with members of low castes such as the Mangs, the Ramusis, the Kolis, and the Sansis.

When the Company's directors read his report, they implicitly praised Sleeman for not repeating the excesses of his anti-Thug campaign: "never in the history of crime and its suppression had there been any other instance of so few arrests, compared with final convictions, or of so much security to the innocent in the pursuit of the guilty" (Tuker 1961, 117). In 1842 Sleeman claimed to have dismantled their gangs. The following year the crowning glory of his campaign, a new law, Act No. XXIV, was passed, targeting "any person accused of the offence of Dacoity, with or without murder, or of having belonged to a group of Dacoits."

The waning of the Thugs was Sleeman's triumphant dawn. He was recognized as the expert in pan-Indian violence: in his words, stranglers and dacoits perpetrated their crimes from the Himalayas to Cape Comorin. The breath of his mission mirrored the dimension of the British Indian Empire. Sleeman, who invented and was responsible for this powerful internal policy, enlisted the cooperation of a large number of native dignitaries and functionaries of the Company and played an important role in the promulgation of the first criminal laws (along with their remarkably vague wording). His network of collaborators, his powers, the efficacy of his methods, the enormity of his task, one that was both unavoidable (order is of essential importance) and interminable (the notion of the "vitality of criminals"), were to convince the Calcutta authorities that the superpoliceman deserved even better than this sort of mission.

From the Stranglers' Fraternity to Criminal Tribes

In spite of the gradual differentiation of different types of delinquencies, the Thugs remained, in the colonizers eyes, the "ideal type" of a specifically Indian criminality. The classificatory concept of "criminal tribes" was the extension of the model constructed by Sleeman. This was evidenced in a speech by Sir J. M. Stephen, who in 1871 introduced the draft of the law pertaining to these tribes to the viceroy's council:

> A family of carpenters now will be a family of carpenters a century or five centuries hence, if they last so long; so will grain-dealers, blacksmiths, leather-makers, and every other known trade. A carpenter cannot drop his tools and become a banya (trader), or a lohar (blacksmith) or anything else. The only means of subsistence open to him other than the trade to which he is born is agriculture. (cited in Pouchepadass 1979, 137–138)

Based on the caste system, the text of the "Criminal Tribes Act" created a delinquent category that was linked to the notion of castes and was entirely defined in penal terms.[103] Its first locus of application were the territories of the Northwestern Provinces, of Awadh, and of the Punjab. It authorized provincial governments, upon agreement with the governor general, to declare criminal any tribe, group, or class thought to systematically perpetrate aggressions to persons and property. This law was then extended to other areas of the subcontinent and allowed forced resettlement of groups thought to be criminal to penal colonies. Their members were required to carry a passport that specified their place of residence, the places they had the right to visit, and the names of the officers with whom they had to meet regularly.

Most of the works on crime and criminality in India in the eighteenth and nineteenth centuries explore the reasons that led the colonial authorities to classify certain groups as delinquent. J. Pouchepadass, A.A. Yang, and Sandria B. Freitag point out the use of the referent *Thug* in this choice. "Their ghost have haunted all other delinquent groups, whether they be dacoit Budhuks of the Awadh, datura poisoners, or the Meenas of Punjab" writes Sanjay Nigam. "Exterminated or neutralized" some forty years previously, the Thugs keep on occupying the position of ancestors in relation to the "tribes, groups and classes" incriminated by Sir Stephen.

Sir Stephen establishes their filiation from the Thugs on the basis of their supposed common sociological identity. The targeted groups were accused of practicing a form of collective crime hereditary in nature. This notion was particularly attractive to the colonizers in that it seemed to correspond to the native one of caste: as B. S. Cohn (1987d) notes, as seen by British administrators, Indian society was a collection of castes, each of them being a solid entity, material and measurable with defined economic and social behavior (243). In presenting his project of law, Sir Stephen gave a "native" style version of Cesare Lombroso's notion that certain people are born criminal. Any delinquent is such "by profession and caste" (Pouchepadass 1979, 137).

Sir Stephen was still thinking about the Thugs as he ended his portrait of the criminal with these words: "His crimes are almost his religion" (cited in Pouchepadass 1979, 138). This "almost" barely softened the finality of the statement. Under the legislator's pen, any crime labeled "Hindu" thus became a crime of religion. He didn't directly attribute religious motives to criminal tribes, he simply let a suspicion float about by using the example of the Thugs as prototypes structuring his discourse.

Who was targeted by this law? Like legislation related to the Thugs earlier, it covered a broad range of groupings. These groups might be marginal by profession, such as peddlers and nomads or they might be marginal by accident, uprooted , having lost their status through famines and wars, such as the Dhekarus of Bengal or the Dongadasaris of the Bellary district. They might also be delinquent segments of specific castes and tribes in the proper sense of the term, as for instance the Doms of Bengal, for whom predatory activities were legitimate (Pouchepadass 1979).

In 1919 the Kallars, whom I evoked in chapter 1, became targeted by this new law. Many refused to register. In 1920 the police murdered about two dozen rebels, and administrators roamed the villages, registering the population by force; that same year, twenty thousand of them were counted. In spite of government statistics showing that only 10 percent of crimes committed in the region of Madura and Tanjore were perpetrated by Kallars, the Criminal Tribes Act was applied to them to such an extent that historians speak of the law as aimed at controlling the Kallar population. The colonizers' unbridled aggressiveness had links with the past.[104]

Indeed the Kallars were the regional model of the "savage Collerie" that was constructed during the British conquest and was thus perpetuated and weighed heavy on their descendants. However, the legislator did not invoke it: he preferred the model of the Thugs that could be applied to the whole of India and that justified his introduction of the famous link, so intangible in judicial documents, between religion and crime.

Marie Fourcade (1993) writes that "spread out in the whole of India, ex-criminal tribes today keep on living thanks to some meager subsidies allocated by the Indian Government, . . . often at the very place of the old British penal colonies. An example are the Kanjarbats of Solapur in Maharashtra filmed by Yolande Zauberman in 1989.[105] . . . Having suffered physical and tacit violence, few among them succeeded in escaping this labeling. They were the eternal victims of an infamous mark that made them the target of accusations by ordinary Indians" (208).

> In the nineteenth century, the Thugs . . . became part of a popular Gothic-Romantic image of India; and as "Thugs" they found their way into the English language. The publicity they received was certainly exaggerated. The phenomenon of "Thuggee" appealed not only to an ordinary sensationalism, but also to the British sense of destiny in India, and it was used to propagate the legitimacy of colonial rule. (Halbfass 1991, 104)

Who Were the Thugs?

OUR SOURCES ON THE THUGS

Accounts Prior to Colonization

Carlo Ginzburg (1989) notes that like medical knowledge, historical knowledge is indirect and has to rely on indices and conjectures. This idea is also held by Gustav Pfirrmann (1970), the author of a doctoral dissertation in philosophy on the religious character of the Thug confraternity. He looked for the assassins in a great number of chronicles and travel books and found in the Indian Office in London sources much older than the one mentioned by the doctor Sherwood in the *Madras Literary Gazette* at the beginning of the nineteenth century. Pfirrmann writes that "the pilgrim Hiouen Thsang (born ca 605 A.D.) came close to being ceremonially sacrificed to Durga on at least two occasions in the course of his journey to India between 629 and 645." He notes that his evidence comes from Stanislas Julien, the author of an undated work on Hiouen Thsang's life and his travels through India. The famous pilgrim had come in India to learn the teaching of Buddhism. He was attacked on the Ganges by pirates looking for their yearly sacrificial victim for Durga: "We were ready, they said, to let pass the time of the sacrifice that our Goddess demands as we could not find a victim worthy of her; but here is a priest with an imposing stature and a charming face. Let us kill him to obtain happiness." The leader of the band sent some of his men to find an altar. Two men pulled out their knives and tied up Hiouen Thsang on it (Pfirrmann 1970, 30–31).[1]

Another time, while Hiouen Thsang was on his way to the town of Pataliputra, he passed by a temple. He was told that no foreigner who entered it would ever come out again. Sir Alexander Cunningham (1814–

1893), director of archaeological research in India, was able to locate this temple twenty-three kilometers from Bhagalpur (Bihar):

> These are no doubt the ruins of the temple seen by Hwen Thsang. The story of its ruin is not known, but it may be guessed with some certainty the presence of the tomb of Sheikh Mari Shah. . . . Hwen Thsang's remark that "people who visited Kahalgaon forgot to leave it," is susceptible of a very different explanation from what he intended. In later times Kahalgaon has been noted as a favourite haunt of the 'River Thugs,' and as dead men tell no tales, there can be no doubt that all their victims who visited Kahalgaon forgot to leave it. . . . So notorious was the name of Kahalgaon as the haunt of Thugs that its name became proverbial. The following verse records the popular opinion: *Bhagalpur ka Bhagaliya Aur Kahalgaon ka Thug Patna ka Dewaliya Tinom nam zad:* "The Swindler of Bhagalpur, the Kahalgaon footpad and Bankrupt of Patna, are Three names very bad." (Cunningham 1882, 15:35)

The account of the seventh-century Chinese pilgrim was thus confirmed, twelve centuries later, by the existence of ruins and the sad renown of the place where they were found.

A second very important allusion to the Thugs appeared in the thirteenth century in Zia-ud-din Barani's chronicle. Vincent Smith mentions it in his history of India. In chapter 2 he tells us about the short reign of Firuz Shah, of Turkish origin, who after being put on the Delhi throne by a faction of nobles took on the title of Jalal-ud-din. He was very soon replaced by his nephew Ala-ud-din, his brother's son, who had him decapitated and had his head paraded on the tip of a lance in front of the army. The British historian writes the following obituary:

> Jalal-ud-din, although he did not deserve his cruel fate, was wholly unfit to rule. One act of leniency was particularly silly. At some time during his reign about 1,000 thugs were arrested in Delhi. The sultan would not allow one of them to be executed. He adopted the imbecile plan of putting them into boats and transporting them to Lakhnauti (Gaur), the capital of Bengal. The story, told by Zia-ud-din Barani, is of special interest as being the earliest known historical notice of thagi. (Smith 1987, 245)

Long before the advent of the British, murder was severely punished in India. The texts of the Brahmanic tradition (which make up the Vedic revelation, including the Veda and the *Upanishads*, along with the *Tradition* and the *Puranas*) differentiated thieves (*steya*) from those guilty of violent crimes (*sahas*), particularly when the victim was a Brahman, a woman, or a child. The victims forbidden to the Thugs pretty much belonged to these same categories. According to this tradition "if several persons violently beat a man, the one who gives the fatal blow is guilty and must be put to death." The strangler was the main culprit, just as he was to be in the colonizers' eyes, but all of his accomplices shared in the guilt (Kane 1968–1975, 3:520–30).

In the Muslim tradition, to kill or wound someone called for either retribution in kind or material compensation in the form of lands, villages, or money. Corporal punishment was expected for a murderer who had acted deliberately and who was in full possession of his mental faculties (Thakur 1978, 32–33). Firuz Shah, in freeing one thousand Thugs, apparently wasn't following the laws described by these authors. Was he motivated by fear of Kali's revenge as the Thugs were to later claim rajahs were? The story remains silent on this. But in condemning them to exile rather than to death, Firuz Shah seems to have followed the practice of compromise so opposite to the positivistic law gradually imposed by the colonizers.

A third author who wrote about the Thugs and was cited by Sleeman was Jean de Thévenot (1633–1667). The account of his journey to India was published in 1684.

> The cunningest robbers in the world are in that country. They use a certain slip with a running noose, which they can cast with so much sleight about a man's neck, when they are within reach of him, that they never fail, so that they strangle him in a trice. They have another cunning trick also to catch travellers with. They send out a handsome woman upon the road, who with her hair dishevelled seems to be in all tears, sighing and complaining of some misfortunes which she pretends has befallen her. Now, as she takes the same way that the traveller goes, he easily falls into conversation with her and finding her beautiful, offers her his assistance, which she accepts; but he has no sooner taken her up behind him on horseback, but she throws the snare about his neck and strangles him, or at least stuns him, until the robbers (who lie hid) come running into her assistance, and complete what she hath begun. But besides that, there are men in those quarters so skillful in casting the snare, that they succeed as well at a distance as near as hand; and if an ox or any beast belonging to a caravan run away, as sometimes it happens, they fail not to catch it by the neck.[2]

In *A New Account of East India and Persia* (1698), published in the same century as Thévenot's work, John Fryer mentions the existence of the Thugs at Surat:

A Pack of Thieves that had infested the Roads a long time, and after some whiles Imprisonment the banyans proffered Money for their Redemption; but the Great Mogul sending an Express, they were led to Execution; they were Fifteen, all of a Gang, who used to lurk under Hedges in narrow Lanes and as they found opportunity, by a Device of a weight tied to a Cotton Bowstring made of Guts (with which they tie Cotton) of some length, they used to throw it about their Necks, they pulled them from their Beasts and dragging them upon the Ground strangled them, and possessed themselves of what they had: One of these was an Old Man with his two Sons, the youngest not fourteen. This being their Practice, they were sentenced, according to *Lex Talionis,* to be hanged; wherefore being delivered to the Catwal of Sherriff's Men, they led them two miles with Ropes about their Necks to some Wild Date-Trees: In their way thither, they were cheerful, and went singing, and smoking Tobacco, the Banyans giving them Sweetmeats, they being as jolly as if going to a Wedding; and the Young Lad now ready to be tied up boasted, That though he were not Fourteen Years of Age, he had killed his Fifteen Men; whereof the Old Man, as he had been a Leader of these Two, was first made an Example for his Villainy, and then the two Striplings were advanced, as all the rest were, half a Foot from the Ground; and then cutting their Legs off that the Blood might flow from them, they left them miserable Spectacles, hanging till they dropped of their own accord.[3]

We might almost be reading word for word Doctor Henry Spry's account, which he wrote two centuries later after witnessing the hangings of the Thugs at Sagar. There is the same joyful attitude, the same bragging by the condemned men. Are these the same Thugs who seized the appetizing Chinese pilgrim to sacrifice him on their goddess's altar, who were exiled to Bengal by Firuz Shah, who sent out one of their own to befriend travelers and lead them into their trap, or again who were hanged by the Great Moghul two centuries before Sleeman?

But things get more complicated as other authors note that in the native languages of the eighteenth and nineteenth centuries, the word *Thug* rarely designated a murderer. It most often was used to refer to a swindler: the word had many usages, signifying acts from the simple misdeed to the ritual or common-law crime. Moreover, Wilhelm Halbfass found that the most ancient Sanskrit sources from the eighth century referred to the assassins by putting them unambiguously into the category of common-law criminals. This paradoxical information touching the very heart of their identity can be found again in a much richer and more elaborated form in colonial sources. What are those sources?

The Depositions

Bheelam Barre Khan,[4] a Thug who had committed thirty crimes, answered the magistrate who was questioning him.

State your name, parentage, caste, profession, age and Residence.
My name is Bheelam Bhure Khan and my father's name was Kadir Sahib. I am a Mussulman and a resident of Hudlugee, Ellake Neepanee, aged 65 years, am a Thug as were my forefathers before me.

In what village were you born?
I was born in the town of Austa, zilla Hyderabad, and when I was ten years of age my father died. My uncle took me to Azunee where we lived for four years and left that place and took up our abode at Ougurda and resided there for the period of 25 years and there I married Moheeoodeen Sahib Patel's daughter [village chief's daughter[5]]. We left that village and I took up our residence at Lohoogaon for ten years and after this we came at Chincholee ellaka Putwurdhun where we lived for 12 years. We lived in Jouree Buree ellaka for two years and nine months when a party came and arrested me.

The magistrate then inquired as to which Thug expedition he had participated in. Bheelam Barre Khan then narrated his crimes according to the scheme I described earlier, with all of its successful and unsuccessful sequences, including simple and complexly imbricated ones.

His account, told in the first person, was supposed to be exhaustive and sincere, and it was expected to open up a window on the identity, or at least the biography, of the narrator. The action was permeated with deception, and there is a surprising element in the narrative: that not one utterance, not one word, betrays the shadow of an emotion. Violence is abstract, the murderer and his fellows kill as if they were smoking the hookah, routinely and silently. The victims are given the same treatment in the story. Even more so than the murderer, they travel through his narrative as if they were shadows. As in all the other depositions collected in the four corners of India by different magistrates, the accused focuses on the inventory of his crimes.

This is a very intriguing situation: in private conversations with Sleeman, Thugs claimed that Kali was their reason to be Thugs. And yet in the judicial procedures, the religious material was either totally obliterated or was present only in tenuous traces. The two universes, the religious and the criminal, were walled off from each other while logically they should have deeply interpenetrated.

In spite of the fleetingness of the information not pertaining to criminal activities that Bheelam Barre Kahn gave about himself, it does call for our attention. For instance, some of his comments indicate that he was repeating pre-existing practices: he was a Thug as his ancestors were before him. He consulted the usual omens before leaving on an expedition. Other comments bring out the lack of stability of his life: he moved very often. Finally, he also shows his insertion into village life: he did marry the chief's daughter.

Secret Language and "Conversations"

There are other, more substantial, sources that add to these precious clues on the social, familial, and particularly the religious identity of the Thugs. They also give a view of their criminal identity that is clearer than that drawn by the dull macabre sequences their interrogators elicited from them.

Sleeman's monograph on the assassins yields two types of sources: Ramasee, the "peculiar language" the Thugs used to communicate among themselves, and the "conversations" the author had with a group of informers to explain some of the language meanings:

> For the present I can only offer, in addition to the above observations, the almost literal translation of some conversations I have had with the approvers in revising the vocabulary of their peculiar dialect for the last time. These conversations were often carried on in the presence of different European gentlemen who happened to call in, and as they seemed to feel a good deal of interest in listening to them, I thought others might possibly feel the same in reading them if committed to paper; and from that time I, for several days, put down the conversations as they took place in the present form. They form the first number of the Appendix, and will be found immediately after the Vocabulary. (Sleeman 1836, "Introduction," 64–66)

This vocabulary was probably collected and these "conversations" held in the prison of Sagar or that of Jabalpur, in the territories where William Sleeman had, since 1835, exclusively devoted himself to the eradication of the Thugs: "having the general superintendence of all proceedings preliminary to trial over the whole field of our operations, which had now extended from Lahore to Carnatic, I was relieved from every other charge" (Sleeman 1836, "Introduction," 57). We have seen him organize the trials and coordinate the pursuits carried on elsewhere by his collaborators. He conducted as well ethnographic and linguistic researches in the course of which he talked with Muslim and Hindu Thugs from different areas of India.

Sleeman didn't give us any details as to the locale or even the season of these conversations, so we can't imagine the scene in a concrete way.

These unusual meetings between repented criminals, brought und[er] escort with iron on their feet, and an audience of invited Europeans, we[re] held at least three times, this with different informers, as indicated by the subsections of the text of "Conversations." Even though very informative, these are secondary in import to the precious list of the words making up the criminals' secret language established by Sleeman.

Ramasee remains mysterious. Sleeman himself owned up to his ignorance as he didn't recognize any Hindi or Persian words in the approximately six hundred terms for which he gave a translation, often accompanied by commentary. Grierson, the author of a famous *Linguistic Survey of India*, originally published in 1927, doesn't mention its existence in his chapter "Unclassed Languages." However, the famous linguist does evoke the "Pendari argot" spoken by the Pindaris we met earlier, in chapter 1. He correctly includes it under the heading "Argots" and notes that argots "are used by criminals and other disreputable people, and are paralleled by the thieves' Latin, and other cant forms of speech found in Europe. . . . The speakers of these argot are of course bilingual. They speak the language of their neighbours and reserve the argot only for special occasions" (Grierson 1973, 1:188). More recently R. R. Mehrotra (1977) studied the question but only peripherally through research of other secret languages. He gives the key to about twenty words.

I owe the hypotheses as to the meaning of the words I am using here and in this volume's lexicon[6] to R. Doktor, a specialist in popular Indian literatures. He has had to be perspicacious, as Ramasee words were distorted both by the speakers themselves and by Sleeman's transcription. J.-L. Chambard, specialist in the Hindi-language popular culture of northern India, kindly agreed to look over his work. In the course of joint work sessions we were able to come up with new hypothetical meanings, eliminate others, and retain yet some others with a greater degree of certainty.

The Thugs thus got to speak through the "conversations" and Ramasee. Of course this was not a reciprocal and free conversation between equals. The questioner was a magistrate and the questioned were defendants. There were thus two distinct groups: the first one felt free to ask questions ranging from the most expected (the where and when of the crime) to the most indiscreet (such as Feringheea's possible "guilty relations" with the beautiful Kalee Babee). The second group appeared to obediently put up with these questions and gave up the knowledge of their secret language to their questioners.

Fiction

In addition to these judiciary and lexical sources there is a work of fiction, *Confessions of a Thug*. It is the autobiography of a Thug, written

r, Sleeman's contemporary and collaborator in the
n. There are many aspects of his narrative that bring
tioned in other sources: thus it can be considered a
1ore so in that the author had direct contacts with the

pages, where I explore these different sources, only the
e extracted from the Ramasee. I have italicized their etymologies ana auded a question mark when some doubt remains. They all
concord with the English definitions given side by side in Sleeman. The
expressions or words between quotation marks are cited from Sleeman.

THUG ACTIVITIES

Thug Names
ONE THOUSAND TRICKS

> *Thag:* a cut-throat, cheat, a pilferer, a robber, a trickster, a sharper,
> a pick-pocket, a swindler, a cunning fellow; *thag lagna:* to be in-
> fested by Thugs in a journey; *thagi:* cheating, robbing, knavery,
> theft; *thagna:* to cheat, to swindle, to rob, to deceive, to trick, to
> dupe, to defraud, to outwit, to gull, to overreach, to rogue, etc.
> *thagna maya se:* to delude, to elude, to wrangle; *thagni:* the wife
> of a thief; *thagmuri:* intoxication used by Thugs to make their vic-
> tims senseless; *thagmuri khana:* to be intoxicated, to faint, to lose
> consciousness, to become senseless; *thagmodak:* sweetmeats im-
> pregnated with narcotic drugs used by Thugs to make their victims
> senseless; *thagvidya:* the art of cheating used by robbers, quackery,
> etc. (*Bhargava's Standard Illustrated Dictionary,* 1946)

The idea of deception dominates the whole of this declension of words
having the same verbal root of Sanskrit origin: *sthag,* to cover, to recover,
to hide, to veil, to make invisible, to make disappear. "The etymological
connection of *thaka* with the Sanskrit root *sthag,* 'to cover,' 'to conceal,'
which has been accepted by . . . numerous lexicographers, may still be
valid, but should certainly not be taken for granted," writes the Indologist
Wilhelm Halbfass in a long note summarizing the issue. He also writes
that at the beginning of the twelfth century, Hemacandra in his dictionary
of Prakrit "uses *thaka* to paraphrase *dhurta,* rogue, deceiver" (Halbfass
1983, 105). Around the same period an author of a Sanskrit dictionary
listed both words as synonyms.

Very early the meaning of "hiding" narrowed into "hiding something
reprehensible," but without excluding other less negative meanings.
These meanings come through in literature. The poet Kabir, writing in
the sixteenth century, states that God is a Thug; another poet from the

Punjab describes the woman who meets her lover as "a sweetness of *thugs;* the lover who kisses her is fooled" (Matringe 1988, 1:27). Here, *thug* invokes an illusion, a seduction involving the idea of irresistible attraction, the impossibility of escaping, thus of being forced, but this inflicted by someone who is loving and whom one loves. The trickery is thus enchantment.

In all these cases, "strangler" is a secondary meaning of the word *thug,* whose meaning remains entirely dominated by the main idea of trickery, one which in different circumstances can lead to pleasure as well as to death.

The historian Stewart N. Gordon looked at two thousand fragments from the oral tradition of central India. He found many stories about robbers, but none specifically about Thugs. Thug was a "common 18th century word meaning a cheat or trickster—anyone from the perennial practical joker to a sleight of hand artist or a coinage swindler. . . . Oral tradition supports the position that the principal meaning of the word thug was not even robbery, much less a particular style of robbery" (Gordon 1969, 408–9). In an article in the *Journal of Indian History,* C. R. Sharma (1976), another present-day historian, notes that the word *thug* could mean "forger."[7] The autobiography of Ardha-Kathnak, an eighteenth-century Jain trader, mentions two travelers accused of being Thugs for having passes faked coins.

At the very beginning of the nineteenth century R. Drummond wrote in his *Illustrations of the Grammatical Parts of the Guzrattee, Mahratta, and English Languages* (1808) that in the language spoken in Gujarat,

> Thug or Tugg (Guz.) [means] An impostor, Swindler. These characters are well known in Guzerat or rather first their depredations on the credulity of the people. Alchemists *(keemeeagur)* deservedly came to be classed with them. The Gosaees and Veiragees and Joota Veidyas (Holy Hypocrites, and Quack-Doctors) to say nothing of Goldsmiths or the Gilders, are the Grant and glaring Actors in all kinds of Cozenage. (Drummond 1808)

In the eighteenth and the beginning of the nineteenth century, in a broad, widespread sense close to its etymological roots ("to hide"), *to thug* thus meant to take advantage of people's credulity by creating an illusion. Stewart N. Gordon writes that the verb *thagna* can often be translated as "to surprise, to subjugate."

FROM THE TECHNIQUE OF MURDER TO THE STATUS OF KILLER

This brings us back to Bheelam Barre Khan and the Thugs' depositions. Their narratives all have to do with one or more premeditated homicides

perpetrated according to specific strategies and a specific killing mode—
that is, strangling followed by robbery. There are many words and expressions drawing from this technical aspect to designate criminals.

Doctor Sherwood noted the existence of the expression in Tamil of *ari
tulucar* (*ari* meaning to cut and *tulucar*, originating from Turkey, meaning a Muslim,[8]) and, of more general use in the south of India, the word
phansigar, in which we recognize *phansi*, noose, and the verb *phamsana*,
to catch, to entrap, to surround, to mislead. This word (*phanseeo*) had
the same meaning in Gujarat. Drummond (1808) notes that the word
was used pejoratively to refer to robbers secretly strangling travelers and
children on the highways. It is significant that it was also used to refer to executioners whose job was to hang individuals condemned to
death.

The same reference to a means of seizing someone with intent to
kill was similar in Karnataka, where Thugs were known as *tanti calleru*,
"sinew robbers." Sleeman wrote that *Thug* was qualified by the different
methods of killing used. The Megpunia Thugs murdered poor folks so
as to kidnap and sell their children; this compound word can be broken down into *meck*, ankle, and *phandiya*, knot. The Persian equivalent,
tashmabaze, means "playing a trick with a strap." "A strap is doubled and
folded up. . . . The art consists in putting in a stick or peg in such a way
that the strap when unfolded shall come out double" (Sleeman 1915, 91).
Here again the criminal was named after the means he uses to kill. The
expression Datura Thugs, which designated Datura poisoners, followed
the same principle. According to Sleeman, the word *thug* was an inflexion
meaning "criminal; it was preceded by that which designates the instrument, the substance, through which the murder is done." Sleeman thus
substituted an unequivocal penal concept to the etymological sense of
"deceiver" at play in the various contexts of the time.

In contrast, in Ramasee Thugs are differentiated by their qualities and
status instead of by these various techniques. In a vein of praise we find
baroo, burka, bora (probably from *bada*, great, powerful), which con-
notes "a Thug of distinction." **Chandoo**, from *chandu*, "one who works
with hemp," from *chand*, knot, trick, fraud—a very telling compound-
ing—designating an expert Thug. There were also Thugs who were "coward, timid, weak." Other words referred to the individual's ritual status
within the group, such as the teacher (**gooroo**), and the apprentice or
the one initiated to the ritual knot (**goor ponch**, from *gur*, esoteric, secret, and *phams*, knot). There is yet a differentiation between someone
who is born a Thug but who doesn't have the status of a strangler: **soon**,
from *sunu*, son, younger brother. In the folk tales studied by Bloomfield,
we also encounter the word **aulae**, from *auliya*, holy man, to designate
a Thug.

The word *thug,* linked up or competing with others helping to specify its meaning, thus covers a palette of diverse modalities which, interestingly, include the ritual mode.

THUGS AND NON-THUGS

In contrast to these sources and to the results of Stewart N. Gordon's and C. R. Sharma's research, the Thug secret language excludes other categories of criminals from their community. There are specific words to refer to people who pillage and to thieves and pickpockets: **bisnee** (homophone of *bisni,* one with bad habits) and **tormee** (which evokes the verb *torna,* meaning transgression, breaking in). A thief is a **kulioo** (from *kalia,* black, dressed in black so as not to be seen) and a **chungar** (opium maker and as well opium smoker). There are three words that specifically denote the separation of these brigands from ordinary society: **dudh/dadh** comes from *dhad,* attack, multitude; **beetoo** from *bit,* low-caste, inferior; **eloo,** from *alag,* separated, distinct, a word also used to designate a victim. Though these robbers' aggressive practice and its dangers paralleled that of the profession of Thug, they remained non-Thugs in Thugs' eyes, as Sleeman correctly translated within the framework of the restricted meaning of "murderer" he attributed to the word.

Thugs' Crimes

Not all Ramasee words appear in the depositions, yet the nature of the vocabulary does confirm them to a substantial extent. The vast majority of the six hundred words that make it up directly pertain to murder: 112 verbs describe murdering actions; 16 nouns describe the terrain; 48 nouns define the functions and the status of the murderers; 38 nouns characterize their victims; 28 designate dangerous situations; and finally, about 70 pertain to the nature of the loot and manner of dividing it.

I proceed to give an account of this data by following the chronological order of the action, one punctuated with incidents endangering the execution of the assassins' sinister program, with which we are already quite familiar. First, there are the formation of the gang and the start of its journey. Travelers appear. The gang performs approach maneuvers, plans the murder, executes it, erases all its traces, and seizes the loot and divides it.

THE GANG: A LEADER AND HIS ACCOMPLICES

In order to be able to gather a gang of Thugs, the leader had to be an accomplished strangler (a **borka,** knowledgeable in rules and omens) and to have several generations of Thug ancestors. He had to be able to set up the material organization of the expedition; he was expected to be "a man who has always at command the means of advancing a month or two's subsistence to a gang . . . one who has influence over local authorities, or the native officers of the courts of justice." He also had to be "a strong and resolute man . . . or a very wise man whose advice in difficult cases has weight with the gang . . . a man of handsome appearance and high bearing, who can feign the man of rank as well." He was an entrepreneur with economic and human resources; "all these things enable a man to get around him a few who will consent to give him the fees and title of **Jemadar**" (Sleeman 1836, "Substance," 263–64).[9]

The gangs were made up of highly variable numbers of members. At times several bands could join together under the leadership of a great chief, who was then given the title of **subehdar** (*subadar*), "but it requires very high and numerous qualifications" (Sleeman 1836, 263–64). This leader also enjoyed privileges: Feringheea never strangled women but always delegated this dirty work to his "slave." A **subehdar** could at times lead hundreds of men through the intermediary of their respective chiefs. When the need arose, the leaders assembled in a council and consulted each other (**katee karna**, from *karti, kati karna*, to whisper) to make important decisions.

Jamadar and **subehdar** are words borrowed from native military terminology. One of Sleeman's informers pushed the military metaphor to the point of attributing the name of "flame" (*shikha*) to the holy pickaxe and the name of "coat of arms" (*nishan*) to the silk scarf, the *roomal*.[10] This ghost army carried deceptively innocent-looking weapons: the pickaxe was attached to the belt along with the scarf, unless this later was worn around the neck. The men who made up this army had specialized jobs to do.

SPECIALISTS IN DEATH

Scouts or spies (**tilha**, from *thilna*, to advance, penetrate; **bykureea**, from *bekar*, without work, idle) checked to see if the road was free and brought back information about travelers (**dhaga le ana**, from *daga*, a ruse, misleading + reporting). Another one of their words, **kautgur** (from *katna*, to cut + *gur*, unrefined sugar) might be an allusion to the rite of sharing the ceremonial sugar, which will be discussed later.

The seducers (**sotha**, from *suthara*, clean, elegant) then came into play. Their mission was to seduce, in the literal sense of getting people away from their paths: to make contact with travelers, to observe them (**tippana**, from *tipna*, to note), to watch them secretly (**choukana** from *chaukna*, to be on the alert, or from *cuk*, trick, mistake), to find out who they are (**rumujna**, from *ramuj*, secret, mysterious) to assess their wealth (**sodhna, sodhlena**, from *sodh*, research inquiry). A trap had to be set (**katee kurna**, to talk, to sweet talk) in order to persuade the travelers to journey jointly with them. In the depositions Thugs said they posed as buyers for horses that merchants hadn't succeeded in selling, and they put down two rupees as deposit to convince them of their good faith. Out-of-work travelers were offered work. Feasts were organized, complete with dancers and musicians, while meat and alcoholic beverages were generously distributed. The travelers' mistrust was put to rest.

This first step accomplished, there was often the need before proceeding to the kill to make use of other tricks that are mentioned in the depositions. Two of these were aimed at taking the victim by surprise: either by waking him or her from sleep (**tankee dena**, from *tangi*, to hang, that is to strangle) or by forcing the victim to sit down (to look at the sky!). There is a third ploy in which the Thugs pretended to be sick so as to distract travelers (**gan karna**, from *ganam*, plot).

In the meantime some men had picked the place for the murder and the burial site (**beyla**, from *bela*, moment, or from *bil*, hole; **maunkurreea**, from *maun*, silence or silent + *kari,*one who renders someone silent). Their job was important: a noun designates an ill-chosen place (**chuckbele**). The grave diggers were called **lugha**, from the word *lupta,* meaning out of sight, hidden; or **kurbakurree** from *kabr,* a Muslim word for tomb. Their actions were described in metaphorical terms: "They clean out the bowl (**kutoree mamjna**)" is found again in another of the words used to designate them (**katoree**). To signal their accomplices that the place was found, they uttered coded words: for instance, **deo, deomun, deoseyn,** in which we find the root *dev,* god.

Everything was then ready. Small teams of Thugs had taken their place at the travelers' side: there was the strangler (**kabita**, from *kabil,* competent, shrewd) also called the "deceiver," "the one who makes one forget (**bukote, bhurtote**, from *bhurkana,* to make one forget, to fool)," or more literally, **char** (from *chor,* thief); the holders of the feet and the hands stood at his side (**oorwala**, from *aur,* side + *vala,* an action), as well as assistants, apprentices, and servants. Their role consisted of helping the strangler, literally making sure that the action of strangling was successful (**gote purajana**, from *ghomtna,* the fact of strangling + *parajana,* to perform an action until its completion). A special word designates the strangler of a horseman: **pooturaet** (horseman) **bhurtote.**

The leader's task was to give the signal to swing into action. He too uttered a coded sentence: **jao katoree mamj lao**, "go clean out the bowl" (in which "bowl" is a euphemism for tomb); or "bring your pipe"; or again "smoke your tobacco," and so on. Some forms of Ramasee follow the same rules of elaboration that argots in general do: one of them consists in attributing a different meaning to a certain utterance taken from ordinary language, a meaning that remains hidden to noninitiates. The aim was to avoid awakening the prospective victim's suspicion as well as to provide clues to identify it and for Thugs to recognize each other without attracting attention, and so on. When a Thug greeted someone by saying *Aule Khan salam,* that person had to respond in kind to show he was a Thug as well. As Sapir (1963) noted:

> Generally speaking, the smaller the circle and the more complex the understanding already arrived at within it, the more economical can the act of communication afford to become. A single word passed between members of an intimate group, in spite of its apparent vagueness and ambiguity, may constitute a far more precise communication than volumes of carefully prepared correspondence interchanged between two governments. (cited in Mehrotra 1977, 44)

This observation is certainly applicable to the Thugs. The brevity of the utterances was usual in this mode of speaking, and the use of the nonverbal register was its ultimate expression. Thus the chief "clears his throat" to warn his accomplices to be ready to pass to action; he "spits" when the situation turns badly or when the murder is postponed.

To give a signal is called **jirnee dena.** According to our hypothesis, this term comes from *chirna,* to split, to tear, to rip a piece of cloth. This same idea of a piece of cloth is found quite logically in several verbs meaning to strangle: **jheer dalna** has the same etymology; **parnakhna,** from *pal,* piece of cloth + *nakhna,* frequently affixed and corresponding to *karna,* to do. Thanks to the famous handkerchief in Thugs' hands, the travelers had little chance of coming out alive from the encounter.

In addition to the expressions based on the instrument of the murder, there are other ones focusing on the action (**leepurna,** from *lipatna,* to surround, to encircle, to clasp; **gorhna,** from *gharna,* to surround), or again strong images of the effects of the aggression: **dhurdalna, dhurohurkurna** (from *dhur,* dust + *dharna,* to hold), the equivalent of our "to bite the dust"; **tubae dalna** (from *topi,* hat) indicates that the hat of the victim has fallen. **Ooharna, wahurna,** derived from the meaning of *varna,* signifies at the same time to encircle and to dedicate in the sense of making an offering to a divinity. It is the only verb that gives to murder the meaning of an offering to the Goddess even while keeping the more technical sense of encircling. It also sometimes happened that the Thugs had to use weapons, as indicated by expressions that include the word for "sword" or "dagger" and end with the verb *dalna,* to send, to throw, or *marna,* to die.

The cleaners (**phurjhurowa,** from *pur,* house, body + *jharna,* to sweep) had the job of completely obliterating all traces of the crime, of "sweeping" the place while the **bojha** (from *bojha,* weight) dragged the bodies to the graves. The grave diggers "rake down the clumps of dirt and spread

them over the graves" (**kondul kurna,** from *kundal karna,* to
cle), while the cutters (**kuthowa,** from *katna,* to cut) swing int

These different functions assigned to individuals within Tl
echoed the professional specialization of the castes in ordinar
but here they only concerned death. This simplified hierarchy w
inated by chiefs and stranglers. From the depositions we learn that the
functions of seducers, holders of hands and feet, cleaners, cutters, and so
on were interchangeable and could often be performed when necessary
by chiefs and stranglers.

There is only one verb (to strangle = to encircle/dedicate to a divinity) and only one function (scout = the one who has partaken of the
holy sugar) that link up with the rites I will discuss later on. There are
apparently no euphemisms, very few double meanings, and so few secrets! The vocabulary of murder is pragmatic and direct. It exposes to
the light of day the murderers' concerns, which did not include a quest
for semantic relations between rites and killings. However, a third word,
a very interesting one, does suggest that this link existed. **Hilla** (from
hilga, close friendship, connection) designates the rank or the grade held
in the course of expedition by the three individuals in charge of the holy
pickaxe, of choosing the place to bury the bodies, and finally of the ceremonial sugar. This link with ritual was thus that of the killing and the
ceremonies surrounding it.

The Victims

The numbers that come out of the Thugs' trials are chilling. "A native
newspaper, *Sumachar Durpan,* of great respectability, in 1833 declared
that one hundred Thugs slaughter, on an average, eight hundred persons
in one month. It is not going beyond the truth to affirm that between
the Nerbudda and the Sutlej, the number murdered every year is not less
than ten thousands" (Kaye 1966, 361). The figures show that on average
each of these mass and serial murderers perpetrated at least 256 murders
in the course of his lifetime (Hutton 1857, 84).

Man or woman, young or old, rich or poor, no one was unworthy of the
Thugs' interest. Of course, they preferred wealthy merchants and treasure
bearers, but the depositions contain many examples of poor folks, usually
holy men, strangled by the Thugs.

The Ramasee lexicon differentiates between two important things: the
number of victims and the profit they represent. Are there too many of
them (**tonkul,** from *thok,* used to refer to wholesale merchandise) to be
strangled? Are there only one, two, three, four? Thugs added the affix *ruh*
(**rooh**), meaning soul, to those numbers that appear appropriate, numbers that seem to match the possibilities of a game of dice. An example
is the much talked about case of the "sixty souls."

Are the victims wealthy (**cheesa,** from *chiz,* something of value), a "blessing from heaven," as Sleeman put it? Or on the contrary, must the Thug "reject" them because they are "forbidden"? Specific professions, gender (female), infirmities (**goneeait,** from *guna,* qualities + *ayat,* without) were supposed to shelter them from being killed. The same applied to someone carrying the bones of a deceased to a sacred river (**gookhee**).

The lexicon differentiates between the travelers who fell into Thugs' hands (**bunij,** from *banij,* trade, merchandise) and those they could not capture (**kuj,** from *kuch,* departure). Two words also designate a suspicious traveler whose demeanor isn't appropriate to his caste and of whom one must be wary: **komil,** from *kamil,* accomplished, knowing; or **bydha,** from *burha,* old, one who knows? Another word remorselessly designates the first murder of an expedition: **sonoka,** from *sona:* gold, excellent thing.

A series of verbs along with nouns constructed from them describe the travelers' attitudes and state when they caused trouble, hindering the successful completion of murders. They sometimes were on their guard and guessed the murderers' intentions. Escaping travelers (like Ram Singh in the previous chapter) are "runaways" (**buhup,** from *behad,* beyond the limits) or "unfinished" (**ardal,** from *ardh,* one half; **adhoreea,** from *adhura,* incomplete). A specific word designates the traveler who escaped at the moment of the strangling: **saur,** from *suau,* "one who has long life," and another the victim who appeared dead but was not: **jywaloo,** from *jiva,* life!

The good strangler, as fast as a magician, had a corresponding good victim, and vice versa. **Soosul, sosal** (from *su,* a positive prefix, and *safal,* fruitful, efficacious) and its opposite, **bisul** (from *be,* a negative prefix, + *safal*), designate the two types of victims. On the one hand, there was the strangler who had well positioned his *roomal,* "neither too high, on the face, nor too low, on the chest" but on the throat, and thus who did not risk having to use knife or sword and thus soil his clothes with blood (**buneana,** from *pani,* any kind of liquid, particularly water). On the other hand, there was the ideal victim "whose head and neck are uncovered" and who behaved well in the course of the strangling, without screaming and struggling. This because it could happen that victims "screamed out horribly" or that they yelled out for help. Paton's Thugs treated a botched or difficult strangling as a joking matter (**bisul** or **bisul parta**).[11]

Legitimate victims with the status of "merchandise" were treated as such. They were assessed from the view point of the material interest they represented, or, if I may put it this way, the possibilities of appropriation they offered, and described according to the obstacles they might present: their presentiments, their cries (**cheyns,** from *chimk,* scream), or again, their escapes.

Even though their jobs might overlap, the Thugs who "chose the place for the murder" bore names differentiating them from the grave digger, **lugha** and **kurbakurree,** whose task was to dig graves so as to safely bury the corpses.

The lexicon distinguishes "square graves" from "round ones" in which the remains are laid out in a circle around a central post; it also distinguishes permanent burial (**pucka kurna,** from *paka,* cooked, done, perfect) from temporary burial (**rhana kur dena,** from *rahna,* "as is"). Temporary burial, obviously risky, is called **rehna, ruhna** (probably from the same root), or again **angjhap** (from *amg,* body + *japa,* funerary room).

Beyla designates the locus of the murder and as well places known to the Thugs where they piled up bodies in the course of various expeditions. In the native state of Awadh, the police found 274 of these mass graves filled with the victims' decomposed corpses (Hutton 1857). Sleeman was able to compile a map of the main **bele** in the north of India. "The monsters" evoke them, he notes, "as sportsmen recollect their best sporting grounds, and talk of them, when they can, with the same kind of glee" (Sleeman 1836, "Introduction," 29–30).

However, there is little specific information on the preparation of the remains except for a verb that designates the tying of the corpses and the tying of the loot in packages (**choundhna,** from *chamdna,* to press, to tie the hind legs of a horse). But we do know that the dismemberers (**kuthowa**) performed their task before piling up the bodies in the graves: "In rocky country where there is little depth of soil, Thugs cut up the bodies of the travellers [**kanthuna,** de *katna,* to cut] severing the head from the trunk and limb that the bodies may not afterwards swell and burst and thus lead to discovery."[12]

The Thugs interrogated by Paton did not limit themselves to this dismemberment. As soon as the victims stopped breathing, "we stab them with a knife in the throat and the eyes that they may never see more . . . that no life may remain . . . and that Bhowanee may have their blood, she delights in blood."[13] In Brahmanic funerary rites, cremation has the goal of transforming the cadaver into a sacrificial victim. "A properly prepared human cadaver is the offering that pleases the god Agni the most" (Malamoud 1986, 443). Likewise, the maimed corpses of Thugs' victims appeared to agree with Kali. This ritual necessity competed with other, nonritual, ones. This very interesting collection of terms and practices pertaining to the treatment of remains, the shape of the graves, the notions of temporary and permanent burial, provides us with precious indications of how important the after-death state was to the Thugs, an import paralleling that of the Brahmanic tradition. The data are unfortunately too fragmentary to make out the religious concepts at play in them.

We are now ready to approach the fourth scene in the story, that in which the Thugs uncover and divide the loot.

The Loot
CONTENT AND RULES OF DIVISION

While the morticians were at work, the division of the loot often was done on the very scene of the crime, because **phur** (from *pur,* place) designates both the place where the victims were killed and the one where the division occurred. They search (**tighunee kurna,** from *tighuna,* triple, to triple, as this search promises to growing wealth), they count (**siharna,** from *siharna,* to accumulate), and they loot (**londh lena,** from *luthana,* to loot).

Ramasee includes a rich palette of words to describe that which was most desired: gold and silver jewels, coral, pearls, money (according to the metals used in it as well as its value and origin), and weapons: shields, knives, swords, guns. The loot also included livestock, packages of clothing "new, old, worn out," cloth, and turbans. All of these saleable goods were "treasures!" In fact, the Thugs also found items of lesser interest in the travelers' baggage items (twenty-three other terms that I have classified under the heading of daily life). These are mainly food (mostly meat, grain, and bread) and kitchen utensils. In India the respect of the rules of purity applies particularly strongly to food so that travelers concerned with these rules often bring their cooking utensils along to fix their own meals.

The division of the loot was a moment fraught with danger. Some Thugs stole it (**kootkurna,** from *kut,* ruse, lie) or hid a part of it. When the goods were in kind and of unequal value, cowries were used to draw lots (**kouree phenkna,** from *kaura,* cowrie + *phemkna,* to throw).

If there was something of great value in the loot (**tome,** from *tumbe,* "for you"), it was the gang leader or the village chief who got it. The Motheea Thugs owed their name to the handful of wealth (*muhti*) they gave their leader before proceeding to divide the rest. A valueless thing was rejected in the same way as a valueless victim (**phank** refers to either one). These preliminaries accomplished, the sharing took place. The gang leader got one tenth of the loot. If he led more than twenty Thugs, he was given an additional portion (**morka,** from *mukha,* mouth, leader). According to the "Conversations," stranglers also received an additional share (5% of the loot), but this isn't mentioned in the depositions. Only the leader appears to receive more than the usual share (**beegha,** from *bagh,* share; **chatae,** from *chamtna,* to take away, to separate; **gar, garbung,** from *kar,* tax but also fraud) given all the others.

There was only one limit to this stealing: Thugs avoided stealing or wearing on their person a good luck charm (**teekula parna,** from *tika,* an auspicious mark + *padna,* to fall) that had belonged to a victim. To wear such an object was thought to be dangerous, as shown by the connotations of **teekula parna:** to unveil, to make visible traces of crimes.

THE DESTINATION AND THE ETHICS OF THE LOOT

The loot had several destinations: it was used to feed the family left in the village; to entice young sons, future gang members, with gifts; to pay for the costs of the expedition, that is to pay back with interest the money the leader had lent to start up the expedition; and finally, to pay for the rituals.

The majority of depositions bear witness to the fact that each of the members of a gang of Thugs joining with another gang and assisting with the murders received an equal share of the loot even though they might not have participated in the preliminary maneuvers. The principles were so mandatory that in the example of Kalee Babee's murder, the Muslims who killed this forbidden and very wealthy victim used force to convince the Hindus to take their share. The best protection against others was, of course, to implicate them as much as oneself. In Arcot the omens were read in company of the whole community, and everyone, the elderly, women, children, received a share upon the criminals' return. Paid to remain silent, young Thugs-to-be or those retired were not only repositories of the secret but also its beneficiaries. The ethics of the loot made it possible to thus parcel out guilt in the form of merchandise and ward off any future betrayal.

The Risks of the Trade

In addition to the greater part of Ramasee devoted to words pertaining to the success of murdering expeditions, there are other words bearing witness to the dangers of the Thug profession.

In the course of dividing the loot, some Thugs stole from others. But much worse, and relatively frequent, was turning in one's accomplices, this sometimes following a quarrel (**khutana, khutae,** from *khota,* false) that erupted during a drinking bout. To these internal dangers was added that of blackmail by non-Thug rivals.

There are several words referring to informers: he is the one who cut himself (**kuthowa,** from *katna,* to cut, or from *kuta,* to tie), or again a **koojaoo** (from *khoj,* research, the one who allows it). But dangers come mostly externally: this is why one must hide, disperse, divide into several groups, and meet later on in a different place. To warn others of danger can be done by waving one's clothes on the road. Then one must escape, run away, seek refuge in the wilderness (become a **jhurowa,** from *jhad,* brush).

The vocabulary clearly emphasizes the dangers of the profession, as evidenced by the entries under the heading "Thugs in Danger" in this volume's lexicon: "Hunter of Thugs," "Thugs' great enemy," "Traitor who knows the Thugs' secrets." There are as well the many pursuits by villagers (**tukrar,** from *takrar,* complaint, etc.) and numerous synonyms designating the police (under the heading "Trades, Castes, Classes").

This sometimes led to murderers' arrest (**cham lena,** from *cham,* skin + *lena,* take). The place where, handcuffed, they awaited their fate was called **doona** (from *dohna,* to accuse, to condemn). As last recourse, they might "persuade an official of their innocence" (**dhaga kurana,** from *daga,* ruse, fraud) by bribing him.

The Thugs were thus far from enjoying the protection that their ties to Kali was thought to give them. They had to defend themselves from all sides to avoid being denounced, blackmailed, dispossessed, imprisoned, and condemned.

"Desperate Criminals"

This summary gives reason to the colonizers. Thugs were fierce criminals. Their crimes followed the same scheme as in the strings of almost identical actions reported in the depositions. They sought out victims, they seduced them over the course of a slow time frame that could span several days, then they eliminated them over the course of a fast and furious time frame as shown by a verb specifically designating the act of killing in this hurried manner. Finally, they divided the loot among themselves. There is an impressive number of words that could be used to account for any possible situation, for the different states of the victim in terms of the different stages leading to his death, for distinguishing the actors' abilities, their efficacy and their functions, the rewards their action brought them. We can almost hear worried breathing. Who will be the next to be duped?

These movements of surveillance, of tracking, of rapprochement with the victims, then their sudden slaughter and their dismemberment evoke the patient progress of the hunter who falls on its prey at the propitious moment and tears it apart to feed on it. A hunter for whom, naturally, the terrain is made up of spaces bereft of human beings: "mountain landscape covered with jungle," "vast uncultivated jungle, ideal for murder." Spaces in which water took on great importance: rivers, streams, gullies, wells. In Ramasee one word designates both a flowing body of water and a camp. In practice we must add that water, in one or another of its forms, also served as grave for the victims. Hostile but propitious for murder, this summarily described wild nature was perceived in a utilitarian manner: **tuppul** designates "the bye-path into which Thugs lead the travellers from the high road in order to murder them without danger." In the depositions vague indications of the places where the murders were perpetrated correlate with the paucity of the geographical vocabulary. This sharply contrasts with the more abundant lexicon available to describe the loot, which thus evidences the murderers' keen interest for the treasures of the civilized world. Concrete, efficacious, often trivial, the Thugs were not bogged down by metaphors and euphemisms; violent, clever but also artless (as these stones left at crossroads to show the way or as this Thug who waves his clothes to warn of danger), there is no trace in their behavior or their secret language of rebellion or any form of protest. The hostility of the external world came from the eccentric position the murderers themselves had staked for themselves. They were the ones who "misled" the world. More fatally yet, they misled each other and thus fell prey to the British game even while clinging to their nefarious habits.

SOCIAL IDENTITIES

The Community
MULTICASTES

In 1832–1833, the trials that were held at Jabalpur included all the Thugs (209 in all) arrested in the plain of the Ganges, in this vast area known at the time as Hindustan. Lists were drawn of the prisoners that were judged by the agent of the governor general. They were grouped according to the following headings:

> 60 Muslims; 79 Lodhees, that is Banjaras caravaners; 5 Brahmins; 4 Rajputs, originally from Rajasthan; 8 Aheers, herders; 6 Bunias, tradesmen; 1 Kachee, Muslim merchant speaking the language of Cutch spoken as well in Sind and Rajasthan; 1 Ghumer, a Gujarat word probably meaning vagabond?; 2 Gosains, Hindu renouncers; 1 Bhurboonya, merchant; 1 Sodhee?; 1 Barbier; 3 Karees, sweepers; 1 Sonar, jeweler; 1 Taylor; 1 Kaet, writer; 1 Kurmi, Hindu peasant; 1 Chuman, tanner; 1 Pathan, from the Pathan tribe originary from Afghanistan; 1 Kular, probably Kallar; 1 Ahuman.[14]

In 1836 another list of the defendants included the following:

> 78 Naiks [see Ramusi Naik in the preceding chapter]; 65 Muslims; 37 Lodhees; 3 Lohars, blacksmiths; 3 Brahmins ; 3 Kachees, merchants from Cutch; 3 Komhars, potters; 2 Kolees, Hindu weavers; 2 Bheels, tribals from Maharastra; 2 Bunias, merchants, lenders; 2 Aheers, herders; 2 Gurureas from gugura, a Thug sect?; 2 Malees, gardeners; 3 Kulars; 1 Baree, seller of cups made from leaves; 1 Kurmi, Hindu peasant; 1 Taylor; 1 Munahar; 1 Romhar; 1 Gond; 1 Chumar, leather tanner.[15]

Title page of *Historical and Descriptive Account of British India,* depicting, from left to right, the four major classes of society in Hindu tradition: priest, warrior, merchant or farmer, and craftsman or servant. From Hugh Murray et al., *Historical and Descriptive Account of British India,* vol. 1 (Edinburgh: Oliver and Boyd, 1832).

These two lists were drawn on the basis of loose criteria, particularly when it came to the Muslims. Their group should have included Pathans and Katchees, who are also Muslim, as well as Lodhees, or Banjaras, who are made up of mixed populations. The administrators also failed to specify the professional occupations and the status of these "Muslims": were they, for instance, recent converts, or were they *ashraf* "of foreign origin, superior to the converted who have owned up to their local origins" Gaborieau 1986, 12)? In the depositions the defendants did, however, sometimes specify that they were sheikhs, which means that they claimed "to be descendant from Arab ancestors others than the Prophet's family"; or again sayyids, claiming by this title to "be descendant from the Prophet, and being part of the upper *ashraf* class" (Gaborieau 1986, 200).

As to the non-Muslims, their finer classification was mostly based on caste criteria. Because the hierarchic classification of castes differed from region to region, it is impossible for me to offer one here. Yet there are indications that the Thugs welcomed people from various rungs of the ladder of status. This ladder is made up of the four great estates of the classical tradition, the *varnas*, starting at the bottom with the servant group, then agriculturalists and people engaged in husbandry, holders of political power, and finally priests. This hierarchy on the main coincides with that of the castes.

These four estates were represented in the lists of defendants. There were Brahman priests from the top of the hierarchy, and from its bottom level leather tanners, who because of their contact with material thought to be polluting belonged to one of the lowest castes and were untouchables. There were also intermediary *varnas:* warriors (second *varna*), such as the Rajputs; agriculturalists (third *varna*), and craftsmen belonging to servant castes (fourth *varna*), though they were not treated as untouchables, such as tailors, gardeners, and so on. Finally, there were people of tribal origins, Bhil and Gond, who were outside the realm of caste society.

What would we find if instead of looking at all the Thugs put on trial in a given year in Jabalpur, we were to look at individual gangs? An example is the gang Captain Borthwick "arrested in 1828 at Okala, at 8 *kos* from Bhilwara (kingdom of the Bhils tribes) and that was traveling from Gujarat to Bundlekhand."[16] The list of forty seven members includes:

> thirteen Lodhees; seven Muslims; seven Aheers, herders; three Kuhars from Kallar; three Kuchees, Muslim merchants from Cutch; two Rajputs; two Kolees, Hindu weavers; two Chumars, leather tanners; one Chobdar, guardian of the palace gates; one Konbee, agriculturalist; one Lohar, blacksmith; one Gurureea; one Dhenook, a Marathi title *deshmuk;* one Goojar, oxen tender.

Lodhees and Muslims were overrepresented within this single gang as it was also made up of people from the various *varnas*, the priestly one excepted. Members included a leather tanner, who was untouchable; two weavers belonging to the servant *varna* (fourth *varna*); eight agriculturalists/oxen drivers (third *varna*); a Rajput (second *varna*).

The gangs did not follow the rules of ordinary society, so they did not have to follow the principle that would require the complementary presence of members of the four *varnas*. And yet they did define themselves in terms of belonging to specific castes during police interrogations. We know that the names of some professions are also caste names. These did not require any secret words because those names in themselves provided the Thugs with a cover. When they are part of the Ramasee lexicon they were often the object of mockery. Skin Scraper, Greedy, Mustache, Cheat, and Muddler correspond respectively to a barber, a merchant, an innkeeper, a jeweler, and a potter. Weren't Thugs supposed to be free from these trivial occupations?

"CLANS, SECTS, AND TRIBES"

Independently from castes, the social identity of the Thugs was also based on the groups and the subgroups they formed themselves. According to Ramasee, they originated from seven clans: **sath-zuth,** where we can recognize the number seven and a corrupted form of the word *jat*, caste. These "clans" are themselves subdivided into "sects." This terminology appears to correspond to an order of magnitude, but there is no point in trying to unravel it as Sleeman nowhere gave any definition of it. The names given to these "clans" and "sects" bring to light the diversity of the groups considering themselves Thugs.

Sleeman didn't comment on the names of the seven clans. But because the names of the sects often had a geographical origin, I am exploring this possibility for the names of the "clans" as well. The clan of the Bursote might have gotten its name from the town of Barsoi (Katihar district, at the far eastern end of Bihar); the clan of the Huttar from Hutar (southwest of this same region); the clan of the Bys from the river Beas in the Punjab; the clan of the Kachunee from the Kachchh region (southwest of Rajasthan); the clan of the Tundil/Tundul from Tundla (southwest of Utter Pradesh, near Rajasthan and the river Chambal), or again from *tanda*, a word we encountered in the preceding chapter and that designates the leader of a Banjara caravan; the clan of the Bulheem/Balheem, from Balimila (in Andhra Pradesh, on the western border of Madhya Pradesh). If my hypotheses are correct, these would thus be areas located in Hindustan, in the north of the subcontinent. The names of the clan of the Gano might come from *gana*, that is a band, a horde? As to the seventh clan, the Bharnts, its name might originate from *bhamdra*, to wander, to walk around aimlessly (like the sect of the Bangureeas, or Banjaras, which we will encounter below and whose name possibly comes from the word *vaghri*, nomad?)

The following list contains Sleeman's information on the origins of the names of the sects as well as our own hypotheses. I have differentiated these latter with a question mark. From east to west and starting in the north there were the following sects in Hindustan:

In Bengal, the sect of the Pungoo/Bungoo, a word in which one can recognize the word Bengal (*bamgal*), and the sect of the Lodaha, caravan leaders (from the word *lodh*, load); in Bihar, the Lodhee/Lodaha; in the region of Rampur and Purnia (Rangpur, Purnea in the British geography of the times), the Motheea, from a weaver caste, whose name derives from the custom of giving to the gang leader a handful (*muhti*) of rupees or other good before dividing the rest of the loot. In Uttar Pradesh, the sect of the Korkureeas, from the place named Korhur (in the region of Kanpur?), as well as the Tundals, probably the same as the Tundils we met earlier; the sect of the Agureeas, from the town of Agra (not far from Tundla in Uttar Pradesh); the Lodhee, and finally the Jumaldahee, living mainly in Awadh and whose name comes from the river Jumna and from *din*, son of: they are the sons of the Jumna. In the east, in what is now Pakistan, the Multaneea, from the town of Multan, and the Qulundera (*qalandar*, wandering dervishes). In Madhya Pradesh, in the region of Gwalior and Malwa, there were the Bangureeas, or Banjaras; the Balheem/Bulheem, whom we met earlier; Khokhureeas (from the Korhur district near Etawah?); the Soopurreeas, from the town of Sheopur (near Gwalior?). In Rajasthan, in the region of Jaipur, Jodhpur, and Bundi: the Gugura, from the name of the river Ghagghar (whose source is in Punjab?); and the Sooseea, members of the Dhanuk (=*dhanak*) caste, wool combers calling themselves *naicks* or *thories* (from the Thar desert?). In Maharashtra: Dhoulanees, whose name might have come from the town of Dhuliya.

It is easier to recognize the geographical origins of the names of the sects in the Deccan area:

1. The Thug sect of Telingana, the Telinganies who lived in a region extending from the Naindair (Naidigama?) to the Nalgonda plateau, a four-day journey from Hyderabad on the road to Musalapatam (Machilipatnam?) and, to their chagrin, whom the other Thugs called the Handeewuls, a sobriquet meaning "they eat out of old and dirty cooking pots": from *hamdi*, argil pots customarily thought to be of the greatest impurity, and *vala*, *val*, meaning something like "the men of the bowl." 2. The sect of the Beraries who lived in Berar from Nagpore (Nagpur, in Maharashtra) to Nandair (Nanded, Maharashtra). 3. The sect of the Duckunies, in the Deccan from Mominabad (Munirabad, in Karnataka) to Pune. 4. The sect of the Kurnaketies, in Carnatic between Satara and Kurpakundole. 5. The sect of the Arcoties in Arcot, from Kurpakundole to Seetabuldeo Ramesur. (Sleeman 1836, 163–64)

Finally, we have without specific geographical designation the Kathurs, from *kathota,* the great bowl, who owed their name to "a man who participated in Thug feasts holding a bowl." To this list should be added the:

> Hindoo Talghat," who were admired by all The Hindoo Thugs of Talghat upon the Krishna River. . . . They are extraordinary men. They have three painted lines on their foreheads extending up from a central point at the nose. . . . They always wear them. They and the Arcot Thugs associate and act together; but they will never mix with us of Telingana. . . . We call them the Talghat men. . . . They have the same omens and language (as we have) and observe the same rules; but we hear that they use the round instead of the oblong grave to bury their victims, the same as the Behar men. They call it the *Chukree;* the Behar men and others call it the *Gobba.* (Sleeman 1836, "Substance," 161–63)

Divisions between clans and sects appeared to be mainly territorial. The "Jogee [=yogi] Thugs" arrested by J. Burrows in Karnataka were subdivided into tribes whose names also had a geographical origin (in their depositions, instead of seven original clans, they spoke of twelve tribes). They claimed to have come from Hindustan and to have been settled in Karnataka for three or four generations. Their given names often ended with *"nath"* or *"dass"* (Poorundass, Ramchundass,[17] and so on). These two terms correspond respectively to protector, patron, master in the terminology of the worship of Shiva, and to servant in Vishnu worship. One of them even had the confusing name of Feringheenath, which can mean either a protégé of the British or someone seeking their protection.

These "Jogee Thugs," who didn't have any caste names (barring a few exceptions—there is a Kinath, from the Banjara caste; a Gungnath, from the sweeper caste, and so on), traveled the roads "in the disguise of religious beggars" and sold pearls and knickknacks. They were exclusively Hindu, as indicated by the suffixes of their family names, and their ties to specific gurus might indicate that some of them belonged to sects.

There were other modes of identification besides place names. These could be professions, as for the nomad-caravan leaders, Lodhees, or Lodahas: Thug informers from Hindustan told that

> their dialect and usages are all the same as ours, but they rarely make Thugs of any men but the members of their own families. They marry into other families who do not know them to be Thugs, their wives never know their secrets, and can therefore never divulge them. No prospect of booty could ever induce them, or any of the Bengal or Behar Thugs, to kill a woman. (Sleeman 1836, "Substance," 180)

Several groups were named on the basis of religious criteria. They were the Kathurs and the Handeewuls, "the men of the bowl," whose names referred to impure eating practices; the Talghats, who wore the sign of a sect and buried their victims in round graves; and finally the Qalendars, wandering dervishes or fakirs, members of a mystical Muslim order. Scorn (for the Handeewuls) or admiration (for the Talghats) show the beginning of hierarchy within the groupings that made up the community.

Finally, there was a third basis for naming, that of the type of criminal practice. The Motheeas owed their name to the fact that they took a bit of the loot prior to its division to give their leader.

The Thugs combined two levels of social identity: they had a caste identity, which located them in relation to the whole of society and which could take the form of a title for the Muslims, such as "sheikh" or "sayyid." And then they had a group identity within their own common criminal Thug community, "the men of Multan" or "the men of the bowl," or a given tribe for the Jogee Thugs. But in contrast to the rebels I discussed in chapter 1, these layers, these accretions of identities also involved a break. Thugs who had a caste identity were visible, recognizable members of ordinary society, but they were also secretly members of their own Thug groups. Some of their discussions pertained to the articulation of these two levels, the visible and the invisible, and on the meaning of the latter.

From Caste to Thug: The Defendants' Viewpoint

The problem posed by this accumulation of identities brings out the differentiation between recent Thugs and Thugs descended from many Thug generations. As a Thug from Hindustan states,

> Some of the Arcot gangs . . . came and settled in Telingana, between Hyderabad and Masulipatam, where they still carry on their trade of thuggee; but they will never intermarry with our families, saying that we once *drove bullocks and were itinerant tradesmen,* and consequently of lower caste. They trace back the trade of Thuggee in their families to more generations than we can, and they are more skillful and observant of rules and omens than we are.

Sleeman then asked the witness: "Do you think there is any truth in their assertion that your ancestors drove bullocks?"

"I think there is. We have some usages and traditions that seem to imply that our ancestors kept bullocks, and traded" (Sleeman 1836, "Substance," 144).

The opposition between ancient and recent Thugs, some of whom were caravanners, which seems to correspond to the opposition between southern and northern Thugs, was transformed in the words of another informer into an opposition between Hindu and Muslim Thugs.

> Here a Brahman Thug, of one of the most ancient Thug families, interposed and declared that he had seen the funeral rites of Musulman Thugs, and that the women who brought the water there chanted all the occupations of the ancestors of the deceased, which demonstrated that they were originally descended from gangs of wandering Khunjurs, or vagrant Muslims, who followed armies and lived in the suburbs of the cities, and in the wild wastes, and that their pretensions to higher descent was all nonsense. . . . Several Musulmans protested sturdily against this. (Sleeman 1836, "Substance," 144)

There was loud protest in the face of what seems to have been experienced as an attack by the Hindu Brahman. Sleeman asked the question again a few pages later:

> Have you, Hindoostan men, any funeral ceremonies by which your origin can be learnt?
>
> "No funeral ceremonies; but at marriages an old matron will sometimes repeat, as she throws down the *Tulsee*,[18] 'Here's to the spirits of those who once led bears, and monkeys; to those who drove bullocks, and marked with the *goodnee* [the needle]; and those who made baskets for the head.'" (Sleeman 1836, "Substance," 161)

This northern Brahman Thug, who refused to be grouped with the Muslim caravanners, introduced a new word to designate them, *Kunjurs*. Russell evokes them in his *Tribes and Castes of the Central Provinces of India*. Like the Banjaras I discussed in the preceding chapter, these Kanjars or Kunjurs have intrigued anthropologists and linguists, and have been the object of a host of fruitless speculations on their origin and name. "A name applied somewhat loosely to various small communities of a gipsy character who wander about the country. . . . The Deccani and Marwari Kanjars were originally Bhats (bards) of the Jat tribe. . . . They are a vagrant people, living in tents and addicted to crime."[19] Russell thinks that the Kanjars were descended from the Doms, a tribe from the north of India and among whom their Muslim members were recent converts. Following the circular principle of dictionaries, under the entry "Thug," the author states that "most of the Thugs are Kanjars," and he puts forth as evidence the description in Sleeman's book of the old matron throwing the *tulsee*. These Kunjurs, as mysterious as the Banjaras, didn't satisfy Sahib Khan, Sleeman's informer. He denied they were his ancestors:

Sahib Khan: By no means. [This marriage rite] only indicates that our ancestors after their captivity at Delhi, were obliged to adopt these disguises to effect their escape. Some pretended to have dancing bears and monkeys; some to have herds of cattle, and to be wandering Khunjurs (Gypsies); but they were not really so; they were high caste Musulmans.

Feringheea: You may hear and say what you please, but your funeral and marriage ceremonies indicate that your ancestors were nothing more than Khunjurs and vagrants around the great city!

Inaent: It is impossible to say whether they were really what is described in these ceremonies, or pretended to be so; that they performed these offices for a time is unquestionable, but I think they must have been assumed as disguises.

Feringheea: But those who emigrated direct from Delhi into remote parts of India, and did not rest at Agra, retain those professions up to the present day; as the Multanies?

Sahib Khan: True; but it is still as disguises to conceal their real profession of Thuggee. . . . I pretend not to know when they put on the disguise, but I am sure it was a disguise; and that they were never really leaders of bears and monkeys. (Sleeman 1836, "Substance," 162–63)

Two interesting interlinked points emerge from this argument: some Thugs "disguised" themselves permanently and pretended to follow a profession that placed them above suspicion. They were motivated by selective strategies (to seduce victims by appropriating an appearance apt to induce trust) as well by plain necessity: the Thugs resembled everyone else in order to practice their secret profession.

But this necessity nonetheless had limits: according to Feringheea, the Brahman Thug from Hindustan, to put on the disguise of a lower caste was one thing, but to adopt its ritual customs was another. For a Thug to submit to them showed the persistence of his previous belonging in the world of castes and implied that his ancestors joined the Thug community relatively recently. Feringheea and some of his Muslim companions differentiated Thugs whose families went back several generations. They had not shed their original caste (Feringheea claimed to be Brahman), but it was subordinated to their Thug identity. In contrast, for more recent Thugs, the trade or caste of origin still persisted in their daily lives. They preserved their memories in their rites or, like the Thugs of Multan, practice the art of Thuggee with the tools of their trade, as when they strangled their victims with the straps they use to harness their bullocks (Sleeman 1836, "Substance," 239).

This distinction boils down to a sharp differentiation between, on the one hand, Thugs recently converted to Islam, of local origin and of whom many are nomadic carriers or traveling grain merchants, and, on the other, ancient Thugs of Hindu origin. This reflects a historical process corroborated by two facts: the Thuggee lexicon is almost entirely of Hindi origin, and the great Muslim invasions date from the thirteenth century.

Thus the origin of the Thugs is not lost in a hazy past anymore than that of the Kallars of southern India. Even though for the time being we lack specific answers on the when and how of their existence and their mode of life, the diversity of the Thugs' links to their profession does point to a historical process. In the course of time, their community must have opened up to the Muslim "invaders," sheikhs and sayyids, or to Hindus, usually of low caste, who had converted to Islam. It is well known, for instance, that the caste of weavers is one among those including the greatest number of Islamic converts in the north of India.

Revolving and Floating Statuses

In chapter 1 I noted that the notion of revolving statuses applied to a large population. In Sleeman, these revolving statuses were the "floating" statuses of nomadic bands that he condemned along with monastic orders, Pindaris, Thugs, and dacoits, these "persons floating loosely upon society, without property or character, with the object of acquiring the property of others" (Sleeman 1849, 268). The word *property* stands out here. I will come back to its import and meaning later.

These reproaches apply to the Thugs as well. In their depositions some informants claimed having served stints of various length in given armies and engaged in agriculture upon returning to their villages. The colonizers interpreted alternation between occupations as a ploy, a cover, to hide their murderous activities. The facts were less simple. Some of the informers' lengths of stay in the village were linked to the success of their expeditions. These Thugs thus cumulated normal and murdering activities. The word **khullee** in Ramasee means a "Thug pursued by his creditors" and clearly denotes the difficulty of living off the land. "Our trade, said one [supposed Thug]to me [Taylor], is to take with us old and new sarees and waistbands and trade with them, getting in exchange brass and copper pots, and gold and silver ornaments; these we exchange again when the rains begin; we don't take our wives; they and the children remain at home as hostages for the rent we owe" (Taylor 1986b, 62). For some others, the relation between the number of expeditions, the earnings, and the lengths of stay in the village, sometimes long, remains unclear. The example of "Hormat Khan, alias Mungulea, formerly of the Gururea caste, a Thug by profession, now a Musulman and soldier in the regiment of Malegaon"[20] well brings out the social mobility of the peasants encountered in chapter 1. The Thugs were not all systematically and continuously engaged in crime. There were great differences between a Thug who rested up in the village only during the monsoon and one who resided there several years between expeditions. These variations imply very different trajectories running the gamut from having entrenched habits to going on expeditions only when forced by difficult material circumstances. The assassins interrogated by Captain Paton in Awadh insisted on the fact that their profession enabled them to eat, that without it their bellies would remain empty.

The insertion of the criminals into sedentary or nomadic society and the tempo of their criminal activities were thus not ruled by a uniform scheme. The fact of being Thug often accommodated other activities—agricultural, military, and so on. This broad palette included hardened Thugs and accidental Thugs; Thugs whose identity was based on an ancestral origin, as was the case for Feringheea; Thugs who still maintained ties with their original professional caste, including Thugs intermingling caste and Thug identities by using the straps of their bullocks to strangle travelers or by observing the rules and rites of their castes. The colonizers who thought that *once a Thug, always a Thug*[21] were not concerned by these disparities. They looked upon the Thugs as a suprahereditary caste whose members partook of a common language and cult. This supracaste, like cults, had marked regional differences, as shown by some depositions as well as by the results of the lexical investigation conducted by William Sleeman. Heredity was obviously not the sole way the group was reproducing itself.

The Family
DESCENT AND MARRIAGE

In almost all of the confessions, after giving his given name, the name of his father, and at times his caste, the defendant uttered the following formulaic statement: "I am a Thug like my ancestors before me." In the rare cases in which the full meaning of this rhetorical formula is accessible to us, I notice that paternal descent was not the only avenue of access to Thuggism. Thus Sayyid Amir Ali testified to being from Fatehpur, located in the territories of the Company. Several Thugs used to visit the area, and one of them, Rohmut, was often a visitor of his father. The defendant called him uncle. When he was about twenty years old, his father died, and he joined his uncle at Sindouse and eventually accompanied him on an expedition..

Gureeb, alias Gurreeha, a Thug *jamadar,* son of Chatun, testified that his ancestors were not Thugs and that he had been initiated into the profession about ten years earlier by his uncle Kheema, *jamadar,* himself initiated by the Banjaras.[22] Another defendant called Punna testified that he was born in Kamsipur in the district of Mynporee (Minapur?), where

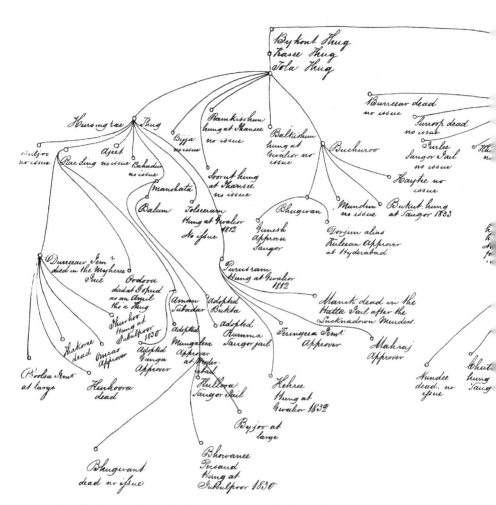

Detail of a genealogy of a Thug family, compiled by William Sleeman. The Brahman ancestor begets two sons (Assa and Seeam), each of whom marries one of the two daughters of a Thug chief. Assa and Seeam are the first Thugs in the family,

his father Bijee Singh was a farmer. His sister married Ghasee, a Thug *jamadar,* but she and her father only learned of his profession two years later. Eventually an older brother joined him on an expedition, and after the defendant's family moved to Sindouse, the defendant and another of his brothers started to regularly join Thug expeditions.[23] Thus, in these three cases kinship ties by blood or marriage led to the adoption of Thug

140

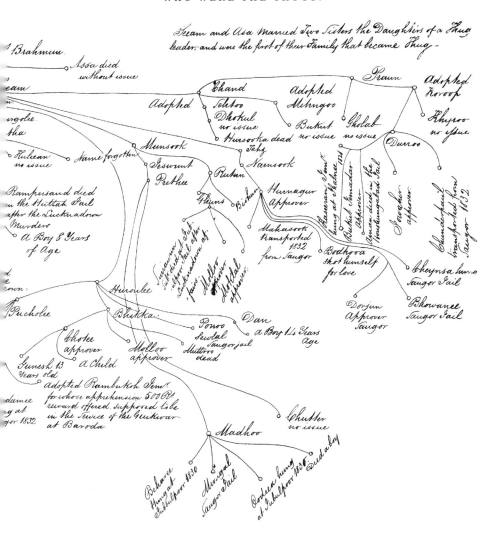

according to the caption in the upper right. This genealogy covers seven generations. From Sleeman, *Ramaseeana* (1836).

identity, this in contrast to the usual situation in other cases, where the
profession is handed down from father to son.

THUGGEE AS A FAMILY ACTIVITY

In another confession elicited by Reynolds the accused, Surwur Khan,
gave the list of the thirty-one members of his gang: twenty-five of them

were related to each other in some way. The *jamadar* Daow had with him his father, Mahomed, and his son Mahee; his four nephews Bhurrea, Sahibun, Hoosain, and Mudar; and his son-in-law Mahomed: altogether seven persons. Hajee, another Thug, was with his brother Mohee; Julle, his father-in-law, and Meeran and Rajee, his two sons-in-law. Another member was accompanied by his brother and his brother-in-law; while Jeffier Khan had with him his three sons and his adopted son. Pootto had his son with him, and finally, Nagooby and Sutwajee were two brothers.

Though the familial character of these bands was not always that pronounced, I haven't encountered a single gang that did not include at least two individuals linked by blood or affinity. I have to point out however, that no gang was composed solely of relatives. How were these things decided? We just don't know.

Interfamilial solidarity could have major effects: thus, when Sayyid Amir Ali's brother informed him that his wife was held prisoner in a village in Sindhia, Amir Ali immediately decided to go rescue his sister-in-law. But this solidarity was not limited to family. On another occasion Amir Ali offered a mare to the wife of a Thug imprisoned at Sagar.[24] As was customary in this sort of criminal society, the family was the gang, and it was the gang leader, the *jamadar*, on whom the members depended. For any given individual, gang and leader remained relatively constant.

The common root of several Ramasee words meaning "village" seems to be *khula*, open space, from *khulana*, to be opened, untied, set aside. This indicates that the Thugs, grouped in families, resided not in the villages, but near each other, an arrangement that strengthened the secret solidarity of the group. But they sometimes could make up whole villages, as the rajah of Jodhpur claimed when questioned by Sleeman.

MARRIAGE

Some very general principles at play in Thug marriage patterns emerge from the "Conversations" reported by Sleeman, though these principles do not seem to have always applied. The Thugs of Arcot didn't marry women descended from the ancient clan of Delhi as they looked upon them "as a caste inferior to them." A Thug from the Delhi clan counteracted this claim: "but we refuse our daughters to them as they refuse theirs to us; and they are in error when they suppose us of low origin" (Sleeman 1836, 162). These kinds of disagreements are common in the Indian context, where marriage is defined by one's status and spouses are usually found within one's subcaste. If the Thugs of Delhi and of the south refused to marry each other, could this mean that Thugs marry within their sects?

The only two specific examples I have don't support the notion of sect endogamy. As we already know, Bheelam Barre Kahn married the daughter of his village chief. Feringheea, a Brahman whose adoptive father was a great Thug leader, was very proud of having married a woman from the "Jhansi aristocracy."

Even though we don't know much about whom Thugs are marrying, it is clear that their family was a major source of economic concern to them. In their depositions they frequently mentioned that in the course of their expeditions they sent one of their fellows to their village to bring some of the loot to their families. This messenger even bore a special name in Ramasee, **maulee** (from *mal*, price, property) or **phoola** (from *phal*, reward). This concern with supporting their families could be the signal to initiate the murders. Mahamud Buksh reported an incident in which his gang faced an opportunity to strangle a group of travelers.. One of the Thugs harangued his fellows: "Shall we go home without something to please our wives and children?" (Sleeman 1836, 234). This forceful reminder of family duty does show that one of the purposes of these murdering expeditions was to support the family members in the village.

The colonizers well understood how to take advantage of these strong family ties: they used them as bait. Feringheea was driven to free his wife, mother, and child arrested by the British: "I could not forsake them—I was always enquiring after them, and affording my pursuers the means of tracing me. I knew not what indignities my wife and mother might suffer. Could I have felt secure that they would suffer none, I should not have been taken" (Sleeman 1836, 234–35).

Even though the rules governing marriages seem fuzzy and variable, the family was the locus of Thug concern. At times they even tried to enlarge it in the course of their expeditions, this in light of the logic of the view that family included members linked by blood, affinity, and adoption as well as fellow gang members.

THE CIRCLE OF CRIME HAS BEEN ENLARGED

In the descriptions of the members of a gang, we often encounter the following after a name: "adopted son of." From whence came these adopted sons? A typical example is the murder of five Gosains who had a four year old boy with them. This boy was saved and given to be adopted by a gang member as part of his share of the loot. Among famous cases of adoption are that of Feringheea and that of the narrator of Meadows Taylor's novel. Both became Thugs after being spared by the criminals and were "raised in the profession." What did these adopted children, often very young, who were given new names on the spot by their Thug captors, know of their own history? Not much, if we are to believe Meadows Taylor's novel.

It could often happen that a little girl became part of one of the criminals' share of the loot. In the course of the Chalesrooh affair, two hundred

Thugs strangled thirty-eight persons out of a group of forty (thirty-one men, seven women, and two girls):

> The daughter of Gunga Tewarree was a very handsome young woman, and Punchum, one of our Jemadars, wished to preserve her for his son Bukholee. But when she saw her mother and father strangled, she screamed and beat her head against the stony ground, and tried to kill herself. Punchum tried in vain to quiet her, and promised to take great care of her, and marry her to his own son who would be a great chief; but all in vain. She continued to scream, and at last Punchum put the *roomal* around her neck and strangled her. (Sleeman 1836, 205)

The marriage plans were thus aborted, this in contrast to a similar event with a different outcome: "The widow of Alfie's brother was strangled, but her daughter, a girl about three years of age, was preserved by Kosul Jemadar, who married her to his own son Hunnee Rae Brahmun, by whom she had two sons, one of whom is still living, and about ten or twelve years of age. Since the death of Kosul and Hunnee Rae she has lived with her husband's mother" (Sleeman 1836, 205).

The fathers thus sometimes took their future daughters-in-law from among their victims' daughters, and these adopted daughters became producers of Thugs: thus the fruits of crime were implanted in the very familial fabric and blood. The generation of the killers and of the victims was separated by death; the next generation mated and procreated.

Thug loot was thus not solely made of merchandise. Occasionally the wives found mouths to feed in the midst of the fabrics and gold and silver coins. Inversely, the victims were not only providers of material goods, they sometimes served as a human resources that the Thugs pilfered at will when the occasion presented itself.

Adoption could have been one of the consequences of the rule including children among forbidden victims. This rule might have been motivated by the desire to perpetuate the group, as well as that of enlarging and enriching the family. The child who entered into the circuit of familial consumption was a form of capital. Whether a daughter-in-law or a son, the end result was to add to the number of Thugs of the household and to make it wealthier. As we have seen, every member of the gang had the right to a share of the loot, and "it even happens that . . . a father is sometimes avaricious, and takes his son out very young, merely to get his share of the booty; for the youngest boy gets as much in his share as the oldest man" (Sleeman 1836, 148).

And yet children were not spared if their survival caused problems: Ghubboo Khan had just strangled the mother of a little girl he wanted to adopt, when one of his fellows advised him to kill her as well "or we should be seized on crossing the Narbuda valley. He threw the child living in upon the dead bodies, and the grave was filled up over it" (Sleeman 1836, 169).

In a similar vein, "on seeing the bodies thrown into the ditch, Jowahir's boy began to cry bitterly; and finding it impossible to pacify him or to keep him quiet, Jowahir took him by the legs, dashed out his brains against a stone, and left him lying on the ground, while the rest were busily occupied in collecting the booty" (Sleeman 1836, 199).

The Thug lexicon doesn't include words to designate real or fictive ties of kinship. Was it because Sleeman failed to ask, or was it unnecessary to have secret words for these types of relationships?

RELATIONS BETWEEN WOMEN AND MEN

The segregation of women and men within the Thug family seems to have been less rigid than that encountered in ordinary Indian society.

ACCOMPLICES? Sleeman was curious, as we are, to know if Thug men and women were accomplices. He was told that southern Thugs never told anything to their spouses for fear that they would reveal their secrets. As to the wives in the know, they were either unhappy about it or quietly acquiescent (Sleeman 1836, 147). Feringheea's wife knew nothing of his activities until the day she was arrested and imprisoned at Jabalpur. Complicity, here again, was a matter of individual cases rather than the general rule. The Jogee Thugs brought their families and oxen along on their expeditions; the wives understood Ramasee, but the men left the camp to make a kill.

In a fragment of the "Conversations," two versions of the story of the murder of four merchants in the home of a Thug illustrates the dangers raised when the wives knew the secret of Thuggee. The Thugs had asked merchants from Awadh to their village in order to sell them stolen merchandise. "They bought a good deal, but Hirroolee's wife wanted to see how we killed people as she had heard a good deal about it, and they were all four strangled for her entertainment I have heard" (Sleeman 1836, 225). Lalmun had a different version of the story. To the story of irresistible feminine curiosity worthy of our biblical Eve, he substituted the idea that this woman was a victim: she was a widow, and when the rajah in power discovered the merchants strangled by the Thugs, he robbed the widow of all her possessions, fined the murderers, and declared that because they were now killing in their own home he was not going to protect them anymore. "I saw the widow afterwards begging her way through Saugor, and she died of starvation at Sehwas in Bhopaul" (Sleeman 1836, 226).

The Thugs did not make a spectacle of their killings; on the contrary they strove to keep them secret, far away from the domestic and village spheres. This story that was making the rounds and that might very well have been fiction was a reminder that women were prone to try to get men to breach the rule of secrecy.

There were however Thug women, and their existence shows that not all the assassins hid everything from their spouses. Ramasee includes a word to designate the female status of **baronee,** "an elder respectable Thug woman." It is the feminine form of **baroo,** "Thug of distinction" (probably derived from the Hindi *bara*, great, important, etc.).

Barring these exceptions, there must thus have been division of labor and, when possible, secrecy between the two genders.

FAITHFUL AND UNFAITHFUL WIVES. It was said that the faithfulness of Thug wives was famous in the whole of India. At least this was what their husbands claimed. "And the fear of the *roomal* operates a little to produce this?" asked Sleeman slyly. The answer: "Perhaps a little, but there have been very few instances of women killed for infidelity among us" (Sleeman 1836, 148).

In contrast, Thug men evoked affairs they had in the course of their sometimes months-long expeditions, though there were remarkably few cases mentioned in the depositions and the "Conversations." Sayyid Amir Ali had some troubles with a *thakur* whose mistress he had seduced away. He spent the night enjoying the performance of a dancer to whom he offered sumptuous gifts before going back home. On another occasion he abandoned his three hundred companions after the murder of thirty-nine travelers, which had brought him a share of ten rupees. He then courted the daughter of the *zamindar* of the village of Shutrunja of the Muhrutta caste, who wanted to keep him with her. Relatives of the father told him who his daughter's suitor was and tried to get him to send him away, but unsuccessfully. But a short time later, a group of eleven men and three women on their way to Banaras passed through the village. He decided to rejoin his companions, and they all came back at night to strangle the travelers.[25]

Thus love didn't keep him away from his professional duties, yet the opposite could also happen. In the course of an expedition, he lied to his fellows to save the life of a woman who was supposed to be strangled and courteously led her back to her village. Like Feringheea he seems to have been faced with quandaries on a number of occasions.

I and my cousin Aman Subahdar were with a gang of one hundred and fifty Thugs on an expedition through Rajpootana about thirteen years ago when we met a handmaid of the *Peshwa*, Bajee Row's, on her way from Poona to Cawnpore. We intended to kill her and her followers, but we found her very beautiful, and after having her and her party three days within our grasp, and knowing that they had a lakh and a half of rupees worth of property in jewels and other things with them, we let her and all her party go; we had talked to her and felt love towards her, for she was very beautiful. (Sleeman 1836, 166)

Thugs were not supposed to kill women or children, but these might sometimes have valuable possessions, as in the case above, or might make potentially bothersome witnesses. The rule was very often broken. When love came into play, everything became more complicated:

It was her fate to die by our hands, [said Feringheea]. I had several times tried to shake off the Moghulanee . . . and I told her that she must go on as I joined some old friends. . . . She then told me that I must go to her home with her near Agra, or she would get me into trouble; and being a Brahman while she was a Musulman, I was afraid that I should be accused of improper intercourse, and turned out of caste.

Question: Had anything improper taken place between Feringheea and the young woman?

Dorgha: Certainly not, or we could never have killed her; but he had a good deal of conversation with her, and she had taken a great fancy to him. She was very fair and beautiful, and we should never have killed her, had he not urged us to do so. Khoda Buksh . . . told us that we must either kill her or let Feringheea go on with her. He would not consent to this, and we agreed to kill her. (Sleeman 1836, 215–16)

The beautiful Moghulanee seems to have been murdered for two reasons: Feringheea had had ritually polluting relations with her, and she was threatening to cause him trouble. All of his companions were in agreement in their claim that the seducer had asked them to murder her against their own wishes.[26]

According to these few fragments it appears that a Thug, following a scheme that is both Indian and Victorian, at times shared himself with female travelers and a faithful spouse who, if possible, was kept ignorant of his profession and who raised his biological and adopted children. Sleeman seemed to be aware of the psychological richness of this situation. He harbored little interest for "old and ugly" women, and he gave his informers advice worthy of a Thug: "Why aren't you content to just kill them?" In contrast, he was very interested by murders of "beautiful and young women." Guilt, frustration, sex, murder: these are associations that blossom in works of fiction. In the documents they crystallize around a central idea: misfortune comes from women. The root for one of the adjectives meaning "dangerous" in Ramasee is *nari*, woman.

THE CRIMINAL FAMILY. I have to admit that this anecdotal exploration of the Thug family is rather disappointing in that it leaves the main questions unanswered. We remain ignorant of how marriages were decided. Relations between women and men appeared to obey principles of inequality at play in Indian society, and yet some Thug women enjoyed a status equal to that of men. Likewise, we are told of secrecy between them. Might this have been more conventional than real? The Jogee Thugs spared women and children the spectacle of their crimes, but didn't keep their activities secret from them. Among them everyone understood the secret language. Here again, different groups followed varying practices.

Yet we do get an indirect glimpse on the special meaning Thugs gave to the family. Not only did the family draw its subsistence from crime, as shown by the **maulee** who returned to the village in the course of the expeditions to bring back loot, but also the family expanded thanks to crime. Far from being set aside and protected as Sleeman's informers at times suggested, it was physically and morally implicated. One of the most striking aspects of this is that it was in the family that victims could be induced to repeat the crime from which they had suffered; it was in its midst that loot victims became a part of the community of their executioners.

Murder was almost exclusively an activity reserved for men, one they performed away from the gaze of women and children. Yet these latter might be have been spared victims, and the boys might be led to become murderers in turn already at age ten. This shows the illusory nature of the dissociation, otherwise presented as customary by the colonizers, between an honorable family life in the village and a delinquent existence elsewhere. The whole of the Thug family was marked by crime.

Thugs and Castes

We get a checkered image involving extremely diverse geographical, religious, and professional origins. Some of the gangs were large, some fragmented and settled in different regions of the north and south of India. Some lived together in groups at the margin of villages, while others were nomads like the Jogee Thugs of Karnataka. But we might also encounter Thugs mixed with the ordinary population, outwardly practicing honorable professions and marrying village chiefs' daughters.

The range of their caste statuses was quite broad, from the Brahman to the humble weaver. Hierarchy was simplified: there was a leader and the rest, all considered equal when the loot was divided. The chief was ritual leader as well as strangler and entrepreneur. Finally, the principle of complementarity of the castes that could have been paralleled by the specialization of the tasks in the course of the expeditions was, for the Thugs, based not on heredity, but on acquired skills and personal ability, themselves contingent upon circumstances. Egalitarianism and social fluidity characterized their communities.

Their profession did tend to become hereditary as is the case for caste, but the reproduction of the group depended on other factors, as shown by the practice of adoption and the absence of specific marriage rules, by economic motivation, or again by the memory of a past in which ancient and recent Thugs existed together. We cannot entirely resorb their heteroclite social image, blurred, incomplete, into the preceding brutal and ferocious description because ruse and violence did obey divine rules.

RELIGIOUS IDENTITY

Foundation Narratives

DIVERSITIES

There are no sacred books for Hindu Thugs. As to the Muslims interrogated by Sleeman, they neglected the Koran to swear allegiance to their Thug group on the sacred pickaxe. "Nothing else on earth could be so binding," they claimed (Sleeman 1836, 155). There were no common spiritual leaders whose words might have been transmitted through a line of successors, *parampara*, according to the principle at play in the formation of sectarian traditions in India (Clémentin-Ojha 1992, 72). Instead, "our Sages alone are consulted, and they consult omens alone as their guides" (Sleeman 1836, 150). Called **gooroo** in Ramasee, they were recruited in the gangs from among the best stranglers. According to the "Conversations," their main mission was to initiate the novice to the "sacred knot," in which one of the ends of the strangling scarf was weighted by a coin, and, more important, to teach him how to throw it. Finally there was no single place of worship, but rather several, be they temples of Kali or tombs of Muslim saints. Sometimes there weren't any: "We neither make offerings to the temples of Davey, nor do we ever consult any of her priests or those of any other temples," claimed Feringheea (Sleeman 1836, 150). Just as Hinduism is thought by some to be made up of the juxtaposition of several religions, Thuggism too presented the image of a diversity of religious attitudes paralleling the group's social heterogeneity.

According to Sleeman, their Hindu and Muslim mythical heroes were honored because their legends exalted theft or murder: Valmiki, the author of the Hindu epic of the *Ramayana*, was cited because he was a thief; this is also the case for the famous Sufi saint, Nizam-ud-din, who lived in Delhi at the beginning of the fourteenth century and whose tomb (*ziyarat*) Thugs visit. This supposed former Thug, known among the assassins for his "magical coin purse" (*dustul ghyb*), which brought him all the riches he wanted, was famous for his miraculous powers and attributes. As the Islamist Simon Digby points out:

> [There are] frequent mentions of the appearance of supernatural beings and narratives of supernatural powers. In a dated and unquestionably authentic narrative of individual conversations of the great Sheikh Nizam al-Din we find a succession of anecdotes of a preacher in a mosque who was so transported by his own eloquence that he flew away from the pulpit to a neighbouring wall; of meetings in deserted places with Khwaja Khidr who has everlasting life; . . . and of the mardan-i-ghaib, "Men of the Unseen" who appear and disappear, and sometimes call away a mortal to join them. (Digby 1986, 62)

These were either pan-Indian heroes appropriated by the Thugs because they resonated with their own culture, or again more obscure heroes such as Jora Naek, his spouse, and his disciple, who were evoked in the course of certain rituals for having stolen an extraordinary sum of 160,000 rupees, which they then shared among all the members of the Thug community. Their cleverness and generosity made them worthy of belonging in the criminals' pantheon.

UNITY

Sleeman's informers were followers of Kali who transcended their various beliefs as well as their territorial and professional distinctions. She might have gone by local goddesses' names, as was the case with the Jogee Thugs who distinguished five of them. She might have taken the name of Fatima, the prophet's daughter, or at least have been identified with her, as was the case for some Muslim Thugs.

Intensive research on the accommodations between Hinduism and Islam brings to light the diversity of the processes at play and shows the depth of the old and reciprocal interactions between the two religions. The Thugs were apparently a variety of a special type; their Muslim members might possibly have been linked to the Nizari Ismaelis, called Khojas on the Indian subcontinent. Their missionaries set out in the thirteenth century to explain the hidden meaning of their doctrine and to "lead their novices to the true path which they presented as the crowning of their previous beliefs." In the process, they incorporated images and concepts familiar to Hindu believers. For these later (and at least partially for the Thugs) "Hindu figures are linked to Islamic figures: Ali is Vishnu, the Prophet is Brahma, his daughter Fatima is at times Shakti, at times Saravati." These Khojas, who "claim allegiance to the imams Nizari issued from the Alumut center in Persia" (Mallisson 1992, 105–9), have ties to the legendary Elder of the Mountain and his Assassins, which Sleeman believed to be at the origin of the Thug phenomenon. This hypothesis deserves to be further explored, but I am here limiting myself to its Hindu aspect.

Kali is a relatively recent goddess in comparison to the other gods of the Hindu pantheon. Her temples, her oldest statues, scattered in the north of India, in Assam, in Orissa, in the Vindhya mountains, and in Rajasthan, date from about the fifth century A.D.

> Some of the names of the Goddess are present in the later Vedic texts . . . but the imposing figure only appears in the epic. . . . She is seen mostly as a virgin, a mountain divinity. . . . The figure is certainly a composite one made up of older personifications of war by what might have been originally certain plants (preserved in Tantric hymns) overlaid with the mother goddess with cosmic tendencies. . . . The Anaryan substrate is larger than any other figure of the Brahminic pantheon. (Renou and Filliozat 1985, 1:523)

In the *Puranas*, a storehouse of legends and myths dating from around the same time as the epics, her treachery and ferocity in combat are exalted.[27] The *Bhagavata Purana* tells that she is the patron of a gang of thieves whose chief, lacking descendants, offer her a Brahman child so as to beget a child himself. But she murders the thieves, cuts off their heads, gets drunk on their blood and plays ball with demons with the severed heads.

The *Markandeya Purana* is by far the most remarkable and famous text about her. It is believed to have been written no later than the ninth century, in a region located in the west of India. She appears in the course of three distinct episodes under different names: Durga, Chamunda, and so on. The first episode, Song 89, the *Devimahatmya*, or "Celebration of the Goddess," glorifies her under the name of Kali and narrates her cosmic combat against the demons. According to P. V. Kane, this song represents "the principal text of Durga worshipers in Northern India" (Kane 1968–1975, 2:738). Her statuary and iconography illustrate the narrative's celebration of her lack of restrain, her orgiastic impulses, her strong taste for gambling and death. She is described as armed "with a sword and snare in hand, . . . carrying a many-coloured skull-topped staff, wearing a garland of human (skulls) . . . with a garment of tiger's skin, exceedingly frightening with her dried-out-skin; with widely gaping mouth, terrifying with (her) lolling tongue."[28] Fighting against the demons Chanda and Munda, she devours their armies:

> taking up the elephants with one hand she flung them into her mouth, together with their rearmen and drivers and their warrior-riders and bells. Flinging likewise warrior with his horses and chariot with its driver into her mouth, she ground them most frightfully with her teeth. She seized one by the hair, and another by the neck. And she kicked another with her foot, and crushed another against her breast. (Coburn 1988, 109)

Her voraciousness is even greater in the next episode. As no weapon could beat Raktabija, her last adversary, she absorbs his blood: "From his stricken body blood flowed copiously, and from whatever direction it came, Camunda takes it then with her mouth. The great Asuras, who sprang up from the flow of blood in her mouth, Camunda both devoured them and quaffed their blood. . . . The great Asuras became bloodless, Oh King!"[29] In this third and final myth "Kali imbibes the substance of the demons, thus establishing a close link of substance between the demons and the terrible aspect of the goddess. One may say that . . . the demon ends as the blood absorbed by Kali within herself" (Das 1985, 31).

In the Thug version, there was a multitude of Asura demons. Kali was overwhelmed: she then "formed two men from the sweat brushed off from one of her arms," and she tore off a piece of her dress to give them to strangle the demons. The killers and their weapon were thus born together and filled the need to kill without spilling blood. Kali's two children strangled Raktabija and his clones, the battle was won; the mission accomplished, rewards followed.

> After their labour was over, they offered to return to the Goddess the handkerchiefs with which they had done their work, but she desired them to keep them as the instruments of a trade by which their posterity were to earn their subsistence and to strangle men with their *roomals*, as they had strangled the demons, and live by the plunder they acquired; and having been the means of enabling the world to get provided with men by the destruction of the demons, their posterity would be entitled to take a few for their own use. (Sleeman 1836, "Ramaseeana," 128)

The Thugs thus earned a return on the human capital they saved from destruction, a return they could hand down to their descendants.

The narrative continues with the usual prohibitions:

The *roomal* they call the *"Goputban,"* and the Goddess told them that they should leave the bodies of their victims on the ground and she would take care that they should be removed, provided they would never look behind them to see in what manner, and that if they observed this and all the other rules she prescribed for them, no power on earth should punish them for what they did. (Sleeman 1836, "Ramaseeana," 128–29)

But the Thugs committed an unforgivable offense. One day as they were walking away from the scene of their crimes, "A slave . . . looked back, and saw her occupied in throwing them [the bodies of the persons murdered] into the air, without any clothes on her body. She was naturally very angry and bid them in the future to bury the bodies themselves; but to use in making the graves pick-axes duly consecrated" (Sleeman 1836, "Ramaseeana," 107).

As shown in numerous depictions, before the transgression of the command to not turn around to look at the Goddess, the corpses, light as play balls, tickled the eroticism of the divine player. After the transgression, the killers had to drag the heavy bodies to their graves and became covered in their blood as they cut them up before hiding them in the ground. The descendants of the carefree stranglers who had been given the *roomal* were thus forced to recruit morticians armed with knives and pickaxes.

The difference in the statuses of the two categories of Thugs was inscribed in the myth: the original strangler was a divine child, while the others were heirs to a transgression and its punishment. In telling how the first Thugs became part of the Goddess's genealogy, the story also pointed to a golden age where one could mete out death without worry.

This adaptation of Kali's myth to legitimize their origin and account for their practices constituted one of the important elements of the worship of the Goddess by the Thugs, a choice of Goddess excluding all the other divinities of the Hindu pantheon. This exclusive choice is an important clue to their religious identity. In India the quest for salvation takes on a diversity of forms running the gamut from solitary renunciation to the formation of sects. These sects are divided into three main groupings linked to either Shiva, Vishnu, or Kali. A movement organized around a cult of a divinity is the prerequisite for the formation of a sect. But this is not sufficient in itself. Did the religious behavior of the Thugs show that they met the other requirements?

Rites and Observances
THE RITE OF PASSAGE INTO THE COMMUNITY

Birth alone did not turn someone into a Thug. Scattered information in the depositions and in the Ramasee lexicon point to the existence of a rite of passage, usually undergone in the presence of the father, or his replacement if he was deceased or was not a member of the profession. Sleeman's informers claimed that this rite of passage happened around ten or thirteen years of age. One of them, Sahib, mentioned three graduated stages: by the end of the first expedition, the child understood that theft was involved; by the end of the second he suspected murder; and by the end of the third, he had seen everything (Sleeman 1836, "Substance," 148). It could happen that this frighteningly short preparation for murder went awry.

Feringheea told the story of Kurshora. At age fourteen he was left at the rearguard of the gang under the care of Hursoka, but at the very moment the signal to kill the travelers was given, he started to gallop toward the main body of the gang.

> He heard the screams of the men, and saw them all strangled. He was seized with a trembling, and fell from his pony; he became immediately delirious, was dreadfully alarmed at the sight of the turbans of the murdered men, and when any one touched or spoke to him, he talked about the murders and screamed exactly like a boy talks in his sleep, and trembled violently. . . . We could not get him on, and after burying the bodies, Aman and I, and a few others, sat by him while the gang went on: we were very fond of him, and tried all we could to tranquilize him, but he never recovered his senses, and before evening, he died. I have seen many instances of feelings greatly shocked at the sight of the first murder, but never one so strong as this. (Sleeman 1836, "Substance," 149)

In his novel Meadows Taylor attaches great importance to this rite of entry into the community. As is the case in Tantric initiations (Gonda 1965, 442–43), the hero's father performs certain rites in the presence of his son, other stranglers, and gang leaders before leading his son to a guru. Good omens are solicited, then the novice has to swear an oath that we can understand as a solemn commitment (*samkalpa*), similar to the deep commitment to which a participant in the Brahmanic tradition must swear for the rite to be completed.

> A pickaxe, that holy symbol of our profession, was placed in my right hand, upon a white handkerchief. I was desired to raise it as high as my breast; and an oath, a fearful oath, was then dictated to me, which I repeated, raising my left hand into the air, and invoking the goddess to whose service I was devoting myself . . . after which a small piece of consecrated Goor, or coarse sugar, was given me to eat, and my inauguration was complete.

154

The father then addresses his son, reminding him that he has sworn to be "faithful, brave, and discrete." He lists the victims the forbidden victims and emphatically concludes: "with these exceptions, the whole human race is open to thy destruction, and thou must omit no possible means to compass their destruction. . . . What remains of thy profession will be shown to thee by our Gooroo" (Taylor 1986a, 46–47).

The second part of the initiation of Taylor's hero is conducted *in situ,* as it consists in witnessing a murder. In the entry in the Ramasee for "strangler," Sleeman paints a dreamlike scene of the passage to action: the novice, feeling finally ready, walks away from his sleeping victim, led by his guru and a few other initiates. At the chosen spot the guru, facing the appropriate direction, beseeches: "O Kalee, *Kankalee, Bhudkalee, O Kalee, Maha Kalee, Calcutta Kalee,*[30] . . . if it seemeth to thee fit that the traveller now at our lodging should die by the hands of they slave, vouchsafe us the *Thibaoo* [omen]" (Sleeman 1836, 76–77).

If Kali didn't respond or if she sent a bad omen, another Thug killed the traveler. But if she sent a left-handed omen, the small group came back to camp, and the guru tied a coin into the end of the *roomal*. This knot, called **goor ghaunt** (from *gur,* ritual, secret + *gamth,* knot), a ritual knot, was ceremoniously presented to the novice. "The disciple receives it respectfully from the high priest in his right hand, and stands over the victim, with a **shumseea,** or holder of hands, by his side. The traveller is roused on some pretense or other, and the disciple passes the handkerchief over his neck, at the signal given by the leader of the gang." The traveler had to have been a sound sleeper indeed to lie still in the midst of all these comings and goings and thus enable the rite to unfold as planned! Sleeman goes on with the story:

> Having finished his work, he bows down before his gooroo, and touches his feet with both hands, and does the same to all his relations and friends present, in gratitude for the honor he has attained. He opens a knot after he has heard or seen a Thibaoo, or auspice on the right, takes out the rupee and gives it, with all the other silver he has, to his gooroo, as a nuzur; and the gooroo adding what money he has at the time, purchases a rupee and a quarter's worth of goor for the Tuponee [closing rite]. (Sleeman 1836, "Ramaseeana," 78)

The new strangler was expected to give a feast for his guru and his guru's family upon his return home. He offered him and his wife clothes, and after a certain length of time the guru reciprocated.

The relationship between guru and disciple was the most sacred there was, claimed the Thugs in the "Conversations." "A Thug might often rather betray his father than the Gooroo by whom he has been knighted

[!]" (Sleeman 1936, "Ramaseeana," 79). J. Paton made a similar comment: "The preceptor who initiates a novice in strangling is afterwards looked up to by the Thug so initiated, who through life will always give part of his spoil to his gooroo. . . . He will sometimes neglect his own father and mother."[31] And yet I found no trace of this privileged relationship in the depositions.

It is tempting to liken the part of the loot the fully initiated Thug gives his guru to the alms the Vedic students gives his spiritual master. Malamoud likens these gifts to sacrificial honoraria, as the student does indeed fill "the role of the sacrificer and his master is for him a divinity" (Malamoud 1976a, 186). The formal structure is identical as it seems that we are dealing with a required gift marking the end of the rite. And yet there is doubt about a Hindu ritualistic origin of the word pertaining to this part of the loot given by the initiated to his initiator because it is not of Sanskrit origin. The word *nazar*, of Arabic origin, originally designated a votive offering, a gift of a particular status; over time it consequently came to mean a ceremonial gift offered by an inferior to a superior. The fact that this is the only word with ritual import that is not of Hindi origin and whose sense became gradually secularized raises a lot of questions. This because Hindu tradition does, of course, have a specific word to designate the "sacrificial honoraria" (*dakshina*) in its liturgy.

The Ramasee lexicon reflects the interest in the Thug novice. Several words designate him: religious words derived from the classical Sanskrit tradition, such as **cheyla** (from *chela*, student, disciple); or from sectarian tradition, such as **margee** (from *margi*, the one who follows the way, the road, the sect member).

The other words designating the future Thug partake of nonreligious semantic fields, which might also imply the secondary role of the guru. **Kotuk** might originate from *kautuk*, meaning curiosity, desire, or anything that stimulates it, any surprising or wondrous thing, as well as festivity, ceremony, especially marriage. Another word emphasizes the contractual aspect of the novice's commitment: **kuboola** comes from *kabul*, meaning consent, approval, contract. Another word yet deals with the exceptional, new aspect of the passage: **nowureea**, from *nav*, new. There's a word for the qualities required of the new Thug: **beetoo** from *bit, vit*, meaning a rascal who seduces with his charm and his words.

Can we conclude that the Thugs were a sect? All sects include a specific theological and liturgical corpus, and their social organization is ruled by the need to transmit this corpus. The person of note, the guru who intercedes between human beings and the chosen divinity, is the keeper of this corpus, and his or her mission is to transmit it to a line of descent of disciples. Guru and disciples constitute a chain (*parampara*), and their relationship is ritualized by a ceremony (*diksha*) whose key element is the transmission of a mantra. This esoteric discourse or text that the guru is transmitting to the novice represents the essence of the sectarian doctrine. Without it the spiritual goal of the tradition cannot be reached because it is the gateway to its practice. It goes without saying that it is not possible to be a guru without first having been a disciple because this type of human group is aimed at perpetuating itself by transmitting the means to put the doctrines of their tradition into practice.[32]

However, the Thug guru did not transmit a doctrine, did not give out its essence through a mantra in the course of an initiation ritual. Likewise, neither the depositions nor Ramasee contain traces of the existence of an uninterrupted chain of masters and disciples. Instead they show separate, autonomous units, each made up of a student assassin and his teacher. Even though this latter was venerated, he was never identified with Kali, in contrast to sectarian traditions in which the guru very often embodies the chosen divinity. In the technical sense of the term, the Thugs did not constitute a sect, despite the fact that many of their traits evoke this possibility. This is made clear by Reiniche, who comments:

> The usage has been to label as "sects" not only those ascetic and monastic orders identifiable to a certain extent by the dimension of renunciation of their members, this in spite of the difficulty of mapping out the contours of their lay clientele, but also currents of worship centered around the particular form of a divinity in the hands of a hereditary and married priesthood, as well as more elaborated forms in which a part of the civil society of a region is merged into a network of temples and monasteries partaking of a unique religious current. (Reiniche 1995a, 10–11)

There is yet more to explore in the Thugs' religious universe. They perform other ceremonies, observe certain prohibitions, perform certain duties. What are they?

PROPITIATORY RITES

Before an expedition, the stranglers met to consecrate the pickaxe (of which one of the names, **kodalee**, is *kudali*, the digging tool used by farmers) that is to be used to dig the graves. This ceremony, which included plant and alcohol offerings, was held in a house with all the windows and doors safely covered, out of sight of any possible onlookers.

> The Thug, most skilled in the ceremonies, sits down with his face to the west, and receives the pickaxe on a brass dish. A pit is dug in the ground, and the pickaxe is washed with water which

falls into this pit. It is afterwards washed with a mixture of sugar and water. Then with *dahee* or sour milk, and lastly with ardent spirits; all falling successively from the pickaxe to the pit. It is then marked from the head to the point with seven spots of red lead, and placed on the brass dish, containing an entire coconut, some cloves, pawn leaves, gogul gum, inderjon, some seed of the sesamum, white sandal wood, and sugar. In a small brass cup close by, is some ghee. They now kindle a fire from dried cow dung, and some wood of the mango or byr tree, and throw in upon it the above named articles, except the coconut; and when the flame rises, they pass the pickaxe seven times through it, the officiating priest holding it in both hands. He now strips the coconut of its outer coat, and placing it on the ground, holds the pickaxe by the point in his right hand and says: "Shall I strike?" All around reply yes. He then says: "All hail mighty Davy, great mother of all!" and striking the coconut with the butt-end of the pickaxe, breaks it into pieces, on which all exclaim: "All hail Davy and prosper the Thugs!"

They throw all the shell and some of the kernel into the fire, tie up the pickaxe in a clean piece of white cloth, and placing it on the ground to the west, all face in that direction and worship it. This done, they all partake of the kernel of the coconut, and collect all the fragments and put them into the pit, that they may never after be eaten.

The omens having been consulted, "the pickaxe is given to the shrewdest, cleanest and most sober and careful man of the party, who carries it in his waist-belt. While in camp, he buries it in a secure place, with its point in the direction they intend to go; and it is believed that if another direction is better its point will be found changed" (Sleeman 1836, "Ramaseeana," 108–9).

Sleeman reported that if the omens were favorable the group held a second ceremony named **kote** (from *kot*, assembly, group). It had to include an animal sacrifice, and it may also have been held as a rite of appeasement to neutralize bad omens. The Thugs described by Captain Paton gave the following description of it:

All murderers who are of the expedition assemble in some secret place, where no one can see them and all take a seat around . . . sometimes to the number of one or two hundreds men! . . . The pickaxe is placed on the ground and a small goat is sacrificed on the spot to the Goddess of destruction by cutting his head off with a sword. The Thug who officiates (as the Priest) is some noted leader who dresses in clean clothes for the ceremony having bathed and fasted since the morning. (The cloth with which they strangle their victims is also left beside the axe.) Spirits are then poured upon the axe and instantly when the head has been struck off, the Priest lays it on the ground. All the Thugs are there sitting around in solemn silence, with their hands joined in the attitude of supplication to Bhowanee then address the head of the victim: *"Bhowanee ugur koosh ho, so bolo*! O Bhowanee if you are pleased with this sacrifice, thus speak!" The severed head then gasps several times which Bhowanee answers, that she is pleased. . . . But if the head of the sacrificed goat makes no reply, we do bend our forehead to the earth. Bhowanee has not accepted our sacrifice, we cannot go upon Thuggee expedition. Sometimes we have three or four times without an answer from Bhowanee. The liver of the sacrifice is then roasted and a portion of it with spirits is distributed and eaten by each initiated Thug. The Oude Thugs do not carry this axe with them but leave it buried on the spot, where the sacrifice is offered.[33]

Paton and Sleeman were in agreement that the nonstranglers, excluded from these rites, were reintegrated only when the animal was sacrificed. The animal was roasted to be consumed, and its liver and head were reserved for the stranglers and the *bhut,* that is the wandering spirits of the dead. As in any well-organized sacrifice, the sacrificer (who is sacrificing for the group) and the place of the sacrifice were each consecrated with water and cow dung, respectively. These traditionally pure substances are mixed with others, such as alcohol and blood, that are less so from the standpoint of Brahmanic orthodoxy, but that the Goddess greatly appreciates.

Mixing the pure with the impure, the Thugs adapted their rituals to the ambivalent, powerful, and wild nature of their Goddess. Reigning over boundaries (in India her statues are often found at the outermost edges of villages), she can travel effortlessly from one territory to another, and she manifests herself equally through life and death.

CLOSING RITE: TUPONEE

Let us assume that the Thugs found good victims and duly dispatched them. We might well ask, as Paton did: "After a murder do Thugs do anything to appease the wrath of the Goddess for their crimes?" Paton, who apparently had not understood Kali's carnivorous leanings, did, however, rightly sense that a final ceremony had to complete the cycle of Thuggee. This ritual was the **tuponee** (from *tap, tapas,* one of the key words of Hinduism: fire, devotion, penance, austerity). The informers explained to Paton:

After each murder or after three or four, we all assemble and four men performs this ceremony in honour of the Goddess. We place the *roomal* with which we strangle on the ground and over the cloth we place sweetmeats and place a ring in a hole made for it (the hand sprinkling water is then moved three times around the articles). The person officiating (he must have been a strangler) then takes up a handful of the sweetmeats and places them in the hand of another Thug, purposely seated near him who also must be a strangler [not a **Tyro**], and thus addresses to him the signal for strangling: *"Sussul Khan chullo!"* The stranglers then eat in silence. Having eaten the sweetmeats, they get up and distribute the *khowas* or remainders to every member of the gang.[34]

This communion meal offered to the divinity and then shared by her devotees was consumed again by forming a circle, as indicated by the word **mururee**, "assembly of the Thugs," from *murri*, the action of tying together the two ends of a rope to make a circle. Like the other ceremonies, the **tuponee** was, of course, held in secrecy. The participants and the locus of the initial ceremony, where only stranglers were invited, were kept secret, and so was the location of the closing ceremony. It was held far away from inhabited areas near the graves of the victims, in the mute presence of noninitiated Thugs. Secrecy was also the rule for the objects of the cult, including the pickaxe, the scarf, the sugar, and the coin, which were buried in a hole dug for that purpose. This excavated altar contrasts with the traditional visibility of the *vedi*, the often-raised altar in places where sacrifices are performed and on which fires are kept lit.

Whether their aim was to consecrate or propitiate, these ceremonies were entirely focused on future or past murders. The instruments (the pickaxe and the scarf), the substances (alcohol and blood), the prominent role of the strangler, the prayers, and the killing of the animal anticipated or commemorated murder. The magical power of sugar during the **tuponee** also cleared the way for a future murder, because after having tasted it the novice, transformed into a Thug, could not go back to his previous state. This consecrated sugar renewed the energy and the determination of the group, whose goal was stated again in the incantation to Kali, the *jirnee*, or the signal to give death. The strangler was only temporarily the main figure of the gang in his role of mediator between the Goddess and his fellows. All sat in a circle for the communion meal ending each of the two ceremonies. The ritual leader merged into this circle, a reminder that all the gears of this killing machine were equally necessary.

OBSERVANCES

During the first seven days the Thugs prepared themselves for the human sacrifice by severing their ties with ordinary life. They stopped eating clarified butter (ghee), meat, and sugar. They stopped shaving, washing their clothes, having sex, and giving alms, and they didn't share their food with a dog, a cat, or a jackal. . . . On the seventh day they had a good meal. During the whole of the expedition they didn't drink milk; nor did they brush their teeth. Dirty and certainly smelling badly, unshaven, the Thugs, like mourners, embodied the impurity of death. But their consecration, which consisted in giving themselves over to nature, was the exact opposite of that undergone by the Brahmanic sacrificer (Malamoud 1976a, 161), who mimics death by making himself into the body of a newborn, naked and hairless. Here again we find a mixture of typically Thug observances, such as the particular choice of animals with whom food could not be shared, animals that were known to carry either frightful or excellent omens, with other prohibitions shared by Brahmanic orthodoxy, such as sexual abstinence and avoidance of meat and dairy products.

The same goes for the list of forbidden victims during these same first seven days, though again the list can vary (Sleeman 1836, 133–34). It was forbidden to murder women as well as Brahmans; this latter prohibition was directly linked to Brahmanic tradition, in which such killing is thought to be severely punished after death. It seems logical that the prohibition against murdering Brahmans was extended to men who were engaged in religious undertakings, such as pilgrims, ascetics, or members of the Nanak sect. However, the list of social categories protected from murder also included groupings whose occupations placed them on the lowest rung of the social ladder (sweepers, oil sellers, bards, writers, female dancers, elephant drivers), as well individuals whose physical disabilities were thought to imply a bad karma (blindness, leprosy, missing limbs, and so on).[35]

In contrast, the circumstances that would prevent a Thug's departure on an expedition followed the prescriptions pertaining to the impurity of personal and family life. A Thug had to postpone his departure in the case of a human or animal birth (cow, mare, goat, cat, dog), or when his daughter had her first or second menstruation, or again when there was a death in the household.

The prohibitions the Thugs were expected to respect were called **eentab** (from *inkar*, prohibition) and **eetuk** (from *etraj*, obstacle, objection). These prohibitions were, of course, connected to the group's recruitment from a variety of castes as well as to its murderous activities, and thus they made up a peculiar assemblage. Some of the criteria were at play in the whole of society: thus the same word, **geeda,** which means "of low caste" and "dirty, soiled, polluted," merges the idea of social inferiority and the idea of pollution, one of the basic tenets of Brahmanic orthodoxy. In contrast, some of the other Thug criteria were at variance or opposite to it. The Thugs were neither in nor out of ordinary society; they inhabited its margins, as evidenced by the deprecatory and exclusionary vocabulary they used to describe it.

Besides these prohibitions, their professional behavior was mostly determined by auspicious and inauspicious omens. These omens were of a changing, fickle nature, this not only from one social group to another, but also from one individual to another, as shown by informants' disagreements reported in the "Conversations."

Omens

Indian gods take on all sorts of disguises to seduce women and fool their opponents. Vishnu followers tell that their god came down to earth to save it when it was taken over by chaos. He then took on a human or an animal form: the word *avatara,* which has entered our own vocabulary as *avatar,* corresponds to this event. The very ancient attention paid to omens in India perhaps echoes these divine metamorphoses and providential descents. The omens consulted by the Thugs were mostly of animal origin and reflected the mysterious ways of the Goddess. A large portion of Ramasee is devoted to their identification and interpretation. Out of the 120 verbs collected, however, only two pertain to omens. "To consult the omens," **rugnoutee,** is derived from *akshan,* sign, omen, or from *raksha,* protection? In **jeetae purjana,** we can recognize the root *jit,* victory, conquest, along with the verb *pahcanna,* to distinguish, discriminate, recognize. The other verb pertains to a disgusting omen, "passing gas" when it happens in the course of the dividing up of the loot or at an assembly of Thugs: **phurka dhuneea/mururee ka dhuneea,** in which **dhuneea** might originate from *dhuni,* smoke.

Omens filled several functions in spite of their apparent triviality (for instance a vulture or a dog seen defecating in the evening was a sign of riches, but a dog doing so in the moonlight meant the opposite). Omens provoked fear and disappointment, but also imparted daring and innocence. By paying attention to them, the Thugs became obligated to execute what the omens dictated, but were freed from any responsibility. The omens had a moderating role because they could at times make Thugs abstain from killing. The group was dependent on them throughout the whole course of an expedition.

If our etymological hypotheses are correct, Ramasee well shows the chain linking good omens with their origin and meaning: **baee,** meaning both "busy road" and "good news," might be derived from *bai,* left, from whence come most of the auspicious signs. This is opposed to **daee,** from *dayi,* right, a normal road lacking the promise of loot.

And yet there was no consensus among the Thugs on the meaning of those signs. Sleeman noted that "What is considered to threaten evil by some, is thought to promise good by others; but on such occasion they all follow the rules of the leader" (Sleeman 1836, "Ramaseeana," 123). Here again the Thug "community" takes on a very loose sense. Of course, everyone agreed that the Goddess was speaking through these signs, but it was up to each individuals to identify these signs and to decide what course of action they entailed. This was particularly the case when the Goddess's omens pointed to a usually forbidden victim:

Nasir, Musulman, of Telingana: "Is not the good omen the order from Heaven to kill them, and would it not be disobedience to let them go? If we did not kill them, should we ever get any more travellers? I have known the experiment tried with good effect. I have known travellers who promised little let go and the virtue of the omen brought better."

Inaent, Musulman: "Yes the virtue of the omen remains, and the traveller who has little should be let go, for you are sure to get a better."

Sahib Khan, of Telingana: "Never! Never! This is one of your Hindostanee heresies. You could never let him go without losing all the fruits of your expedition. You might get property, but it could never do you any good. No success could result from your disobedience."

Nasir: "The idea of securing the good will of Davey by disobeying her order is quite monstrous. Do Duckun Thugs not understand how you got hold of it? Our ancestors were never guilty of such a folly."

Feringheea: "You do not mean to say that we of Murnae and Sindouse were not as well instructed as you of Telingana?"

Nasir and Sahib Khan: "We only mean to say that you have clearly mistaken the nature of a good omen in this case. It is the order of Davey to take what she has put in our way: at least so we, in the Duckun, understand it." (Sleeman 1836, "Substance," 196–97)

All these rites and observances allowed the Thugs to be outside the law governing the rest of the society: "No man's family can survive a murder committed in any other way [that is, other than by knowing and attending to omens and rules]; and yet Thugs have thrived through a long series of generations. We have all children like other men, and we are never visited with any extraordinary affliction" (Sleeman 1836, "Substance," 155). Yet escaping from the dictates of the law required one thing: to faithfully obey the rules instituted by the Goddess—to accomplish the rites, to not kill forbidden victims, and to respect the omens.

Religious Practices and Guilt

Thugs sometimes had to make difficult choices. To blindly respect the rules might lead to their being deprived of substantial loot, to not respect the rules might lead to their exclusion from the Thug community, **nuga kar dena,** meaning literally to be naked, that is, to be sent back to a state of nature—or even worse, as the following narratives explain.

TO OBEY EVEN WHILE DISOBEYING

So some Thugs cheated. They did this not at the level of thought by elaborating a sophisticated casuistry, but by transforming the facts themselves, by given them an appearance that conformed to the rules they were supposed to follow. This masking often entailed costs: proper appearances could be expensive.

If a group of treasure bearers appeared and they were unfortunately accompanied by a cow, the Thugs pretended that they had made an oath to offer this cow to a Brahman. The treasure bearers, not wanting to bring down divine punishment on themselves by keeping pious men from fulfilling their religious duties, would agree to sell them the cow. As soon as they were divested of the animal, they could be immediately murdered, as the Thugs then could avoid breaking the rule prohibiting the killing of travelers "accompanied by cows" (Sleeman 1836, "Substance," 172).

When it came to the killing of a disabled person or a woman, an unscrupulous Thug might be highly paid to commit the deed (Sleeman 1836, 143 and 174) while the rest remained at a distance. Thus, though the rule was broken, the rest of the Thugs, having not performed the murder or witnessed it with their own eyes, were less guilty. Another way of avoiding the guilt of a forbidden crime was to refuse a share of the loot.

It was also possible to call upon Brahmans and rites. In the case of the murder of the beautiful Kalee Babee, the Hindu Thugs, who had been reluctant to kill her, performed ceremonies of atonement upon their return to the village. Lalmun narrated:

> Feringheea's father, Purusram Brahman, was there; so was Ghasee Subahdar, a Rajpoot; so was Himmut Brahman. When they came home to Murnae, Rae Singh, Purusram's brother, refused to eat, drink or smoke with his brother till he had purged himself from this great sin; and he, Himmut and Ghasee gave a feast which cost them a thousand rupees each. Four or five thousand Brahmans were assembled at that feast. Had it rested here, we should have thrived; but in the Affair of the sixty [Souls], women were again murdered; in the Affair of the forty, several women were murdered;

the Musulmans were too strong for the Hindoos; and from that
time we may trace our decline.

Maduree, who died last year in the Saugor jail, was the man who
strangled Kalee Babee. . . . Himmut, after the Surgooja affair, got
worms in his body and died barking like a dog. Kosul died a miserable death at Nodha. One of his sons has been transported from
Saugor, and the other died in the jail. His family is extinct. Look at
Purusram's family; all gone! And Ghasee Subahdar's also! (Sleeman
1836, "Substance . . . ," 173–74)

The rite was aimed at erasing a past fault, while the masking maneuver
was aimed at making it appear in the present as rule-obeying behavior.
Both were aimed at changing the nature and perception of the event. The
Thugs were not content to mislead just human beings, but the Goddess
was not fooled by these ploys, and her vengeance was terrible.

CRIMES AND PUNISHMENTS

Death took on horrible forms matching the importance of the broken
rules. There are many such examples scattered throughout the "Conversations." The guilty was transformed; his transgression became visible
on his body. "If any man swears to a falsehood upon a pickaxe, properly
consecrated, we will consent to be hung if he survives the time appointed;
appoint one, two or three days when he swears, and we pledge ourselves
that he does not live a moment beyond the time; he will die a horrible
death; his head will turn round, his face towards the back, and he will
writhe in tortures till he dies" (Sleeman 1836, 155). As the eating of the
ritual sugar transformed a man into a Thug, transgressing the laws of
Thuggee transformed the Thug into a monster: Himmut, who participated in the murder of Kalee Babee, "dies barking like a dog."

Yes; that demon is well remembered to this day, we have all
heard him a hundred times described by the survivors.

I saw him only once myself. I was awake while all the rest were
asleep; he came in at the door, and seemed to swell as he came
in till his head touched the roof, and the roof was very high, and
his bulk became enormous. I prostrated myself, and told him that
he was our Purmesur, (Great God) and we poor helpless mortals
depending entirely upon his will. This pleased him, and he passes
by me; but took such a grasp at the man Munghulee, who slept by
my side, that he was seized with spasms all over from the nape of
the neck to the sole of his foot. (Sleeman 1836, 220)

Bodily havoc, collective hallucinations, these delirious symptoms
linked to guilt were a manifestation of the compulsory nature of divine

rules. The ruses used to get round them showed the energy the Thugs were willing to expend in order to preserve appearances. We know that practices such as cheating and lying were rarely attributed to the victims, that is, to others. They mostly applied to the members of the group and to the Goddess.

All of those beliefs, rites, and observances were inspired by crime. They all had as their goal to legitimize it (through the founding narratives) and to regulate it, this in both the quantitative and the formal sense. The times, the places, and the victims were chosen in terms of the Goddess, who was constantly beseeched to make her wishes known. The Thugs were anything but anarchists; on the contrary, they were restrained and under divine surveillance. They had duties, obligations; they had to perform rites, say prayers, and give thanks. The constraining power of this edifice was a fragile one as it was not controlled or maintained by an authority respected by the whole of the community. Each gang leader was his fellows' temporary priest, the sole guardian of their religiosity. The opportunities for profit could obviously become irresistibly tempting. So there was cheating, a forbidden murder was masked into a legitimate one, principles were transgressed, and the breach that had been opened could be fatal. In the stories circulating among the Thugs, the guilty barked and lost their humanness. Thugs tell the British, who were in the process of destroying their community, that one of the reasons for their downfall was that they had disobeyed the rules of Thuggee.

THE HARSHNESS OF THE WORLD

The most telling characteristic in the Thugs' mental universe was probably the key place omens held in it. Thugs had to be constantly on the lookout for omens that might at any time negate the efficacy of rites, depending entirely on the flux of time and on the Goddess and her moods—that is, on her immediacy. This is the opposite of the Brahmanic tradition, in which rites, when performed scrupulously according to all the appropriate rules, predictably and mechanically yield the desired results. Through a donkey's bray or a jackal's cry, the Goddess permitted what she forbade and forbade what she permitted. There was a gap between the premeditation of the murder and the precariousness of the signs that determined or suspended it. This gap reflected a harsh vision of human life on which the Thugs focused in its tragic and ephemeral nature: a dog turd might save life, a vulture dropping might erase it.

Omens, like Thug observances and ceremonies, constituted a complex set into which murder was embedded and was thus allowed to bask in the rays of sanctity. Even though the information we have on their society keeps us from classifying the Thugs as a sect, their ritual practices and their worldview do partake of the tendencies and currents in Hindu tradition.

The Boats of Salvation

Sacrifice has held center stage in Indian religious thinking ever since the time of the oldest traditions. It is through sacrifice that the relation with the divine is defined and the paths to the absolute are laid out. "As the organizing principle of everything that exists, sacrifice tends to include in itself this very totality it is organizing" (Malamoud 1987, 11).

The *Brahmanas*, the liturgical commentaries on the Veda, tirelessly repeat that "the sacrifice is the boat for safe passage."[36] Madeleine Biardeau, borrowing an image dear to many members of the Orientalist school, claims that sacrifice is "the common tree trunk of Hinduism" (Biardeau 1976). If this is the case, then Thug devotees were indeed nourished by the sap of Hinduism.

To believe in the efficacy of the rite, to have faith in priests who are competent and respectful of the exactitude (*satya*) of the rites, is required for this complex and coded ritual to bring the desired fruits; this ritual process, Sylvain Lévi has argued, is a mechanistic one. Even though sacrifice is presented as the sole path of salvation, as the sole mean of reestablishing equilibrium between creditor gods and human debtors ("When they sacrifice, human beings are buying back their bodies from death" [Lévi 1966, 131]), some mythical narratives have dwelt on the potential pitfalls of sacrifice. Thus Manu's "sacrificial folly" that leads him to offer vases, bulls, hosts, and spouse is condemned by the god Indra. The myth seems to raise the possibility of human sacrifice even as it argues that it is a boundary that must not be breached. British Orientalists wrongly dismissed the possibility of such sacrifice. We now know that human sacrifice, *purusamedha*, was "systematically taught and regulated." It seemed to obey the same rules at play in the famous sacrifice of the horse (*ashvamedha*). The victim, animal or human, was smothered "by a special officiant, the *samitr*, that is the pacifier, who is expected to keep the victim from crying out" (Lévi 1966, 133). There is no proof that these prescriptions have ever been followed. Like Colebrooke did in the past, present day scholars remain cautious on this issue. And yet, could this "pacifier" be the ancestor of the Thug stranglers, who too feared their victims' cries?

RENUNCIATION

Sacrifice does not allow individuals to escape from the cycle of rebirths to which human beings are fated as long as the fruits of their actions, their karma, have not reached maturity. In the *Upanishads* (the closing texts in the Veda that were written around the same time as the *Brahmanas*) and their Vedic exegesis, there emerged a new solution that proposed to end all ritual activity so as to no longer cause long-term effects and to be, at the moment of death, definitely freed from the servitude of rebirth. In contrast to the master of the house, the ideal sacrificer, the renouncer, strove for chastity, for an absolute detachment from passions, and for the avoidance of any pollution linked to violence. To the licit murder of the sacrifice is opposed the nonviolence, the nondesire to destroy life, the *ahimsa* of the renouncer, who goes so far as to filter his water (to avoid inadvertently consuming living organisms) and who only eats vegetable food (Biardeau 1976, 60).

In parallel to this path of renunciation, another one was established: that of yoga. It is characterized by the idea that the *atman*, the self, can detach itself from the material world through certain techniques. The yogi hopes to gain deliverance. Through concentration and asceticism, through transcending the realm of physical reality by passing through several planes of consciousness, the yogi unites (from the verbal Sanskrit root, *yuj*, to unite) and becomes one with the Absolute, which, in some of the *Upanishads*, takes on the forms of Vishnu or Shiva, the two great gods of the Hindu pantheon.

This lays out the conditions for a personal relationship between the yogi and his chosen god. In the *Shvetashvatara Upanishad*, the word *devotion* (*bhakti*) appears in the sense that it would have later on (a devotion as great for the guru, the spiritual master, as for the god), along with the ritual phrase that was to become typical of the devotee, the *bhakta*: "to that God . . . do I, eager for liberation, resort for refuge."[37] The Thugs said the same thing about the Goddess: "I hold her name in my heart before leaving on an expedition, in my heart I hold her name."

POLLUTION AND VIOLENCE

There is another little-known revealed tradition, that of the *Agamas*, which teaches that the divine is not one or the other of these two great gods, but a couple (Biardeau 1981, 1663), the male member of which is Shiva. According to these Tantric Shivaites, the world, represented as energy, *shakti*, must be neither renounced nor corrected. Among initiates the sole mode of devotion that is valued is that of the hero, *vira*, "who passes directly through the zones of greatest danger to rise with the help of nature . . . and to accept a non-dual celebration of the world" (Zimmer 1953, 449). Heroes free themselves in the here and now, and their liberation is manifested by "breaking away from the eight bonds of pity, error, shame, family, morality, caste, tenderness, and fear" (Renou and Filliozat 1985, 1:594, para. 1218). Their aim is to be *jivanmukta*, liberated living beings. There is a great emphasis on "heroic" rites in the *Tantra* dedicated to Kali that originated in northern India (Goudriaan and Gupta 1981). What are the implications of the term *heroic* here? Liminal experiences, the reconciliation of opposites; esoteric practices; secret language said to be "of the dusk"; *samdhya-basha*, profane actions made of elements forbidden in everyday life, all confer extraordinary merit to initiates: they extricate them out of the human order.

Tantric Shivaites include groups who "take refuge" only in the Goddess. In their eyes she is the unique source of the universe, the one who makes it possible for Brahma to create, for Vishnu to preserve, and for Shiva to destroy. She ensures the deliverance of the world and the return to the Absolute. She presents herself under extraordinarily varied names and appearances: Kali the Black, "an old black woman pulling her tongue and dripping with blood," as well as Durga the Inaccessible, "a beautiful young woman, blue of skin, mounted on a tiger or a lion." Then there is Chinnamasta, who in her lower left hand holds her own head "with wild hair, dangling red tongue, menacing teeth." A jet of blood comes out of her neck and ends up on the lips of the head; "two other stream of blood, coming from the sides of the neck, pour into receptacles held by two female figures," companions that Kali created for herself by making them spring out of her own body (Malamoud 1987, 8). There's also Gauri the Golden; Candi the Violent; Parvati, Daughter of the Mountain; Kumari the Virgin; and Devi the Goddess—her frightful representations are the most widespread.

These *Tantrikas*, known as *Shaktas*, are organized into a multitude of sects and welcome persons of all social origins. "Even the lowliest of the Untouchables can receive the Tantric initiation and become a member of the worship circle" (Woodruff 1929, 292). They see Kali as a mother who is punishing as well as nurturing. She represents destructive time, death and life blended together. "A Tantric aspirant who wants to follow the course described in the Kalikula should feel attracted to the unpredictable, the antinomian, the idea of salvation through gruesome experience, in short, the 'heroic state' (*virabhava*)" (Goudriaan and Gupta 1981, 75).

These cults, originally adhered to by a small number of initiated renouncers, "were to gradually take on more Brahminic forms, more speculative and abstract ones . . . in which rites are softened or symbolically reinterpreted so as to render them inoffensive and acceptable to society at large" (Padoux 1992, 67).

This process links up with the one that within Brahmanic orthodoxy tends to give sacrifice a euphemistic representation so as to obliterate its violent aspect and mask its heterodox element. "But this latter is always present in it, where it will tend to represent the secret esoteric depth of the doctrine and practices, the one where the greatest dangerous forces hide, forces that might themselves be at the root of the power of the divinities celebrated by the esoteric cult." This is expressed by a thirteenth-century description of the behavior of Shivaite Brahmans in Kashmir. These Brahmans were "internally Kaula, externally Shiva, and in the life of the world, vaidika," that is, orthodox (Padoux 1992, 68). This program of dissociated behavior and practices could well have been the ancestor to that of the Thugs.

This religious landscape, upon which I have barely touched here, does suggest the diversity and the antagonistic nature of the boats of salvation found in India. And yet the central and perennial idea of the violence of sacrifice, expressed or alluded to in various ways, lies beneath the accretion of beliefs. Tantric heroes from all classes and all castes have to go through "frightful experiences." In this sense, the Thugs were indisputably among the best ones. After all, they did consider the victims they killed as sacrifices to the Goddess, "as a Priest of Jupiter remembered the oxen and a Priest of Saturn the children sacrificed upon their altars" (Sleeman 1836, "Introduction," 7–8). As the last bastion of their religious identity (besides their founding narratives, their rituals, and their observances), did the assassins' motives confirm the sacred character of their crimes?

SACRED STRANGULATIONS

The Thug Viewpoint

The Thugs claimed a positive function for Thuggee: thanks to it, they said, fewer human beings die, because if they were at the mercy of Kali's fury, they would all die. The Thugs put the responsibility onto the gods:

> "It is God who kills but Bhowanee has the name of it."
> "God is all in all, for good and evil."
> "God has appointed blood for her (Bhowanee) food, saying: 'khoon tu kao,' feed thou upon blood. In my opinion this is very bad, but what can she do, being ordered to subsist upon blood!"
> "Bhowanee is happy and more so in proportion to the blood that is shed."[38]

GOD IS TO BLAME

Muslim and Hindu Thugs claimed that a unique, omnipotent, and undifferentiated principle, that is, everything in everything, in good as well as evil, set forth the Goddess and ordered her to feed on blood. They might perhaps have been echoing a cycle of Hindu myths about the origin of evil, according to which God either voluntarily or involuntarily created evil and then got rid of it by imparting it to either mankind or demons. "What could the Goddess do, being forced to subside in this way?" asked one of the informers without giving an answer. The outrage meted out on the murdered bodies was due to her voracious nature. "Bhowani is angry when we do not spill the blood of our victims, she loves blood" (Sleeman 1915, "Conversations," 157).

In the *Bhagavad Gita*, the god Krishna beseeches Arjuna to engage in battles. Arjuna explains that the faith he has in his god makes him innocent of the evil his duty requires him to do. "When your mind becomes fixed on Me, you shall overcome all difficulties" (*Bhagavad Gita* 1976, Canto 18, verset 58). Man "is neither born nor . . . dies at any time" (*Bhagavad Gita* 1976, Canto 2, verset 10). The Thugs echoed this as they repeated: "*Admi ke marne se koe nurta nabeen.*" "No man is killed by man's killing, all who are strangled are strangled in effect by God" (Sleeman 1915, "Conversations," 157).

This world is not for man without sacrifice; we must sacrifice to invigorate the gods, because "one who enjoys the gifts of the Devas [Gods] without offering them [anything in return] is indeed a thief" (*Bhagavad Gita* 1978, Canto 3, verset 12), says the blessed Krishna. The accused interrogated by Paton also took pain to differentiate themselves from thieves. Through Thuggee, which in this context might take on the meaning of sacrifice, everything they obtained was a gift from God:

> Six approvers at once shake their heads: "We do not steal! . . . We never steal! What God gives us, he gives us in Thuggee! God is the Giver, we never steal!"

Rambux: If you would put down there 50 rupees I would not steal it. I only take it after strangling a man! No thieving! If I had to pay rent to the Company and owed 200 rupees Revenue, I would get it from Thuggee on the roads, and not from a Banker! why should I steal him? I know not how to steal, but I have learnt thuggee!

Jheoodeen: There are many thieves in my village but I would not go with them. My father a Thug used to counsel me: Do not join them! They take money without thugging!

Bhuram: A *chor!* A thief! But a Thug rides his horse! Wears his dagger! *chor ee nah!* thieving? never, never! I despise a dacoit, a robber! *Aur kya?* What else?[39]

The word **bunij**, merchandise, which Thugs used to designate their victims, denoted circulation and exchange. Was it the correlate of the difference between stealing and Thugging?

The Thugs also denied their personal responsibility with an etiological narrative paying homage to Kali's uncontrolled fury. According to them the earth would have been devastated "in a single day" if Bhagwan had not been watching over it. They added that they were created to ensure this watchfulness and claimed to be the intercessors between their Goddess, whom they had the job of feeding, and the god seemingly overwhelmed by its creature. If the Thugs were to stop sacrificing, death would strike everyone. "Bhowanee must be fed and since the British Government has been suppressing our trade of murder Bhowanee has begun with her own hands to devastate the country with disease and death. Men are everywhere propitiating her, people in the villages are dying by 20s and 40s within the last five years of the suppression of the Thugs." By ensuring a continuous supply of victims to the Goddess, the Thugs restrained her natural voracity. Yet their sacrifices were never sufficient, as "she requires more extensive food!" than the few people killed by the Thugs.

> "The day after to-morrow 12th October hundreds of thousands of goats buffaloes sheep will be slain as sacrifices to Bhowanee in Lucknow, Calcutta and everywhere." "I saw with my own eyes at Bindachul (Mirzapur) . . . 200 or 400 goats sacrificed to Bhowanee and the blood was taken by her, before whose image a crowd of about 50 Sukhees (men dressed in women's clothes) were dancing."[40]

Kali is excess. She is constantly hungry, "as we would be if we were not practicing Thuggee," added some informants.

The devotional stream of which the *Gita* is the bible recommends acting on behalf of one's chosen divinity. The Thugs followed its lessons as they seemed to know that the divinity takes on the responsibility for violence only if devotees renounce the fruits of their actions. Krishna reassures Arjuna that Arjuna won't be responsible for the massacres of war if he sincerely offers his actions to Krishna. The Thugs too maintained this internal attitude: "Bhowanee is approved by God and thereupon we who place our trust in Bhowanee are pardoned."[41] In theory the Thug closing ritual gave expression to this indispensable sincerity. In the course of the ritual they were supposed to offer their loot to the Goddess so as to be able to enjoy, as was customary, the "leftovers" properly consecrated after a portion had been set aside for her.

THE FULFILLED TRAVELER

The Thugs didn't fear the *bhuts*, the unappeased spirits of their victims. According to them, a strangled traveler was a fulfilled one. Violence, meted out in compassion, freed the traveler from the cycle of transmigrations. There are very ancient references to this disquieting eschatology. Wilhelm Halbfass (1991) retraces its history. In the eighth century, Kumarila alludes briefly to the *Samsaramochaka*. Kumarila was a commentator of the *Mimamsa*, a manual of discussions on the socioreligious duties spelled out in the *Dharma*, itself based on the injunctions in the Veda. The *Samsaramochaka* were liberators from the flow of rebirths, and for them violence, *himsa*, was meritorious. Kumarila contrasts them with others for whom violence cannot be meritorious. In his demonstration aimed at supporting the preeminence of the commandments of the Vedic revelation over all other ethical considerations, the Liberators, along with the rest of the defenders of *ahimsa*, are mentioned only as an example of mistaken interpretations of the Vedic *Dharma*. This is because the sole sources of the *Dharma* are the injunctions and prohibitions of the Veda, "specified according to the occasion of the act and the qualifications of the actor, and they cannot be translated or reduced to general commonsensically 'reasonable' rules and principles concerning . . . violence and non-violence" (Halbfass 1991, 90–91). Kumarila does not tell us more about these liberators from the flow of rebirth, nor do any of his commentators. But we find other references one century later in Jayanta's *Nyayamanjari*. "Jayanta mentions the *Samsaramochaka*, whom he characterizes as 'devoted to the killing of living creatures' and 'as acting from delusion,' side by side with the Buddhists. Whatever their distinguishing features may be, both have in common that their traditions are outside the Veda and nothing but a fraud" (Halbfass 1991, 99). The *Samsaramochaka* appear in other texts, where they are often compared to Jains as similar examples of people with mistaken religious attitudes. In the twelfth century another author, Malayagiri, writes:

> The "liberators from samsara" argue that killing and even torturing can be a genuinely meritorious activity, motivated by compassion and altruism and guided by therapeutic skills. . . . Here, the Samsaramochaka poses as a benevolent doctor in the wider context of karma and rebirth. His victims are patients; being an expert physician, he knows that he has to administer a harsh medicine in order to bring about a change for the better.
>
> This would seem to be basically compatible with Kumarila's brief and cryptic reference. First of all, it illustrates the failure of *lokaprasiddhi*, "common acquaintance," to provide reliable criteria for the distinction between right and wrong in ethics and religion. Beyond this, it reflects Kumarila's conviction that dharma cannot be defined in terms of utilitarianism or altruism. . . . The Samsaramochaka may present himself as the ultimate altruist and utilitarian. . . . In Malayagiri's perspective, the "liberators from

samsara" are, of course, not really good and compassionate doctors. Their altruism is a travesty. Instead of delivering the victims from their bad karma, they will intensify their "afflictions" and thus keep them in the bondage of karma and samsara. Perhaps the most obvious association would be with certain Shivaite texts, in which bloody rituals are described and explained, and in which the killing of living beings, including humans, has a religious function and value. (Halbfass 1991, 99–101)

Halbfass particularly mentions the *Netratantra*, in which, in chapter 20, the female powers, the Yoginis, kill human victims. Hélène Brunner, who studied this *Tantra*, tells us that Shiva states in it that "they are acting upon his orders"; they kill human beings "to offer them to him in sacrifice." The victims have been created for this purpose. Lines 8 and 9 of the chapter even specify that the Yoginis sacrifice their victims so that they may be delivered. "They are thrown into the world of transmigration only to be returned to Shiva" (Brunner 1974, 184). It is also says that the Yoginis act to "help" the victims, to liberate them from their sins, from the shackles of worldly existence. Thus they are not really killing them, but rather are "uniting" them with Shiva.

One of Jayanta's contemporaries, Bhasarvarjna, who also upheld the Veda as the ultimate source of truth, alluded to "the sacred texts of the Thugs"(*thakashastras*)!

This statement seems to be the oldest extant reference in Sanskrit to the sect of assassins. There is no authority in the texts of the Thags and similar groups. They "are produced for a visible purpose by somebody stricken with passion and other afflictions," . . . and they illustrate the dangers of not being under the guidance of the true source, i.e., the Veda. The references in the works of Bhasarvajna . . . have neither been noticed by the historians of religion, nor by the lexicographers who have tried to trace the history of the word. (Halbfass 1991, 103–4)

Yet these mentions are fascinating. Just like the liberators from the flow of rebirths, the Thugs claimed that the positive character of sacrifice benefited the victim. They attributed the benefits of sacrifice not selfishly to themselves (as a long life, riches and happiness, and so on) but generously to the victim, and it does not even appear that these meritorious murders ensured Thugs any benefits after their own death.

In contrast to the other explanations of Thuggee, this one corresponds to the elaboration of a specific doctrine, one moreover backed by texts mentioning the Thugs by name as being its disciples.

Outside Views
THE INDOLOGISTS

Wilhelm Halbfass does not even mention the possibility of a colonial invention of the Thugs, though this might be because he was interested only in uncovering the traces of their ancestors in written documents. He comments on the oldest known Sanskrit reference to the sect of assassins as follows:

> We may question the authenticity of Bhasarvajan. . . . Nevertheless, it seems reasonable to assume that he did not invent the reference to the Thags, and that they had indeed been cited by earlier antagonists of the authority of the Veda. . . . There is, however, a passage in Bhavya's *Tarkajvala* (available only in a Tibetan translation) which might be interpreted as a reference to the Thags. It mentions a tradition of "deceivers" (*slu byed pa*) who practice ritual killing. Some time after Bhasarvajna, the Thags, as well as their practices and even their "sacred traditions" (*thakagama*) appear again in several Jaina works. (Halbfass 1991, 103)

Other Indianists have advanced hypotheses on the socioreligious origins of the assassins whom the colonialists discovered in the nineteenth century. Richard Karl von Garbe (1857–1927), whose work Halbfass cites, refers to views advanced by Sir John Malcolm:

> Independent of the thieves and robbers who dwell in Central India, there have been, for many years past, annual incursions of vagrants from other countries. Amongst the most numerous of these bands are a tribe of Brahmins, from Bundelcund, who take the name of the sect of Canoje: they are at once mendicants, pilfering thieves, robbers and murderers. A number of them are usually found in that singular association called Thugs, who are well known in Hindustan, and have of late years become very formidable in Malwa and adjoining provinces, with many of the petty chiefs of which this extraordinary society was, during its late troubles, intimately connected. A description of these robbers and their usual proceedings, while it shews their character, will suffice as an example of the bands by which the provinces of India, in the condition this country has lately been, are liable to be infested, or rather invaded. (Malcolm 1972, 2:186–87)

Garbe writes that "it would not be surprising if the murderous enterprises of the Thugs usually rest into the hands of the priestly classes" (Garbe 1903, 187). Gustav Pfirrmann, whom I cited earlier, is struck by the animism of Thug beliefs. He thinks that Thuggee is a cult of tribal origin that would have gradually spread to other layers of the population during the Middle Ages. Assassin Brahmans or Sanskritized aborigines? None of these authors offers any convincing proof of their theses. Yet in their view, as in that of Halbfass, it is the cult of the Goddess that turned the Thugs into brigands.

HISTORY AND ANTHROPOLOGY

There were Thugs, there is no doubt, and this gang of marauders practiced a crude religion of their own; but there was nothing peculiar about it. Criminals all over the world have some kind of religious notions of their own.

—O. P. Bathnagar (1966)

Like O. P. Bathnagar, some Indian historians hold that the Thugs' "crude religion" should be explained in general human terms, while in contrast others, including J. N. Farquhar, see the Thugs as a part of Indian and Hindu social history and explain them accordingly. Farquhar speculates that the Thugs are "an ordinary criminal tribe and that the first Thugs would be ignorant Hindus who had been worshipers of the goddess before they formed the society to strangle and rob unwary travellers" (Farquhar 1908–1926, 12, 261). Christopher Bayly expresses doubts, though without giving his reasons, that "Thuggee was an organized conspiracy, let alone one which was based exclusively on the worship of the ferocious goddess Kali" (Bayly 1990c, 227). In contrast, Percival Spear, Vincent Smith, Sir Francis Tuker, and George Bruce, all historians of the colonial school, adhere wholeheartedly to the conspiracy view, as can be expected.

And yet in spite of the doubts of a number of scholars, the problem of sacrifice does remain. Even though human sacrifice in India was not an everyday practice, it was no colonial phantasm either. Even today this sort of event is occasionally reported in newspapers.

Jorge Luis Borges, after reading *Confessions of a Thug*, phrased the issue in the form of a chicken and egg question: "Were the Thugs brigands who sanctified their profession with the cult of the goddess Bhowani, or was it the cult of the Goddess Bhowani that turned them into brigands?" (Borges 1923, 1154). Indianists tend toward the second part of the question, but let us next look at the first possibility.

RELIGION, MURDER, DECEIT

A stout Mogul officer of noble bearing and singularly handsome countenance, on his way from the Punjab to Oudh crossed the Ganges. . . . he was mounted on a fine Turkish horse and attended by his butler and groom. Soon after crossing the river, he fell in with a small party of well-dressed and modest-looking men going the same road. They accosted him in a respectful manner, and attempted to enter into conversation with him. He had heard of Thugs and told them to be off. . . . The next morning he overtook the same number of men, but of a different appearance, all Musulmans.

A familiar plot unfolds again: "Putting his hand on his sword he bid them all to be off." Yet the day after next, all these people were sleeping in the same *serail,* and the group

> became very intimate with the butler and groom. The next day, when they had got to the middle of an extensive and uninhabited plain, the Mogul in advance, and his two servants a few hundred yards behind him, he came up to a party of six poor Musulmans, sitting weeping by the side of a dead companion. . . . They were poor unlettered men, and unable to repeat the funeral service from the holy Koran—would His Highness but perform this last office for them, he would, no doubt, find his reward in this world and the next. The Mogul dismounted. . . . A carpet was spread—the Mogul took off his bow and quiver, then his pistols and sword, and placed them on the ground near the body—called for water and washed his feet, hands and face, that he might not pronounce the holy words in an unclean state. He then knelt down and began to repeat the funeral service, in a clear, loud voice. Two of the poor soldiers knelt by him, one on each side in silence. The other four went off a few paces to beg that the butler and groom would not come so near as to interrupt the good Samaritan at his devotions. All being ready, one of the four, in a low undertone gave the signal, the handkerchiefs were thrown over their necks and in a few minutes all three were dead—the Mogul and his servants—lying in the grave in the usual manner, the head of one at the feet of the one below him. (Sleeman 1915, 81–82)[42]

Religion was used as a stratagem in this narrative collected by Sleeman. Yet we have just seen that religion can also provide the Thugs' legitimation. Where did consecration stop and profanation begin? The boundary is fuzzy.

Trickery and religion are linked by secrecy, and thus by the capability of unveiling. Are the priests not entrusted with the secret language of the gods? Is it the magician not *indrajalin,* that is, the one "possessing Indra's net," who gives birth to the reality of illusion? Both priests and magicians draw their authority and their power, practice their seduction through their access to the gods, to the secrets of the sacred. They are indispensable to their fellow human beings for obtaining life after death, for bringing on rain, for protecting against misfortune. To those ends they perform dances, prayers, offerings, and rites create representations. . . . They must be paid in return. Can we get a sense of the price for their services? R. R. Mehrotra gives a description of the favorite tricks used in the 1970s by the Pandas of Banaras, who were priests specializing in the performance of funerary rituals (Mehrotra 1977, 19–52). They would choose a pilgrim from among a group they had picked up, often already at the train station, and a Panda priest would bring him secretly to visit a divinity. The Panda would sing mantras, the sacred verses, then give his delighted victim a bouquet of flowers. He would hide some rupees in the bouquet. They would both rejoin the group, and at a given moment, the priest would take the flowers back from his victim and publicly "discover" the rupees. He would bless the tricked pilgrim for his generosity. A norm would thus be established, and all the other pilgrims would feel obligated to give at least as much to the priest to go pray in turn to this particular divinity (Mehrotra 1977, 43–44).

This scam mirrors the mechanism of Thug trickery. The Thugs either called upon compassion (they feigned illness, or ritual breakdown as in the story of the Moghul horseman) to get the victim to "give" care, prayers, and so on, or they offered pleasure or a service (often protection of the travelers) that appeared to be a disinterested gift. The beneficiaries were at first suspicious, but because nothing was asked of them in return, their mistrust abated. The victim was a party to a transaction in which a free gift (that the victim gave or benefited from) was the first step to the murder.

Emile Benveniste (1973, 66–67) writes that "in Indo-European, the notions "to give" and "to take" converged, as it were, in gesture" ("*cf.* English, *to take to*," that is, to take in order to give to). "The root *do-* means 'give' in all Indo-European languages" except in Hittite, where *da-* means "take. . . . The other languages constructed *do-* with the idea of a destination, which results in the sense 'to give' [*donner,* to give, in French]."[43] Was Thug trickery inspired by this ancient linguistic confusion between the kindred senses of giving and taking, a confusion that for them took on the form of violence (physical or mental), hidden under the external appearance of nonviolence?

Even a female lover's kiss (sometimes called "Thug sweetness") could be described in those terms. Her goal is to catch the lover, to dispossess him, at least for the moment, by giving him pleasure. The stolen kiss, the strangled traveler, and the magic trick all seemed to be guided by the same principle: to cover, to hide (*thagna*) the gain that was sought or the violence to be exerted by giving something, or by provoking the gift of something.

The word **bunij** (from the Hindi *banij,* trade, occupation), commonly used by the Thugs to designate the victim, provides an additional argument. The verb that corresponds to this substantive, *banijna,* means to buy, to sell, to subjugate, in which the opposite meanings of selling and buying appear to melt into that of subjugation. If we agree that selling and buying are particular modes of giving and taking, then it might be legitimate to link **bunij** and the Avestan word *baog.* The Thugs might have believed their activities to be painted on the walls of the famous subterranean temples of Ellora, but I think I recognize them in the history of this Old Iranian word from whence might have come the word by which they designated their victim. The Gothic verb *bugjan,* which also means sell "to buy" in the sense of "to free, to buy back someone," has a fabulous etymology, as Benveniste shows:

> We think that Gothic *bugjan* "buy" is to be compared with the root attested only, but in a very clear way, by Old Iranian: Av[estan] *baog-,* which has abundant derivatives in Iranian and signifies "undo," "detach" a girdle, a garment, and later "set free" and finally "save." The Av[estan] verb *baog-* exists with several pre-verbs: it supplies the agent noun *baoxtar,* "liberator." It has a material, as well as a religious sense. . . . Very soon the religious sense was emphasized: liberation through the intervention of a god, of a "saviour," who must come and deliver captive creation. It was to express the idea of salvation, redemption, liberation, that the word was employed, particularly in the vocabulary of Manichaeism. (Benveniste 1973, 111)

Was that not the program of the liberator from the flow or rebirths? He took and gave, bought and sold, saved, delivered, untied.

THUGS NOW

There are today in India some social practices that evoke the sliding of meaning between transaction and transcendence within the exchange system, and of which the Thugs appear to have drawn extreme consequences. Lee Siegel, in his book on magic in India, writes that the magician

> cultivates the religious association; performing near a mosque on Friday, the Islamic day of public worship, he'll whisper incantations that sound like the Arabic of the Qur'an or invoke the name of the Prophet, "Peace be upon Him"; in another part of town, near a temple later that day, he'll praise Shiva, Rama, or Krishna, and claim to have accrued his magic powers at the cremation grounds. The street conjurer is now, as he has always been, often a mock

holy man; he knows there's money to be made in religion. (Siegel 1991, 3)

The Pandas,[44] whom I mentioned above, are even more interesting. At Banaras they are treated as Pindaris(!), as rapacious stranglers, extortionists, and fake holy men. In the spoken language of the town, *panda* means thief, crook, bloodthirsty, and so on. However, they are different from magicians and ordinary criminals in that they are priests and benefit from legal sanction and social patronage. Among them, some of the less educated and perhaps even non-Brahmans have developed a peculiar argot that includes some Sanskrit when they perform ritual acts, some Hindi when they speak to pilgrims, and plain argot when they communicate among themselves. Pandas pass from one register to another according to the need of the situation: their language being "both (overtly) sacred and (covertly) profane" (Mehrotra 1977, 26). Among the oldest words in this argot, R. R. Mehrotra has identified borrowings from the Ramasee of river Thugs, the "Bangoos" Sleeman mentioned as operating between Patan and Allahabad! Some of the words have changed meaning; some have not. The strangler, *bhartote,* today designates the Panda from the temple of Kashi Karwat; *orhana,* "to strangle" in Ramasee, means for them "to beat," *bhela;* the grave digger, killer, or strangler (*martakar, bhartota*) designates the Panda extorting money. To kill, *martana,* now means to scam a pilgrim; *marti,* "fated to die," now designates the would-be victim of this scam; the corpse, *marh,* means the same but recalcitrant, difficult, victim; a customer who has been scammed is a dead customer, *maral majhi.* Finally, just as the victim of the Thugs is called *bunij,* merchandise, the Panda who defrauds a pilgrim is respectfully and misleadingly called a "businessman," *rojgar!*

Banaras is the city where people come to die or at least to have their sins forgiven before they die. "As the saying goes, 'Death in Kashi is Liberation'" (Eck 1993, 325). The Panda argot, like that of the Thugs, is associated with death. Like their ancestors, in the temple of Shiva at Kashi Karwat the Panda nicknamed the Strangler used in the past to free pilgrims from the flow of rebirths:

For a considerable period it was believed that death at this place would immediately lead one to emancipation from the chances of rebirth. Some pilgrims are said to have availed of this easy means rather too literally by handing over all their belongings to local *Pandas* and getting themselves killed by a big saw which was provided in a large underground apartment for this purpose. When this came to the notice of the government, the district authorities closed the passage leading to the underground apartment with iron-gratings which were removed only once a week under police supervision for purposes of cleaning the place. (Mehrotra 1977, 25–26)

The Thugs' sham altruism was not of the same order as that of the Pandas, even though their aims were similar. Thugs' victims were coerced; those of the Pandas are apparently voluntary. Therein lies a tenuous difference. If the fire of devotion and the desire for deliverance lead some people to have themselves voluntarily cut up in pieces, much as in the self-decapitations evoked in Indian tales, I am tempted to think that in this context the Thugs were not that odd when they pretended that they strangled in order to "fulfill" travelers. It is hard not to contrast their discreet cruelty—they strangled by surprise—with the ostentatious cruelty of the Pandas and their great saw. In contrast to the Pandas' escalation of violence into unimaginable torture, the Thugs seemed to have partially incorporated the injunctions aimed at attenuating the violence of sacrifice: they "smothered" their victims according to the ancient usage, by making sure they were not able to see death coming.

We know that there are more orthodox, less horrifying ways to permanently escape from the cycle of rebirths. Nonetheless, from the Thugs to the Pandas "sacrificial folly" remains one way. So even though the identity of the Thugs' ascendants remains obscure, the identity of the Pandas' ascendants is pretty clear.

Crime, Sect, Caste

In the legend of the king and the thief Kaladushaka, these two characters are both opposed and complementary. The thief lives on the periphery of the inhabited and cultivated world while the king is its central axis; the first is excluded while the other embodies the whole of the community. Their opposite natures are reflected in kings' frequent attraction to asceticism and thieves to "pollution, wildness, violence," yet again paradoxically, these two realms belong in the same wild spaces, the forest or the jungle. The tale resolves the two protagonists' conflict by showing them linked in the end by their devotion to the "lord of the thieves."

Jacques Pouchepadass (1979) argues that in India criminal culture often involves the confusion of "two orders of reality, renunciation and delinquency" (134–35). And yet the renouncers renounce voluntarily "while criminal groupings are faced with forced exclusions." As it lays out the difficulties in Thugging, Ramasee does bring out quite clearly that the enemy of the Thugs, except for traitors among them, was the dominant culture from which they deviated and which they mistrusted.

"Everything organizes itself as if an analogous situation created analogous social forms," continues Pouchepadass, who uses the word *con-*

tamination to explain the relationship between renunciation, sects, and criminal groups:

> The multi-caste recruitment of [criminal groups] restores a social identity to individuals expelled from their groups of origin. [This social identity's] legitimacy stems from the intense adherence of its members to a system of values and norms based on predation, an adherence legitimized through a rite of passage. The group's criminal culture is equivalent to a vision of the world which basically expresses itself in religious terms; it has its own founding inspiring heroes. (Pouchepadass 1979, 134–35)

The Thug case belongs in this general configuration described by Pouchepadass. But it also differs from it in that the Thugs were possibly the heirs, the continuators of a sect. This has been suggested by Dirk H. A. Kolff, and it does appear that this is the way the Thugs looked upon themselves. And yet they were not a living sect.

In the course of the "Conversations," Sleeman asked them how it was they were getting hanged since the Goddess was protecting them. They answered that the Company was more powerful or luckier (*ikbal*) than they were. But they added a much more interesting comment. They all said they had stopped obeying the rules of the profession; their actions were no longer inspired by them. They were neglecting the rites, no longer consulting omens or performing the proper rituals, and they indiscriminately murdered Brahmans, women, and children. And they proved their point by telling of cases that led to hangings in which the prohibitions had been tossed by the wayside. Thugs from other regions, and mostly their own ancestors, used to follow these prescriptions. But Thugs no longer respected anything, their devotion had eroded, been neglected, forgotten. The ties linking them to Kali had been obscured: should they obey omens in the case of forbidden victims? They no longer knew; they argued among themselves. And yet they kept on claiming "that Davey instituted Thuggee and supported it as long as we attended to her omens, and observed the rules framed by the wisdom of our ancestors, nothing in the world can ever make us doubt" (Sleeman 1836, "Substance," 187). They saw themselves as links in a devotional filiation. But they were the end the line.

At the time they were speaking they constituted an open, competitive community to which society appeared similar to what Touraine (1974) would later depict as a market in which each individual seeks to profit from brutally pragmatic behavior aimed at concrete gains. The competition went hand in hand with doctrinal upheavals, rivalries, and conflicts between gangs and translated into their self-destruction in the confrontation with the British.

The system of distribution, the internal logic of their belief system, had collapsed: the goods stolen after the murders were no longer a divine payment in exchange for the sacrificial victims. The Thugs were taking without giving. Their religious construction had broken down; because they pushed the Goddess away from their actions, there only remained assassins and victims. At one point they had been authentic devotees, true *shaktas*. They were no longer so; they had been abandoned by their Goddess for having neglected the rules of their vocation. The cult of Bhowani did turn them into brigands.

In their own eyes the Thugs were one of the collective expressions of the "quest for salvation in the world" invented by *Bhakti* devotional thinkers. Yet it is possible that Thug practices and goals ended up standing for a drastic change within that quest itself. What could have caused them to pass from their quest for salvation to their unbounded lust for loot, from engaging in ritually controlled violent actions to committing mass crimes? How did it happen, and when? Our sources are mute on this point, but they do make it possible to see that this passage, this change, was latent in the parallel society established by Kali's exceptional devotees.

The individual quest for salvation in the world affirms the possibility of a direct relationship with the divine; it is in itself subversive of the Brahmanic order and the castes it implies as well as of the need for Brahmans' mediation in order for others to reach the divine. In the course of time, "the relation individual-collectivity has been managed in such a way as to lead to the softening of the radical opposition society/individual-out-of-the-world set forth by the inventors of renunciation in their challenge to Vedic ritual" (Reiniche 1995a, 10). One of the sociological consequences of this absorption of heterodox religious ways by Brahmanic orthodoxy is that the sect, in theory opened to all those sharing its views, tends to close up, to become itself a caste (as in the case of the Giri Sannayasi studied by Véronique Bouillier in Nepal).

There is an endless number of possible combinations of social and religious identities, as illustrated by the Muslim Bhartrharis Jogees of the Gorakhpur region in Uttar Pradesh. These hereditary renouncers, these ascetic householders who do marry and have children, lay claim outside of their sect and caste to a surprising third link, that of their double Shivaite and Sufi religious adherences (Champion 1995)! These multiple identities might appear contradictory and incoherent were we to forget that the society these groups are inhabiting is hierarchized in such a way that multiple identities appearing frozen in a paradoxical pile-up are actually deployed one by one as particular circumstances warrant.

This was true for the Thugs, who had perfectly incorporated this principle of shifting identities and viewpoints offered by Indian society according to the set, subset, and segment in which an individual might be situated. But the Thugs were in a state of rupture from the ordinary world because the transgressions, the horrendous liminal experiences, in which they indulged and the inversion of the values that they obeyed had anything but been tempered. Moreover, this rupture was hidden, subterranean: their alternate society and the violence of their cult were transported elsewhere, far from their villages in the intermediary space linking them. This necessary secrecy, which anchored their cohesiveness, was at the same time one of the factors in their decay, as it required they occupy positions that were extreme and antagonistic within society. Thugs had to be at once ordinary and extraordinary.

The cumulation of these two orders of identities, those of caste and sect, seems to have produced an effect similar to that in the examples I listed above: the Thugs' sect too became fragmented into castes. Some Thug groups, as for instance the Multanis, practiced endogamy. Individuals came to be defined by their Thug ancestors rather than by their voluntary joining of Thuggee. For instance, Feringheea, who objected to seeing gangs made up of all sorts of individuals lacking Thug pedigrees, adopted an attitude of exclusion characteristic of caste. The sect was recuperated, partially digested by the dominant caste model. This would explain the coexistence of these numerous "clans, sects and tribes" described by Sleeman as so many particular units with their regional linguistic legacy (we can read in Sleeman's appendix that a given Ramasee word can be pronounced a certain way in the Deccan, and another way in the North, and so on) and their own interpretation for their corpus of rules.

Geographical dispersion and attachment to ordinary society led to the disintegration of their community identity. The extreme tension between a quest for salvation requiring horrendous secret rites and the need to effect social practices conforming with the dominant social model in order to be able to pursue this quest might have induced the transformation of the devotees into habitual brigand-assassins (in the narrative of the Chinese pilgrim Hiouen Thsang's travels, as well as in folk tales and the theater, these devotees only perform sacrifices occasionally, sometimes only once yearly). As the Thugs acquired a caste identity and became integrated into society, their original sectarian identity might have gradually dissolved. This could be one of the sociological hypotheses—a new myth?—of this "fatal slope" that led them to mass serial crimes.

As to human sacrifice itself, the notions imbued with religion, derived from the verbs "to take" and "to give," might perhaps be its very distant origin. But if we look at it less speculatively and in a shallower time frame, it appears that sacrifice was probably dictated to the Thugs by these transgression cults dedicated to the Goddess in her terrible form.

Before massacring human beings, the Thugs sacrificed them to feed her so that she would feed them in turn. The traveler then bore the name of **neeamut,** a legitimate dead. However, at the moment of their encounter with the British, the Thugs blamed the neglect of the rules of Thuggee for the fall of their community: the practical function had won over the ideological one.

Part II
The Colonizers
between
Science and the
Imaginary

In this second part of the book I am leaving the accused so as to take a look at their judges and their representations of the Thugs, as well as at the avatars of these representations in the field of our own imaginings. Who were those men who succeeded in turning the assassins into perpetrators of the most odious crimes in the whole history of humankind, and in the process made those crimes fascinating? What images have they left us? Why those particular images? And are we still their captives?

William Sleeman was in a peculiar position. He was both an administrator and a policeman, and he presented himself as meting out justice for the sole goal of eradicating the Thugs. The campaign he orchestrated became his primary mission for several years, and his career turned so brilliant only because he was fighting this scourge of the empire so efficaciously—he had become its specialist. A great part of his prestige however, stemmed, not so much from his actions against the Thugs as from his pen, particularly his scholarly books. The first one, Ramaseeana, *in which he claimed to give the most objective and exhaustive known description of the assassins, spread his fame all the way to England.*

Three years later, in 1839, Meadows Taylor, an occasional collaborator of Sleeman in the territories of the nizam *of Hyderabad, published the first novel on the topic. His* Confessions of a Thug *made him famous both in India and in England, where Queen Victoria herself was eager to read his book. Continually republished since its first printing (as recently as 1986 by the venerable Oxford University Press), the book presented this fictional confession as if it were an authentic account.*

The two founding texts of "Thuggology" thus saw the light of day almost simultaneously. One had the trappings of science, while the other was opened to the imaginary. The ties uniting Ramaseeana and Confessions of a Thug raise the fascinating and still topical question of the contiguity, the link, between history and fiction. Born from the same impetuous movement of condemnation and curiosity as well as from the desire to share an uncommon experience, the monograph and the "true" novel pointed to different political and intellectual stakes as well as different narrative techniques and personalities. They produced representations of the Thugs that were blatantly horrifying and discretely contradictory.

These unresolved contradictions within the discourses on their origins might be one of the reasons why present-day authors of literary and film fiction in the West still find them interesting. The metamorphoses of the Thug topos show the variations in Western perception of the Orient as well as the history of this perception. Though the assassins still appear as the symbol of an irreducible and terrifying otherness, the evil they embody took on a political coloration even as cracks appeared in the colonial illusion of progress and modernity.

Before I started the study of these past and present representations, I wanted to get better acquainted with their initiators, Sleeman and Taylor. Comparing these two colonialist exemplars enabled me to uncover the relationship between the cleavages of colonial society and the order of its intellectual priorities, to define its center, the dwelling place of liberal ideology, of individualism and science, and its periphery, where the imaginary and ambivalent idols of Victorian morality were relegated. The epistemology of their discourse on the Thugs involved researching the means available to Sleeman and Taylor to realize their meeting with India. It involved getting to know their links to their country of origin as well as to the society of their temporary residence.

FOUR   William Sleeman and Meadows Taylor

Parallel Biographies

Malcolm predicted that even though the conquest had been relatively easy, the consolidation of the conquered empire was going to be hard. William Sleeman and Meadows Taylor help us understand why and how conquered India remained so. These two individuals out of a mere two thousand were striking representatives of the forgers of this consolidation in the 1830s. Members of this "handful of British," to use the favorite expression of the time, were leading one of the biggest armies in the world and used it to disarm and control the country. Sleeman and Taylor, even while occupying various positions in the civil administration, never ceased to fight rebels and brigands and remained connected to the army all their lives long: the first ended up a general, the second a captain.

Circumstances kept their experience from being straightforward. They were no longer the glorious conquerors of the preceding administration. Their mission was neither simple nor easy. They were expected to administer and make the ground fructify, as well as to impose colonial authority in far-away districts that shortly before were obeying other powers. As long as they followed their government's directives and their superiors' occasional reports deemed their work satisfactory, they enjoyed a great deal of leeway. Their happiness, their personal interest, and the aims of . the state were an almost perfect match, even if impatience, at times frustration, occasionally troubled this harmony. Like most of their fellows, they were aware and proud of their responsibilities and were confident they were achieving their goals: they all reported that the people they were administering were holding them in high esteem. These were authentic and fervent colonizers.

Taylor's and Sleeman's careers were quite different: the first was to be for the whole of his life a "local recruit" assigned to the territories of he *nizam* of Hyderabad. The men of the Company were never to look upon him as one of their own. In addition to his lack of professional and moral recognition, Taylor was materially less favored than Sleeman. This latter, who joined the colonial army by the front door, found his actions rewarded with higher and higher ranks as he was entrusted political missions of the highest import for the empire. Yet Taylor did experience some fame thanks to his talent as novelist, and we still know him today mainly through his novel on the Thugs. Sleeman's many reports and essays are at present of interest only to historians of colonialism, as the "truth" of India they propounded was rejected long ago.

SIMILAR LIFESTYLES

The Threat of Death

These differences between our two characters partly disappear in the realm of a private life ruled by natural constraints and social usages. Among the constraints the most important was incontestably the constant threat of dying: chronic fevers (dysentery, malaria), riding accidents, and exhaustion regularly brought them to the brink of death. India was very harsh. In mid-century only one civil servant out of seven lived to go back home and enjoy retirement. Sleeman told that during the war in Nepal in 1816 three hundred men of his regiment, stricken with fever, had to leave the battlefield; five European out of ten died (Sleeman 1915, xxi).

Death could at times come in other guises. Taylor admitted he had been prey to uncontrollable agitation when, using a daring ploy, he kidnapped the rebellious rajah Narayan Rao from a fort filled with armed men ready to fire at the slightest sign from their leader. Sleeman escaped three attempts on his life, the first one, at Lucknow, thought to be by a Thug. They both lived to a ripe old age after having escaped many dangers, most of which were anything but picturesque, and they lost many of their children, close kin, and friends. Taylor's wife died in 1844 after only eleven years of marriage. To these losses and physical trials we have to add painful separations from young surviving children who had to be sent on a six-month journey to Europe to get a good education and, mainly, to escape the deadly epidemics and the debilitating heat of India. In the end, both Sleeman and Taylor set sail for England for health reasons. Sleeman did not make it: he died off the coast of Ceylon on 24 January 1856.

A Disciplined Way of Life

They were both faced with similar hardships while driven by the ambition to succeed, and they shared a similar discipline in their way of life. They were strict in a social milieu in which laxness was the rule. Fanny Parks, always looking for the picturesque, wrote:

> What can be more wretched than the life of a private soldier in the East? His profession employs but a little of his time. During the heat of the day, he is forced to remain within the intensely hot barrack-rooms; heat produces thirst and idleness and discontent. He drinks arrack like a fish, and soon finds life a burden of existence, to escape from it transportation appears a blessing. The great source of all his misery is the cheapness of arrack mixed with *datura*. (Parks 1850, 1:149)

Sleeman and Taylor were not only sober "even at the risk of appearing antisocial" but they didn't gamble either, even though Taylor claimed it to be the general practice among his fellow administrators (Taylor 1986b, chapter 4). Their dislike of the social circuit ran deep: Sleeman complained about the duty young officers of the Company had of entertaining the wives and female kin of Company members (Tuker 1961, 28), and Taylor appeared to enjoy only salons in London.

It is true that the solitude reigning in their districts was not conducive to parties. Maybe they were presenting as personal choice something that circumstances were forcing on them? Whatever the case, they frequented mostly restricted circles of friends to whom they were remarkably loyal. As was the practice among the members of the company, these friends were professional colleagues, often relatives who had also chosen the India adventure:[1] the doctor Henry Spry, whom Sleeman invited to see Thugs being hanged, was his cousin. His nephew James Sleeman succeeded him in the post of general director for the suppression of Thugs and dacoits. William Palmer, who was to be Taylor's assistant at Nurdroog in 1856, was his brother-in-law. This moderate sociability and these frugal habits enabled them to be almost totally devoted to work. We have Taylor's possibly embellished description of his daily schedule, which he sent to his father:

> Up at 5 A.M., and go out about the survey of the roads. In by 8 o'clock and answer letters; English and Mahratta, till ten; bathe and breakfast over at eleven. Then to cutcherry work, trials, etc. till 6 P.M., without stirring—often, indeed, until seven. Dine and sit an hour or so with Palmer, if he is there, or with some native friend, by way of a rest, which brings up the time to half-past eight or nine. Then to my room, and work at translations or other business till eleven or twelve. Count up all this and you will see there is no time for anything except hard work. (Taylor 1986b, 265–66)

Learning

The two men rested only when they were terribly ill or exhausted, and their few, but long, breaks, matched the intensity of their efforts. Taylor spent three years in London; Sleeman left for a year (1835–1836) to Simla, in the Himalayas, "seeking his health."

They sometimes went hunting bears or tigers or wild boars; Taylor painted and stuffed birds for his ornithologist uncle and studied astronomy. Sleeman became passionately interested in geology, economics, and utilitarian philosophy. Both came to be quite interested in botany. These self-educated men kept on learning. They studied Indian languages, of course, but also European ones: Taylor spent his evenings at Hingoli, "a station with no distractions," to read Italian and French along with his wife, while Sleeman practiced French, perhaps a bit too much, with his wife Amélie, who was supposed to have spoken English very poorly.

Their thirst for knowledge was boundless, but the ways they looked upon their learning were different. Taylor regretted never having received a formal education and often felt lacking in comparison to the educated men whose company he frequented. If only, he bemoaned, "I had been among such men always. . . . I should have been very different!" (Taylor 1986b, 84). He felt this was a lack he could never fill. Sleeman, just as driven to knowledge, believed he was in the possession of a substantial portion of it and indignantly berated his colleagues for not following his example.

> The ignorance of the first principles of political economy among European gentlemen of otherwise first-rate education and abilities in India is lamentable. . . . No excuse can be admitted for a civil functionary who is so ignorant, since a thorough acquaintance with the principles of political economy must be, and indeed, always is considered as an essential branch of that knowledge which is to fit him for public employment in India. (Sleeman 1915, 157)

Like Taylor he admired thinkers, but unlike the novelist he counted himself as one of them, in his words, "a thinking man."

Finally, letter writing used up a good part of their daily schedule. They communicated locally with colleagues and superiors, and with family members in England. The letters Sleeman wrote his sister during his Himalayan stay were to be published in a seven-hundred-page volume! Taylor claimed to have written, between 1853 and 1857, 34,474 letters, of which nine thousand between himself and his assistant were written, of course, in Marathi! Was he under the spell of Indian mythology when he laid claim to this astronomical figure?

This is thus the thread that helps us imagine the seasons of Sleeman and Taylor, whose courage, determination, curiosity, and colonialist choices are representative of those of the Europeans ruling India at the time.

THE PRIVATE SPHERE

In order to complete these portraits I still need to make an incursion into the more secret domain of their affective and sexual investments. These are seldom mentioned in the sources at my disposal, so I will be brief.

Sleeman and Social Usages

In his forties Sleeman married at Jabalpur a nineteen-year-old French woman of noble origin, Amélie Joséphine, the daughter of Count Blondin de Fontenne, who had to abandon his extensive properties and flee the French Revolution. The couple had many children, including numerous daughters, though few of them survived, and two sons, of which only one survived. In *Ramaseeana*, he evoked the Thug nightmares that pursued his wife, who had actually slept on the graves of murdered Thug victims. But there was no place for her in that kind of book. I would have expected to find more traces of her in the book he wrote during their long stay in Simla. But he alluded to her presence only once, to mention that she was asleep! "After the dust of Tehri, . . . the quiet morning I spent in this secluded spot under the shade of some beautiful trees, with the surviving canary singing, my boy playing and my wife sleeping off the fatigues of her journey, was to me most delightful" (Sleeman 1915, 147–48). This might be pure coincidence, but I am tempted to see here the mark of a puritanical attitude that disappears when sexuality is no longer a factor. He dedicated this book to his sister and wrote in it that the greatest source of pleasure for the British exiled in India are letters from their sisters.

His relationship with God seems to have to have lain midway between the conjugal bond, private and secret, and the sororal bond, private but proclaimed. Religion was as much a matter of personal conscience as of conventional usage. The norm, he claimed, is to believe what your mother taught you.

Romantic Taylor

Sleeman hid his feelings behind social conventions. For Taylor, in contrast, affectivity and emotions were the powerful wellspring of his public and private life: he did not hide them even while being prisoner of a Victorian rhetoric at once exalted and prudish.

At age twenty-five, he married his great friend Palmer's daughter. She too was of noble descent, though not of the same status as Amélie Blondin de Fontenne: "Mr Palmer's father, who had been secretary to Warren Hastings, had taken part in all the most eventful scenes of early Anglo-Indian history, and had married, as was very usual then among English gentlemen, a lady of high rank, one of the Princesses of the royal house of Delhi" (Taylor 1986b, 68). Taylor and his wife had several children, of whom a number died in infancy. About his wife's death in 1844 after a sudden illness, Taylor wrote: "Of that time I cannot write. It is many years ago, and all the scene with its sad details rises fresh before me. I tried humbly to bow to the will of God; but I had lost in her not only my loving and beloved wife, but my steady, true friend, my comfort and my happiness" (Taylor 1986b, 163).

Some years later, on the road to Hyderabad, one night when he had trouble sleeping, he had a premonitory vision: a face and a silhouette he had once loved appeared to him, but old and sad.

> The dress was white, and seemed covered with a profusion of lace, and glistened in the bright moonlight. The arms were stretched out, and a low plaintive cry of "Do not let me go! Do not let me go!" reached me. I sprang forward, but the figure receded, growing fainter and fainter, till I could see it no longer, but the low sad tones still sounded. . . . I wrote to my father. . . . He wrote back to me in these words: "Too late, my dear son. On the very day of the vision you describe to me, she was married." (Taylor 1986b, 203–4)

It was possibly from his mother that he inherited his premonitory dreams, his oaths, and his romantic impulses. He had to leave her while still very young and was never to see her again. She remained for him an object of adoration and love all of his life. As was the case for Sleeman, the mother was the one who taught the young child about God. The memory he retained is in no way lukewarm or rational: "From her I learnt the doctrines of the Church and the sublime sacrifice and atonement of the Christ; and how lovingly and carefully she taught us will, I am sure, never be forgotten by my brother or myself, and led to the feelings I have all my life experienced of love and humble devotion to our glorious Church" (Taylor 1986b, 10).

During his happy and unhappy periods he evoked either his mother or God, or both together, with effusion and resignation. Taylor was marked by the specific sensitivity of the evangelical current of Christian renewal that had originated in the eighteenth century. The evangelicals held a dark vision of human beings as driven by appetites and conventions. The sin that lay in them could only be neutralized, set aside, through the individual's striving toward God. Neither priest nor ritual could be of any help (Stokes 1959, 27–30). Only a personal journey involving the physical and mental experience of evil could lead to the illumination of a spiritual rebirth. "Work requiring industry, frugality, and perseverance, was an end in its own right." To the adherents of this militant religion, this fighting gospel of the time "also afforded the material means of furthering the Kingdom on earth" (Stokes 1959, 30).

As Taylor himself wrote, his mother was puritanical. His grandfather was strongly antimilitaristic, and as a child Taylor was cruelly beaten in every school he attended. There is no doubt that he was brought up with the strict moral principles he adhered to. For instance, he was scrupulously honest, which caused the *nizam's* minister, Chandroo Lall, no end of merriment. His belief that life was controlled by secret causes outside the realm of reason, his hyperemotionalism, and his taste for the supernatural, for dreams and prophesies, went hand in hand with his moral rigidity. This sort of austere education aimed mainly at "saving one's soul" often led to manifestations of collective hysteria, as shown by the following strange episode. At the time, Taylor was fifteen years old and worked for Yates and Brothers at Liverpool:

> I was returning to the office late one evening, when, passing by the door of a chapel, and hearing groans and cries, I looked in. A person stationed at the door invited me to enter and "save my soul." The place, a large one, was in profound darkness; a candle here and there only made the gloom more impenetrable. People of both sexes were sitting in the pews, and shrill piercing cries arose of "Save me!" "I'm going to hell!" "I'm damned!" "The devil has me!" "I'm burning, burning!" "Go away Satan!" "Jesus has got me!", and the like, with prayers so profane and shocking that I dare not write them down. Sometimes one got up, man or woman, and gave his or her experience of sins and crimes, horrible to hear, but which, nevertheless, fascinated me. I know not how long I stayed, but a girl sat down by me at last and whispered: "Come and kiss me, you beautiful boy—come away." I gained the door, and fled rapidly in the darkness up the street. (Taylor 1986b, 12–13)

This unforgettable incident might have contributed some of the motives at play in certain of the passages in the *Confessions of a Thug*. The pressing and dangerous love the beautiful Shurfun feels for the main character evokes the erotic and forbidden demand made of him by the strange girl in the church.

The virile image Sleeman gives of the Thugs is quite different. They are only fleetingly interested in beautiful adventuresses. Their wives occupy in the shadows the traditional roles of faithful spouses and housewives, and they embodied the stable values of marriage and reproduction, which seemed to resonate in the apparition of Sleeman's sleeping wife, Amélie de Fontenne, in his book. In many respects, Sleeman seems to have anticipated the traits of Victorian respectability while Taylor reflected the murky desires it hid.

God and the Colonizers

"Moral independence," so prized by the British elites, "enshrined in their laws, constitution and protestant religion" (Bayly 1990b, 151), leads to seeing individual success as a manifestation of divine approval. God was visible in history, particularly "in the miraculous subjugation of India by a handful of English" (Stokes 1959, 30–31). Sleeman and Taylor, each in their own way, made of God the witness of their work. They offered him the fruits of their labor: the extermination of the Thugs, the happiness of the natives, and the fertility of the land.

Sleeman's self-satisfaction did not come solely from his class background and successful career. It also came from his conviction that a distant and benevolent God approved of him, particularly of his attack on idolatrous assassins. In his "Conversations" with them he was told: "If God helps you, you'll succeed, but the territory is vast and favors the Thugs." Sleeman protested. His own will was one with the divine will because man is the repository of reason in the image of God.

For Taylor, on the contrary, his personal fate escaped him; his terrible God was never far away, particularly in his absolute power over life and death.

The Neo-Nabobs: Two Images

First the official image: in 1856 the future empress of India bestowed the cross of the knightly order of Bath on William Sleeman and expressed the intention of giving him the title of baron upon his return to England. Taylor too, late in life, was the beneficiary of this royal meritocracy. In 1869 he bragged that his work "was delightfully interrupted by an announcement from the Secretary of State that Her Most Gracious Majesty the Queen had been pleased, on the 2nd of June, to appoint me a 'Companion of the Most Exalted Order of the Star of India'" (Taylor 1986b, 369–70). Victoria did recognize that the two men were among the best of her subordinates.

Then the hidden image: our two characters were almost at the end of their stay in India. Denis Kincaid, a member of the Company, reminisced about Taylor:

At Shorapur ruled Meadows Taylor, enormous and benign, relishing the devotion and gratitude of a province and the various pleasures of a well-stocked harem. He sat at his ease in a great cane chair, puffing at his hookah, fanned by *chowries* and thought of Lady Blessington's salon and the evening when he met that odd Louis Napoleon. . . . He enjoyed his visits to England, he liked gratifying the ladies with new and ever-stranger stories of India, and he was flattered by the astonishment and awe with which his white *topi* hung with gold braid was greeted in the streets of Europe. But he was happy to be back again in his kingdom, surrounded by his subjects and his girls, all rivals for his favours. When my grandfather stayed with him, the old gentleman was particularly satisfied with the newest recruit to his household, a fifteen-year-old Maratha girl who was uncommonly skillful at "mulling" his eyebrows. (Kincaid 1973, 175)

The mellifluous Taylor, surrounded by his young servant girls, exiled in his distant kingdom, here again let his status of employee without a contract show through. He continued the despised nabob tradition of the preceding generations, to which belonged his wife's grandfather, Palmer, the husband of a Delhi princess. In contrast, the political agents, residents, and other officials of the Company bemoaned the political fate that forced them to engage in ostentatious parades and other displays in the style of native nabobs. In spite of their avowed scorn for them, the colonizers claimed they were forced to engage in them so as to rival the native magnates and impose their authority on them. Sleeman thus dismissed as "mere trifle" his official arrival into Lucknow accompanied by a parade of three hundred elephants in splendid armor along with three regiments led by European officers.

Sleeman had the long-term nickname among Company people of "Thuggee Sleeman," an oxymoron linking the crime and its judge. Taylor claimed that his own troops acclaimed him as *Mahadeo baba ke jai,* "long live the son of the god Mahadeo!" Whether true or the stuff of legends, Sleeman's and Taylor's nicknames are like the signatures that botanists used to attribute to plants. They show how they were perceived and point, at least in part, to their very different visions of India.

WRITING AND POWER

In addition to family and social factors, personality and ambition also played a decisive role in the disparities of their trajectories. Writing was incontestably one of the means at the service of both their ambitions. At that time it was the activity needed for communicating at a distance and a powerfully efficacious weapon for those knowing how to manipulate it. Sleeman used it in all its registers—anonymous letters, reports, correspondence, and books. Every one of his missions, thoughts, discoveries, the various categories of Thugs including the Budhuk dacoits, the poisoners, and the children's kidnappers, Ricardo's theory of rents, and wolf-children, all were the objects of individual reports that were often published. His biographer, Sir Francis Tuker, writes that before being given the leadership of the anti-Thug campaign, he literally flooded the government with letters, so much so that, foreshadowing his future role, his correspondents gave him the nickname of "Thuggee Sleeman."

Writing was part of his pattern of action. The three main books he wrote were milestones to the three great stages of his career. In 1836, at the height of his victory over the Thugs, he published *Ramaseeana*. That same year he began his monumental work on India in the form of letters to his sister, *Rambles and Recollections of an Indian Official*, which was to be published in 1844, four years prior to his being made Resident of Lucknow. Finally, in 1852, while he was resident, he supervised the first edition of his travel diary in Awadh, *A Journey through the Kingdom of Oude*, which like his preceding book was almost seven hundred pages long. In all three works he focused on denouncing India's troubles. *Rambles*, like the spandrel beam of a church, stood in the middle position between the two other books. This middle consisted in the list of all the ills India was prey to. *Ramaseeana* and *A Journey*, on either side of *Rambles*, represented the extreme state of decadence, of barbarism, of decrepitude to which India's main ills had led: religious fanaticism and oriental despotism, crime and anarchy—all this, of course, before to the authors came to the rescue!

The Company's man devoted a large part of his life to thinking in terms of his own public relations, of showing off his knowledge and ensuring acknowledgment. In his work he laid out his political and intellectual orientations, practiced reason, and paraded his knowledge. He demonstrated the validity and the interest of his ideas by his own actions, which he either described or anticipated. He was sovereign in the police sphere in which he operated, and in *Ramaseeana* he dwelled on his victory over a secret society infiltrating the colony from one end to another. In *Rambles* the panoptic observer of India laid out what needed to be done for its future. In the devastated kingdom of Awadh, he was the eye of authority itself. He was engaged in the struggle for control of history—that is, the quest for and the maintenance and reproduction of domination. Each of his works provided him with the opportunity of shedding his old social identity and claiming a new one, thus to change his relations with others. His institutional identity was in a constant state of progression and soon left far behind his earlier identities as a cadet of Baraset, and then as a humble magistrate overwhelmed with work in his first post in the newly annexed provinces of central India.

The intellectual and political ambition of this historical agent,[2] receiving and diffusing the lights of power and progress, make comparison with Taylor almost irrelevant. But it is interesting, precisely in that this exemplary and fervent colonialist, who too ended up decorated by the queen of England, remained obscure. He regretted it and believed it could have been otherwise. He claimed that if he had not been transferred to another post at the very moment he discovered the assassins he would have been "the first to reveal the horrible crime of thuggee to the world." He was cheated of this by Sleeman, by the "good fortune of the major." This incident, one of many he recalls bitterly in his autobiography, was a consequence of his status as a local recruit. This status not only was frustrating, but also alienated him. He shared the goals and values of the men of the Company, but they treated him as an inferior. He protested only timidly the injustices he suffered as he depended on those men and identified with them. He worked night and day; he wanted to prove that he was their equal, but he was never to be. He then went native and turned nabob.

My speculations fit in well with his strange writing career, which starts with *Confessions of a Thug* in 1839, which he followed with a silence of more than twenty-five years. In London, M. Bentley, publisher to the queen, accepted his book to be published, but with changes: as Taylor notes,

> Much had to be curtailed and condensed; a great deal was pronounced too horrible to publish. . . . Her Most Gracious Majesty the Queen had directed sheets, as they were revised, to be sent to her—and having become interested in the work, wished for further supplies as soon as possible. . . . Returning to London in Spring, I found my book had been received with much greater interest and success than I have ever ventured to hope for; and not only did the London papers and periodicals take it up, but the provincial press teemed with flattering reviews and long extracts from it. It was curious to hear people wondering over the book and discussing it; and evidently the subject was a new sensation for the public. It passed rapidly through the first edition and a second was in preparation. (Taylor 1986b, 117, 120)

Thus Taylor got to experience glory through his novel and thanks to the horrible assassins. But this had no effect on his colonial career, and upon his return to the territories in his charge he found himself still in the same state of undesirability as he had been in previously. He was correspondent for the *Times* in India, but he gradually abandoned his pen to devote himself exclusively to his job. He began to write again only after leaving the colony. His production then became very abundant. *Tippoo Sultan* is a history of the kingdom of Mysore. *Ralph Darnell* (1865) is the story of a young Britisher seeking his fortune in India, working for the Company! In *Seeta* (1872) the author adopted an Indian viewpoint and described the struggle to get rid of the British yoke. *Tara: A Mahratta Tale* (1874) is the story of the conflict opposing the Hindu Mahratta kingdom to the Moghul. *A Noble Queen, a Romance of Indian History* (1878) deals with the history of the rivalries between the Moghuls and the Muslims in the kingdoms of the Deccan.

These late works were certainly not a springboard to the official status that had been denied him and for which he had stopped yearning, and neither were they a platform to speak to the powerful of this world and debate the great ideas agitating them at the time. His *Confessions of a Thug* was not aimed at denouncing the degradation of India. From his very first work, Taylor did not link his writing with the system of action of the dominant power and ideology. He constructed a parallel universe that did not openly challenge the dominant order, but that, nonetheless, invalidated its prejudices.

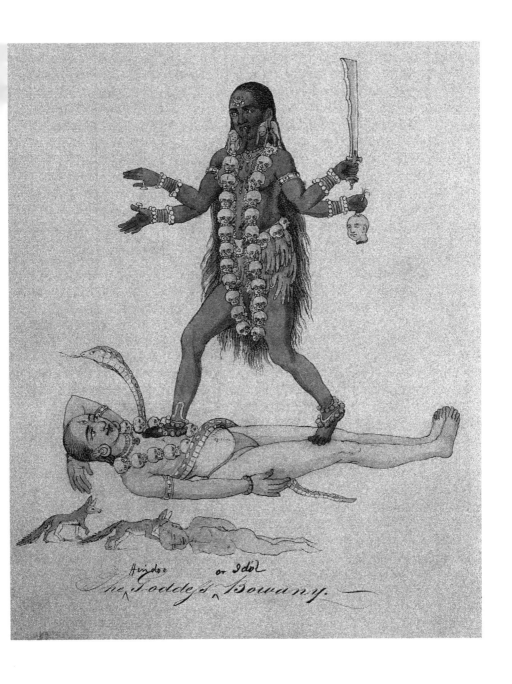

Drawing of Shiva, the ascetic god, trampled by the goddess Kali. He is called Shiva-shava (*Shava* means "corpse"). With her two right hands, Kali repels fear and conjures up strength. Artist and date unknown. Reprinted by permission of the British Library (Paton's papers, Add. 41300, no. 58824).

Drawing of Thugs strangling a traveler on horseback. Artist and date unknown. Reprinted by permission of the British Library (Paton's papers, Add. 41300, no. 41188).

Drawing of Thugs piercing dead travelers with their swords before taking them to the burial place chosen by the gravedigger (*lugha* in Ramasee). Artist and date unknown. Reprinted by permission of the British Library (Paton's papers, Add. 41300, no. E 29361).

Drawing of Thugs gouging out the eyes and piercing the bodies of dead travelers, either to make sure they are dead or to please Kali, who "adores blood." Artist and date unknown. Reprinted by permission of the British Library (Paton's papers, Add. 41300, no. E 34077).

Drawing of travelers' corpses being loaded up as so many bundles before burial. Artist and date unknown. Reprinted by permission of the British Library (Paton's papers, Add. 41300, no. E 34079).

Drawing of murder technique used by the Thugs: the strangler (*kabita*) is assisted by the holders of the feet or the hands (*shumseea* in Ramasee). Artist and date unknown. Reprinted by permission of the British Library (Paton's papers, Add. 41300, no. E 34078).

Drawing of Thug "dismembers" (*kuthowa* in Ramasee) performing their appointed task on murdered travelers. Artist and date unknown. Reprinted by permission of the British Library (Paton's papers, Add. 41300, no. E 58825).

Drawing of Thugs kneeling in a circle and performing the *kote* ceremony. Artist and date unknown. Reprinted by permission of the British Library (Paton's papers, Add. 41300, no. E 58823).

William Sleeman and Thug Science

Rambles and Recollections of an Indian Official, published in 1844, mark-ed an important stage in Sleeman's career. He traded in his identity as Thug specialist and policeman for that of specialist of India. In this work he laid out his vision of the subcontinent in which he had by then lived for thirty-five years. He discussed major economic, political, and moral questions and offered concrete and theoretical solutions to them. His ob-servations, analyses, and reflections put him at the heart of an intellectual space shared by the colonizers. They enabled him to fully identify with the ruling class, and at the same time, they give us access to it.

The study of representations I am starting here requires getting to know the main traits of this work. *Rambles,* published after *Ramaseeana,* his monograph on the Thugs, constructed a frame of reference. Sleeman, the ardent defender of liberal ideology, described ills and advocated solu-tions for an India in which the Thugs were very much alive. We can get a better understanding of why he made them his target in the light of what we learn in *Rambles* about his interests, his value system, his certitude about the positive nature of colonialism, and his devotion to science.

SLEEMAN AND INDIA

The Land and the People

I am much attached to the agricultural classes of India generally, and I have found among them some of the best men I have ever known. The peasantry in India have generally very good manners, and are exceedingly intelligent, from having so much leisure and unreserved and easy intercourse with those above them. (Sleeman 1915, 59)

In *Rambles*, Sleeman was full of praise for the "peasants." Land was one of his great preoccupations and one of his most regular sources of pleasure. Not only did this passion stem from his family legacy, but it was also part of the culture of the "internal empire," as Christopher Bayly puts it. There had been a convergence of economic interests shared by Protestant Scottish and Irish elites and English ones, and this convergence came with shared intellectual interests that included agriculture. In his *The Gentleman Farmer*, the Scot Lord Kames presented agriculture as the ideal condition for a gentleman because it stemmed from a natural right and made it possible for him to avoid the corruption exemplified by the "ardour of the Indian Nabob" (Bayly 1990b, 85).

Sleeman and Taylor, issued from the military class, both wished to belong to the civil service. In addition to their personal motives, they understood that the future belonged to surveyors' tools and accounting books. Belonging to the civil service involved participating in the most determining enterprise of their century, the one aimed at "preserving" the empire, as Malcolm euphemistically wrote in his call for a mode of organization strong enough to defeat archaism and disorder. Sleeman's attribution of remarkable qualities to peasants might have stemmed from his and fellow colonizers' conviction that the colonial edifice rested entirely on a foundation of land taxes. The whole of the radical current dominating the decade of the 1830s rested on the esoteric claim that a land tax was "the most legitimate fund for the payment of [the state's] . . . public establishments" (Sleeman 1915, 571). What does this mean?

THE LIBERAL SCHEME

The British were actually advocating a principle that had been part of the Moghul tradition. They used it on their own behalf as they extended to all their territories the privilege of collecting land taxes, which they had first obtained in Bengal. But the colonizers' underlying theoretical and ideological views were different from those of the Moghuls. James Mill had described Hindus as feudal or semifeudal, and they were seen as "half-civilized" members of "stationary" Asiatic peoples (Stocking 1986, 44). It was thought that in order for a subsistence economy to be rapidly transformed into a market one, landed property had to acquire a monetary value, and individual owners had to be free to sell, buy, or mortgage it. This "liberating vision of economy as a private market domain, a vision which goes along with the expansion of the state public sphere" (Pouchepadass 1991, 44), intersected with three core notions: private property, free exchange, and the theory of land rent.

PRIVATE PROPERTY. The aim of Sleeman's struggle against Thugs and brigands was to protect private property. The thrust of his anti-Thug campaign lay in "the protection of human life and private property." Lord Kames's creed, embodied by his gentlemen farmers, was a source of order, prosperity and happiness. Anything that threatened it had to be eliminated. On many other occasions Sleeman's analyses aimed at proving that all evil stemmed from the fact that private property was not solidly established. During the great famine of 1833 (one of the years at the height of the Thug trials), in Bundelkhand, he blamed the native government for the situation as it was the sort that "allows no man the free enjoyment of property" (Sleeman 1915, 148).

FREE TRADE. The Thugs' looting hindered the free circulation of goods. Free trade was the second of the three leitmotivs of the dominating liberal current, and Sleeman passionately praised its virtues. When the same famine reached Sagar, Sleeman the ethnographer noted that Indians were less savage than he had thought as they died with "the patient resignation with which the poor people submit to their fate . . . and the almost absence of those revolting acts which have characterized the famines . . . such as the living feeding on the dead, and mothers devouring their own children" (Sleeman 1915, 152). Sleeman the economist, on the other hand, condemned the behavior of an officer of the Company who, out of fear of letting people die, "had been continually interfering to coerce sales and regulate prices, and continually aggravating the evils of the dearth by so doing" (Sleeman 1915, 156). Sleeman described himself, yet again anonymously, as the man of the hour. He decided that the laws of supply and demand had to be maintained without the interference of anyone in a position of authority.

> The magistrate now issued a formal proclamation, pledging himself to see that such granaries should be as much respected as any other property in the city—that every man might keep his grain and expose it for sale, wherever and whenever he pleased. . . . After issuing this proclamation about noon, he had his police establishments augmented, and so placed and employed as to give to the people entire confidence in the assurances conveyed in it. . . . In the morning the bazaars were all supplied, and every man who had money could buy as much as he pleased. (Sleeman 1915, 154–55)

It was thought that this imposed free trade, obeying the objective laws of the market by excluding the moneyless, promoted the development of trade and industry, another lively source of happiness for the colonizers. India was a merchant kingdom and had to remain so. No tax on goods should hinder its flowering. As James Mill wrote in 1832:

Nine-tenths probably of the revenue of the Governement of India is derived from the rent of land, never appropriated to individuals, and always considered to be the property of governement, and to me that appears to be one of the most fortunate circumstances that can occur in any country because in consequence of this the wants of the state are supplied really and truly without taxation. (cited in Stokes 1959, 91)

Sleeman was a faithful disciple of Mill's ideas when, early in his career, he replied to a question about why he liked India by saying that besides fresh air, what pleased him the most were the "light taxes" (Sleeman 1915, 485).

A NEW LAW OF ECONOMICS. The third part of the creed came from the discovery of a new law of economics elaborated first by Malthus and then by Ricardo and which they called land rent. Sleeman was familiar with it and wrote an essay on it. It was the law of land rent that made light taxation possible, but it had to involve the existence of private property. James Mill and all the enthusiastic Benthamites saw colonial India as a laboratory where this discovery could be applied, a discovery that took on alchemical properties as it was said that this law could change sand into gold. What did it stand for and to what did it lead?

Land rent was what was left after the cost of labor, the investments (seeds to plant and so on), and the interest on capital have been subtracted. It was the surplus, the net profit that usually belonged to the landowner. The colonial state decided to appropriate this for itself even while guaranteeing the landowner the permanent ownership of the difference between this net profit and what the state took. The newness here was that this profit was calculated in currency and not in kind: it was a monetary sum whose value depended on the market and that was no longer a part of the products of the soil as had traditionally been the case.

The precise calculation of this rent could be based only on rights to land that clearly differentiated between private and collective customary rights. But this distinction was not made in India, where these rights were multiple, interwoven, uncertain, and precarious, "made on different grounds, some by rates of produce, some on estimates of gross produce, taking a half or a third as the right to Government; others on a classification of soils and rates applied, some on the year's produce, a great number on bargain," and so on (Fraser, cited in Stokes 1959, 98). Compiling property registries and deeds involved long and intensive investigations on the ground. This made for the Herculean task of Sleeman, tax collector, as well as the endless work days of Taylor in his early posts.

"If the whole of the rent of land were taken by the state it would not diminish in any way the profits of the Cultivator" (Ryan to Bentinck, cited in Stokes 1959, 132). Yet this rent that British thinkers saw as panacea led to disagreement at the level of its application, for James Mill, along with Ricardo, thought the state should be able to benefit from the expected rise of surplus taken in by the owner, and thus the rent should be revised often. But both these thinkers were at the same time deeply anti-aristocratic. So they felt that the state, holding the "natural monopoly" of the rent, must address itself uniquely to those small landholders known as *ryots* in India.

This viewpoint was shared by T. Munro in Madras, Elphinstone in Maharashtra (both Scottish) and Metcalf in the newly acquired provinces in the Deccan. They were opposed to the system devised by Cornwallis in which the class of people collecting large amounts of revenue from land were made into the landowners and favored interlocutors of the British tax collectors at the time of the Permanent Settlement in Bengal. In contrast, these three administrators wanted a more personal relationship between Company agents and the less-favored strata of small landholders. Bentinck too spurned the great landholders, the *zamindars* and *talukdars*, these "nonproductive hordes," as artificial creations of the Moghul empire and preferred the peasantry. But, as all the historians of the Raj point out today, there were large gaps between these theoretical declarations and the often flowery rhetoric in which they are couched, and what was actually accomplished in reality. After some attempts and a few disasters, Bentinck realized that if he tried to get rid of all the intermediary classes between the colonial power and the small landholders, this would be likely cause widespread protest. A first compromise was agreed upon (Regulation IX, 1833); it sought the middle ground between principles and customs, between utopia and actual situations. The British gave up assessing the yearly tax on individual farms on the basis of their production for the year and instead opted for a tax amount based on the land taxes paid for the previous twenty years. The tax collector's interlocutor was no longer the small peasant, but were groups of villages put under the authority of an intermediary appointed and paid by the state. Finally, the sum owed was fixed for thirty years. Sleeman went along with this approach, which was said to be conservative.

THE POOR GET POORER

What were the economic and social consequences of this land policy?

These consequences varied and can only be uncovered region by region, according to the quality of the soil, social organization and its relation with the various colonial and local authorities, and the personal philosophies and practices of the British functionaries in charge. Eric Stokes, in his study of the economic causes of the Mutiny in northern

India, showed the surprisingly large economic variations between the regions of Delhi, Meerut, and Muzaffarnagar (Stokes 1986). Compromises between the colonial state and local conditions took a variety of forms, so that even though we might partly believe Taylor's boast of having considerably added to the revenues of the state, enlarged areas under cultivation, and satisfied all concerned in the Berar area, Sumit Guha (1985) is pretty convincing too. He is far from sharing Taylor's optimism, as shown in his study of the agrarian situation in the Bombay area between 1818 and 1841.

Since the fall of the *peshwa* the demand for agricultural products had greatly fallen, and this had been followed by a decline in prices. In 1823 Pringle, the assistant tax collector for the Pabal district, mentioned peasants who were selling their grain at half the price they did in the previous twenty years. One of the reasons was the dislocation of the *peshwa's* court, which ended numerous local crafts, particularly weaving. Cultivated areas stagnated as peasants left the lands of the superimposed state to find lands free of taxes. Tax collectors zealously tried to increase land revenue in response to their superiors' sole focus on maximizing it: "If there be no decrease of revenue and the assessment be duly realized, you will be rewarded accordingly. The cultivation should, if possible exceed that of the preceding year, but at all events, there should be no decrease. If there be any, you will be considered deficient in your duty and dismissed."[1] There was no forgiving of the tax, except for the totally destitute. The way the tax was collected added to the peasant's burden: crops were seized until the tax or a substantial deposit was paid. This situation forced peasants to rely on lenders and intermediaries, and if peasants failed to produce the required sum, their lands were seized and sold.

According to the historians Sumit Guha, Christopher Bayly, Eric Stokes, J. Breman, Burton Stein, and others, the colonial state did not react with any substantial change in the flow of agricultural products and crafts. Instead, it adjusted to the situation by tempering its harshness and lowering the tax by 20 percent in the years 1836–1837. But even in the moderate form of the tax, the rapaciousness of this state is evident. It not only deprived some of the poorest peasants of their lands, but also destabilized the upper classes as "there was no place in the new system for that hybrid figure, part entrepreneur, part official, and part territorial magnate" (Guha 1985, 52).

SLEEMAN'S LIBERALISM

THE MIDDLE GROUND. Sleeman alluded to the polar opposites of *zamindar* and *ryot* as he chastised the government for acting "unwisely in going, as it has generally done, onto [one or the other of] two extremes, in its settlement of the land revenue" (Sleeman 1915, 64). His ideal was the middle ground advocated by Lord Bentinck, which Sleeman applied successfully in his own district in the Sagar and Nerbudda territories, where he found the "urbanity and intelligence" lacking in other districts (Sleeman 1915, 133).

This middle path acknowledged the existence of an intermediary class of landholders expected to pay "a moderate and fixed tax" to the government, which then left them a "private rent," the sole guarantee, according to Sleeman, that capital would be reinvested.

> Those cultivators are, I think, the best, who learn to depend upon their stock and character for favourable terms, hold themselves free to change their holdings when their leases expire, and pretend not to any hereditary right on the soil.
>
> One of these cultivators, with a good plough and bullocks, and a good character, can always get good land on moderate terms from holders of villages. (Sleeman 1915, 59)

Sleeman appeared to ignore that some peasants owned neither plough nor bullocks, as was the case with some of the Thugs we encountered. Like Metcalf and other conservatives, Sleeman wanted to ensure and protect what he believed was the perennial idyllic nature of the village community.[2] In his view, the first requisite to achieve this was the creation of a middle class, modeled on the one from which he himself originated, and which he thought was the basis of all things great and good in European societies. The same idea can be found in James Mill, who argued that the "middling ranks" were the "chief source of all that has exalted and refined human nature" (Stocking 1987, 33).

It is interesting to find out what, in Sleeman's view, these "intermediary classes" stood for. They were landowners who collected the tax from a set of villages or a region as well as "the agricultural capitalists who derived their incomes from the interest of money advanced to the farmer and cultivators for subsistence and the purchase of stock [and] were commonly men of rank and influence in society" along with "honest merchants," "peaceful and hard working entrepreneurs" (Sleeman 1915, 572). The middle class was thus made up of all those having access to money and the market and investing their profit in works of public utility and in factories. This social category, from which most of the sahibs themselves originated, was synonymous with economic and moral progress: like James Mill they believed that "it was the middle-classes of modern European civilized society in which the liberation of human reason from the forces of instinct had progressed furthest" (Stocking 1987, 35).[3]

THE EXCLUDED: THE POOR AND THE POWERFUL. The people excluded from progress were primarily those who had failed to enter the market economy. Indians reproached Sleeman on several occasions because "under Company's domination there is no employment (*Company ke amal men kuch rozgar nahin*)." It was true, he admitted, and he deplored the famines and the fact that a growing number of people were sinking "into the lowest class of religious mendicants, or retainers . . . and . . . are roaming over the country in search of service" (Sleeman 1915, 365, 367). However, these people remained outside of his concerns, unless, of course, they turned into brigands, who were (of course!) wealthy, but illegitimately so.

Page after page, his attention and anger were focused on the wealthy, the rajahs, the parasitic large landowners, holders of hereditary rights to collect land rent. "As a citizen of the world," wrote Sleeman, "I could not help thinking that it would be an immense blessing upon a large portion of our species if an earthquake were to swallow up this court of Gwalior, and the army that surrounds it" (Sleeman 1915, 264). No potentate, big or small, was exempt from his contempt. Rajahs were not only barbarian and superstitious, but also boring, weak of character, "grotesque," "clown like," of "weak intelligence," and moreover, "addicted to *bhumiavat*." For instance, the rajah of Orcha "is a man of no parts or character, and his expenditure being beyond his income, he is killing his goose for the sake of her eggs" (Sleeman 1915, 115). They were in constant conflict over inheritance of lands, and none of them showed the least interest in their subjects. They totally lacked in education and, Sleeman concludes, were unfit to serve the Company.

> Nothing tends so much to prevent the accumulation and concentration of capital over India as this feudal aristocracy which tends everywhere to destroy that feeling of security without which men will nowhere accumulate and concentrate it. They do so, not only by the intrigues and combinations against the paramount power, which keep alive the dread of internal wars and foreign invasion, but by those gangs of robbers and murderers which they foster and locate upon their estates to prey upon the more favoured or better governed territories around them. (Sleeman 1915, 578–79)

THE MARCH OF PROGRESS

Sleeman did not exactly go along the extreme view that emerged after 1830 on "the backwardness, dishonesty and corrupt character of Indians," according to which "India and Indians were sunk in a hopeless morass of corruption, . . . and vice " (Cohn 1987a, 437). He believed instead that British laws could get rid of the "undesirable segments" of society and transform the others. His wish was for the centralized colonial state to speak to the whole of the middle classes, the intermediaries between the supreme authority and the "masses" it was ruling. To the question of who should work the land, the authors of ancient Greece and Rome responded: "slaves." Sleeman claimed that slavery did not exist in India (mistakenly so, as it existed in many disguised forms), and his answer to the ancient Western classical authors' question was that the land should be worked by peasants equipped with good plows, and so on. The middle classes were called upon constitutionally to be the representatives of this productive lower class. Sleeman's ideal society was one in which the gradation of ranks was maintained; it was a hierarchical utopia governed by an enlightened elite. This utopia was dynamic, oriented toward abundance, the production of goods, and the increasing of wealth, and it participated in the modern idea of progress. This was no Garden of Eden where human beings only had to reach out to harvest the fruits of the earth. The organization of work, industry, and science were its unavoidable dimensions. England offered the model all should follow,[4] and Jabalpur, "town of manufactories" thanks to the repented Thugs, was this model transposed in India.

This utopia aimed to eliminate the burden of need, of war and despotism (Finley 1990), and Sleeman thus advocated that the upper rank of the extant social body be lopped off. There was no need, he argued, for this aristocracy, for whom "arms more than law prevailed; and courage preferably to equity and justice, was the virtue most valued and respected" (Hume, cited in Sleeman 1915, 397). Their members refused to "trade their swords for ploughshares" as well as to get rid of the bandits and thieves, who surreptitiously, in Sleeman's representations, had become substitutes for the poor, for dispossessed peasants and craft producers, for workers tied for life to their bosses through their debts, and for all those who "sink into the lowest class of religious mendicants." The poor as such were thus tacitly expelled from Sleeman's sight, and there remained only those famous kings and robbers trampling on private property rights, preventing the free flow of goods, and moreover, sinking a shameful portion of their revenues into unproductive socioreligious rites and ceremonies, as for instance the rajah of Orcha, who spent fortunes "marrying a pebble with a bush."[5]

The liberal grid "relied on the laws of mercantile exchange and of the natural sharing of interests in order and the general happiness" (Dumont 1983, 102). This scheme was anti-aristocratic because the aristocracy shared none of these interests and did not obey these laws. It was also antipoor as the poor remained outside the promised well-being. The poor offended Sleeman, who kept on repeating that "there has never been a government that gave so much security to life and property." He did qualify the situation by admitting that it was in a "state of transition," but he minimized what remained to be done. In a report of a conversation with two merchants, he had them say: "all we want is a little more of public service, and a little more of trade." He assured them that a happy tomorrow was already here. After all wasn't he safely traveling in India? Didn't the people he was questioning on the main claim to be happy (Sleeman 1915, 439–40)? Throughout his analyses he pointed to the progress accomplished by the government. He was the witness to and the spokesman of its success.

Sleeman claimed the "paternal enlightened government" he so praised merely changed the machinery and mode of procedure by which these civil rights were secured and these duties enforced (Sleeman 1915, 65). In fact, the aggressiveness of the project was inversely proportional to these reassuring statements. Its aim was to dislocate local institutions, to give birth to a new class, to hollow the power out of the Indian crowns, and to eliminate the poor turned into monsters or dangerous classes allied with the native authorities.

Beliefs

Religious beliefs and practices might be a theme as important as the one I just evoked. I believe there is no single chapter in Sleeman's work in which the issue is not mentioned. His intolerance for these beliefs and practices was emotional and compulsive. According to him, India's "extravagances" were rooted in religion, and he produced an oppressive inventory to make his point.

THE RELATIVE SUPERIORITY OF ISLAM AND INFERIORITY OF HINDUISM

Sleeman used his Muslim friends to denounce the Hindu religion. He was a monotheist like them and had no doubt about the superiority of the prophets. Both Sleeman and his Muslim friends acknowledged the extraordinary tolerance of the Hindus who did recognize Christ as the son of God and Mohamed as his prophet. Sleeman paid tribute to this spirit of tolerance, which he assumed helped the British to be so well accepted in India, but all the rest of Hindu beliefs and practices came under his constant attack. First, "in nothing do the Hindu deities appear more horrible than in the delight they are supposed to take in their sacrifice— it is everywhere the helpless, the female, and the infant that they seek to devour" (Sleeman 1915, 101). Sleeman used the Thugs to claim sacrifice to be a common practice, and he quotes one of his precious informers as telling him "there is no sin in offering human sacrifices to the gods where none have been offered; but, where the gods have been accustomed to them, they are actually annoyed when the rite is abolished, and visit the place and people with all kinds of calamities" (Sleeman 1915, 101).

One of the imaginary corollaries of human sacrifice is cannibalism. Sleeman linked the two in the following "well mannered" dialog:

"I understand, Kehri Singh, that certain men among the Gonds of the jungle, towards the source of the Nerbudda, eat human flesh. Is it so?"

"No, Sir; the men never eat people; but the Gond women do."

"Where?"

"Everywhere, Sir; there is not a parish, nay, a village, among the Gonds, in which you will not find one or more such women."

"And how do they eat people?"

"They eat their livers, Sir."

"O! I understand; you mean witches?"

"Of course! Who ever heard of other people eating human beings?" (Sleeman 1915, 68)

Sleeman was obviously persuaded that the Gonds, of which some tribes lived in the newly annexed territories of Sagar and Narmada, "performed human sacrifice" as the British claimed to have discovered around 1835 (but never did witness [Bates 1992]) in the course of their struggle against the rebels of the areas of Ganjam that I discussed in chapter 2. However, though the British claimed the Gonds tore off pieces of their victims' flesh before quickly burying them in their fields, they never mentioned cannibalism.[6]

THE POWER OF THE GODS

In *Ramaseeana*, on page 187 of the "Conversations," Sleeman tells his Thug informers: "we hope it will end in the entire suppression of this wicked and foolish system; and in the conviction on your part that Davey has really had nothing to do with it." One of the victories he was ardently striving for was to extirpate their beliefs. He wanted to put an end to the sinful, clouded link they stubbornly claimed united their crimes and their Goddess. He was told "that Davey instituted Thuggee, and supported it as long as we attended to her omens, and observed the rules framed by the wisdom of our ancestors, nothing in the world can never make us doubt."

In *Rambles* his favorite targets are the numerous gods and goddesses, spirits, vampires, and ghosts feared by credulous people who went to extremes trying to obey the dictates of their mad demons. Sleeman's insatiable curiosity was matched by his near systematic indignation over these "notorious absurdities" and their power over all classes of society.

The Hindoo religion reposes upon an entire prostration of mind, that continual and habitual surrender of the reasoning faculties. . . . With the Hindoos, the greater the improbability, the more monstrous and preposterous the fiction, the greater is the charm upon their minds; and the greater their learning in the Sanskrit the more are they under the influence of this charm. [They believe that] all is written by the Deity, or by his inspiration [and that] the heroes of these fables are demigods, or people endowed with powers far superior to those of the ordinary men of their own days. (Sleeman 1915, 175)

In India, Sleeman claimed, an individual did nothing without consulting a priest, while in England an individual did nothing without consulting an attorney. This Sleemanian quip set Indian society, ruled by divine fables, in opposition to British civil society, ruled by law. In India religion was destroying the use of reason and turning away from knowledge. The superiority of Christianity stemmed from its encouraging both, or at least from its not hindering either one of them. The Christian faith belonged to the private sphere of personal "conscience," while other religions permeated social life. Christianity did not put an obstacle before grasping "reality," while the followers of the other religions held for true that which was false, and vice versa. They preferred fanciful explanations to "natural analogies" and could not be convinced otherwise.

THE PITFALLS OF REASON

Sleeman's repulsion for idolatry led him too to fall into error. Not all of the beliefs he reported involved human sacrifice or cannibalistic feasts. Nonetheless, he perceived them all as marked by these stigmata so that he seldom challenged himself to understand what his interlocutors were expressing through them. His only response was skepticism and scorn. For him, facts and symbols remained separate entities, and he failed to understand their interweaving. This attitude is blatant in his writing about peasant discontent. He classified their reproaches and criticisms under the headings of "folklore" and "popular opinion" in his chapter 58, titled "Declining Fertility of the Soil. Popular Notion of the Cause." Writing about the terrible blight affecting wheat in the Narmada districts, he reports that his "little friend, the Sarimant" told him of the following rumor:

The people at first attributed this terrible calamity to an increase in the crime of adultery which had followed the introduction of our rule, and which, he said, was understood to follow it everywhere; that afterwards it was by most people attributed to our frequent measurement of the land, and inspection of fields, with a view to estimate their capabilities to pay; which the people considered a kind of *incest,* and which he, himself, the Deity, can never tolerate. The land is, said he, considered as the mother of the prince or chief who holds it—the great parent from whom he derives all that maintains him—his family and his establishments. If well treated, she yields this in abundance to her son; but if he presumes to look upon her with the eye of desire, she ceases to be fruitful; or the Deity sends down hail or blight to destroy all that she yields. (Sleeman 1915, 193–94)

Sleeman goes on with his own causal explanation: a phantasmagoric electrical theory on the scientific causes of the blight, and he admits he is powerless to prevent it. A bit later in the text, the author comes back to the issue of poor harvests. To ward them off, at night in Central India peasants ask Brahmans to come exorcize the fence posts placed by British functionaries to calculate the areas of the parcels (to register them and to tax them) or, barring that, they simply pull them off. One day in 1833, one of the famine years, a Brahman, "a very holy man," is determined to find out from the goddess the reason for this avalanche of catastrophes and starts to meditate.

After three days and nights of fasting and prayer, he saw a vision which stood before him in a white mantle, and told him that all these calamities arose from the slaughter of cows; and that under former governments this practice had been strictly prohibited, and the returns of the harvest had, in consequence, been always abundant, and subsistence cheap, in spite of invasion from without, insurrection within, and a good deal of misrule and oppression on the part of the local government. The holy man was enjoined by the vision to make this revelation known to the constituted authorities, and to persuade the people generally throughout the district to join in the petition for the prohibition of *beef-eating* throughout our Nerbudda territories. . . . A petition was soon drawn up and signed by many hundreds of the most respectable people in the district. (Sleeman 1915, 202)

Sleeman was persuaded that the attribution of disasters such as epidemics, penury, poor harvests, and so on to British colonial practices such as measuring the land or eating beef was superstition. Incest with the earth and the massacre of cows evidently were neither crimes nor disorders. In his eyes, the symbolic forms the protest took negated the grievances they were expressing. "These people were all much attached to us and to our rule, and were many of them on the most intimate terms of social intercourse with us; and, at the time they signed this petition, were entirely satisfied that they had discovered the real cause of all their sufferings, and impressed with the idea that we should be convinced, and grant their prayers." According to Sleeman, the complaints of the earth were nothing but old wives' tales. He was stuck in his views and wrote brutally: "The day is past. Beef continued to be eaten with undiminished appetite, the blight, nevertheless, disappeared . . . and the people are now, I believe, satisfied that they were mistaken" (Sleeman 1915, 203).

As in Europe, in the literature on witchcraft extant at the time, in which believers were thought to be idiots (Favret-Saada 1977), the scholar observer-narrator was the inverted image of the witchcraft victim. Sleeman refused to accept the causality proposed to him. And yet it could not have escaped him that these causes, "this rubbish" of beliefs, were directed at the colonizers and their actions in India. He hid behind religion, which he decreed to be false. At the same time, in contrast with the Thugs, he exalted religion as he declared their crimes to be ritual ones. In both cases religion was the culprit. Sleeman used it to both hide and reveal, according to the opportunity, the context or the viewpoint he had chosen for the occasion.

Sleeman attempted to prove in his book that he had the resolve and was capable of bringing about the needed changes, that he was at once a "thinking man," an educated man capable of reflection, and a practical man capable of action. The value of his analyses on the progress he had already brought about or on the dysfunction, the aberrations that were still resisting this progress, was based on their "truth," a truth that was the primary justification of his discourse.

He was so convinced of this that he made of "truth" the object of his work on India. India science was a continuation of Thug science. *Rambles* enables us to broach this epistemological issue using the author's own views as well as his methods and the value he attributes to them.

Knowledge and Truth
RAMBLES AND RECOLLECTIONS OF AN INDIAN OFFICIAL,
BY MAJOR-GENERAL SIR W. H. SLEEMAN

The long title of his book points not to India as the subject matter of the book, but instead to a literary travel genre quite popular at the time. The first word of the title, *Rambles*, evokes a travel diary and refers to the leisurely, linear, and slow wanderings that have presided to the writing. A map inside the book traces the stages of the journey, from Jabalpur to the Himalayan mountains, and delimits the terrain of the author's explorations.

The second word of the title, *Recollections*, points at once to the intellectual activity stimulated by these wanderings, as musings and emptying one's mind open up access to the past, and to the harvest of thoughts and observations the author is presenting in the very work. It points to the personal nature of the enterprise.

Holding second place in the hierarchy of typographical bodies is "*of an Indian Official*," which transforms the information preceding it from picturesque and intimate into the opposite framework of state institution. It is here that a twice-removed image of India is presented: once removed because it is bereft of its normal geographical function, as there is no mention of the space in which the journey occurred, and twice removed because *India* appears not in the preeminent form of a substantive, but instead as the secondary form of an epithet qualifying the traveler rather than the space. Is this appropriation, subordination, or symbiosis? Probably all of these at once.

Finally we have "by Major-General Sir W. H. Sleeman": the military rank and the patronymic make their appearance in the third rank of this materially highlighted hierarchy.

This progression from the general (*Rambles*) to the particular, from action to agent, with the central position occupied by the status—the *Indian Official*—is reminiscent of the revolving images of the ancestor of motion pictures, the early zoetropes whose images could be projected and that were so popular in England at the time. As the images projected by the title revolve from the first to the second and third tiers, the two lower levels retrospectively erase the bucolic and subjective connotation of the first level.

It is not certain that Sleeman himself was the author of the title. Yet its elaborate private and public montage did correspond perfectly well with what he aimed to communicate to his potential readers. In his preface, this time going from the particular to the general, he wrote that his aim was to "interest and entertain" his sister, to whom the letters that made up the bulk of the work were addressed, "along with the rest of my family," and finally, a large anonymous public that too could find learning and interest in it. The progression was ambitious and the program well worn: to learn while being entertained. The bait he used to draw readers was that of the "truth." His sources for this truth were first others and then himself.

ETHNOGRAPHIC METHOD

History was, without a shadow of a doubt, Sleeman's favorite discipline. Borrowing a definition from Bolingbroke, he wrote that history is philosophy teaching by example,[7] and he abundantly cited historians who influenced his thinking. India, where Sleeman saw native states as archaic and the territories under British rule as modern, offered him a favorable locus of observation. For him, India was at once past and present, decadence and progress, and he believed he could easily infer the lessons of history on the spot.

Sleeman's second source of truth lay in the field, where he practiced direct observation. One source were "respectable peasants" with whom he talked shop (rights over land, taxes, crops, inheritance, and so on) and argued with variable success for his progressive theories. Another was the learned elite, which gave him access to practices and customs linked to religion. It included Muslim merchants, also of the "respectable" sort; Muslim learned doctors; Brahmans, among whom was a "very learned Sanskrit scholar"; heads of monasteries; school directors; and rajahs, like the "little Sarimant" pensioned by the British, "of average intelligence, short of stature" (but whose handsomeness and elegance Sleeman admired) or again the "delightful Ramchand Rao" whose superstitious beliefs about men transformed into tigers and vice versa were a source of amusement for the rational investigator (Sleeman 1915, 127). Sleeman took pains to make clear the status and the esteem in which he held the intellectual and moral abilities of his interlocutors, and he made what he perceived as the lameness of their reasoning and the stupidity of their behavior appear all the more desperate in that they were honorable, educated, and intelligent.

In the course of his interviews and encounters Sleeman wore a number of masks corresponding to the three levels I have described in the title of his book. His wanderings and his status of wanderer went well with the peasants. He came to them to hear their true, sincere opinions. Some resisted him: "A man cannot, sir, venture to tell the truth at all times, and in all places." Sleeman, like the wolf seducing Little Red Riding Hood, reassured them: "You may tell it now with safety, my good old friend; I am a mere traveller (*musafir*) going to the hills in search of health" (Sleeman 1915, 412).

It was as an Indian official that the major general Sir W. H. Sleeman connected with the rajahs of the kingdoms he traveled through. Here the representative of the British government announced his arrival, got himself welcomed with great pomp, followed the rule of etiquette that he did not appreciate, and despised his feeble minded hosts.

The more open man was certainly the one conversing with his friends in the elite. With them discussions were always well-mannered, urbane, lofty, and elegant. There were no confrontations or joking as sometimes happened with the peasants he encountered, but, as with the latter, he was the one who initiated and controlled the exchanges.

Sleeman often mixed testimonies and explanations with his value judgments. He used various strategies to present his often speculative explanations as objective truth. Thus, to back his deprecatory statements on Indian society, he relied on carefully chosen informants and reinforced

their statements by adding his own, at times in the form of a qualifi-
cation. "Shiva and Parvati are Adam and Eve," a learned Brahman told
him. "I believe it," concluded Sleeman. In other cases he took refuge in
the consensus of general opinion, a tactic we have already encountered.
In his chapter 2, he writes:

> It is now pretty clear that all these works are of comparatively re-
> cent date, that the great poem of the Mahabharata could not have
> been written before the year 786 of the Christian era, and was prob-
> ably written so late as A.D. 1157; that Krishna, if born at all, must
> have been born on the 7th of August, A.D. 600, but was most likely a
> mere creation of the imagination to serve the purpose of the Brah-
> mans of Ujjain, in whom the fiction originated; that the other in-
> carnations were invented about the same time, and for the same
> object. (Sleeman 1915, 11)

We can well wonder whether his readers were capable of taking his
qualifications into account. The "I believe it," and "I think," and "we can
say" do point to the words of the Indian official and the major general.
Though they imply hypothetical thinking, they also authorize the reader
to embrace his claims on the ground that he is their source. Thus he
turned the very expression of his doubts into means to have his viewpoint
accepted, this based on his status, experience, and authority. Sleeman
was well-versed in the art of persuasion and lying, and he succeeded in
Rambles in producing a remarkable exercise that, to us, casts a heavy
shadow of suspicion on his supposed truth-seeking agenda.

VERACITY

"Veracity," truthfulness or lack of it,[8] refers to the true or false quality
of speech in human relations. Sleeman's methods included the search
for general laws through observation of the particular, as well as comparison, and on their basis he came up with an analysis of veracity we
might nowadays call "anthropological." Veracity is not a value in itself,
guaranteed by some sort of moral or divine transcendence; rather, it is
a social and relative notion determined by the status of the researchers
as well as their times and places. In the chapter Sleeman devotes to this
question, he claims everyone is lying. The "savage" and "semi-savage"
Indian tribespeople, the members of village communities, native soldiers
in the army, bandits and thieves who were practicing a primitive hori-
zontal truthfulness with truth inside and lies on the outside. Sleeman
even asserted that while in the past in British criminal courts the guilty
did not know of the "virtues of lying," things were quite different in his
day. The truth, he believed, could no longer be expected to come out of
the courts (except when the court was presided by Curven Smith, the

Solomon of the assassins, he implies in a later chapter). British judges were fooled, the fear of public opinion no longer existed, and so on. Only merchants found grace in his eyes. They partook of the truth because numbers were receptacles of exactitude and their account books held no trickery or errors. The author's unbounded affection for figures and for the merchant class fitted in with Bentham's utilitarianism, founded on a philosophy of an "arithmetic of pleasure," based solely on quantity rather than quality. Sleeman thus subordinated the value of truthfulness, that is, its usefulness, to the general good. In politics, which he defined as the art of dissimulation and artifice, he distinguished the trivial lie from the necessary one, the "lie that brings peace" as the poet Sa'di wrote.

Sleeman's grating analysis is disquieting to his present-day readers. Indeed, what are we to make of Sleeman's commitment to the truth when he implies that everything he reports as coming from others is true and so is everything that comes from him. He takes pains to reassure us: "When I go into a village and talk with the people in any part of India, I know that I shall get the truth out of them on all subjects as long as I can satisfy them that I am not come on the part of the Government to inquire into the value of their fields with a view to new impositions, and this I can always do" (Sleeman 1915, 400). We already encountered this "open sesame" that he felt free to use whenever he wanted when he declared to the peasants that he was just "a simple traveler seeking my health." In the title of his book what is highlighted is the disinterested, authentic aspect of his quest, his rambles and reminiscences, but the edifice is held up by the authority conferred by his status and rank. They were the means that enabled him to obtain the truth from others, even as he denied their effects. As to the content of this truth, it was entirely determined by the major general's concerns.

LIBERAL ETHNOLOGY

Rambles includes eyewitness accounts, observations, moral judgments, demonstrations, and propaganda—a blend that is frequently found in past and present travel books[9] and that makes of Sleeman's book a precious sample of liberal ethnology. According to the historian T. Trautmann (1992),[10] this sort of ethnology coming to the fore in the 1830s was dominated by the idea of progress, which the genre broke down into three components: property, liberty, and knowledge. *Rambles* is clearly organized along these three axes.

In this genre, knowledge was no longer legitimized by God or his dogma; instead, it was a quest for truth, that is, a quest for the objective laws ruling this world. This quest, applied to society, had two aspects. The first was ideological. The author pointed to what knowledge must aim for: private property, order, the rise of middle classes, and so on. Dominated by his desire to transform society, to make it fit with his dogmas, either through persuasion or by throwing it to the hounds of public opinion by ridiculing it, Sleeman assessed the terrain according to its degree of conformity to his views. The second aspect of the quest was pragmatic, and the author revealed himself to be an excellent observer. He did perceive the overlap of civil law and religion in India: "Their civil laws and their religion are in reality one and the same, and are contained in one and the same code. . . . By these codes, and the established usages everywhere well understood by the people, are their rights and duties in marriage, inheritance, succession, caste, contract, and all the other civil relations of life, ascertained" (Sleeman 1915, 65). He even wrote that the colonizers were "working in the dark." Present-day historiography concurs: "The British might have been governing, but it was the Indians who ruled" (Markovits 1991, 203). Thus in some cases, precious for us, "truth" is exposed, but most of the time it is exposed unintentionally, as in his analysis of the "popular causes" of peasant discontent. Sleeman's discourse amplifies the colonial cognitive scheme according to which colonial authorities are seldom seen as distinct from the information they report.

SLEEMAN AND THE THUGS

Ramaseeana had an even more ambitious program of truth than *Rambles,* as Sleeman claimed everything in it to be true and everything about the Thugs to be revealed in it. Was this program fulfilled or betrayed? What do Sleeman's Thugs teach us about the new fields of intellectual experience of colonial society?

Useful Lies

Ramaseeana, or a Vocabulary of the Peculiar Language Used by the Thugs with an Introduction and an Appendix Descriptive of the System Pursued by That Fraternity is introduced as a monograph on the culture of the Thugs gathered through their "language" and their "system." It is made up of two books. The first, in chronological order, includes a short preface with general remarks on humankind, on human institutions in India and in the West, and on the Thugs. Then an introduction of more than sixty pages describes the "system" and celebrates the history of the repression of the assassins from its hesitant beginnings to the time the author took charge and orchestrated the campaign. In his notes Sleeman provides complementary elaborations on Indian superstitions and makes various commentaries, but mostly he includes copies of full texts and dated and certified "true copies" of official and private correspondence pertaining to them. This introduction is followed by the Ramasee lexicon (140 pages).

The second part of the work is made up of appendices. The first one, a bit over 120 pages long, is made up of the transcription of the "Conversations" Sleeman held with Thugs. The others are official archives: correspondence, summary tables of sentences, interrogations, and confessions, descriptions of certain cases, lists of gang members, procedures that were followed by some magistrates, and so on. Each documents bears a date and a signature.

Paul Ricoeur has argued in *Temps et récit* [*Time and the Narrative*] that the historical method relies on three specific connectors, those of the calendar; the succession of the generations; and archives, documents, and traces (1985, 3:chapter 4). The analysis of the different parts of Sleeman's book in relation to its whole shows that these three connectors are indeed present. However, the way Sleeman uses them calls for the following remarks. The linguistic materials announced as being the mainstay of the work are first set in the framework of the discursive form of the preface and the introduction, and then of the documents of the colonial anti-Thug enterprise. As we have seen, the criminals' depositions are made up of the accounts of both their offenses and their repression, and likewise, the history of the campaign envelops the culture of the criminals—it smothers it. And yet this history is not mentioned in the title except in very small print and in third position: *and of the Measures Which Have Been Adopted by the Supreme Government for Its Suppression.* As in *Rambles and Recollections,* the cleverly composed hierarchy of the title holds a trap. It calls attention to on one thing (the strange language of the criminals) so as to better show another (the civilizing mission).

How is Ricoeur's second connector, the link between generations, given form in Sleeman? In order to totally amaze his reader with the colonialists' victory over the Thugs, Sleeman projects an asymmetric time in which the past of the Thugs is very long and that of the colonizers very short. The colonizers' brief past is evident in that Sleeman pays homage only to the preceding generation (Doctor Sherwood, Lord Hastings, and so on) in contrast to his discussion of the Thugs, whose practices are grounded in immemorial times: those of the myth of Kali and the frescoes of the caves of Ajanta and Ellora, to which Sleeman adds the time of the Crusades through that of the "Old man of the mountain." The Thug generations he lists do not reach as far back as these distant times, but they still cover several generations. In contrast to the genealogy of the colonizers that includes fathers and sons, the Thugs' genealogy encompasses vast temporal dimensions. The present, with its winners (Sleeman and his team) and its vanquished, its condemned Thugs and its judges, its dead and its living, is only the more glorious for it. This glory is projected onto the near future as the counterweight to the criminal excessive "principle of vitality," which the author was determined to keep on fighting. The colonizers' victory, actual and future, representing the temporal horizon of expectations of the book, is all the more striking in that its past is so shallow, while the past of the Thugs has the unfathomable temporal depth of myths.

The third mediator, according to Ricoeur, is the documents. On this point *Ramaseeana* is unimpeachable. Documents abound in it. Sleeman disappears behind this mountain of evidence. In fact, though, his invisible presence is a constant one. He was the one directing these conversations by asking questions of the criminals (and by sometimes answering them himself!). It was he who recorded them, as for instance the Ramasee lexicon that the conversations were aimed at clarifying. He was, finally, the main authority in the struggle against the Thugs, the instigator of all these archives produced and assembled. Everything came from him; everything went through him and came back to him.

But he was not alone. His collaborators, the members of the supreme government, the Thug criminals, or again the audience of Europeans watching these conversations, were also participating and controlling the elaboration of these documents. The evidence offered came with all guarantees of validity. Of course, it is possible that its very monumental aspect was aimed at silencing any suspicion, perhaps even at discouraging the reader from reading them so that the proof would lie solely in the quantity. But there is no point in trying to guess at intentions. I would rather draw attention to the enormous disparity between what we can learn from these documents on the Thugs and what Sleeman tells us about them in this introduction.

THUG PORTRAIT

To compare these two categories of texts amounts to comparing two kinds of Thugs: Sleeman's Thugs and their secret twin. Inside the same work, like Dr. Jekyll and Mr. Hyde, the Sleeman who is lexicographer and ethnologist is the prisoner of the writer. The writer takes full advantage of the trust stemming from the scholarship of the lexicographer-ethnologist, but on the main disregards his findings.

In chapter 3, I too gave a translation[11] of Thug culture on the basis of these same documents. Of course, I cannot see the distortions that I might have put in it, but in contrast I can point out his: I can describe the procedures he used and bring out the main traits of his fabricated picture of the assassins.

In *Rambles* Sleeman declares his passionate interest in history. In *Ramaseeana* the history of the Thugs is that which he attributes to them. In the "Conversations," his informers deny that Thuggee is of Muslim origin and that their community is divided into seven clans that have spread throughout India. Sleeman claims the opposite in his introduction. He argues that the Sagartii (a body of horsemen mentioned by Herodotus as accompanying Xerxes' armies in the fifth century B.C.) were the ancestors of the thieves described by Thévenot (which Sleeman spells on three occasions as Thievenot!). The Sagartii horsemen's "only defensive weapons were a dagger, and a cord made of twisted leather with a noose at one end," while Thévenot's thieves "use a certain rope with a running noose, which they can cast with so much sleight about a man's neck when they are within reach of him, that they never fail, so that they strangle him in a trice" (Sleeman 1836, "Introduction," 10).

Sleeman too disposed in a trice of the problem of the enormous temporal and spatial lag between the groups described:

> Though there is a vast interval of time between the Persian invasion of Greece and the travels of Thievenot, and of space between the seat of Sagartii and that of the ancient capital of India, I am still inclined to think that the vagrant bands who, in the 16th century infested the roads . . . between Delhi and Agra, came from some wild tribe and country of the kind; and I feel myself no doubt, that from these vagrant bands are descended the seven clans of Mahommudun Thugs, Bhys, Bursote, Kachunee, Huttar, Ganoo and Tundel, who, by the common consent of all Thugs throughout India, whether Hindoos or Mahommuduns, are admitted to be the most ancient, and the great original trunk upon which all the others have at different times and in different places been grafted. (Sleeman 1836, "Introduction," 11)

Did Sleeman draw his inspiration from James Tod, who, according to his 1825 work, thought the Scythians were the ancestors of the Rajputs as well as of the Germanic people and the other tribes of nascent Europe (Tod 1971, 1:74 n. 2)? Here again he presented his speculations as solid claims so they could take on the force of truth. Most of the time, however, he used more subtle mechanisms. His Thugs do undeniably appear to share a surface similarity with those I describe in part I of the present book, but their traits have been touched up, reframed, while some elements have been magnified and others erased.

His informers stated that their pickaxe was so sacred that it had jumped magically into the hands of its holders out of the well into which it had been placed the day before an expedition. But they acknowledged that they had never seen this phenomenon. They stated that it was true because they had heard the story from their fathers.[12] They thus differentiated between facts and the principle at the base of their beliefs. Sleeman neglected this distinction. He drew his conclusions not from the whole of the information, but from a single one of its elements. Likewise, he used the example of the friendly and distinguished Feringheea to draw a conclusion he claimed applied to the whole of the group.

> The circles of society in which these assassins by profession live and move are conciliated by their lavish expenditure of the booty they acquire on their annual expeditions, and by that amiable deportment which they find necessary to enable them to win the confidence of their victims while abroad, and which they continue to preserve at home, where they are commonly the most scrupulous in the discharge of their duties in all relations of life—the most liberal promoters of all social enjoyment, and the most rigid observers of everything relating to caste and religion. (Sleeman 1836, "Preface," ii)

Feringheea stood for all the Thugs, and the Thugs stood for the whole of India. They were the horrible symptom of the evil gripping the whole of the social body:

> The dreadful trade of murder by which they earn their incomes, even when known or suspected, as it commonly is, hardly ever makes them odious; for the want of sympathy between men of different castes, or different places of abode is, unhappily, the grand characteristic of Indian society; and as long as these assassins forbear to murder in and about the places where they reside, and conciliate or keep in ignorance the local police authorities, they are sure of being cherished as among the dearest members of society. (Sleeman 1836, "Preface," ii)

This distorted discourse follows the principle of the useful lie. In *Ramaseeana* as in *Rambles* the ever-present idea is that of degeneracy. This new explanation is an alternative to that of polygenesis. It justifies the providential intervention of the colonizers and provides "an alternative explanation for the manifest human diversity. . . . Thus could hierarchy and unity coexist, . . . just as aggressive ethnocentrism and Christian humanitarianism coexisted in the general cultural attitude toward non-Western peoples" (Stocking 1987, 45). The Thugs were the most telling example of that degeneracy, as confirmed by the discovery of a new medical science.

PHRENOLOGY AND COLONIALISM

With Sleeman's cooperation and upon the request of George Swinton, the general secretary of the supreme government in India, who was very interested in the new comparative anatomical science, the doctor Henry Spry, the very one we came across earlier observing with fascination the

Thugs before and after their hanging, had the heads of seven of them cut off. They were sent to Scotland to the phrenology society. British observers interpreted the Thugs' impudence before their death as evidence of their guilt. Phrenology[13] was to provide a confirmation.

Phrenology had ardent supporters in Britain, particularly among members of the medical profession, who defended it as "emphasizing observation, absolutizing 'objective facts,' and stressing accessibility, practicality, and progress" (Cooter 1984, 73 and chapter 1). The examination of the Thug skulls is the subject of an article written by M. Robert Cox, the conservator of the Edinburgh museum, and his nephew, M. Combe. The article was published in the *Journal of Phrenology* of Edinburgh. The authors sought positive correlations between the shape of those skulls and the murderous habits of the assassins. They had read Spry's and Sleeman's reports, and they seemed as convinced as they were that the Thugs' behavior could be located halfway between nature (physical heredity) and culture (education). They bent their observations every which way to fit this subtle intertwining and discovered mysterious "organs" of various sizes corresponding to it:

> One peculiarity is, that destructiveness is not a predominant organ in any of them; and yet they were murderers. This fact, although it might appear to a superficial observer in opposition to their character, is in reality perfectly consistent with it. . . . The skulls show that combination of large organs of the animal propensities with comparatively moderate organs of the moral sentiments, which predispose individuals to any mode of self-gratification and indulgence, without restraining them by regard to the rights and welfare of others. The Thugs belong to the class of characters in which I would place the captains and crews of slave-ships, and also the more desperate among soldiers; that is to say, men who individually are not quite so prone to cruelty, that they would of themselves have embarked in a murderous enterprise unsolicited; but who, when temptation is presented to them, feel little or no compunction in yielding to it. (cited in Spry 1837)

After minimizing the physiological symptoms pointing to the criminal tendencies of the Thugs, the scientists nonetheless wrote that the assassins' skulls "are of smaller size than the European average. Circumstances more suitable for the cultivation of the lower feelings and unfavourable for the strengthening of benevolence and conscientiousness, than those of the Thugs, it is impossible to conceive." But "in many cases the practices of the Thugs are little if at all dictated by them." Thus the phrenologists had to deal with culture again, and they ended up going along with Spry and Sleeman:

Dr. Spry states it as his opinion—and the opinion exactly accords with my own conclusion, drawn from the examination of the skulls—that "many boys go on the roads as Thugs because their fathers do, and not from inherent ferocity of disposition." The influence of the priests is very great in leading to the enormities detailed by Dr Spry. When the *instructors* of the people are men "not ashamed to declare openly, that untruth and false-swearing are virtuous and meritorious deeds when they tend to their own advantage," it is far from wonderful that the naturally weak morality of the *instructed* should become still more weak. Nor is it at all surprising, that the authority of men looked up to with awe, for their promises of eternal felicity, should be very influential in giving life and vigour to the animal propensities. The love of approbation is a powerful stimulant to the commission of the atrocities of the Thugs. (cited in Spry 1837)

This statement is then followed by an extract from the *Calcutta Literary Gazette* of a description of the ritual in which the "priest" ceremoniously gives the scarf to the future strangler. Next, there is a long description of organs and behavior (such a "Dirgaul's head has the organ more developed than either of the others") as well as of "propensities" and events, the whole scattered with gems such as "The sexual propensities are strongly developed in the whole seven" (Spry 1837, 2:168–72). Sleeman's expertise and then that of Dr. Spry were used to construct an ethnological, sociological, and moral projection of Thug crimes, which presented them as the product of sick and decadent Indian culture and society. The phrenologists' expertise assigned a physiological cause to this decadence, but their physiological explanations were not paid very much attention at the time. The discourse of "degeneracy" in the racial sense was to prevail at a later date (Metcalf 1995, 90). There was to be agreement that the "sexual propensities" deduced from the examination of the Thugs' brains crowned this "truthful" discourse, which nonetheless had the odd characteristic of being foreign to the most elementary rules of scientific reasoning as well as being grotesque in the literal sense of the word (Foucault 1999, 11–12).

Under the diagnosis of phrenology, cultural heredity tended to take on the natural sense that Sleeman was foreshadowing: "The notion that acquired characteristics could be inherited was widely accepted. . . . Given the belief that the habitual behaviour of human groups in different environments might become part of their hereditary physical makeup, cultural phenomena were readily translatable into "racial" tendencies. . . . The determinism implicit in the race idea was biological only in a secondary way" (Stocking 1987, 63–64). Phrenology led to the formulation of an almost racial view on the Thugs, a step taken by the very Christian Captain Paton. But phrenology had not yet imagined the culture of a group to be the product of its genetic capital. It found confirmation of culture in nature and not the other way around.

> Nourished in the shadow of Cuvierian comparative anatomy and the phrenological movement, physical anthropology by the 1840s had begun to emerge as a distinct approach to the study of human variability. Although much of its data had been collected in loosely descriptive natural historical or purely anecdotal terms ("a gentleman in Bombay assures me . . ."), a considerable amount of comparative anatomical material had also been collected, and various measures developed that seemed to give precision to racial comparison. (Stocking 1987, 65)

The application of this discipline to the Thugs is frightening, in part because of its macabre material aspects: the mutilation of the assassins after their hanging and the decomposition of their packaged heads during the very long journey from India to Scotland. And then it is frightening on account of its ominous political implications: the alliance that was then forged between the new science and Swinton, the general secretary of the government, was to have quite a future. For the time being the holders of this contrived knowledge were containing their creativity within the boundaries fixed by the colonizers, but soon the phrenologists' descendants were eagerly making explicit what had lain at the back of earlier like-thinking minds that found it convenient and comforting to see caste as race. In Europe in 1895, in the Reichstag, the phrenologized Thugs, organic monsters matching the mental portrait painted by Sleeman, provided one of the arguments for Representative Ahlwardt, the spokesperson of the anti-Semitic group. He compared the Jews to the Thugs and praised Sleeman for having exterminated (*ausrotteten*) "the whole of the sect," because, like the assassins, "any Jew who has not committed a crime is probably going to commit one in the future" (Hilberg 1988, 24).[14]

Scientific Discourse

The time has come to wonder about the existence of this discourse itself. By the time Sleeman published his book, the fate of the assassins was fixed for all intents and purposes. From a strictly utilitarian viewpoint, knowledge of their secret language did not affect the course of the campaign waged against them. What was his reason for undertaking the arduous scientific task of collecting words, of checking and rechecking them? Did it benefit him in some way? Was context a factor? What were the ties woven between the groups confronting each other in the political and intellectual arena where Sleeman was positioned?

THE ORIENTALISTS

In the years preceding the publication of *Ramaseeana*, reform currents met with the resistance of some scholars and politicians who had a vision of India different from the colonizing mission and its priorities. They were the so-called Orientalists, and since the discovery of Sanskrit texts they had nourished their vision at the very source of the great texts of Indian civilization. "There was a time when, of all human explorations, only humanism had not yet had its Columbus, its Copernicus, or its Newton" (Schwab 1950, 17–19). These scholars were responsible for the extraordinary sudden European interest in India. Orientalism became fashionable in France, then in Germany. In 1803 F. Schlegel stated: "Here [in India] lies the source of all languages, all thoughts, and the whole of history of the human mind; everything with no exception originated in India" (Schwab 1950, 79).

This was not the case in Britain. Even though it caused the rise of this infatuation, paradoxically it was not to experience the movement of "Oriental renaissance" or "Indian renaissance." Why did England in the 1830s, with the arrival of the generation of the sahibs, turn its back to the fabulous scholars whose work and research went on, of course, but no longer provoked in public opinion the burning curiosity that had greeted their first discoveries? Why did the British prefer Sleeman's monograph on the Thugs? Why did Queen Victoria and the British salons give such a glowing welcome to Meadows Taylor and his novel about the stranglers' sect? The ethnographic and fictional discourses on the crimes perpetrated in the present displaced philology and the exploration of the literary monuments of the past. How can this lack of interest be explained? What is its meaning?

CONSERVATIVES VERSUS LIBERALS

At the end of the eighteenth and beginning of the nineteenth century the Orientalists provided the impetus for the founding of a number of institutions to educate Muslim elites (Islamic law was taught at the *madrassa* of Calcutta from 1781), Hindu elites (ten years later Sanskrit, law codes, and literature were taught at the Sanskrit College of Benares), and finally, the British elites. From 1800 on at Fort William College in Calcutta, future judges and administrators of the Company, among whom was William Sleeman, could learn Sanskrit, Arabic, Persian, and six vernacular languages. But in Britain evangelists and utilitarians were displeased by this type of education and this way of spending the annual subsidy diverted from public funds. Already in 1792 in his *Observations on the State of Society among the Asiatic Subjects of Great-Britain*,[15] Charles Grant demanded that English, the most efficacious weapon in the struggle against "error," be taught. English was supposed to enable Hindus to reason and to dissipate the absurdity and falsity of their myths. From 1820 on, articles on education inspired by James Mill, who was appointed examiner at the Court of Directors in 1819, defended the idea that "the great end should not have been to teach Hindoo learning but useful learning" (Clive 1987, 345). For different reasons, but still converging with James Mill and Reginald Heber, the bishop of Calcutta, author of a famous *Narrative through the Upper Provinces of India* (1843), decried the fact that the students of the colleges of Calcutta and Benares were learning "geography that enumerated six earths and seven seas supported on the back of a huge tortoise" and advocated, instead, the study of English grammar, Hume's *History*, Western geography, and Christian dogma (cited in Clive 1987, 349).

These protests and this advice were strengthened by the Bengali elite's aspirations. Land owners, merchants, bankers, and craftsmen all supported the British government and wanted to learn English (Ahmed 1965). But the Orientalists' choice continued to prevail. They refused to descend from the top of their Mount Meru. In their view, "the metaphysical sciences, as found in Sanskrit and Arabic writings, were fully as worthy of being studied in those languages as in any other; and . . . poetry was a legitimate object of study" (Sharp, cited in Clive 1973, 348).

In 1828 Lord Bentinck set out to impose moral reforms and at the same time reduce the expenditures of the Company. In order to do both at once, he inserted in the new Charter of 1833 the provision that any Indian could be called upon to fulfill an official function "regardless of his religion, birth, descent or skin color." These new recruits were referred to as *babu*,[16] a Bengali term "with a slightly deprecating connotation used to designate a superficially westernized native" (Yule and Burnell 1968). They worked for the colonizers and, of course, needed to learn English, "the key to all improvements." The governor general had moreover made this a necessity by replacing Persian as the official language with English.

The Anglophiles were convinced of the superiority of Western literature and sciences and of the need to teach them to the colonized elite. They and the Orientalists confronted each other with passion and determination. As always, the linguistic battle involved the adversaries' ideological and political options though, paradoxically, it only affected the language of instruction and not its content. On the one hand, the Orientalists, labeled by their opponents as elitists, conservatives, extreme Tories, Islamic Hindus—and even sometimes white *babus*!—wanted the British to acquire the knowledge of Indian culture so as to gradually assimilate into the Indian context. They defended the idea according to which classical Oriental languages were the sole means of "revitalizing" regional literatures and vernacular languages, the basis and the tools needed to introduce Indians to Western knowledge. In the opposite camp Bentinck, Trevelyan, and Macaulay opposed the vernaculars "dangerously linked to Sanskrit." They represented the popular party, the liberal, ultraradical Whigs. Their wishes were exactly opposite from those of their adversaries: Indians had to thoroughly learn English Western culture so as to be able to progressively assimilate to Europe. The issue then boiled down to the question of whether the British should be Indianized or the Indians Anglicized?

The Calcutta press, the same one that had printed Sleeman's anonymous 1830 letter on the Thugs, heatedly defended the Anglophiles and their "spirit of innovation." They won in the Supreme Council of the Company in London in 1835. In October 1836, the year of the publication of *Ramaseeana*, Macaulay wrote to his father:

> Our English schools are flourishing wonderfully. . . . The effect of this education on the Hindoos is prodigious. . . . It is my firm belief that, if our plans of education are followed up, there will not be a single idolater among the respectable classes in Bengal thirty years hence. And this will be effected without any efforts to proselytize; without the smallest interference with religious liberty; merely by the natural operation of knowledge and reflection. (Clive 1987, 411)

At that time, the Westerners all believed in the unity of mankind. "The pre-Darwinian period in Britain is one in which, after a century of retreat, the biblical tradition resumed a kind of paradigmatic status" (Stocking 1987, 44). Sleeman too adhered to this notion when, as we have seen, he claimed that Shiva and Parvati are Adam and Eve, or when he denied the antiquity of the founding texts of Hinduism in order to claim the absolute anteriority of the bible. And yet a split occurred within this framework. The mosaic scheme of the Orientalists, represented by trees and branches, had been replaced by the utilitarian scheme of the "ladder of civilizations" advocated by James Mill in his *History* (1826). The historian Tom Trautmann (1992) ironically notes that the "scheme of the stairs" has been substituted for the "scheme of the tree." Human history thenceforth moved only in one direction as time became an arrow flying toward progress.

ORIENTALISM AND ETHNOLOGY

Sleeman was close to the liberal Anglophiles, but in his monograph on the Thugs he borrowed some of the weapons of his enemies, the conservative Orientalists. He combined them with others so that his work partook of the disparaged but prestigious recent discoveries in India even while being deeply demarcated from them.

This was the case for philology. Of course, the comparison between the Ramasee specialist and the Sanskrit scholars is preposterous in that Sleeman only aimed at establishing a lexicon, a word list, and not at describing a system with its specific grammar. Sleeman's philological contributions obviously belonged in a much more junior league! And yet he and his public had no qualms about crossing over: they preferred to speak of the "secret language of the Thugs" rather than just their vocabulary.

Moreover, the atmospheres in which Sleeman's and the Orientalists' research was conducted don't seem to have been that different. Until Wilkins, Sanskrit had been out of bounds for European knowledge; there was an aura of impenetrable mystery surrounding this language, "dead, sacred, liturgic and learned, reserved for the high priestly caste, illustrated by an immense mysterious literature, written in characters whose key remained unknown. Formidable prohibitions defended this treasure from the impurity of Europeans" (Schwab 1950, 39). The prison where Sleeman's interrogations were held, his assassin informants, and his aim of making accessible that which had not been had similarities with the Orientalists' trajectory, with its inquiries, danger, crossing over into the unknown, and finally its victory. The status of the informants they both used was not as different as might seem at first glance: the Orientalists had recourse to the pandits, that is, learned Brahmans, while Sleeman questioned criminals, among whom the figure of Feringheea, the Brahman Thug, stood out. He had more knowledge than his fellows of the arcana of his fraternity. Thus Feringheea was a side door that too would give Sleeman access to native scholars' knowledge.

And what were Orientalists doing? They translated mythologies, revealed the norms of Hindu society, and so on. The assassins too had their mythology and their norms. The methods of inquiry and the climate in which they were conducted have an undeniable feel of kinship with each other. But Sleeman differentiated himself and surpassed his elders: his object was not a dead language but a living one, though not a perfect language, instead a criminal argot. R. R. Mehrotra (1977), rightfully so, considers him the precursor of students of criminal argots that "may be defined as 'specialized language used by organized, professional groups operating outside the law; these groups normally constitute criminal subcultures, and the language is usually secret or semi-secret.'"[17]

Sleeman not only surpassed his predecessors, but he also inverted the sign attached to their discoveries: Sanskrit was made inaccessible to non-Hindus to protect it from their "impurity," but with the Thugs impurity had changed sides. Their language was secret only to better protect their impure crimes. As in fairy tales, the treasure finally discovered was awash with atrocities.

The seductive impact of *Ramaseeana* on public opinion certainly drew from a series of oppositions: the actuality of a living language and of human sacrifices is pitted against texts from the past, against Sanskrit and metaphysical speculations. The discontinuity was enormous, but, to Victorian eyes, was not the marginal culture of the present that Sleeman was unveiling the degenerate form of the past uncovered by his predecessors?

In fact, we are dealing with much more than discontinuity, as we are faced with the confrontation of opinions. One question cropping up constantly was whether Hindu religion promotes human sacrifice. *Ramaseeana* responded with a frightful "yes." Colebrooke did not deny the existence of this "unconscionable practice," but denied that it was legitimized by the Veda.

Sleeman as well used philology to invalidate what the Orientalists had held to be true since the beginning of the century, that is, that all Indian languages are derived from Sanskrit and that all the peoples of India have the same origin. Already in 1816 the missionary William Carey had argued that the idea that all the languages (Tamil, Telugu, Orissa, Bengali, Punjabi, and so on) originated from the Sanskrit was erroneous; rather, each of these languages was specific to the province from which it got its name (Grierson 1926, 11–12). In 1817 Ellis established the existence of the family of Dravidian languages spoken in the south of India, which are completely independent from Sanskrit. Around 1850 another language family was identified: that of the Munda languages. These linguistic researches sapped the first Orientalists' mythical India and substituted an India that was multiple, protean. In the same movement, philological science opened up the way for an internal ethnology[18] that made it possible to define the kinds of groupings existing in the population. Ramasee opened up the possibility of adding a new category to these groups: that of a "community" of an autonomous "fraternity" of criminals.

Sleeman went beyond the field of philology by also adopting the objects and methods of ethnography. Access to the Thug way of life, to their practices and thinking, was gained through inquiry, observation, and direct contact. Here again, a certain demeanor was required. Writing about a woman whose son had died, poisoned by the Datura Thugs, he noted: "I listened with all the coldness of a magistrate who wanted merely to learn facts and have nothing whatever to do with feelings" (Sleeman 1915, 82). This problem having been resolved, truthfulness having showed its face, telescopes having been correctly pointed at the sky, or at the Thugs, everything became visible. Like the sky, Thugs did not lie; they hid nothing when Sleeman directed his scrutiny at them. It was not only that *Ramaseeana* was all true, it also contained everything: "I am satisfied that there is no term, no rite, no ceremony, no opinion, no omen or usage that they have intentionally concealed from me; and if any have been accidentally omitted after the numerous narratives that I have had to record, and cases to investigate, they can be but comparatively very few and unimportant" (Sleeman 1836, "Introduction," 1).

This truthfulness and exhaustiveness, the key words of the work—did Sleeman really achieve them? Certainly in parts. In the "Conversations," for instance, Sleeman went to the trouble of noting what he heard, including the disagreements Thugs were having with each other and with him, and of showing the importance of Feringheea, his "good informant," well-versed on the norms of the community. Thus he was able to offer his readers a first look at the oral aspect of the information he had acquired, on the basis of which he was able to classify, to establish lists of words, and to assign a meaning to them. The ethnographer admitted honestly that Thug science came from this small circle of men.

Though Sleeman's Ramasee is one of those written orderings of the spoken word Jack Goody has written about (Goody 1977), it does not guarantee a passage to the level of the whole community as Sleeman claimed. Moreover, it is not a "secret language," but rather a thieves' argot whose origins are less opaque than he claimed (he was probably waylaid here by his limited knowledge of Indian languages[19] rather than by his broader concerns). And then the Thug identities I have sought to apprehend show that Sleeman's limitations were in more areas than that of linguistic knowledge. The image he paints of the Thugs is both intense and full of holes; it reflects his utter indifference for certain aspects and his extreme curiosity about others.

He was limited as well by the illusion of objectivity, denying distance and any possibility of error between observer and observed. Sleeman the observer believed transparency could be instantaneously achieved when he set his gaze on the observed. This illusion stemmed both from the official's sense of superiority and his belief that nothing escaped from his gaze, as well as from his denial of the impact of his presence and everything he represented on the process of communication itself. As he faced his peasant or criminal informants, Sleeman excluded himself as a representative of the colonial state and convinced himself that he was acquiring truth through his sole personal authority. This denial was shared by his peers. Missionaries did not ever question their own beliefs as they railed against idolatry and the evil of Hindu gods and sought to substitute their own God, saints, hell, and legends from the Bible for native divinities. When the Company became indignant at the endemic violence plaguing India, it did not take into consideration that its own violence and perverse effects were part of the country's suffering.

Sleeman embodied the new type of scientists who deeply impacted the beginnings of the discipline. Eurocentric and convinced of his superiority, persuaded of his magical power to deny the impact of his own authority (implying "I am not who I am"), he conducted research replete with "truths" and rationality mixed with folk and scholarly notions of causality, laws, and principles that were locked into his political mission. And yet he did succeed in bringing to light some information on the universe of the assassins and in broadening the field of our knowledge about them, himself, and his peers.

Science and Colonialism

At the turn of the nineteenth century a whole set of new objects of knowledge, new concepts, and new methods was emerging. In economics there was the analysis of the forms of production; in political science, the separation of civil society from religion; in criminal law, the idea of a fair gradation of punishments as advocated by Beccaria. In the domain of life there was the positing of the relationship of character with physiology that came with comparative anatomy and phrenology. Finally, in the field of discourse there was the discovery of new language families (Foucault 1966, 264–65). The colonizers, administrators, judges, and doctors explored, elaborated, constituted, and appropriated these new fields of knowledge and experience.

These multiple agendas of truth[20] were put at the service of the colonial state, as was the case with Sleeman, for whom official ideology formed the dominant interpretative grid for his ethnology of India. However, the state did not need to dictate what he should research or what his methods should be. His thirst for knowledge and his freedom to seek it exceeded the state's expectations. And in the end no one expressed surprise at the distance, the disparity even, between, on the one hand, the popularization of the cliché representing the Thugs as a fanatical horde organized against humankind, and on the other, ethnographic and philological information that partially corrected this cliché and made it possible to glimpse the fact that the murderers did have a history whose internal logic was not that imagined by their European observers.

In 1853 J. W. Kaye summarized the stages of the British presence in India:

> We have been for nearly two centuries connected with [the natives of India] by ties at least of commerce, before we knew very much more about them that they were a race of black people, with bare legs. . . . In time we came to look upon them as a people to be subdued; and then, having subdued them we began to regard our dusky subjects as so many millions of revenue-payers. . . . Then after another lapse of years we looked upon them as a people to be governed. . . . But it is only within very recent times that we have

thought it worth our while to know anything about the natives of India and to turn our knowledge into profitable account. (Kaye 1966, 354)

In Kaye's eyes Sleeman was the exemplary symbol of this recent stage. In my eyes he represents the tangle of what Max Weber calls the scientific and the political. This double link is visible in his writings in the power he sought to gain through his intellectual weapons and in the juxtaposition of erudition and disinformation, of truth and lies, of lucidity and blindness, and of cynicism and guilelessness.

Sleeman was a great admirer of Hobbes, and his intense relationship to political authorities might have stemmed from the philosopher's view that "the proper life of man is not that of an individual, it is that of a being which is closely dependent upon the State, so closely that it cannot but identify itself for a part with the Sovereign" (Dumont 1986, 84). In the same vein, Sleeman's scientific curiosity about the Thugs (and later about wolf-children), from which he undeniably drew moral benefits, possibly came from a desire to capture the state of nature, "solitary, poor, nasty, brutish and short," that preceded "proper" life and on which Hobbes reflects in Leviathan(cited in Dumont 1986, 83).

The Thugs were close to this state of nature for two reasons. Their notion of natural right partook of a natural order ruled over by a divinity who had power of life and death over her creatures so that they were bereft of individual autonomy and responsibility. And then, their "lives of crime" could be described in a mechanistic language as, in Dumont's words, "a system of movements of desire and passions" from which rationality, that is comfort, security, the development of faculties, and so on, was excluded. But the Thugs did not kill to eat. Their gain could not be reduced to that, and Sleeman did pierce this secret. This is why he saw them rather as embodying an intermediate stage between natural and civilized, political human beings, this expressed in a phrase their ethnographer-judge freely applied to them: "man is wolf to man." This statement denounced not only the ferocity of human relationships, but also its cause, the fact that human rationality remained "impure and mixed with animality" as long as the social contract and the establishment of the state had not come about (Dumont 1986, 107–12).

SIX   # Meadows Taylor's Imaginary Discourse

Published three years after *Ramaseeana*, the *Confessions of a Thug* was the send-off for fictional works inspired by the Thugs. This "truthful" account of the life of "Ameer Ali, the Thug" was an unprecedented instance of a deposition not completely subjugated to the aim of the police interrogation. Aesthetic emotion and erotic pleasure play an important part in it, along with the picturesque and the description of customs, the notion of fate and the tragic. In spite of this, the narrator's crimes, their circumstances, and their protagonists, his complicities and his faithfully narrated strategies are reminiscent of the roughness of the trial testimonies, though the quest for Ameer Ali's own identity and the mystery of his family occupy almost more place. The reader is in suspense: Will Ali recover his lost memory? Will it make it possible to go back in time? This fictional matter draws *Confessions* toward another shore, that of the imaginary. Are we dealing with here, as we are with *Ramaseeana*, the same imbrication of history and fiction, one that is at any rate unavoidable in any construction of the past (Ricoeur 1985)? What are the means Taylor uses to demarcate his Thug from the model bequeathed by Sleeman? What new representation does he propose?

HISTORY AND FICTION

From the very first line of his introduction, Meadows Taylor warns his reader: "The tale of crime which forms the subject of the following pages is alas! almost all true; what there is of fiction has been supplied only to connect the events, and make the adventures of Ameer Ali as interesting as the nature of his horrible profession would permit it" (Taylor 1986a, 1). The "alas! almost all true" expresses a regret that from the outset puts the author above any suspicion of having produced a fraud, the more so in that he acknowledges that fiction plays a role in the writing of his book. Fiction enters at first discreetly with the utilitarian purpose of smoothing over transitions, but then its presence becomes incommensurable when it aims at adding to the interest of the book.

And yet the claim to truth that tops Taylor's liminal sentence is its decisive element. The attraction of the *Confessions*, their persuasive force, lies first of all in this truth claim made in both preamble and conclusion. Ameer Ali himself ends his narrative with this unconditional statement: "I have told all, nor concealed from you one thought, one feeling, much less any act which at this distance of time I can remember" (Taylor 1986a, 545). We can recognize Sleeman's comments almost word for word: "I am satisfied that there is no term, no rite, no ceremony, no opinion, no omen or usage that the Thugs have intentionally concealed from me" (Sleeman 1836, 1). Moreover, Ali's worth as an example of murderousness make his sincerity all the more attractive. Taylor throws in yet another piece of bait in the same first page of his introduction. The Thug who perpetrated "more than seven hundred and fifty nine murders, sighs: 'Ah! Sir, if I had not been in prison twelve years, the number would have been a thousand!'" (Taylor 1986a, 1)

In the depositions one can at times read, without any reference to any specific date, statements of the sort: "We walked for four days." "Two months went by." For Ameer Ali as well as for the Thugs (and most people), the flow of life was only minimally indexed to the calendar. The text, 545 pages in the volume edited by Nick Mirsky, was not conceived like a journal and does not include a single date, except for one that is incomplete: "18.." This tenuous relationship with calendrical time is not accidental. It bolsters the authenticity of the narrative, whose temporal context is laid out in the introduction: "I became acquainted with this person in 1832. He was one of the approvers or informers who were sent to the Nizam's territory from Saugor, and whose appealing disclosures caused an excitement in the country which can never be forgotten. I have listened to them with fearful interest" (Taylor 1986a, 318). In the first chapter Ameer Ali evokes an event that occurred thirty-five years previously, when he was five years old. This age is confirmed by Taylor on page 265, when he finally states that his narrator is "thirty five or forty years old." Except for a few time markers—the death of his mother Myriam when he was nine, his initiation at age thirteen or fourteen, his first expedition at age eighteen—it is impossible to make out precisely the duration of his actions.

To show that the confessions are authentic, Taylor restates the arguments used in the criminals' trials as he writes: "his own confessions were in every particular confirmed by those of his brother informers, and are upon official record" (Taylor 1986a, 1) Indeed, Sayyid Amir Ali did give an official deposition in Sagar in 1832, one of the depositions recorded by the ubiquitous Sleeman. The handling of time, the existence of a reference document, the official status of the person recording it, clearly reassure the reader. While Sleeman draws history toward fiction, Taylor does the opposite and works at housing his fiction in history.

However, historical characters (Chitu, the Pindari!) and events (the death of the nabob of Lucknow, the British presence) are mixed with characters and events that lack this historical status, so much so that history is presented in a neutralized mode rather than a denotative one. Taylor inserts various epigraphs at the start of some of his chapters. Some are drawn from Shakespeare (*Richard III, Othello, Hamlet, King Lear,* and so on) as well as from old songs and folk sayings—all working to complete the temporal and spatial "unframing" of the narrative. Finally, Sayyid Amir Ali's official deposition, the longest one I am aware of,[1] is six times shorter than the one taken down by Taylor. The two depositions do, however, have some points in common: in the official deposition the criminal. who was around fifty years of age, had became a Thug by accident upon the death of his father. At age twenty he had gone to join the household of his uncle, who then took him on his first expedition. He was imprisoned at Lucknow for twelve years. He had romantic adventures and killed a large number of people. In Taylor's story, there is an accident, but it's not the same, and neither is the way his time in prison ends nor the importance of his love interests nor even his crimes! To whom did Ameer Ali lie? It does not matter; he is a melting pot of several of his fellows and many of their adventures through which the document became a novel.

In the last paragraphs of his introduction Taylor discusses the reasons for the disparity in the size of the depositions: "I hope, however, that the form of the present work may be found more attractive and more generally interesting than an account of the superstitions and customs only of the Thugs" (Taylor 1986a, 10). We should read this to mean that he was hoping to best his rival. His references and a note show that he was writing *Confessions* after having received and read *Ramaseeana:* "I take this opportunity of acknowledging the obligations I am under to Colonel Sleeman for much valuable information and also for a copy of his work" (Taylor 1986a, 5 n. 1). So even though he could not ignore the colonel's authority in Thug matters, the author of the *Confessions,* who was enacting a sort of revenge for his elder's "lucky star," took it upon himself to bring to the specialist's administrative and accounting report the art and the pleasure it was lacking. The rarity of his interjections in Ameer Ali's long monologue should not mislead us. Taylor is silent because he speaks through his protagonist. His is a narrative voice belonging to the narrator's lived time as his imaginative variations unveil the protagonist's virtual resources. Their source does lie in history; they were inspired by it even as they detached themselves from it. Taylor tells his readers of a life that was told to him, and he also tells them what might have happened.

Foucault shows that the evolution of judicial and religious institutions during the eighteenth and nineteenth centuries led to a demand for the guilty's avowal, that is, their acknowledgment of their state of being, rather than their straightforward confession.[2] In "this vast total narrative of life" everything had to be owned up to; nothing could be omitted. Of course the aim was still to bring infractions to light, but the whole of the procedure of examination was now aimed at the body, at its buried desires, its defects and stigmas. The observer had to detect and describe impulses, enjoyments, pleasures, and complacencies (Foucault 1999, 169–77). It is this apparatus of avowal that Taylor substitutes for the confessions and "Conversations" of his predecessor, who most of the time shunned dealing with his informers' individual feelings and identities.

MEADOWS TAYLOR'S INDIA

In contrast to Sleeman, Taylor does not use Thuggism as a pretext to vituperate against Indian society, institutions, and religions. Sleeman expresses only a limited admiration for the spectacles offered by India, but Taylor is enthusiastic about them. In his eyes Indian landscapes are grandiose, the land is richly cultivated, and there is no pleasure as great as that of galloping in its immense spaces. The monuments he comes across trigger fervor and regret; the busy large cities, the well-stocked markets, the crowded streets awaken his eagerness as spicy treats, fragrant oils, sorbets, and pilafs make his mouth water. The beauty of women and their *ghazals*[3] completely unsettle him. This India, vast, sensual, delicious, also dazzle Ameer Ali, who is our guide in the course of surprising interludes in the famous sites he visits as a curious and well-educated traveler.

Taylor's opinion of the people is more circumspect. So as to suspend any premature judgment, he uses the technique of creating an evil double for all the good characters, or again he creates the same moderating effect by using a sample. Thus the nabob who introduces Zora to Ameer Ali is an impressive warrior, affable, generous with his hospitality, and having a keen political perception. His double is the nabob of Jalaun, "the Thugs' mortal and bitter enemy." Giving in to British pressure, this nabob brings Ismail, Ameer Ali's father, to trial and condemns him to die shamefully, his head crushed by an elephant's foot. And yet for years he sheltered Ismail in his kingdom even though he was fully aware that he was a Thug, and extracted high taxes and sumptuous gifts from him. The Pindari chief, Chitu, whom Ameer Ali and his fellows decide to serve, is a brave warrior, just and tireless, an ambitious strategist who organizes an alliance to kick the British out of India. One of his generals, Ghuffoor Khan, is his double. Khan is driven by savagery, lust, greed, and the passion for carnage—all traits the colonizers attributed to the Pindaris. But even this monster plays the sitar admirably and can recite verses from the poet Hafiz.

Among the people approached by the Thugs in Taylor's book, there is a rich palette of "simple and honest" folks; but many others rival the murderers in their duplicity. Among the Thugs themselves hardened, cruel brutes like Ganesha contrast with Ameer Ali or with a Peer Khan, who "dies of sorrow" after seeing his ten-year-old nephew die from the shock of witnessing the horrifying spectacle of strangled travelers. The case of Surfuraz Khan, another of Ameer Ali's friends, whose conversion to asceticism and charity stem from similar dramatic events, is yet the most surprising (see also Fanny Parks 1850, 399).[4] He tells the young and beautiful slave of a victim he has just strangled: "I have no wife, nor child: thou shalt be both to me." But she spits in his face: "Strike! Murderer and villain as you are, strike!" And so he strangles her.

> He accompanied us to our home, got his share of the booty which he immediately distributed among the poorer members of the band, and after bidding us a melancholy farewell, stripped himself of all his clothes, covered his body with ashes, and went forth into the rude world . . . in the guise of a Fakeer. I heard, years after, that he returned to the spot where he had killed the girl, constructed a hut by the roadside and ministered to the wants of travelers. (Taylor 1986a, 256–60)

Taylor does not vituperate against any particular social category, not even that of the Thugs, whom he seemed to find perfectible. The society that Taylor's hero Ameer Ali frequents and crisscrosses is diverse, mobile, and active. Trade is flourishing, mounds of booty are there for the taking, and letters of credit are honored. Thanks to the many travelers and caravans, news moves quickly; interpersonal relations are often friendly, easy going, trusting. It is an India where the pleasure of conversation is appreciated, where people who know how to tell stories (and Thugs are masters in this department) can find success and acquire a good reputation.

In this world, caste only rarely determines moral behavior ("Bhojpoorees! Then I dare say they are Thugs," says Ameer Ali on only one occasion [Taylor 1986a, 440]), and birth does not definitively determine function. On the model of "last year I was a weaver, now I am a Sheikh, next year if prices go up, I'll become a Sayyid," Ameer Ali is a Sayyid and Thug one day, he is a Pindari the next, and later on he is a fake ascetic. When he gets out of Lucknow prison, he "disguises himself as a qalandar" and lives from alms before getting a new gang together.

Taylor thus is not using Ameer Ali's career to criticize India, nor even its superstitions (outside of Thuggism, of course!). But he does indirectly pay homage to the colonizers. Their grip closes around the criminal as the narrative unfolds; a price is put on his head, he is denounced. In the final pages, he is finally taken to the Sagar court to appear in front of a judge, "a tall, noble-looking person he was." It is Sleeman, of course. The trial is conducted with fairness, the depositions faithfully transcribed, justice rendered. This homage frames the *Confessions:* "to preserve my life, which was forfeited to your laws, I have bound myself to your service by the fearful tenure of denouncing all my old confederates. . . . Few now remain at large" (Taylor 1986a, 11).

Even though he is following the official stance regarding the Thugs, Taylor does adopt the native position by subtly showing that the British too are undesirable invaders. A treasure bearer becomes passionately angry against them as well as at the weakness of Baji Ra, who was defeated at Kirkee. He exclaims disconsolately: "They are advancing, they're going to take over the Marathi empire!" Chitu and, to a lesser extent, Ameer Ali are anti-British. In front of the ruins of the abandoned stronghold of the kingdom of Bedar, Ameer Ali bitterly laments the decrepitude of the present; the colonizers' victories have been the death knell of this splendid past:

Where were now the princely state, the pomp of royalty, the gallant warriors who had . . . so oft bidden defiance to hosts of invaders? All were gone, all was now lonely and desolate, and the stillness accorded well with the ruinous appearance of the scene before us. Not however that the walls were dilapidated or overthrown; they remained as firm and solid as ever; and here and there the muzzle of a canon pointing from a loophole or rude embrasure showed that they were still capable of defense, though, alas! defenders there were none. (Taylor 1986a, 238)

In the book one of the Britishers' least honorable assets are the natives, the traitors, the *kafirs* who enlist in their armies, or even worse, who play a double game, like this Soobhan Khan, "paid both by them and by us," who makes use of his contacts with the colonizers to sell information to the Thugs in exchange for a part of their loot. The insiders' viewpoint comes through in the form of comical questions as Ameer Ali, who in the course of the narrative enjoys dipping his fingers into succulent pilafs, asks: Why do the British eat with forks? And what could be the meaning of "hip, hip, hip," these mystical onomatopoeia they utter when they drink alcohol? Just as the Britishers usually look down upon the natives, these natives too find the colonizers to have bizarre customs. And those colonizers' mortal enemies, the Thugs and the Pindaris, harbor motivations that are more political than they app   to be. This personal narrative voice, respectful of India, of its charms as much as its wounds, contrasts sharply with the "objective" discourse with are familiar with.

Now that I have sketched out the decor, the time has come to unveil the aspect of Taylor's Thug criminal that is both unexpected and feverishly romantic.

TAYLOR'S INTRUSIONS

About halfway into Ameer Ali's monologues, Taylor interrupts him and describes him. He is a magnificent man, he tells us.

> His figure is slight, but it is in the highest degree compact, agile and muscular. . . . His dress is always scrupulously neat and clean . . . his waist tightly girded with a shawl. . . . In complexion, he is fair . . . his face is even now strikingly handsome . . . his forehead is high and broad; his eyes large, sparkling and very expressive . . . his nose is aquiline and elegantly formed, his mouth small and beautifully chiseled, and his teeth are exquisitely white and even. . . . His manner is graceful, bland, and polite—it is indeed more than gentlemanlike—it is courtly, and I have not seen it equaled even by the Mahomedan noblemen, with many of whom I have associated. . . . His language [Urdu] is pure and fluent, perhaps a little affected from his knowledge of Persian. . . . He prides himself upon it, and holds in supreme contempt those who speak the corrupt patois of the Dukhun, or the still worse one of Hindostan. (Taylor 1986a, 265–66)

This flattering portrait of the Thug gives the author the opportunity to recognize that he himself is not able to render Ameer Ali's speech, particularly in places where "his eloquence kindles and bursts forth in a torrent of figurative language, which it would be impossible to render into English, or, if it were rendered, would appear to the English reader, unused to such forms of speech, highly exaggerated and absurd" (Taylor 1986a, 265).

In spite of Taylor's own limitations and those imposed by censorship, the fiery atmosphere and the vision evoked by the three amorous episodes Ameer Ali narrates seems to be extracted from Indian or Middle Eastern folk tales.[5] Of the three women protagonists, only the third is assassinated because of her indiscretion—a fate reminiscent of Blue Beard's three spouses. For both male characters, crime is something they are collecting. One of them murders his wives, while the other strangles travelers he meets along his way. But the analogy stops here. In contrast to Blue Beard, Ameer Ali as ogre is seductive but no pervert.

Drawing by Emile Bayard of the execution of Ameer Ali's father, ordered by the rajah of Jalaun under pressure from the British to punish the Thugs he had been protecting. From Louis Rousselet, "L'Inde des rajahs," in *Le Tour du Monde* (1864–1868).

Love: Venal, Legal, and Tragic

Love appears in the few breaks between murderous activities. It presents itself in the exquisite traits of very beautiful women, with eyes slanted like those of a doe, and who, as soon they are gazed upon, awaken instant passion. They ask for Ameer Ali's help and protection for a variety of reasons and claim that their happiness, even their lives, depend on him. Beauty, dependence, and passion: regardless of the difference in the trajectories of the three women, they echo each other as so many variations of the summarily defined femininity they share.

> Like the full moon emerging from a cloud, Zora sailed towards us with a slow and graceful motion. How shall I describe to you, Sahib, her exquisite movements! Every turn displayed her form to greater advantage, and I gazed till my soul was fairly entranced. But how much more was I affected when she began to sing! Having performed the dance, both the slow and the quick, she ceased; and after a prelude by one of the musicians behind her, she broke out into an impassioned *ghazal*. It was one I was very fond of myself. I listened till I could have fallen at her feet, and worshiped her as a Peri[6] from heaven. My soul was so intoxicated with the blessed sounds I heard, that I was insensible to all around me. (Taylor 1986a, 107)

Zora the courtesan, the Thug's first love, uses him to free her from the clutches of a jealous petty nabob who is mistreating her. At the risk of his life he organizes her escape, but the passion of the *ghazal* singer, of the voluptuous dancer, survives only one night after he leads her to Hyderabad. He then makes these melancholy remarks:

> Sahib! that was the last night I passed with my beloved. . . . The whole of our intercourse remains on my memory like the impression of a pleasing dream, on which I delight often to dwell, to conjure up the scenes and conversations of years past and gone,— years of wild adventure, of trial, of sorrow, and of crime. . . . I can again hear her protestations of unalterable love, her entreaties that I would soon return to her; and above all I remember her surpassing loveliness, and the look of anguish . . . as I left her, after a long passionate embrace. (Taylor 1986a, 180–81)

Ameer Ali is to never see Zora again. She has paid him with a few nights of love for the freedom to climb the social ladder, to perhaps become the "captive" of the *nizam* of Hyderabad, whose petty nabob claims to want her for himself. Ameer Ali has been cheated, he has made a mistake. But he bears no grudge because, like him, Zora the courtesan follows the logic of a profession that involves the use of ruses and false promises. He is left only with an unforgettable memory.

Ameer Ali's disappointment and humiliation are quickly forgotten with the appearance of a servant girl who begs him to help her mistress, who is in great danger. Azima immediately declares her love for the visitor. She was bought from her parents by a senile and tyrannical husband. If Ameer Ali does not help her, she will kill herself: "I have prepared a bitter draught, and tomorrow's sun will look upon my dead body." "Allah forbid, lady. . . . Fly with me this instant, and I will lead you to a father who will welcome you, and a land far away where your flight will never be discovered" (Taylor 1986, 222–23).

There is a repeat of the flight scenario, but this time it is met with success as it is soon followed by marriage. Azima does experience a bit of hesitation just before the ceremony: "I am another's wife—how can this be done?" "Forget this hateful marriage! Azima, these objections will kill me. Am I not your slave?" (Taylor 1986a, 236). The two lovers forget their respective pasts, and the wedding proceeds as tradition requires, in the presence of a mullah and with the blessing of Ismail, the groom's father.

The two adventures follow each other in a sequence that shows that these two female archetypes of the courtesan and the wife can substitute for each other. Azima offers immediate and permanent consolation for the pain inflicted by the fickle Zora. Thanks to this faithful love, which appears in the nick of time to heal his wounds, the lover keeps an unchanging memory of the brief, and for that all the more powerful, pleasures of the preceding woman, even as he marries another.

The third woman Ameer Ali encounters, some years later, is a more complex figure. Zora and Azima only see Ameer Ali's appearance. The first does not guess he is immensely wealthy, the second marries him without knowing he is a Thug. Like the two others, Shurfun seduces Ameer Ali from the moment he sets eyes on her. She is exceptionally beautiful, all the more so in that he gets only a glimpse of her as she lifts part of the curtain that hides her.

Ameer Ali has stopped at a stall in the Jabalpur market. He smokes a hookah like any ordinary man resting from the day's toil. In fact, he is looking for prey, for travelers who might travel with him. It is then he sees Shurfun's face, "radiant with beauty" (Taylor 1986a, 319). He is seduced, but reasons with himself: Thugs do not assassinate women. Surprised by this sexual prey who cannot be *bunij*, he goes back to camp. Shurfun is excluded in the name of the rules of the profession, but from the start, sex and death are linked. This first sequence, in the course of which desire is negated in the name of duty, is to have an inverted outcome: desire is to be satisfied and duty betrayed. Ameer Ali succumbs to the advances of the young and beautiful widow, but he regrets it. She then pursues him and offers him her fortune and marriage. Ameer Ali resists.

"Beware," said she, "how you deceive me, for I know your secret, and if you are unfaithful I will expose it; your life is in my hands, and you know it."

"What secret," cried I with alarm, "What can you mean?"

"I know that you are a Thug," she said in a low and determined voice; "my slave has discovered you, and a thousand circumstances impress the belief that you are one upon my mind."

"Then, Shurfun, since you have discovered us, I have no alternative; we must be united." (Taylor 1986a, 315)

The Thug then declares: "I was determined I would take no active part in her death, for I could not bear the thought of lifting my hand against one whose caresses I had allowed, and whose kisses were, I may say, still warm on my lips" (Taylor 1986a, 318). Peer Khan and Budrinath take care of her. Shurfun and her entourage, no less than fifteen people, are strangled. Like Blue Beard, Ameer Ali kills to protect the secret of his past and future murders. Shurfun's complicity is impossible, monstrous, diabolical. A Thug wants to be loved for his appearances, not for what he is. Disguise is as indispensable in love as it is in his profession.[7]

The Two Narrators

In the official confession taken down by William Sleeman, the narrator, who also found himself in the Hyderabad area, told that in the course of his ninth expedition he was then on very friendly terms with Moneea, a dancer from Huttah, and gave her sixty rupees. He brought her to Chutterpore, where he gave her a scarf he bought for 150 rupees. Then he went back to his village, from which he had been absent ten months. He stayed home for the whole of the rainy season. Later in the deposition he alluded to a meeting with a dancer in the course of another expedition. He spent an evening admiring her charms and then asked her to visit him during the night. The pandit who was watching over her discovered it and, being suspicious as to the defendant's profession, sent soldiers to capture his gang. They were taken and spent the night in prison. The next morning Sleeman's Amir Ali showed him receipts from customs and other papers having to do with the horse trade, and their captor let them go, believing they were horse traders.[8] For Sayyid Amir Ali, enjoyment of the beauty of women came at a high cost of gifts and dangers.

Taylor's Blue Beard is a lover of *One Thousand and One Nights* with colors, smells, and music. In his book it is Taylor's voice that predominates: his character frequents places with which he himself familiar, and some of his experiences are close to his own, as shown by passages from his autobiography. The Thug first sees the city of Hyderabad from the same

Nineteenth-century engraving by M. Gaton Woodville of a dance performance. Did Zora, the courtesan with whom Ameer Ali falls madly in love, appear to him in the form of such a sensual dancer?

hills from which young Taylor used to admire it when he was awaiting his fate. The city's beauty takes the breath away from both of them (see Taylor 1986b). Shurfun's demands are reminiscent of that of the young girl he met at the church in his youth and of her pressing her invitation in this consecrated place while he was working at Yates and Brothers. His emotions, his personal experiences are rendered in a flowery language. Taylor is faithful to his folk-tale models, particularly to their rhetoric and their code of love.

The gaze is decisive and passion absolute from the very first glance. Love and death are closely intertwined. Seduction is played out in predictable gradual stages. Zora, expert in the art of singing and seduction, makes us think of the women described by Vatsyayana in the *Kamasutra*.

Azima, faithful, loving, devoted, and discreet is the very image of the accomplished wife (who further gives birth to a son). As for Shurfun, who is in control of her wealth and her person, she represents an unusual type of independent widow.

In the course of these amorous episodes, the three women clearly show that Ameer Ali stands for the Victorian Taylor, and this makes of Shurfun the most interesting case. When she proposes to marry her lover, knowing full well he is already married, he answers that this marriage would be "unhallowed and disgraceful." Such an answer does not fit Koranic law, which allows polygamy. Here Taylor commits a strange cultural error. But mostly, when Ameer Ali decides to execute Shurfun, Taylor emphasizes her freedom to pick her lovers, this in complete contradiction with the submissive ideals of British womanhood of the time.

TWO ROMANTIC TALES OF THE TIMES

Ameer Ali, who could fit so well in the literature of his own culture, is not without relation to our own. In 1818 Victor Frankenstein created a deformed and criminal giant out of "dead tissue" and electrical energy, and in 1886 Dr. Jekyll drank potions of his own making and morphed into the demonic Mr. Hyde. These monsters of modernity, creatures of the western scientific world, formed the framework for the chronology of the romantic discovery of the Thugs in 1839. If we take the first third of the century as a time marker, another configuration appears. *Frankenstein* and the *Confessions* taken together became the foreshadowing of recurrent anxieties. At the end of the nineteenth century the theme of evil resurfaced with a similar vigor under the same disguise as that of the mad scientist (Dr. Jekyll) or a serial murderer whose crimes and rapes are ordained by the medieval myth of Dracula, Prince Vlad V of Valachia. Like that of Ameer Ali, the figure of Dracula the Devil is not oriented toward predicting the future of humankind, but rather toward shedding a disquieting light on its past.

The authors of this new teratology put side by side religious obscurantism and the pull of the desire for knowledge, this by choosing to depict and to explain "exceptions in the moral order." In a world submitted to the law of progress, they, along with figures such as Baudelaire and Edgar Alan Poe, stood against the tide as they claimed that evil is an integral part of human nature:

There is in man a mysterious force unaccounted for by modern philosophy. And yet, without this unnamed force, without this primordial drive, a multitude of human actions remain unexplained, unexplainable. These actions attract us only *because* they are evil, dangerous. They possess the pull of the abyss. This primitive,

247

irresistible force, is natural Perversity causing man to be constantly at once homicide and suicide, assassin and executioner. (Baudelaire 1964, 113)

Like the Thugs and the vampires, Mary Shelley's and Stevenson's characters are driven by this mysterious force. They cause just as much terror from their location at the troubled margins of knowledge and belief, where familiar landmarks have ceased to exist. But their aims, their means, the locus of their actions are the extreme opposite from those of the Thugs. Victor Frankenstein and Dr. Jekyll seek to unearth the laws of life through the force of their intelligence, their reasoning, their ingenuity. It is curiosity that obliterates in them all moral and religious considerations. Their transgression lies in transforming into a field of experience that which should not be, that is, in breaching the very laws of creation. Frankenstein usurps God's prerogatives when he gives birth to a monstrous chemical and electrical Adam. Dr. Jekyll does likewise when he turns into a ferocious and criminal Hyde. "These are blasphemous versions of the myth of creation" (Lecercle 1988, 20). The two narratives stigmatize scientific hubris and assign limits to its ambition. They bring to mind the famous Rabelaisian adage, "science without conscience brings ruin to the soul." While Frankenstein and Dr. Jekyll act as if God were dead, the Thugs on the contrary are the instruments of an omnipresent and evil goddess. The moral barrier that the scientists lack is erected by the Thugs as a guide to action. And yet there is an identical catch in these very different stories; it is fascination for violence and death.

Romantic scientists' characters put the world at risk with their otherwise laudable aims of giving life or of understanding its mystery, of making progress what Victor Frankenstein calls "natural philosophy." Their mental universe, involving their faith in science, which they saw as synonymous with progress, was not different from that of Sleeman and Western readers in general. In contrast, the Indian Thugs' goals were depicted as neither imaginary nor good. Their beliefs defied reason. In fiction as elsewhere, the split was made between the West, the self, harbinger of the future; and the Orient, the other, the elsewhere, the blight of the past in the present. These exceptions to the moral order, these representations of evil and the abnormal came from culturally heterogeneous and geographically distant places, and though they projected the potential transgression of civilized men, they were denouncing the very present barbarism of the Thugs. Bearer of a split from the Western world, the stranglers were set in opposition to the mad scientists who were only nefarious drifters from science, freed in imagination from the control of the human community.

This is my bird's-eye view, suggested by the most popular works of fiction of the nineteenth century, works that were all to be abundantly used in the cinema of the twentieth. I will limit myself to discussing two of them, *Confessions a Thug* and *Frankenstein; or, The Modern Prometheus*, as their main characters embody these oppositions and were to have surprisingly numerous resonances.

Ameer Ali and Victor Frankenstein: Resonances and Dissonances

Even though Clerval, Frankenstein's friend, has the "design to visit India, in the belief that he had . . . the means of materially assisting the progress of European colonization and trade" (Shelley 1978, 427–28), and Victor Frankenstein himself finds solace in reading the Orientalists, Mary Shelley's novel does not belong in the exotic genre. Rather, it set in opposition the discourse of religion, that is, the limits it assigned to the desire for knowledge and power, with the discourse of science. Victor Frankenstein "was prey to a Faustian arrogance and thus doomed to become haunted by an ungrateful Creature in whom we have to see the return in diabolical form of the God whose prerogatives Frankenstein is usurping" (Lecercle 1988, 41).

There is no such opposition between science and religion in the *Confessions*. And yet it does contain a discordant discourse, that of unbelief. Ameer Ali has no respect for Kali. "You are always prating about these foolish omens, as if success lay more in them than in stout hearts. I believe them not" (Taylor 1986a, 207). He only tolerates rites to please his fellows, and many a time he tries to persuade them that a negative omen is of no import. He thus leaves little room for the action of the Goddess. If "Victor the scientist opened the door for human beings to be their own creators, then scientific progress was to glorify the creature and marginalize the creator" (Lecercle 1988, 44). Ameer Ali believes that human beings are their own destroyers, that we can do away with the idea of sacrifice, with violence mediated by the divine. Death is (almost) a profane business. "Almost" because Allah guides his hand. But this principle is general and distant, acquired once and for all and never questioned. It is, of course, quite different from the close dependence in which his companions see themselves in relation to their divine patroness, who is at least theoretically constantly consulted and obeyed.

This deserted place, however, is not left vacant. Rather than the goddess, it is the desire for renown and glory that dictates Ameer Ali's behavior. His crimes take on the appearance of victories won over worthy adversaries in difficult circumstances. The nabob Subzee Khan, who met a violent death, is one of them. He fascinates Ameer Ali. "I often wished that I had met him as a friend, or enrolled myself under him, when I might have followed his banner and . . . endeavoured to equal his deeds of valour" (Taylor 1986a, 249). Because he cannot share the fate of such an admirable victim, he claims to dare eliminate him. He tells Budrinath: "It may be something new to kill a Nuwab, but think, man, think on the glory of being able to say we had killed Subzee Khan, that valiant among the valiant: why, our fathers and grandfathers never did such an act before" (Taylor 1986a, 252).

He is daring; death has meaning only if one can defy it, play with it, take risks. The thought of inflicting death when the victims have no possibility of escape repulses him. The murder of two travelers doomed for having unexpectedly come on the scene makes him "sick." "I watched them; they stood up mechanically when they were ordered to do so, and stretched out their necks for the fatal *roomal*, and were slain as unresistingly as sheep beneath the knife of the butcher" (Taylor 1986a, 298). He looks upon his own death the same way. At Sagar he first rejects the offer of becoming an informer: "Death has no terrors for Ameer Ali, yet shame, everlasting shame has! . . . I was to die, but how? Not like a man or a soldier, but like a miserable thief" (Taylor 1986a, 538).

He probably exults the most when marching at the head of a unit entrusted to him by Chitu, as leader of one thousand splendid horsemen, "devouring mountains and drying up rivers." His physical courage, his respect for the soldier's code of honor, his understanding of military situations earn him the Pindari's praise on several occasions. The circumstances that lead him to leave Chitu's command are unexpected. The brutality of one of Chitu's lieutenants, Ghuffoor Khan, disgusts and anger him so much he decides to assassinate him. "He is a devil . . . unfit to live." Soldier by day, Thug by night. After this killing for "retributive justice," as he puts it, he perpetrates a number of others; but he is denounced in the end and has to flee.

This miscreant forsakes Thuggism, not because it brings in less profit than war but because he loves acts of bravery and the dangers of battle. He has a constant need to satisfy a desire for adventures. Three years after leaving Chitu the rajah of Jalaun cajoles the wealthy Thugs who have now become tax collectors over a vast part of his land. "Many persons from distant parts of the country, hearing of our mild and equitable mode of government, came and settled with us in our villages. Still a restless spirit was within me; . . . and again I longed to be at the head of my gallant fellows, and to roam awhile, striking terror in the country" (Taylor 1986a, 408).

Glory is of greater import than booty, and so is risk over comfort. Ameer Ali is driven by adventure, daring, the desire to be unconstrained by rules, taboos, and omens, except the need to preserve honor. Frankenstein too shuns material gains: "Wealth was an inferior object, but what glory would attend the discovery if I would banish disease from the human frame and render man invulnerable to any but a violent death!"

(Shelley 1969, 4). Ameer Ali, his exact symmetrical and contrary oppo-site, with few humanitarian concerns, precisely embodies the limit of this ambition. The sorcerer's apprentice persecuted by his creature, like the criminal persecuted by horrendous remorse, are both victims of the "dia-bolical return of the gods," whose prerogatives they have either usurped or neglected. They have had to endure similarly horrendous experiences. "To examine the causes of life, we must first have recourse to death. . . . Now I was forced . . . to spend days and nights in vaults and charnel-houses" (Shelley 1969, 51). In order to create the creature, and then the spouse the creature demands, Victor Frankenstein performs his nause-ating work. He gathers recovered bones, organs, and pieces of putrefied flesh. The job he is taking on is no less horrifying than the death rattle of Thugs' victims, whose bodies need to be quickly undressed, pierced with pickaxes to prevent them from swelling up, and dragged and thrown in a heap into holes.

The strongest, most marking experiences are located within this neces-sity of crossing the ideal limits of life and death, as the scientist explicitly states (Shelley 1969, 54), a "crossing" that translates into "experiencing" in the case of Ameer Ali. How often, facing the spectacle of trusting travel-ers behind whom the stranglers, ready for action, are standing, has Ameer Ali marveled at the tangible presence of this boundary? "To me, it was wonderful. I knew he was to die that night, and yet he was arranging his sleeping-place. . . . The pipe and the story passed round. . . . What could he have suspected? That he was in the hands of those from whom he was to meet his death?" (Taylor 1986a, 51–53).

Disbelief, the defiance of the rules of morality and religion, their boundless ambition finally lead the two characters into misfortune, soli-tude, and death or its equivalent, prison for life. They feel sadness and remorse, but against all expectations this does not appease the "irre-sistible force that makes of man at once homicide and suicide, assassin and executioner" (Baudelaire 1964, 113). They swear to avenge them-selves: Frankenstein against his creature, who has murdered his loved ones, and Ameer Ali, who states: "Had not my heart become hardened by oppression and misery? They have aroused within me a spirit of revenge against the whole human race" (Taylor 1986a, 529).

Ameer Ali and the Creature: Correspondences

"The monster is at once good and evil. For one used to horror stories where devils are clearly devilish, even though they can also be at time quite seductive, the monster is a strange character. Capable of the most violent anger, of the cleverest ruses, he is at the same time reasonable, thinking, and even affectionate" (Lecercle 1988, 27).

Shakespeare's verses used as epigraph to chapter 38 poetically describe this same paradox regarding Ameer Ali: "Oh what may man within him hide, though angel on the outward side." On the visible side Ameer Ali is this angel, as beautiful as the creature is ugly! But what does his heart hide in the inside? He asks Taylor: "You think my heart bad, then?" "Certainly" replies Taylor. But Ameer Ali defends himself. Let us listen; he almost tells the truth:

> "Have I not ever been a kind husband and a faithful friend? Did I not love my children and wife while He who is above spared them to me? And do I not even now mourn their deaths? Where is the man existing who can say a word against Ameer Ali's honour, which ever has been and ever will remain pure and unsullied? Have I ever broken a social tie? ever been unfaithful or unkind to a comrade? ever failed in my duty and in my trust? ever neglected a rite or ceremony of my religion?"
>
> "But the seven hundred murders, Ameer Ali, what can you say to them? They make a fearful balance against you in the other scale."
>
> "Ah! those are a different matter," said the Thug laughing, "quite a different matter. I can never persuade you that I was fully authorized to commit them, and only an humble instrument in the hands of Allah. . . . Would they have died, without it being His will?" (Taylor 1986a, 267)

Good and bad, yes. Bad because of his crimes, his efforts to accomplish them, his diabolical ruses; but good for the reasons he states. His confession starts out as a blaspheme: he dearly regrets the excitement and the pleasures of his past life. But gradually, as he tells more of his story, he too, like the Creature, reveals that he is as unhappy as he is friendly and succeeds in eliciting our sympathy and compassion (Taylor 1986a).

In his analysis of *Frankenstein* Jean-Jacques Lecercle shows that the Creature, a sort of embodied oxymoron, is constructed from contradictory information and discourses. These are not the same ones that make up Ameer Ali. Indeed, at first sight, this latter is not at all like the Creature, who is "without family, country, childhood, excluded from the chain of being. . . . Doubly abandoned by God, who did not create it and against whom it was created" (Lecercle 1988, 29). In contrast, Ameer Ali was incorporated into the community through the appropriate rites so that Thuggism is for him synonymous with belonging, with being linked to the chain of his peers. And yet while the cult of Kali brings the Thugs closer to each other, it also cuts them off from the rest of humankind, as the young boy's father solemnly and without circumlocution reminds him in the course of his initiation ritual.

To this group marginality, Ameer Ali adds his own personal distance: "I am soldier by disposition, a Thug by profession." There is contradiction in the fabric of his person and in the plane of his motivations. He is an atypical Thug: a Thug without being a disciple of Kali, a Thug for want of being a soldier. This does not keep him from being the best among Thugs and from loving them dearly. He is overwhelmed by his father Ismail's love, and he returns it with a childish devotion: "My father, said I, you need say no more, I am yours; do as you will with me" (Taylor 1986a, 32), he tells him before his initiation. It is thus not for want of the social contract that he becomes bad, and neither, in contrast to the Creature, is it because God has abandoned him. But they both lead to the same results.

Among all the dissonances that distance Ameer Ali from the Creature, there is yet an assonance greater than murder that brings them together. "And what was I? Of my creation and creator I was absolutely ignorant" (Shelley 1969, 102). Ameer Ali too ignores everything about his origins. The question "Who am I?" permeates his *Confessions*. We readers know the answer from the start, as Ameer Ali, following chronological order, narrates his "first memory" in the first chapter. The anamnesis he then undergoes is a repetition of a preceding one that occurred while he was in prison at Lucknow, shortly before his arrest at Sagar. It frames his narrative, though it comes up only at its end. During the greater part of his life he forgets. The mystery thus is centered on the subterranean and determining manner in which his life, unbeknownst to himself, has been ruled by this memory.

Intermittent Memories

"I have an indistinct recollection of a tall fair lady whom I used to call mother . . . also of a sister who was younger than myself, but of whom I was passionately fond." He is five years old at the time. He also remembers setting out on a trip with his parents accompanied by an escort of soldiers. After three or four days the caravan stops at a town. The little boy plays in the street. A "good-looking man of middle age addressed me. . . . 'You shall ride a horse, too, one of these days, and wear a sword and shield like me.'" The next day the man and his band travel with the caravan of the child. The little boy rides on the horse that his new friend has lent him. The third day his friend advises the boy's father to send back his escort. Ameer Ali then gives the young soldiers "an old rupee" for his little sister, asking them to tell her to wear it around her neck so as not to forget him. The next day, very early, well before dawn, Ameer Ali again climbs with his friend Ismail onto the beautiful horse. Ismail gets down to drink and tells the child to keep on going by himself.

Before I had got well across the stream, I heard a cry, and the noise, as if of a sudden scuffle. It alarmed me; and in looking back to see from whence it proceeded, I lost my balance on the horse and fell heavily on the stones in the bed of the river, which cut my forehead severely. I bear the mark now. I lay for a short time, and raising myself up, saw all the men, who I thought were far on before us, engaged in plundering the booty. I now began to scream with all my might. One of them ran up to me, and I saw it was the ill-looking man [Ganesha] I have before mentioned. "Ah! we have forgotten you, you little devil!" cried he; and throwing an hand-kerchief round my neck, he nearly choked me. Another man came up hastily—it was my friend. "He must not be touched," he cried angrily to the other, and seized his hands; they had a violent quarrel, and drew their swords. . . . I was so much frightened that I lost all consciousness, and, as I suppose, fainted. I was recovered by some water being forced into my mouth; and the first objects which met my eyes were the bodies of my father and mother, with those of the palankeen-bearers, all lying confusedly on the ground. . . . I only recollect throwing myself on my dead mother, whose face appeared dreadfully distorted, and again relapsing into insensibility. Even after the lapse of thirty-five years, the hideous appearance of my mother's face, and particularly of her eyes, comes to my recollection.

After traveling for a long time, Ameer Ali is entrusted to the care of Myriam, Ismail's wife. "In fine, I was formally adopted by them as their own, and my sufferings were speedily forgotten" (Taylor 1986a, 13–18).

Ismail's frequent absences intrigue him so much that one night he spies on him and overhears a strange conversation. It opens his eyes on two mysteries. First his own, as he hears Ismail tell his friends: "He was the son of. . . ." But he can't understand the rest spoken in Ramasee. And then the mystery that the men in the group share in their incomprehensible language. "Who could my parents be? I had gathered from the conversation, that Ismail was not my father . . . but all was dark in me" (Taylor 1986a, 25). This question fades in favor of the other one—that of Ismail's activities, where Ameer Ali directs his attention. Ismail opens up to him about them. "I have now no alternative but to make you such as I am myself" (Taylor 1986a, 30). Thus Ameer Ali adopts his adoptive father's identity and for almost the whole of his life as a free man believes that he is his real son.

And yet his penchant for the life of a warrior does emanate from his biological father, the proud Pathan. The glory he frenetically pursues and that leads him to constantly expose himself, to have his name known, might also be the symptom of his quest for identity. For the same reasons he is drawn to repeat the initial situation that changed the course

254

of his destiny. After his son's death, he yearns for all the male children of strangled victims. On the first opportunity it is none other than Ganesha, the Thug whom he now hates and had already disliked in the original scene, who grabs the child he wants and violently throws him on the heap of corpses, killing him just as he had wanted to kill Ameer Ali in the past—and exactly as Sleeman's informers' confess doing.

The veil opens up, in part, in the course of an expedition that accidentally leads Ameer Ali into a village that, along with its inhabitants, seem familiar to him. The powerful talisman he seizes from one of the travelers from this village, whom he strangles with his own hands, reminds him of the battered rupee he in the past entrusted to his father's soldiers to give to his young sister. The face of this very beautiful woman is familiar to him. The signs multiply, but he doesn't believe them. After he has broken two interdicts, the murder of a woman and the stealing of her talisman (in Ramasee, *teekula*), misfortunes pile up. The veil lifts halfway when Ismail, condemned to death by the rajah of Jalaun, confesses to his adopted son that he is not his father. Ameer Ali, branded with a red hot iron, is led to the border of the kingdom. His freedom is of short duration. He is imprisoned at Lucknow. There, an old Thug stitches together the bits and pieces of his intermittent memories and of Ismail's confession.

The *Confessions* ends on a "fatal revelation":

> Ismail was married, but had no children. . . . He used often to say to us, that he regretted your father had left your sister behind when he undertook his fatal journey to Indore.
>
> "My sister! cried I." . . .
>
> "Yes! . . . You might get news of her at Eklera, if ever you get out of this cursed hole."
>
> Why did not my heartstrings crack in that moment? Why did I leave to drag a load of remorse with me to my grave? . . . Sahib, after this fatal revelation, I know not what I did for many days. I believe I raved, and they thought me mad. . . . My hair turned grey, my form and strength wasted . . . a kind of burning fever possessed me. (Taylor 1986a, 524–26)

Ameer Ali, like those people whom Baudelaire so appreciated, is a dissonant being.

The Social Bond

In his report on wolf-children in India (Sleeman 1889, 87–97), Sleeman claimed that they could not be recognized by their real parents because thieves (again!) lay in wait at the entrances of caves where they lived to rob them of their jewelry and clothes. Criminal savagery took the relay of natural wildness.[9] Sleeman heard rumors of several cases, all identical. Having learned to live with their new protectors and walking on all fours and growing long hair all over their bodies, the animal-children could never again get used to human society. They escaped from it or died young.

Like the wolf-children, Taylor's Ameer Ali keeps only a trace of his previous life: the scar from his fall from the horse at the moment of his parents' murder. Oblivion, encouraged by his new family, submerges this memory, which would have at any rate kept the orphan from living with Ismail, his sole protector. Ameer Ali thus dons the pelt of the Thugs. For Taylor, man is a wolf for man not because he is evil, but because he is cut off from society. Deprived from the pleasure society could give him, he turns the "bloody laws of mankind" against it. The narrative contradiction also has its chronological side; circumstances made the monster, and they denatured a natural personality that was good (Lecercle 1988, 36). Neither in Mary Shelly nor in Meadows Taylor is evil seen as a natural perversity or a mysterious force. Rather, it is the result of a disastrous family story in which birth (or survival) of the characters has been marked by murder. The Creature and Ameer Ali are the products of an inverted sacrifice. Victor Frankenstein gives life and so does Ismail by tearing the child away from his programmed death. Frankenstein uses putrefied flesh, while Ismail kills the parents. Both characters are born from the work of death. They will have no other choice, then, than to be the conduit of the violence of which they are the victims. The horrible assassin starts out as martyred child.

But the family, assassinated or denied, is not only the point of departure, the origin of their violence. It is also the privileged and terrifying locus on which this violence is unknowingly aimed. Like Oedipus, both the Creature and Ameer Ali kill a member of their family without being aware of it: the Creature's first murder is of William, Victor's brother, and thus at least his imaginary paternal uncle, while, as we know, Ameer Ali strangles his sister. There is a triple barrier between them and their families: the murders that exclude them from it, their birth that cut them off from their ascendants, and finally the lack of descendants. There is no spouse for the Creature condemned to total solitude, a solitude that also marks the end of the Thug's life. He has no close family as he never can replace his dead son, and he has lost his wife Azima, who died of sorrow when she found out she was the wife of a murderer. His daughter, entrusted to a mullah, is to never see him again and know who her father is. He also lost his extended family and his friends when he became informer.

The contradictions within these "good and bad" characters originates in family history. The child and the Creature started out as tabula rasa. They became wolves because society, as extension and metaphor of the family, forced them to spread evil.

Taylor and his Novel's Character

I was wondering in chapter 3 about the lives of the children adopted by the Thugs after their parents' murders. The *Confessions* offer a possible answer to this question. But by making his character into the victim of this practice, Taylor subverts the official image of the Thugs, whose ethnography and then whose science held that their propensity for crime, inscribed in the circumvolutions of their brains, had been handed down from one generation to another. His Ameer Ali escapes this determinism. He is the victim of chance, or of fate, as he repeats numerous times. This monster in human form has morally left the camp of evil: he regrets his past, remorse is eating at him. In the course of the *Confessions*, Taylor explicitly pushes his reader to adopt this viewpoint. He does this in various ways that involve communicating his own emotions to the reader so as to break through the barrier of their disapproval: "Although the mind would ordinarily reject sympathy with the joys or sorrows of a murderer like Ameer Ali, one so deeply stained with crime, . . . yet for the moment I was moved to see, that after the lapse of nearly twenty years by his account, the simple mention of the death of his favourite child could so much affect him, even to tears, and they were genuine." Taylor also emphasizes the honorableness of his character and the lack of the ignominious duplicity that was thought to be an atavistic perversity.

> Ameer Ali is a *Bhula Admee* even in the eyes of his jailers; a respectable man, a religious man, one who from his youth has said his *Namaz* five times a day, is most devout in his life and conduct, is most particular in his devotions, keeps the fast of the *Ramzan* and every saint's day in his calendar, dresses in green clothes in the *Mohorun,* and beats his breast and tears his hair as a good *Syud* of Hindostan ought to do; in short, he performs the thousand and one ceremonies of his religion, and believes himself as sure of heaven and all the houris promised there as he now is of a good dinner. (Taylor 1986a, 263–64)

Finally, Taylor compares the Thugs to other groups dwelling at the margins, such as organized criminals, mercenaries, pillagers, and rebels. "The free bands of Germany, the Lanzknechts, the Banditti, the Condottieri of Italy, the Buccaneers and Pirates, and in our own time the fraternity of Burkes and Hares (a degenerate system of Thuggee, by the by, at which Ameer Ali, when I told him of them, laughed heartily)" (Taylor 1986a, 264). As I elucidated this passage, I too had to laugh when I discovered in the *Harrap's Standard English-French Dictionary* that the verb "to burke" means "to smother or strangle someone in order to sell his cadaver to be dissected, as Burke was doing in Edinburgh."[10] Could these Scottish Thugs at the service of a science taking on the guise of a new Kali with decidedly infernal tendencies have been the phrenologists' secret purveyors?

Predictably, however, Taylor closes his narrative with the representation of an equitable colonial justice that locks up Ameer Ali forever. It also sends the "mean" Ganesha to the gallows, and it is then his turn to die like "a sheep under the butcher's knife." Was the justice meted out on the Thugs objectionable? Ameer Ali's confession is already quite troubling as it shows the exception to the moral order to be born from an individual history, from a horrifying and secret story relayed by the "bloody laws" of society. Taylor's further interjections and innuendos in the body of this confession [*aveux*][11] sap the official discourse on the Thugs even while recognizing that it does apply to some of them.

Romantics and Barbarians

Ameer Ali's strange pitfalls, his tragic fate, his ambivalent nature, his compulsive relationship with murder, makes for numerous affinities with the romantic ideal influenced by the "gothic flame."[12] "The discovery of Horror as a source of delight reacted on men's actual conception of Beauty itself; the Horrid, from being a category of the Beautiful, became eventually one of its essential elements, and the 'beautifully horrid' passed by insensible degrees into the 'horribly beautiful'" (Praz 1978, 10). The British eighteenth century was at the forefront of this new perception of the sublime generated by pain, exalting "the Pleasure derived from Objects of Terror" and "those kinds of Distress which excite agreeable sensations."[13] Baudelaire's *L'art romantique* elaborates this aesthetic of the exceptional and the paradoxical. To the readers of the *Flower of Evil* (1868), he addresses the famous verses in which we can sense the shadow of a Thug: "Boredom. —His eye filled with unwilled tears / He dreams of scaffolds as he smokes his hookah."[14] Fascinated by the socially fallen, by the marginal, by assassins, the poet translates Edgar Alan Poe, and De Quincey's *On Murder Considered as One of the Fine Arts* (1963), in which the Thugs occupy a choice place. Interested by eccentricities, Baudelaire claims that modern beauty lies in strangeness, in the odd; pleasure involves surprise. In words that evoke Ameer Ali, Octavio Paz explains the nature of this modernity. It is consciousness of change, a consciousness synonymous with misfortune.

> In the past . . . men could escape eternity. Modern man is condemned to the instant, to instability. He has no rest. No matter: there is a moment where time, since it cannot stop, turns on itself; an instant that is not outside of time but before history which is the other side of the present. It is the original instant; in it modernity unfolds as a timeless antiquity: the time of the savage. In destroying

the idea of eternal beauty, modernity opens the gates to the world of the barbarians. . . .

The moment of origin doesn't suspend time: it is the other side of actuality just as barbarism is inverse of civilization. Each of these realities is prisoner of this relation and depends on the other: the savage is only the viewpoint of the civilized. (Paz 1983, 115–16)

Mary Shelley's and Taylor's characters, "monsters tattooed by death," so different from each other and yet linked by surprising correspondences, open the gate of the world to the barbarians. By turning time around as Octavio Paz describes, the deformed Creature, so agile in climbing mountains, so fast a runner, so resistant to the cold, so powerful, and so big, represents the dawn of humankind, a time closer to animality than to the Adam and Eve of the Genesis. Ameer Ali, the inheritor of a bloody cult devoted to a cannibal goddess, also represents this dawn, where the inchoate god of the Christians is absent.

The Mythologizing of the Thugs

Mary Shelley's belief that her narrative involved "so many exquisite combinations of human feelings" (Shelley 1969,13) has fallen by the wayside; now readers look at her work as a modern myth. From 1910 to the present,[15] hundreds of films have been made in which the Creature keeps on questioning his creator and the public: Who am I? Ameer Ali too asked this question, but his has not had the same repercussions in the West. Why? The answer perhaps lies in the distinction Mary Shelley established between the possible and the credible. "The event on which this fiction is founded has been supposed, by Dr Darwin and some of the physiological writers of Germany, as not of impossible occurrence," she wrote in her preface. The father of the theoretician of evolution looked positively upon her fable as scientifically thinkable even though materially unrealizable. In Shelley's view, this source of inspiration offered more freedom than did the credible: "The interest of the story . . . was recommended by the novelty of the situation which it develops, and however impossible as a physical fact, affords a point of view to the imagination for the delineating of human passions more comprehensive and commanding than any which the ordinary relations of existing events yield." She notes that the *Iliad, The Tempest,* and *Paradise Lost* follow the same rule: "I have thus endeavoured to preserve the truth of the elementary principles of human nature, while I have not scrupled to innovate upon their combinations" (Shelley 1969, 13).

Ameer Ali is obviously not possible in the same and very new sense as the Creature made by the scientist, a modern Prometheus who uncovered the secret of life. He is merely credible. He does not fit as well the definition of the myth as an imaginary solution to a real contradiction. This because he is an answer so permeated with historical truth that Taylor even attempts to make us believe he is a witness worthy of being believed. Moreover, the contradiction he does embody is only a moral one. It does not reflect, as does that embodied by Victor Frankenstein, the conflict between science and conscience sharpened by the century of scientific discoveries that was at play in the romantic premonition of the young novelist.

Dracula (first published in 1897), another important modern myth, does not embody this conflict either. Like the Thug, Dracula's story sets the opposition between good and evil in religious terms. But the vampire is a phantasmagoric character and is eternal by his nature; "his centuries-old age is an abyss that gives the best possible image of the myth" (Lecercle 1988, 76). In contrast, Ameer Ali is an ordinary man, close to death at the end of his narrative. His confessions, his denunciations have emptied him of substance, prison has doomed him to a desertic existence "without pleasure, worries, pain." Dracula threatens to "invade London, to settle in the heart of the Empire and to destroy its values" (Lecercle 1988, 76). Ameer Ali is the last representative of a danger that has been eliminated in a very distant colony. He could have served as model to other narratives on Kali's stranglers. This was not to be the case; Ameer Ali has no direct heirs. His ambivalence is too embarrassing and his vision of India too indulgent.

In this way, Taylor invented a new universe of exotic literature, first by using his direct experience of India and its culture, then by expressing his admiration for them, and finally because he refused to be their privileged and omniscient observer. He preferred the role of theater director, the one who made facts "more attractive, more interesting." Just as he himself was colonized by the culture surrounding him, Taylor the nabob colonized his character with the values and key ideas of his own culture regarding the family, psychology, and the unconscious. He turned his Thug into a modern hero pulled in different directions, close to us and thus opposed to Sleeman's extreme dehumanizing vision of a state of nature that preceded the age of reason.

SEVEN   # Later Thug Adventures

HOW THUGS BECAME THE STUFF OF MEDIA

Since their discovery, the Thugs have become the stuff of various media. Works of fiction, press accounts, and visual representations, as well as serious studies in history and ethnology, all have contributed to the fame of the criminal idolater and the heroic colonizer. A quick overview of this highly diversified process of representation shows that it is not surprising that we find the Thugs in present-day Western-made adventure films set in India. *Ramaseeana* and the *Confessions* each has had its descendants corresponding to its original type of either scientific or fictional discourse.

Sleeman's Heirs

Among Sleeman's heirs I am not including here the numerous travel books, encyclopedias, and other works in which the Thugs are mentioned in whole chapters, articles, or paragraphs, because these often repeat word for word what by now we know almost by heart. Sleeman, as we understand too well, is taken as the sole authority on Thug matters, and it is to him that other colonizers, historians, ethnologists, and chroniclers of India turn for information. In 1857 James Hutton pilfered extensively from *Ramaseeana* in his *A Popular Account of the Thugs and Dacoits*. During the next century Sir Francis Tuker (1961) with *The Yellow Scarf: An Account of Thuggee and Its Suppression* and George Bruce (1968) with *The Stranglers: The Cult of Thuggee and Its Overthrow in British India* do likewise. However, they also read their hero's correspondence and consult archives.

The word *Thug* was probably introduced in France during the first half of the nineteenth century. It was used in the journal *Anthropologie*, which published the translation of an article bearing the enticing title "Du meurtre religieux et philosophique dans l'Inde" ("On religious and philosophical murder in India"). The article, which summarized *Ramaseeana*, had come out in the Edinburgh gazette.[1] This article on the stranglers' "philosophy" (that is, Kali's cult) was the third one on the topic. The preceding ones evoked the arrests and executions of the Thugs, who sang "songs whose refrain is: Glory to Bindachul, glory to Bhowani!"

Sleeman's grandson, the colonel James L. Sleeman, also had access to "family papers" to write his *Thug, or a Million Murders* (1933), but these papers do not seem to contain more information than the official papers do. James Sleeman's was the only work of this type translated into French; it was published by Payot in Paris in 1934 as *La Secte secrète des Thugs, Le culte de l'assassinat aux Indes* (The secret sect of the thugs, the cult of murder in India). Its cover illustration depicts "the great goddess of the Thugs" of the temple of Bindachul, "from a drawing by Miss Fanny Parks" (the tireless traveler with whom we are familiar).

These books all pay homage to William Sleeman for his victory over the stranglers, his literary works, and his "immense knowledge of the languages and religions of India." They are strongly tainted by the sensationalism of his "anonymous" article published in the Calcutta gazette and in particular by his trivial and striking metaphors, such as his comparison of the freedom and independence of the Thugs with that of "a gentleman in an English pub," or again the comparison in his anonymous letter of the Thugs to hares making their burrows near kennels when they settle close to the seats of British courts of law, and so on. These metaphors were to have long-term careers, particularly in Sleeman's direct descendant, as James Sleeman also turns the Thugs into familiar figures for the Western reader. He states that "it must surely compel the most skilled and ruthless Chicagoan gun-man to feel the veriest amateur by comparison" (Sleeman 1933, 1). He brings up with the utmost seriousness "the strange history of Dr. Jekyll and Mr. Hyde . . . [but] the actual dual personality of the Thug must surely be more so," and he puts down Stevenson's novel in favor of his own as "these true tales of Thuggee must surely appeal to those who prefer fact to fancy" (Sleeman 1933, 4).

All these authors call upon History and its ally, Science. One of James Sleeman's chapters, titled "one million murders" attempts to establish the number of victims of the Thugs "by using the law of averages" and the mysterious fact of "the curiously level standard maintained by Indian statistics" (Sleeman 1933, 233).

> For the purpose of arriving at a correct estimate we will . . . assume 10,000 [victims]. . . . Neither shall we assume this be the annual toll

of three hundred years of killing but the most modest estimate of 10,000 Thug victims a year for a hundred years. In other words, in order to err on the side of caution and to avoid the least trace of exaggeration, the estimate of a million murders is based upon one-fourth of the area of the country over which the Thugs operated, and for one-third of the period only during which this hideous faith is known to have existed. (Sleeman 1933, 236)

This literature is repetitive, arrogant in its principle (all of the authors believe they possess the truth), and imaginary in its claims. The authors' whims might lead them to exaggerate or obliterate a given detail or even invent new ones. The Thugs' mode of communication is said to be "telegraphic" (Caunter 1836), so that speed and the invisibility of technical miracle is added to their coded signs. They trade their loot carelessly, are lazy, and engage in debauchery. They might be "moralists, priests, artists," "sweet, affable, honest in their dealings and excellent citizens"[2] though unfortunately in the sway of pagan beliefs, or alternatively, as for George Bruce1968, mentally sick people whose "schizoid state" produces "a hypnotic effect, linked to emotional and moral insensibility." Their group is at times Westernized (an "association," a "confraternity," a "guild," a "league," a "nation," a "race unto itself") or, on the contrary, indigenized (a "caste," "clans," "tribes," or a "mixture of castes," or again a group made up of "several ranks of society"), and so on.

These modern Orientalists are Sleeman's vassals. They do not read the sources and do not propose different hypotheses. In their view, the affair of the Thugs has been correctly settled once and for all, and the British empire can be proud of the justice it has meted out to them.

Taylor's Heirs

The Thugs are only one motif among many in the prolific Anglo-Indian literature, and it is amusing to note that perhaps because Taylor's book has been reedited regularly his heirs have mostly expanded outside of India. One of the most famous among them is incontestably the Italian novelist Emilio Salgari (1862–1911), who was nicknamed the Italian Jules Verne because of the immense popularity of his adventure novels. Kali and the inhuman Thugs appear in his *I Misteri della giungla nera* (The mysteries of the black jungle), published in 1895, then in his three-volume "Malaysian cycle," *Li Avventure di Sandokan.*

In 1859 Méry published *Les Etrangleurs de l'Inde* (The Stranglers of India), a fictional reportage in which he attributes to Taylor the discovery of "the infernal secret of their ritual burials."

These monsters have nothing in common with the human race. . . .
They seem to have been issued from the mating of hyenas with ba-

boons. A thin copper membrane barely covers their hideous skele-
ton, they have claws for toe nails, their flat hair is glued on their
depressed foreheads, a knot of angular and wrinkled muscles attaches their heads to their shoulders, and two ambers burn under
their eyelids. (Méry 1859, 30)

In "daily installments of a novel whose readers unavoidably want to
know the outcome after reading the beginning" with runs of several thousand, the stereotype of the strangler was first spread in *Le Juif errant*
(The wandering Jew) (1844–1845) by Eugène Suë, then in *Le procès des
Thugs* (The trial of the Thugs) (1879) by René de Pont-Jest. The illustrations of these novels were linked to the representations produced by
pre-Orientalist travelers who saw in Hindu gods monsters very much resembling those of their own culture (Mitter 1977).

After independence in 1947, John Masters, an officer of the Company
for fourteen years, left India and settled in the United States. His novels set in India have been compared to Kipling's and were best sellers
between 1951 and 1961. Masters represents an important figure for the
popular image of India in America, and his writing is said to be "flam-
boyant" (Ramsdell 1983). *The Deceivers*, which reopens the Thug topos,
and *Bhowani Junction* were to be turned into films. In France in the
1960s there was a lively interest in the Thugs in children's literature. They
made their appearance in comic strips and in novels for adolescents. Bob
Morane, Henri Vernes's hero, in books published by Marabout Junior,
fights the stranglers in the "complete stories of his exciting adventures"
with graceful titles such as *La marque de Kali* (Kali's mark), *La couronne
de Golgonde* (The crown of Golgonda), and *Les joyaux du maharajah* (The
maharajah's jewels). The Thugs had become a subject for popular adolescent literature.

Thug Images

The turning of Thugs into media images also involved visual representations, such as the portraits of tattooed Thugs or drawings of Thugs in action painted with watercolors and used to illustrate Paton's manuscript,
as was the fashion of the time for travel diaries. George Bruce used some
of those drawings, as I also do here. The London British museum and the
Central City Museum of Jaipur in Rajasthan (Bayly 1990, 228–29) both
possess groups of statuettes "in wood, clay, and cloth" set on bases made
by a native artist from Madras in the year 1847 and representing small
scenes of "Thugs murdering their victims." The prince Alexis de Soltykoff,
in his *Voyages dans l'Inde*, published in 1851, told how these sorts of statuettes were made. At the Lucknow prison, the director showed him

Photograph of repented assassins demonstrating their craft for the camera in 1874, after the end of Thuggism. This photograph gave the false impression that the Thugs were still plying their trade at the time. Reprinted by permission of the British Library (IOL 355/1, 53d 8560119).

very well made statuettes of colored plasters, representing all sorts of massacre scenes perpetrated by Thugs. The artist who is a low caste Indian, was coming regularly to the prison by order of the Officer and used as models scenes that Thugs were acting out, taking up their positions with a certain amount of satisfaction, as they reminded them of their past prowesses when they were free. These admirable little groupings which were laid out on a table in front of me were so realistic that they made me tremble. (Soltykoff 1851)

Travelers went see the Thugs in the same way as they went to see the Taj Mahal. Alexis de Soltykoff bought the portrait of an eighty-nine year old man who boasted having strangled 999 persons and who "had stopped at this number only because he was proud of it." The criminals were made into objects on display in a gallery of curiosities. These elegant, rigid, and miniaturized tiny-toy-sized figurines made of "colored bits of plasters" were similar to those representing ethnic types and trades sold to tourists in present-day India.

In the 1860s, the Thugs were caught by the photographic camera and became more real than ever because it was believed photos could not lie. In the course of sessions organized by the School of Arts and Manufactures of Jabalpur Thugs again playacted the criminal acts that had been their specialty, but this time in front of the camera. In his book Sir Francis Tuker used the photos taken by a certain F. Beato in 1855. We see three assassins—though of course they are by that time "repented" ones, having been in prison for more than twenty years. They are bent casually over a victim lying on the ground, supposedly already dead. We are far from the secret jungles and their footpaths: on the left, there is the base of a column and in the background, a door.

The photo of "A Group of Thugs," by Samuel Bourne (c. 1860), is particularly interesting as the "fierce" expressions they were obviously requested to put on is the very sign of their criminal identity. In P. Thomas's book published in 1966, *Secrets of Sorcery Spells and Pleasure Cults of India,* this photo is part of an infernal trio made up also of a picture of a statue of Kali and one of a "*sadhu* or wandering beggar"! On the cover jacket of the last English edition (1988), this time touched up and in color, the Thugs have turbans and wear bright green, turquoise, yellow, and brown clothing. They are sitting cross-legged and barefoot on a lovely flower-patterned rug. Here this picture stands alone, but has been cropped and reframed. The three wise and old men that were on the left and right sides of the picture have been erased so that only the mean looking ones in the middle remain. They glare threateningly; one of them raises his right knee, and one of his hands rests on it as if he were getting ready to pounce and kill. We only have the photographer's word that these ordinary-looking men with turbans are Thugs! There is no longer any need to show them in action: their name suffices, though it is written in large letters. The stereotype has become quite widespread, at least in Great Britain (Tartakov 1979).

After the photographers it was filmmakers' turn to claim the Thugs. In 1939 the film *Gunga Din* was made. In the 1980s *Indiana Jones and the Temple of Doom* was all the rage. In 1990 television got into the act with an Italian-British-Indian coproduction, *I Misteri della giungla nera* (The mysteries of the black jungle). This made-for-TV film was popular enough to be shown on French television again in 1993.

From the time of Sleeman's discovery of the Thugs at the beginning of the nineteenth century in Jabalpur and Sagar to the present time in

Europe and the United States, the image of the religious assassins has been propagated in various forms ranging from the historical to the fictional, from the written to the visual, and finally to cinematographic representations. This reassessing of the struggle between good and evil in colonial and neocolonial contexts, this tireless rediscovery of Kali's stranglers is still surprising. Why this perseverance? Can it be explained with the argument that all colonial representations are beholden to the ideological split between Orient and Occident? Is it enough to simply argue that the Thugs are a good topic, a theme in some ways attractive?

Of course, as Thomas De Quincey quipped (1963, 25), people began to see that a successful crime is made up of more than the two dense characters of the victim and the assassin, plus a knife, a money purse, and a dark alleyway. The Thugs thus satisfy expanded new demands. But the effect sought is no guarantee of success: the film *The Deceivers,* based on John Masters's very popular novel, flopped even in England. The morbidly virtuous De Quincey brings out the import of composition, lighting, and shadows, as well as poetry and feelings in this genre. Other factors external to the intrinsic quality of the works themselves can favor their success. First, the Thugs did exist; then they fit in well with the outlook of the times, as the Gothic current remains very popular; finally, they match Western expectations and fears: is not India, the land of spirituality, also violent, chaotic, and unpredictable?

Though these written and cinematographic works do carry information about collective imaginings on the "East/West" relationship , they nonetheless are not, as is often believed, a storehouse and refuge for the clichés inherited from colonialism. With these works the relation with truth changes angle of vision and is given a new lighting.

FRENCH IMAGININGS

France and India

The French have a special relationship with India. The British took it from them in the eighteenth century. In the nineteenth century the Oriental Renaissance I evoked in chapter 5 finally revealed to the French public a brilliant civilization that had remained close to its sources. This heady discovery might have aggravated feelings of regret for a loss resented as unfair. The disappointed French envied the British, whom they generally looked upon as scornful, if not outright racist, toward the Indians. They felt a strong resentment that percolated through the equivocal way the Thugs were regarded in nineteenth-century popular novels.

This nostalgia for India was still present shortly before World War II. Claude Farrère, a member of the *Academie Française,* gave free rein to

Photograph of Thugs in captivity after the end of Thuggism, taken by Bourne and Shepherd ca. 1870. The photograph, reframed and with colors added, appears on

"bitterness, anger, and a feeling of absurdity" in his *L'Inde perdue*, (Lost India), published in 1935. Jacques Weber, who wrote a history of the French trading posts in India in the nineteenth century (1988), shows that Delamare, in his book *Désordres à Pondichéry* (1938), was depicting the Pondichéry establishment as an enterprise in successful colonization in

the cover of *Confessions of a Thug*, reprinted by Oxford University Press in 1985. Reprinted by permission of the British Library (IOL 28/2, 51).

which the French-style assimilation policy "made an art of living together possible," an art that flourished in the black city, "the city of love," containing "precise French architecture mixed with the ritual images of gods and elephants." This apologia went hand in hand with a focus on the disastrous past: Delamare devoted no fewer than "seven pages in analyzing

Undated drawing by A. de Neuville from a photograph taken in the Aurangabad prison in 1889, depicting another group of Thugs as unfriendly looking as the one in the preceding illustration.

the cause of the failure of the French colonial enterprise in India, through a brief summary of its history in the eighteenth century," and represented the white city of trade, "a forgotten, fallen, capital," as a "city of silence and regret" (J. Weber 1993, 383–85).

Because they do not possess India, French writers "dream it more than they know it, draw from its exotic universe without concern for its Indianness." French fiction generally shows a "brutal desire to unite with India and capture it in its most seductive aspects" (Champion 1993, 57–58). The reader might perhaps remember that the first Thug the French encountered was that beautiful and treacherous woman described by the traveler Thévenot in the seventeenth century! She laid in wait between Agra and Delhi and pretended distress so as to seduce and rob the naive traveler. At that time she was not yet bearing the nefarious name of Thug. We need to wait till 1844–1845 for Eugène Süe to open the door of French fiction to the stranglers in Le Juif errant. This serial novel met with extraordinary popular and financial success as the circulation of the paper that published it, Le Constitutionel, soared from three thousand to more than forty thousand. It provoked the jealously of Balzac, who planned to write "two or three major works that would overthrow the false gods of this ersatz literature" (Lacassin 1983, 4). In Süe's novel the prince Djalma, whose "features are both of great nobility and charming beauty," is dispossessed by the British. He is "first imprisoned by them as a state prisoner after the death of his father Kadja Sing, killed fighting" (Süe 1983, 128). He then goes into exile on the island of Java. Like his friend the general Simon, he is a victim of the criminal intrigues of the Jesuits settled at Pondichéry who have Thugs in their pay. Eugène Süe, who referred to Sleeman, wrote that "the Thugs are linked to a dark and invisible power in the name of which they spread everywhere, *so as to make corpses,* to use one of their savage expressions." But Süe, in spite of being a dandy, was also a convert to socialism. His stranglers were even more clearly oppressed than those of Taylor, whom he met in London (Mirsky 1986, ix). In Süe's eyes, Thuggism, which the Thugs call "the good work," was a response to the internal tyranny of Indian society. "There is no doubt that such a religion can only flourish in countries practicing the worst kind of slavery as India does, the most pitiless exploitation of man by man. . . . Perhaps this homicidal sect perpetuated itself in these regions as the only possible protest of slavery against despotism" (Süe 1983, 141)—to which Süe added the exploitation by the colonizers. Three of his Thugs escape from India with their chief Feringheea (spelled Feringhea in the novel), and they are planning to spread the good works in Java and in all countries of oppression, misery, corruption, and slavery, as "the Dutch are as rapacious as the British" (Süe 1983, 142–43).

1877: A Thug Trial in a Serial Novel

René de Pont-Jest,[3] an author and a legal columnist for the *Figaro*, fascinated by distant lands and criminal issues, devoted a much more central place to the Thugs than did Eugène Suë.[4] However, there is an additional reason for us looking at his *Procès des Thugs* (Thug Trials),[5] published in 1877: there has probably never been a case in which the Thugs have been so thoroughly crammed into an author's phantasms. The Thug topos transplanted in France severed all ties with Thug history. However, Pont-Jest did read the classical works on the topic. He was filled with the revulsion Sleeman felt for the assassins, and he perfectly understood the romantic interest of Taylor's repented hero. Perhaps to hide what he owed each of them or simply to capitalize on the fame acquired by Feringheea in Eugène Suë's serial, he called his hero by the same name and gave him the ambivalence of Ameer Ali. At the same time, he created an almost-namesake of Ameer Ali, "Hyder Ali," to whom he attributed the ferocity of Ganesha in the *Confessions!*

Pont-Jest's India overflows with exoticism. It has all the seduction of a French-style Indian dream; it is prodigiously diverse, it has supernatural mystics, and it is the scene of the unleashing of extravagant passions. In the first part of the serial novel, titled "Feringhea," the Thugs are presented within the pomp of a trial held in Madras in 1850, in which the main person accused, Feringheea, is tried while there is a crowd waiting to celebrate the expected punishment. In the second part, "The Avatar," Nadir, Feringheea's son, becomes the Thugs' leader and persuades them that "the tiger of Sagar will crush the British lion" (Pont-Jest 1879, 357). He leaves for England under a pseudonym to learn to know his enemies. The third part, titled "Satan's Legacy: The Avenger," turns Nadir into one of the secret leaders of Irish Fenianism making common cause with the working class against big capitalists. Discovered by the British police, Nadir flees to India, where he hides with his two wives, one English and the other Indian, and then decides to give up on violent action in order to devote himself to teaching the Hindu people.

I will limit myself to discussing only the first and second part of this serial novel and its author's vision of the Thugs, a vision as unbridled as it is exploitative.

JUDICIAL THEATER

The trial is held after a preliminary hearing chaired by Lord Bentinck in person, in which the deposition of Feringheea, the leader of the Thugs, was heard. The trial itself lasts four months, and at its close "the city of Madras was illuminated the whole night as in a feast day." This trial that leads "to the ruin of a whole creed, a whole race," is that of "the India of Brahma called before Christ's tribunal," that of the "Far East and its superstitions called before civilized Europe" (Pont-Jest 1879, 8–11).

"The most horrible cause that human justice has had to judge" (Pont-Jest 1879, 8–9) is heard on a set where a gigantic spectacle is played out, with its scenes, its key and secondary actors, its costumes and accessories, and even its choir represented by the public. Action is united in the sentence "without appeal" that is rendered after the overwhelming condemnation of the Thugs' misdeeds. The locus is united by "a hall with a sober architecture" in the government palace transformed for this occasion into a criminal court. Temporal unity is the only element of the trial that is not respected; time is distended, dilated, so as to accommodate the monstrous truth produced by more than one hundred defendants.

In this permanent theater parade witnesses and defendants of all nationalities and both genders, British, French, Indian, Chinese, Russian, Dutch, of all professions and castes, sepoy, barber, fakir, snake charmer, tradesperson, servant, pariah, sailor, pigeon raiser. The author lavishes particular care on the description of these "Orientals," who resemble the stickers exhibiting the worst sort of prejudices—and here it verges on the grotesque—that were given at the time in Europe as a bonus with the purchase of exotic products.

> The Hindu fakir wears as belt a steel cord on which hangs a heavy chain attached to a ring soldered around his right ankle. This strange personage holds his right arm raised up and the fingernails of his closed right hand are so long that they have penetrated his flesh.
>
> "I did not ask you to raise your arm," said the president.
>
> "It would be impossible for me to lower it," my Lord, replied the Hindu. "I had sworn to stay two whole years with my arm up, and at the end of this time my arm became stiff like an iron rod; I can't lower it anymore." (Pont-Jest 1879, 8–9)

The overexcited, eager, and impatient public includes Britishers as well as Hindus of all races and castes, and it reacts noisily all during the proceedings. The court trying the Thugs is turned into a popular tribunal. In the course of this gigantic inventory, emotional, convulsive narratives filled with suspense, twists and turns, and last-minute revelations describe the crimes of "a whole race" (Pont-Jest 1879, 9). We are told that the same trials with the same sentences are held all over India. Madras is only the epitome of the triumph of civilization over "the tigers with human faces." The white race lays bare the defects of a sect identified with the conquered race, and in so doing relegates the crimes linked to the conquest to a distant past. The court is the keeper of the law by which it judges the cases. It is a law that claims to protect reason, rather than the

LE PROCÈS

135267

DES THUGS

1ᴿᴱ PARTIE

FERINGHEA

PAR

RENÉ DE PONT-JEST

10 centimes	100 livraisons	50 centimes
LA LIVRAISON	2 LIVRAISONS PAR SEMAINE	LA SÉRIE DE 5 LIVRAISONS

UNE SÉRIE TOUS LES QUINZE JOURS

Title page of René de Pont-Jest's *Procès des Thugs*. Title pages in successive editions of the book were aimed at hooking readers on serial novels. René de Pont-Jest, *Le Procès des Thugs* (Lyon: Victor Bunel, 1879).

rights of the strongest, in the face of native violence. It is also a law that Pont-Jest concocted as entirely bereft of any referent to Indian culture.

THE TORTURE GARDEN

Pont-Jest's Thugs are torture masters; their confessions are exuberant demonstrations of the slow and tortuous paths that sometimes lead to death. Hyder Ali is *"Rundee an Julta,"* that is, "Women Burner" (Pont-Jest 1879, 81). as he nicknames himself. Pont-Jest, drawing from a skewed historical perspective, confers to his Thuggism a semblance of ortho-doxy by calling upon the rite of sati. He dwells on the fiction of the three burnings he creates and does not hesitate to imagine carnival-like and grotesque situations, such as that of the fakir with the paralyzed arm summoned by the judge. Here he has a character whose Thuggism is floundering cut off his own head by using a *karavat*.[6] His wife, who has just witnessed the suicide, calmly sits down next to her husband's decap-itated corpse and devotedly "takes his head on her lap" (Pont-Jest 1879, 85) while her feet are held over red-hot coals before she is thrown into the pyre!

The French-style Thugs are torturers of women, and their depravities partake more of the Marquis de Sade's universe than the Indian sectar-ian one, as illustrated by the sacrifice of forty young women spread on the ground in front of Kali and forming a carpet of "perfumed" flesh on which tread their executioners. The often implicit lubricity in at least one instance verges on necrophilia, in the case of the wife of a Macao Chinese first bitten by snakes and then thrown to wild pigs. "They jumped on her and with their snouts dug into this woman's body; their teeth ripping it apart as they fought over pieces of her quivering flesh" (Pont-Jest 1879, 147).

What a long road has been traveled from Ameer Ali's loves to the psy-chopathological debauches of Pont-Jest! They made theirs the duke of Blangis's maxim: "Pleasure comes solely from evil, not from its object" (Belaval 1976, 24). This India rivals the China octave Mirabeau creates in his *Jardin des supplices* (Garden of tortures) (1957).

ASSASSINS AND VICTIMS

The Thugs on trial have other peculiarities: they recruit their members outside of India, as this Irish Fenian who came to help them out, or this Van Lynden, a Dutch merchant from Java. Their victims of choice are preferably father (Ivan), husband (Mang Tseu), lover (Miss Clara), brother (Sir Temple), servant (Gilbert and Soulami). Anyone can become by choice or constraint the Thug of the person to whom he is linked by blood, marriage, or loyalty. This unsavory assortment of adventur-ers and perverts embodies "a Hindu evil" enriched with all the crimes of humankind. The Madras trial takes on the guise of a Last Judgment in which the representatives of order have the task of cleansing the world of the chaos of violence and sex. The author, who robs Taylor's work without citing him and who only gives Sleeman a small role in his novel, has taken literally Sleeman's statement about the Thugs: "The more it's unbelievable, the more it's true."

THEATER OF APPEARANCES

Pont-Jest had yet another agenda: he planned on incriminating the British, who, in his view, did not deserve India. Though they succeeded in cleansing the country from its fanatical practices and beliefs, the sons of the soon-to-be-hanged condemned are to one day fight those whom they saw as usurpers wrongfully judging their fathers. This theater of justice is a theater of appearances. The key to this twist lies in Feringheea, who has star billing in the performance we have just witnessed. Feringheea's story is the copy, adorned with Oriental baubles, of that of Ameer Ali. Feringheea was not destined to become a Thug. He was born in a marble palace filled with elephants and servants. At age twelve he studied in Benares with pandits who taught him "the history of his fatherland and the hatred for the oppressor" (Pont-Jest 1879, 22). He was then kidnapped and led to Thuggism. After having been initiated in its mysteries and having taken the ritual oath, he was made "to strike with a long Malaysian dagger, a person completely covered with long gauzy veils that two priests were holding in their arms" (Pont-Jest 1879, 51). He then discovered that the body was that of Goolab Sohbi, the woman he loved. It is then that he swore to kill one thousand victims for Kali and to follow the path laid out in his childhood by the Benares pandits.

Feringheea partakes of two destinies, of two histories, of two races even, as shown by "his proud and intelligent face, his extremely elegant body and his Greek type" (Pont-Jest 1879, 11). Incredible circumstances have turned him into the informer in the trial, but he bows to English law only in order to better strike it down later. And soon we will see the Thugs, now sporting a messianic aura, put their violence and cruelty at the service of a just cause, that of the fatherland. This complete reversal is accompanied by a strange detail: it is done through a coalition between Catholic Fenians and idolater Thugs. Did Pont-Jest see them as sharing a common hatred for the British, or more obscurely as sharing a boundless love for God that leads them to unite in the struggle against the British? Was this confusing alliance aimed at making the point that Hindus have more affinities with French Catholics than with their Protestant colonizers? Probably. In his other works Pont-Jest claims the intellectual and affective superiority of the French influence on their colonies and is persuaded that, thanks to this, the native population of Pondichéry is no longer the same as that of the rest of India. The Thugs who struggled against British conquest are thus avenging the French, from whom this conquest was taken away. And Nadir, who prefers the power of education to violence, strips the usurping colonialists from the moral justification of their enterprise. Thus *The Trial*, a colonial novel of a lost colony, fed with the illusion that the British do not deserve India, turns the Thugs into ardent patriots cleansed from their past crimes.

THUGS IN THE MOVIES

A discussion of films is the last stage of this exploration of the Thug topos in the realm of the imaginary. I am discussing here only a portion of this production, that is, three feature films and a made-for-TV one, spanning more than sixty years. The first film, George Stevens's *Gunga Din*, came out in 1939; Spielberg's *Indiana Jones and the Temple of Doom*[7] came out in 1984. *The Deceivers*, by Nicholas Meyer, came out in 1989 and was closely based on the excellent novel by John Masters (1952). Finally, Kevin Connor made *I Misteri della giungla nera* (The mysteries of the black jungle)[8] for television.

Predestination and Chance: The Contaminating Effect of India

In *Indiana Jones* and in *Mysteries of the Black Jungle*, the heroes are pre-destined for extraordinary adventures. Here the Indian imaginary meets the Western one. Indiana Jones learns from the village head that he has been predestined to land there and that he belongs to the fantastic filiation of the divine *avataras*:

"Shiva has led you here," he tells him.

"We haven't been led here, our plane crashed," protests Indiana.

"No," responds the chief, "we have prayed Shiva for a long time to recover the lingam. It's him who made you fall from the sky; it's why you will go to the Pankot palace to get the lingam and bring it back to us."

These commending words come to make sense to the archaeologist when he recognizes on a fragment of the Shiva manuscript the mount Kailash, the cosmic mountain in Hindu mythology that is the residence of the god and of Shankara (the wise old man we encountered in chapter 1 of the present book, who, thanks to his magical powers, reduced to ashes the hordes of *kapalika* ascetics). The Sanskrit text that accompanies this map and that Indiana easily translates tells that very long ago Shiva[9] gave the wise old man five magical stones in the shape of lingams[10] so as to fight against the forces of evil. The film fiction is consistent with this legend in its claim that the small Himalayan village where Indiana Jones lands is holder of one of these crystal phalluses that once belonged to Shankara. The film barely embroiders the story when it adds that this precious relic was stolen by Evil, who rules over Pankot, that is, the barbarian sect of the

Thugs. Because it was stolen, rain has stopped falling, the streams have dried out, and misery is everywhere. Chance is thus negated. Convinced by the manuscript he is reading, which backs the words of the chief, the archaeologist accepts entering into the myth proposed to him.

The Mysteries of the Black Jungle tells the saga of the Corishant family from 1843 to 1859 and its struggle against Mohan Singh, the leader of the Thugs, who has designs on their youngest daughter, Ada. To show that the fate of the Indian hero, Tremal Naik, too is predestined, the film draws from famous narrative situations. The kingdom of Rangnagar has been devastated, pillaged, and burned by the rajah Mohan Singh's troops. Tremal Naik, then a little boy and heir to the crown, is saved by the brave Kamamuri, who then plays the role of adoptive father. Both their lives are turned topsy-turvy: the warrior gives up the insignia of his function while the child king leads with him the life of a humble fisherman. It is the equivalent of the "exile in the forest" of the kings of the epics *Ramayana* and *Mahabharata*. The fishing expedition that leads the adolescent boy, sixteen years later, toward an unknown temple where he discovers Ada, the young English woman kidnapped to be sacrificed to Kali, is also fashioned after this literary motif, in which the king gets lost in the woods and encounters something that drastically changes the course of his life.

Spielberg plays with the theory of reincarnation and makes it the explicit and implicit force at play in the decision taken by Indiana Jones, who is now part of a divine filiation. As for Tremal Naik, he is of kingly lineage, but he learns it only belatedly. Temporalities and modalities are different, but they all tend toward the same goal: the heroes, led by mysterious forces originating form Indian legends, have as their mission to destroy evil.

Sorcery, spells, calamitous incantations, torture, deceit, magic, and sadism: in the sway of the Thugs India is the receptacle of powerful and obscure beliefs that, this time, contaminate the Western heroes and harm their integrity. Indiana Jones; Ada, the young English woman of the *Mysteries;* and William Savage in *Deceivers* fall under the sway of the terrible Kali. When the temple empties after a horrific human sacrifice, Indiana, faithful to his project of returning the glass phalluses to the villagers, grabs hold of the ones placed at the foot of the goddess. He is soon captured and forced to drink his own blood. In a daze, he is about to commit a human sacrifice. Ada too, kidnapped by Mohan Singh, who gives her to Kali, is dispossessed of her own self.

This theme is also at the core of the *Deceivers*, but it takes on an entirely different meaning: William Savage, in black face, dressed Indian style, becomes Gopal the Thug. After eating the consecrated sugar he passes to action: he kills and experiences incredible pleasure akin to sexual orgasm; he thus morphs in front of our very eyes into a horrible criminal. Two men inhabit him, a Thug and a Christian torn by remorse. He sways between good and evil, gives in to one, then to the other. The Thuggization of Indiana Jones or of Ada seems bland in comparison. Even though in a daze and with no control of themselves, they still do not cross the fatal threshold leading to the guilty pleasure of killing. In contrast, the process by which William Savage turns native leads to his permanent transformation: when he returns to colonial life, he throws away the cross that Hussein had given him for protection, and he can no longer communicate with his wife. His impious experience cannot be expressed and dooms him to solitude. Contaminated by India, he cannot regain his previous identity.

From Commemoration to Colonial Parody
GUNGA DIN

George Stevens notes in his film credits that *Gunga Din* is based on "Rudyard Kipling's work." And yet Kipling had no interest in the Thugs. In the preface of *The Jungle Book,* Alexis Tadié suggests that the novelist might have read William Sleeman's report on the wolf-children to construct his main character (Tadié 1994). But there's no mention of Thugs in Kipling's enormous body of works, only of highway robbers, the dacoits. The filmmaker thus puts together a collage: Kipling's fictional characters along with a colonial motif that Kipling did not use. Among the borrowed characters is Gunga Din, the water boy, who does his job in the course of clashes between the British army and the Thug army. Stevens also uses three soldiers very much akin to Kipling's *Soldiers Three* (1930) with other names but with the same deep friendship for each other and the same sense of humor and taste for fighting.[11] The figure of Kipling appears in the military camp of Muree (present-day Pakistan) at the end of the film after the Thugs are finally exterminated and the dead buried. With his famous glasses, here made bigger with large dark frames, he writes "The Ballad of Gunga Din" at the mess table.

In spite of its innovations, this new filmic assemblage remains faithful to Kipling's "imperial fibre" and reinforces the symbolic meaning the extermination of the Thugs had for the British. Before the playing of the funerary taps, the colonel reads the poem in front of the remains of the devoted water carrier and ends on its last four verses:

> You Lazarushian-leather Gunga Din!
> Though I've belted and flayed you,
> By the livin' Gawd that made you,
> You're a better man than I am, Gunga Din!
> —Kipling 1982a, 618

Thugs in the movies. *Above: Gunga Din* (1939), a panegyric of the imperial army. *Below: Indiana Jones and the Temple of Doom* (1984), singing the praises of American anticolonial humanism.

The poem sends back to the apologia for the British empire that is evident in the opening shots of the film. There, we see flags flapping in the wind and a statue of Queen Victoria as empress of India while an off-screen voice pays homage to the eternal colony and its humble servant: "During the sunny days I spent in India in the service of His Gracious Majesty, fate has led me to make the acquaintance of the most loyal man I have ever known." The legendary British victory over the Thugs is thus faithfully rethreaded in the film. Placed in Kipling's giant shadow, in his uncritical approval of colonialism, the film constitutes a hymn to the glory of the army that made the advent and consolidation of colonialism possible.

THE DECEIVERS

To commemorate an event implies respect for calendric time: *The Deceivers* follows this rule as it claims to be "based on a true story" in the opening credits, which attribute more than two million victims to the stranglers (thus twice as many as did Sleeman's grandson!). William Savage, who throws himself against all odds into the struggle against the Thugs and whose name obviously echoes that of William Sleeman, borrows much from his historical model. The action occurs at the same time period, in 1829, and in the same region of Madhya Pradesh, around Jabalpur. He has to overcome the same sort of difficulties his model did before being able to act. The rule is not to interfere in native affairs. Savage angrily cites Lord Amherst: "Do nothing, have nothing done, and don't let anybody do anything!" He arrests without convincing evidence a group of travelers whom he assumes are Thugs. He is ordered to set them free in spite of the result of his interrogation of the prisoners. One of them, Hussein, confesses to all the secrets of the fraternity. But Colonel Wilson, his superior, wants to have his insubordinate subordinate transferred to another district. Just as happened with Meadows Taylor, the Thugs are going to slip through his fingers!

At this point Savage breaks with his two historical models: with Hussein's help he transforms himself into a Thug. Upon his return, Colonel Wilson confronts him with Bentinck's famous statement. But the colonel substitutes Savage for the collective "we" used by the governor general: "You have a great task to accomplish!" he tells him as he appoints him head of a special department for the extermination of the Thugs. Like that of Ameer Ali, William Savage's trajectory is inscribed directly into the facts of history and respects its temporal framework. The explicit theme of the fictional film is that of the colonizer who in turn becomes a colonized victim: return to his family, captive of his murderous experience, Savage is torn in two and, as we know, remains a Thug in his mind.

INDIANA JONES AND THE TEMPLE OF DOOM

At the heart of Lucas's and Spielberg's story is the founding Hindu myth of the *avatara* instead of a nationalist and imperialist writer or a copy of Sleeman. This shift toward the colonized's mythology leads the Americans to Hindu spirituality and to ally themselves with it to destroy the Thugs. The filmmakers then shift again, this time in the opposite direction and closer to the present, or at least the recent past, as they suggest that the Thugs are the exotic equivalent of the Nazis.

This connotation comes out of the sequence of the three Indiana Jones films, of which *The Temple of Doom* is the second. In *Raiders of the Lost Ark* (1981) and *Indiana Jones and the Last Crusade* (1989), Indiana Jones fights against Nazis who want to steal the tablets of the law from the Ark of the Covenant as well as the Holy Grail, thus planning to consolidate their domination over the world thanks to the magical power they contain. In *Temple*, he fights against Thugs who have no longer anything in common with their ancestors and who this time have stolen a lingam, the phallic symbol of the god Shiva. Like their Nazi model, they celebrate in grandiose and terrifying settings their will to power and want of conquering the world by becoming the masters of a spiritual symbol linked to the very origin of their civilization. Indiana Jones and his two companions, Wendy and Half Moon, thus find themselves at the crossroads of Indian and present-day Western myths. And yet they are not struggling only against the Thugs, but are also in opposition to the colonizers, to whom they are superior because of their intelligence and their purely humanitarian motives.

After leaving the village, a place of distress and innocence, the three characters arrive in the kingdom of Pankot, a place of corruption and turpitude. During the dinner Indiana reminds the other people at the table that a century earlier (thus around 1830), the kingdom was the center of activity of the Thugs. He suggests that the disappearance of the lingam from the village might be linked to the Thugs' revival. Captain Blumburtt, his beer-bellied body impeccably dressed in his military uniform, claims that His Majesty's army has long since destroyed the Thugs and their monstrous cult. He agrees that the Thugs did exist in the past, but his shortsightedness keeps him from accepting the possibility of history repeating itself. Thus he misses the opportunity of being the worthy representative of the empire. As in *Gunga Din*, his kilt-dressed bagpipe-playing troops arrive in the nick of time to rescue the hero in danger. But here there is no longer any need for the colonel himself. As a self-satisfied victim of false appearances, with an attitude that, of course, benefits the impious kingdom he has come to "inspect," his role is without any trouble kidnapped by the clean-handed Americans.

Whether the films are an homage, a commemoration, or a parody of the British empire, they do on the main seem to represent it as a great and glorious human adventure. Of course, things are not that simple.

Thugs as Rebels?

In *Indiana Jones* Kali keeps only her name and her human-heads necklace from Hindu imagery. Her statue incorporates various elements, including some borrowed from Christian demonology.[12] She is colossal,[13] and her hideous head is crowned by a papal tiara. The headdress of her great priest too fits this satanic inspiration: four horns frame his face, a shrunken human head is embedded at the level of his forehead, and a necklace of teeth adorns his chest (these images obviously are of Amerindian origin rather than traditional depictions of the goddess). This demonized Hindu goddess is served by a Christian devil expatriated in India, whose pseudoreligious name has surreptitious links to the religious Islamic title of Mola (=*mullah*) and the name of Ram, the Hindu epic hero of the *Ramayana*. Oozing the sordid light of human servitude, the kingdom of Pankot, like that of Mohan Singh in *Mysteries of the Black Jungle,* is an aggregate of Oriental despotism, hate-filled anticolonialism, idolatrous religiosity, and black magic.

The great priest, happy sacrificer, and satanical organizer of this megalomaniac's project intends to "massacre the British imperialists, crush the Muslims, and then cause the god of the Christians to crumble into dust." His plan is identical to the ones in the *Mysteries* and *Gunga Din* showing that their leaders want to regain the power they were stripped of ("We have been humiliated," screams its avenging priest, who sends his followers to sabotage telegraphic communications so as to isolate the British). In *Gunga Din,* as true soldiers of the goddess, they even practice armed terrorism and confront their enemies on the battlefield. In these three films in which the Thugs are reborn after having been vanquished by Sleeman, they fight against the established colonial order as they did in nineteenth-century serial novels. These rebels, sullied by their frightful reputation, can only propound an indefensible cause. Films, like literary fiction, manage the colonial legacy even as they subvert it with a contradictory hypothesis: Thuggism as an unworthy form of protest against the colonizers.

ORIENT AND OCCIDENT

The imaginary Thugs are a stepping stone for formulating, bolstering, and legitimizing certain Occidental stances regarding the Orient. Two belief systems, two images of India confront each other. The first belongs to the assassins, to human sacrifices, to their drive for power. It is criminal, frightful, violent. The second is humble and good as in certain characters in Taylor, in *Gunga Din,* or in *Indiana Jones.* The villagers in *Indiana Jones* are reduced to praying to the gods to act in their stead, and their powerlessness even affects their children, who are held prisoners in the mine of Pankot. They servilely dig tunnels while the young Chinese Half Moon immediately uses the digging tool put in his hands to break the lock securing his chains. Village spirituality is weighed down with fatalism and demoralization. Their faith in divine goodness thus corresponds, in fact, to giving up.

Indiana Jones shows the messianic role of its hero in an infantile Orient abandoned by a decrepit Europe. The hero's nonchalance is only surface deep as the humanist archaeologist's attitude is in fact deeply colonialist. The whole of India falls at his feet: the India of the Thugs, which he destroys, and that of the villagers, who ask him to act in their stead. *Gunga Din*, through the postmortem promotion of the ridiculous water carrier into soldier of His Gracious Majesty, exhibits the same condescension. The faces of the village head and the water carrier are bathed in a cinematographic light connoting the same weakness of character, the same submissive acceptance, the same guilty nonviolence.

The Mysteries of the Black Jungle takes another path: the Thugs are beaten thanks to the close collaboration of the "good" Indians and the British. The rapprochement of Occident and Orient occurs with difficulty, but finally prejudices are overcome. The marriage of Ada, the colonel's daughter, to Tremal Naik, the brave son of the king, and the adoption by the Corishant couple of an Indian little girl are signs that they are all ready to mingle intimately with each other and that racist barriers have fallen. Kevin Connor, in an otherwise conventional exotic film, shows a progression in which human beings, rather than the gods' avatars, play the essential role. It is a progression in which military aggressiveness is not momentarily set aside in front of the remains of the water boy; rather, it is progressively and permanently replaced by the respect for the other. Finally, in this story no characters have lost themselves in the culture of the other to the point of irremediably losing their own integrity.

None of these works dare feature a Thug like Ameer Ali. The Thugs, indeed, remain the murdering horde described by Sleeman at the beginning of the nineteenth century. The other images grafted on them (Pont-Jest's sadism, Aztec sacrifices in Indiana Jones, armed terrorism in *Gunga Din*) are so many variations—political, religious, sexual—of their monstrosity. They have become a suitable figure to embody this particular form of evil, that is, violence under the guise of religion, and to use it to denounce its perenniality, its universalism, and its madness.

But the renewal of the colonial theme comes with two new propositions: the Thugs are also rebels led by power-hungry religious chiefs or iniquitous kings. They are bad rebels, Robin Hoods obeying Satan instead of God. And yet in these imaginings Thuggism is not only the horrid beast arisen from the darkness of the distant past, but also a protest that might have no outlet of expression other than murder. Popular fiction does offer a possible alternative to Sleeman's ersatz description and Taylor's individual case. Like them, it condemns the assassins, but it also suggests that evil lies neither in superstitions thought to be of divine origin nor in the tragic development of a family history. It is the consequence of a process of domination leading the oppressed to turn on their oppressors.

This proposition complements the erosion of the colonizers' image as it loses its moorings from the images, past and present, that colonialists have had of themselves. In Pont-Jest or in the rustic bagpipes of a Blumburtt operetta, the colonizers' myopia and their smugness are disastrous. *The Deceivers* denounces their fragility; *Gunga Din* shows that war is the only outlet for their virility. Finally, in *Mysteries of the Black Jungle* Colonel Corishant is first racist, scornful, and abusively authoritarian before becoming a good person. The glorious and smooth image of the empire and its builders has cracked. Neither the army nor its leader nor the ideal of progress nor benevolent paternalism nor the moral force of the employees of the Company particularly shines through in these portrayals of their cynicism, blundering, futility, meanness, and vulnerability.

In this sense works of fiction are "a critique of the social narrative, a rectification and broadening of collective memory" (Ricoeur 1985, 3:175). The Orient is neither the fascinating enigma the Orientalists sought to decipher nor an inverted mirror of the Occident, as Sleeman claimed. The confrontation is no longer a binary one between nasty Thugs and colonizers filled with good intentions. The imaginary renders the original scene more complex; it corrects its Manichaeanism and invents new mediations and new alternatives. It does this even to the point of an extreme metamorphosis of the Thug topos, a point at which these new imaginings pass over to the other side of the mirror, like William Savage, the Westerner burned in his turn by the fascination of violence and death.

Conclusion

According to Louis Dumont, the key to the Indian social system is the renouncer, the emaciated personage of the *sannyasin* "with his begging bowl, his stick and his orange robe" (1966, 350). Seeking personal salvation and liberation from the flux of transmigration, renouncers voluntarily step out of the social world that has held them in a tight network of debts and obligations, particularly toward their ancestors and descendants. They break from consensual relations and invent other ones that ordinary society eventually appropriates. This is a process through which nonviolence, along with its correlate, vegetarianism, are gradually substituted for bloody sacrifice. The ideal stage of life preceding renouncement is that of the forest hermit (Hulin 1992). Hermits and their spouses settle in the forest, where they still perform part of the sacrificial activities. They find their food in nature, their hair is unkempt and unshaven, they dress with animal skins and tree bark, and they engage in extreme ascetic exercises. If we have to look for a distant model for the Thugs in Brahmanic thought, it might perhaps lie in this hermit who, though still following rites, transcends the cultural values of purity.

And yet in comparison with these orthodox paths to salvation pursued outside of secular society, the idea of "the sacredness of the transgression" advocated by the Thugs amounts to a drastic break about which we know relatively little. There is speculation about a link between the *Tantras* and the *Aranyaka,* the latter a text that is "secret, dangerous and read in the forest away from the community," providing forest hermits with an esoteric elaboration of Vedic doctrine (Renou and Filliozat 1985, 294). The hypothetical nature of this link is brought out by the fact that the *Brahmanas* date from around the ninth to the eight century B.C. and thus are much more ancient than the first Tantric texts, believed to date from around the ninth century A.D. However, according to Charles Malamoud the Tantric soteriological break would have begun much earlier, as seems to be evidenced by the inclusion in Brahmanic mythology of two interpretations of the rite of reconstitution of the body of Prajapati, the ancestor of both sacrifice and human beings. The first interpretation emphasizes the male character of the rite, while the second, an esoteric one, attributes its ultimate meaning to the plural mode of femaleness. "The female plural also characterizes the Tantric sacrificial scene organized around the headless goddess" (Malamoud 1987, 27–28). Already at the very heart of the myth of the dismembering and reconstruction of Prajapati we can make out the trace of an enormous power attributed to femaleness that might be at the core of the beliefs of the Shaktas and the Thugs.

These traces, these fascinating clues, point to a possible origin for Thug religion, particularly if we consider the possibility that in the ninth century Jayanta might have been referring to the Thugs in his mention of "the liberators from the flow of rebirths," whom Jayanta characterizes as "devoted to the killing of living creatures" (Halbfass 1991, 98). The importance of Tantrism is unanimously recognized by scholars of India, but its secret traditions and practices remain more difficult to access and thus much less explored than those of Brahmanic tradition. Our doctrinal knowledge of the Thugs' religion thus remains allusive and limited, though not entirely conjectural.

Likewise, the issue of the Thugs' place within Indian tradition and of the scope of their activities (Halbfass 1991, 104) is only imperfectly understood. However, recent research has been able to shed light on some aspects of their practices. By showing that the crucial role of the ascetic orders was not specifically Hindu, at least in northern India in the period encompassing the fourteenth century to the beginning of the twentieth, Peter van der Veer (1994, 25–77) helps us understand the other intriguing aspect of the stranglers' fraternity, namely its inclusion of both Muslims and Hindus. The similarity in the organizational schemes of Muslim and Hindu religious confraternities, as well as that of the overall identities of fakirs and of ascetics show that these groupings have mutually influenced each other. The Thugs appear to have reflected this. They intermingled Shaktic and Sufi elements. They traveled the same trading and pilgrimage routes as the fakirs and yogis did and made sure to stop for the Hindu celebration of *dussera*[1] as well as for the Muslim celebration of *mohorum*.[2] Sleeman constructed his religious system on the basis of the information given to him by Feringheea, his Brahman informant, even while imagining without any evidence that Ḥasan-e Ṣabbāḥ, the wise old man of the mountain, and his sect of assassins were the Thugs' ancestors. Nonetheless, this link probably merits exploration.[3] Today unlike the colonizers we are no longer surprised at the existence of a Muslim-Hindu "fraternity" whose members, as we have seen, were cooperating even while maintaining their distinct religious identities.

More recent works in history and anthropology have made the ideal figure of the renouncer Dumont described much more complex, but in the process they have somewhat trivialized the assassins. We have seen holy men lead monasteries as well as armies, fight ferociously against their enemies, sell themselves as mercenaries, or engage in profitable trade. They could marry and live in the world or lead a life of celibacy in temples and monasteries.

The multiplicity of social and religious forms at variance with the dominant caste ideology gives morphological credibility to the Thugs' lack of hierarchy and strong egalitarian tendency, while there is cognitive credibility in ontological criteria of purity and impurity taking second place to notions of auspiciousness and inauspiciousness linked to the flow of time, accidents, and chance. The emaciated ascetics in search of salvation thus had fearsome doubles who did more than inhabit the tales collected by M. Bloomfield. The Benares Pandas who use some of the Thugs' argot in their speech might be one of their present-day continuators. These priests specialize in funerary rituals and also appropriate religion for shady, and in the past murderous, aims. One example is the forced closing of the temple of Kashi Karwat dedicated to Shiva, which had in its basement a "big saw" the Pandas used to kill devotees seeking permanent salvation after first handing over all of their worldly goods to them.

Filmmaker Satyajit Ray depicts this Indian trickster drawing on divine authority and symbols to organize his ploys. In *Mahapurush* (The holy man, 1965) the sensual and obese Birinchi Baba rudely abuses his disciples, while in *Joi Baha Felunath* (The elephant god, 1978) his emaciated counterpart sows ills on the sacred shore of the Ganges at Benares with the complicity of a wealthy and criminal trafficker.

The Thugs are more than a religious enigma; one of the numerous topos converging on them has them linked to political power. As might be remembered that French popular fiction clearly plays on this link by turning the Thugs into revolutionaries with independence on their agenda. In contrast, British writings on Indian national history use the Thugs to propound a drastic separation of Indians from political aims. In 1936 the Britisher G. MacMunn claimed a Thug revival when terrorists tried to murder the viceroy, Lord Hardinge, with hidden bombs during his official entry into Delhi:

The *bomb-parast* is an individual who placed a bomb or a hand grenade in Shiva's sanctuary so as to worship him along with Kali, the Hungry, and to enjoy in advance the blood that is to flow. In Bengal, the trials of these assassins show how the Hindu student, physically and morally victim of premature sexual activity, responds to the propaganda of crime, and worships the Goddess through the power of nitroglycerine. . . . The cult of the hand grenade is similar to that of Bhowani and Kali, the patron saints of Thuggism whose thirst for blood spared no one. (MacMunn 1936, 210–11)

This brings to mind Sleeman's blindness toward the rituals of peasants protesting against the land-surveying and cow-eating colonizers. He shared a view that reduced protest to its religious form and emptied it of its political meaning. The British thought the natives were unable to think in political terms, and they measured their imagined immaturity and primitivism by this supposed mental deficiency resulting from superstition. MacMunn embraces these same enduring presumptions. In 1961 the author of the introduction on the cover of Sir Francis Tuker's hagiography claims that the problem lay less in weakness than in error: "Without titans like Sleeman, India would have remained a subcontinent of feudal and antagonistic despots, unable to form a nation. This biography is a reminder that India was awaiting the British to put it on the path of Independence" (Tuker 1961). Recent decolonization had forced a change in argument, so Tuker projected a reel that, instead of showing Thugs as terrorists, focused instead on their valorous exterminators and on denouncing Oriental despotism. The prejudice remained intact; the British were still thought to be the sole holders of political knowledge, and they were needed to guide the Indian nation.

Still within this same perspective of the self-proclamation of colonial superiority I would like to discuss and conclude on the theme of the monstrosity of the Thugs. This pervasive theme is central to the long-debated question with which my research deals, namely that of the relationship between history and the imaginary.

To the colonizers the Thugs' extermination evidenced the impact of science on the power of human beings. Morality justified the guilty's punishment. Knowledge accumulated on the criminals transformed the punishment into a gain for humankind, into the victory of enlightenment over obscurantism (Blanckaert 1992, 64). Scientific ethnology and colonial ideology hypostatized the old antagonism between good and evil into the overlapping categories of modernity and tradition, and of normalcy and abnormalcy. But the campaign against the assassins, the grandiose and brutal scene onto which they were projected, their affinity with Western romantic heroes, did not stem solely from historical circumstances the colonizers labeled "providential" and from the law enforcement concerns they claim were motivating them. Radhika Singha

(1998) has brilliantly shown the judicial and political gains this affair garnered for the British.

In the plane of the imaginary, the story making about Thuggism is also linked to a tradition that is at play in the gothic literary current of the nineteenth century and in our present-day fascination with serial killers.[4] It is a representation of violence specific to Anglo-Saxon culture and is rooted in the stock of Germanic, Scandinavian, and Celtic legends highlighting the essential fragility of the civilized world and the continuing threat of the monsters' return. Man is a wolf to man: the criminal symbolizes a direct and solitary opposition to society. At any time "a crazed warrior covered with blood" (Duclos 1994, 26–27) can appear, intent on destroying a civilization defending itself through a strict system of laws.

The colonizers' representations of the Thugs appropriated, even while slanting and exoticizing it, the figure of the "crazed warrior," pushing it toward abnormality and monstrosity. According to Foucault, the sequence of images making up this domain starts out with that of the human monster, then that of the individual in need of correction, and finally that of the masturbator. The monster violates the laws of nature and society through his or her very form. It is Frankenstein, a "new natural form of counter-nature" who leaves the law with no other resource than violence, "outright extermination." This human monster that went back to the dawn of time was to become the principle of intelligibility for all forms of abnormality: "What is the natural monster whose shadow blends in with that of the petty thief?" (Foucault 1999, 8). This is the problem raised throughout the nineteenth century.

The Thugs encompass all of the terms of this evolutionary scheme. They combine the human monster whose field of apparition is at once juridical and biological with its second avatar, the delinquent, and finally with the sexual degenerate. But they are a unique form in this scheme. They are physically attractive and elegant (compare the historical Feringheea with his fictive counterpart, Ameer Ali), and their intellectual level is high. They are neither misshapen nor idiotic, nor are they devoid of moral sense. Finally, in contrast to their Western model, they are neither rare nor solitary. They are thus unlikely human monsters, lacking any external signs that might betray their nature. They are the monster's inverted and ordinary form, one that renders the monster invisible and thus particularly dangerous. This because these men who inspire trust and respect are professional mass and serial killers. It is in this that their monstrosity lies: in their actions, in the cold-blooded way in which they perpetrate them, and in the duplicity, the ambivalence they have mastered in order to accomplish their aims—traits that a later historian (MacMunn) was to attribute to their "premature sexuality."

This set of iniquitous actions and habits projects onto the monster the fear that gripped the observers when they realized that they did not know the natives in spite of ruling over them after vanquishing and subjugating them (Kaye 1966). Could the colonizers be sure of the obedience, tolerance, and friendliness of the peasants with whom Sleeman conversed under a tree? For a time, thanks to the monster, the fear that arose after the 1857 Mutiny could be forgotten and repressed. The Thugs were thus the foundations of a ritual of conjuration in the sense that they made it possible to give a name to this anxiety and turn it into a possibility that could be quickly controlled, a source of fear that could be definitely eliminated. The campaign of extermination against them thus was beneficial not only because it legitimized a state based on individual rights, but also because it provided a psychological bonus in the form of a substantial surplus of moral comfort that spread to the whole of the colony. Its members were to derive a quasidivine power from making visible the invisible, from uncovering that which lurked beneath appearances, and from pushing aside this fear for a long time to come.

In the guise of scientific knowledge the explanatory apparatus erected to account for the Thugs had an additional effect, in Foucault's words: "to spread the power to punish to other things besides crime." The psychiatrizing of the judicial process, in particular in the course of the nineteenth century, shifted the offense onto "its abnormal base, its ancestors, its rear guard" (Foucault 1999, 8). In the West the medical expert's task thus became the unveiling of the delinquent's past, of his or her childhood and of its excesses and lacks. This shift did not affect individuals in India, as they were seen as deprived of autonomy and freedom, their "beliefs" reducing them to cogs in an idolatrous machine. This deindividualization added to generalizations, such as "all Indians are potential Thugs," that authorized the observer to change temporal and spatial scale. The "other things beside crime" were first of all Kali, the ancient cannibal Goddess, and then metonymically the whole of India, riddled with evil. At bottom, finally, the Thugs were monstrous because they embodied Indian cultural abnormalcy. The colonial expert thus added to his police and judicial functions that of psychiatry practiced at the bedside of the colonized culture. He was to be able to perform only a partial cure. Indian culture was essentialized similarly to the delinquent in the paradoxical form of "an individual in need of correction but defined by his or her incorrigibility" (Foucault 1999, 54). India required numerous and specific treatments, but they were all bound to fail. Cultural difference provided both the impetus to action and its closure, its limits. The boundaries of this difference could be pushed back, but never eliminated.

A second aspect of the apparatus of explanation aimed at naturalizing Thug crime through the phrenological study of the assassins' brains. This approach remained marginal. Though it is true that the later sociological classification of "criminal castes and tribes" did hint at an implicit biological frame of reference, the construction of Thug monstrosity drew first of all from arguments of historical and cultural environment. And its efficacy was all the more powerful in that the former warrior "covered in blood" had donned the judge's robe or the peaceful walker's outfit and had come to project onto the other that which he himself no longer wished to be.

The Thugs had a very different perception of this play of mirrors between them and the British. They did not expel to the outside that which they refused to acknowledge in themselves. On the contrary, they identified with their enemies, they abolished all difference: were they not like them smitten with hunting human beings? The inconvenient "we" emerging from this is very interesting. The Thugs did not see the British as nonhuman, and they attributed their victory to a luck and power that they themselves had come to lack. They looked upon their adversaries in terms of their own worldview and mode of action. The British, on the contrary, aimed at completing their separation by calling upon two complementary symbolic operations: they projected their own reflection onto the other so as to expel it from themselves.

Thug "monstrosity" does not belong only in the curio cabinet of history. Though on the surface it appeared to lack a physiological basis, such basis was implicit in its "scientific" elaboration and in sophisticated ritual processes. In fact, cultural racism was to become the dominant mode of thinking in India after 1857 (Metcalf 1995). This legacy survived the colonial past as the story of the Thugs reveals mechanisms of thought that are still with us today. This can be seen at present in France, where an ideology of difference and identity has taken over for the biological argument after the latter lost its pseudoscientific credibility during the 1980s (Taguieff 1999, 12). This can also be seen on the Indian political scene, where religious nationalists, gurus, swamis, and ulemas use Hindu and Muslim religious aspirations and idioms to further electoral goals aimed at defining exclusive collective identities of which they would be the guarantors and embodiments. The other would thus be excluded and relegated to an imagined incommensurable and inalienable difference.

Thug Lexicon or Ramasee

The words making up this means for secret communication are predominantly of Hindi origin. Our working instruments were the *Bhargava* Hindi-English dictionary (1946), the Varma Hindi-Hindi dictionary in five volumes (1962), Grierson's book *Bihar Peasant Life* (1926), and *An Atlas of India* (Muthiah and Ramachandran 1990).

The influence of Urdu is minimal. We have identified only four words: water pipe: *hukkah;* offering or gift: *nazrana;* grave: *kahr;* thing: *chiz.*

English transcription leads to certain regular though nonsystematic deformations: *a* may be transcribed into *u* in English, as in *Jubulpure* instead of the correct *Jabalpur; m* into *b,* as in *Narbada* instead of *Narmada; b* into *v; d* into a retroflex *r; j* into *g* or *k; r* into *l; p* into *b,* and so on.

SEMANTICS

Most of the words have maintained their original meaning. When there is a slide in meaning, the mechanisms observed are the usual ones of metonymy or metaphor.

Metonymy

An object stands for a person, as when Brahman is **hurva,** from *harva,* a sacred necklace. A quality stands for a person: soldier is **rungwa,** from *rang,* color + *wa,* agential. Content stands for the container: copper pot, **dhungee,** from *dhan,* grain + *ki* genitive.

Metaphor

It is found mainly in names of trades, as "skin scraper" for barber, "bird of prey" for merchant, "crooked" for jeweler. It is used as well for parts

295

of the body, such as "coconut" for head and "bag" for stomach; it is used for "tear drops" for rain outside of the rainy season.

Double Meaning

It is rare and mostly applies to murder: **bunij**, occupation, trade, designates the victims; **bunij ladhna** means to murder the victims. To choose the place of murder is called "to wash the cup," **kutoree manjna.**

MORPHOLOGY

Composition does not play a major role, except in the case of a few examples of combined words. Traveler on horseback: **pootraet**, from *bootrayyat*, a peasant wearing boots, a horseman. Beginner, initiate: **nowaarrea**, from *nav*, new, *va* agential + *iya*.

Some of the combination words are portmanteau words combining fragments of two words: **togri**, from *topi*, hat + *pagri*, turban; **tormee** (assassins), from *torna*, to break, to violate, to transgress, to force + *jurmi*, criminal.

Suffixation

There are many popular suffixes, such as *ya* and *ia*, which show belonging: **Agureeas**, Thugs of Agra. The suffix *a*, *wa* agential is from *vala*, the one who practices a trade, or somebody's function: **kuboola**, servant of Thugs; **phoola**, one bringing money to his family; **jhurowa**, a Thug who runs away. The qualifying suffix *i* appears in **Kachunee**, Thugs from Kachchh; **Multanee**, Thugs from Multan. We see the conceptual nominative *u* in **thibaoo**, omen from the right. The abstract mark *ai* indicates "the fact of being something," as in **kathai**, the function of dismemberer; **kabitae**, the function of strangler; **bykureeae**, the function of spy, and so on.

We notice a tendency toward suffix adjunctives, particularly for agentials, where standard Hindi would not have them: **kuthae**, verb *katna* + *uai;* **maulee**, *mal* + *ui;* **chandoo**, *chand* + *uoo.*

Verb Forms

Hindi uses auxiliary verbs that it adds to the verbal root to modify its sense; similarly, Ramasee uses a limited number of these high-frequency auxiliary verbs. These are mostly *dena*, to give; *karna*, to make; *dekhna*, to see; *dalna*, often in a completive sense; *hona*, to become; *jana*, to go; *padna*, to fall; *lena*, to take; *nakhna* (Rajasthani/Marwari), to give, to throw.

Moreover, in a specific manner, Ramasee creates verbs from nouns by adding the suffix *na:* **choudhana**, *chunri* (painting technique, and, by extension, the fold of a cloth) + *na*, to tie up the arms; **chourukna**, *chor* (thief) + *uk* + *na*, to denounce.

Ramasee also adds auxiliaries to nouns where this is not practiced in standard Hindi: **phool dena,** *pal dena,* to tell the time, to set an appointment; **tighunee karna,** *dekhni karna,* to seek.

HOW TO READ THE LEXICON

Sleeman presents his lexicon in alphabetical order. To better show its interest I have organized it by themes: ordinary society (types and castes), Thug society (status and roles), verbs describing Thug actions, nouns linked to these actions, the terrain, time, and so on. The list of verbs, the most revealing and striking in terms of Thug activities, is found in the third section.

Within each theme, entries are in alphabetical order and given the meaning Sleeman indicated.[1] Each of these English words is followed by its Ramasee equivalent in bold letters, and the etymology I propose here is in italics. The least convincing etymologies are followed by a question mark. Because most of the origins are from the Hindi, I only note exceptions (Rajasthani = Raj.; Gujarati = Guj.; Marathi = Mar.; Urdu and Persian, which I spell out, and so on).

Sleeman's conjectural explanations are in quotation marks.

1. ORDINARY SOCIETY

Women/Men
Boy: **chimmota,** from *chimukla* (Guj., Mar.), boy; **tinnooa, tinna,** from *tanu,* son; **chingana/chinha,** from *chingi,* sparks, and, by extension, boy.

Girl: **chimmotee,** from *chimukli* (Guj.), girl.

Man: **munkhela,** from *manav + kula,* human + race, caste, birth.

Man, non-Thug: **dudh (dadh?),** from *dhad,* an attack, a multitude?; **beetoo,** from *bit,* lower caste, inferior; **eloo,** from *alag,* separate, distinct.

Man, old: **khodda,** from *burha, old?*

Man on horseback: **pooturaet,** from "boot" (English word borrowed by Hindi); or from *put,* clog + *rayyat,* peasant.

Man or woman, crippled: **awkhur,** from *ek + aur?* (bad omen if encountered the first day of an expedition [Deccan]); **bydha,** from *burha,* old.

Man or woman without nose and ears: **goneeait,** from *guna,* qualities + *ayat,* without.

Man who is carrying the bones of his relatives to a holy river: **gookhee,** from *guru + ki?* (Deccan).

Man who knows the Thugs and whom they should avoid: **jhummanta,** from *jana-mana,* well-known.

Woman: **chowan,** from *javan,* young (Deccan), or *joban,* breast, and, by extension, woman; **indermunn endh,** from *aimdri,* woman from Indra's court, from *indra + manav,* descended from Indra's court.

Woman, non-Thug: **kajjee,** from *kamchni,* dancer.

Woman, old: **dholin,** *dholin,* woman drum player; her tears are called **now,** from *rona,* to cry.

Woman, Thug: **baronee,** from *badi,* big.

Trades, Castes, Classes

Ascetic: **minuk,** from *mauni,* ascetic who has made a vow of silence.
Ascetic, Byragee: **churagee** (Deccan), from *hairagi* and *chira,* ascetic's robe, bark.
Ascetic, Gosain: **minukeea,** from *mauni,* same meaning.
Banker: **rahookar, sahookar,** from *sahukar,* a wealthy man, a moneylender.
Barber: **khorchee,** from *khamroch + i,* one who scratches; **khal khossea,** *khal,* skin,
and *khamroch,* skin scratcher; **mykureea** (Deccan), from *mukha,* face.
Carpenter: **kutkola,** from *"katna,* to cut *+ kala,* art."
Fakir or a religious mendicant: **lukeer,** from *lakir,* lines in the hands, and, by exten-
sion, one who reads them, a palm reader, such as the fakir, a Muslim mendicant.
Goldsmith: **tirkeea** (Deccan), from *tircha,* that which is not straight, thus that
which is dishonest.
Hindu: **bindan,** from *bindi,* a mark on the forehead.
Innkeeper: **muchhooa,** from *mumcha,* mustache; **bhutteeara,** from *bhatiyara,*
innkeeper.
Launderer: **lendkeea** (Deccan), from *lomda,* a shapeless mass, a bundle, including
a bundle of clothes packed into a large sheet to give to the launderer; **siskar**
(Jumaldahee, Lodaha, and Motheea Thugs), from *siskar,* the whistling sound
produced by the launderers as they let out air from their lungs when beating the
washing on a stone to clean it.
Marathi: **chireyta,** from *chira,* an ascetic's clothes; **tongur,** from *dangar,* low caste.
Muslim: **khosman,** from *usman,* non-Muslim?; **hawur/jhanwur** (Berar), from *ya-
van,* Muslim; **licka** (Deccan); **suthna,** from *sunna,* circumcision.
Pickpocket: **kuchooa,** from *katwa,* one who cuts, a money-purse cutter.
Policeman or guard: **barkundanze,** from *badka,* strong *+ andesha,* suspicion;
chuprasi, from *chaprasi,* pawn, official messenger; **dhonkee,** from *dhamkana,* to
threaten, to reprimand; **dantun,** from *damt,* tooth, one who has teeth; **khydura,**
from *khatra,* threat; **najeeb,** from *nazir,* inspector; **narta,** from *narak,* hell, one
who behaves infernally or from *narkit,* a jerk; **roukee, roukeea,** from *rokhna,*
to arrest, one who arrests; **thola,** from *thala,* bag, and, by extension, prison, or
from *thula,* fat, fat-bellied.
Potter: **thapteea** (Deccan), from *thapna,* to tap.
Priest, Brahman: **chummun,** from *chaman/chiman,* Mar. Brahmanic name; **hur-
wa,** from *hari + wa,* man of God, or *harva,* one who wears a sacred necklace
(*har*).
Rajput: **jangura** (Deccan), from *jamg,* combat; **mukkaur,** from *mukha,* face, and,
by extension, chief.
Scholar or a Marathi: **chireyta,** from *chira,* ascetic's clothes.
Seller, alcohol: **dhulal** (Deccan), from *dalal,* intermediary.
Seller, oil: **teylee,** from *teli,* oil merchant; **ekburda,** from *ek,* one *+ burha,* old?
Smith: **lohar,** from *lohar,* same meaning.
Soldier: **rangooas, rungwa,** from *ramg + wa,* in color (his uniform is red); **narta,**
from *narak,* hell, infernal; a body of soldiers: **nughoo,** army (Doab, Oudh, Bihar),
khour designating a body of soldiers in Awadh and a path, *khura,* in Bihar.
Thief: **kulioo,** from *kala chor,* literally, black thief, meaning a notorious thief, or
from *kalia,* black, dressed in black as camouflage; **kullooee,** to steal; **luppooa,**
from *lupna,* to hide.
Thief or pickpocket or someone living from loot: **bisnee,** from *bisni,* one with bad
habits; **tormee,** from *torna,* to break, to violate, to transgress, to force, or from
dhurt, sly, clever; **chungar,** from *chamd,* prepared opium and, by extension, an
opium smoker, or from *chamd,* a trick, fraud, one who practices fraud.

2. THUG SOCIETY

Status

Deprecatory term for a Thug from Telingana: **harndeewal,** "from *hamdi,* pot of earth" + *vala,* "one from the pot"; also for a Bangureea Thug: **khokureea,** from an onomatopoeia, *khokar,* suggesting a bird call from the Guj. word *khokro,* hollow, worthless.

Rank or grade of the three men respectively responsible for (1) the place chosen to bury the corpses, (2) the sacred pickaxe, and (3) the ceremonial sugar: **hilla,** from *hilga,* close friendship, connection. The status is applied jointly to the three men as well as to each one individually.

Thug: **bora** (Bihar, Bengal, Jumaldahee, Lodaha, Motheea, Bungoo), from *bada,* big; **bisnee,** *bisni,* one with bad habits (also thief, pickpocket, any category of looters); **tormee,** from *torna,* to break, to violate, to transgress, to force, or from *jurmi,* criminal (also any sort of thief), probably a combination of two words; **aulae,** from *auliya,* holy man.

Thug by birth who has not yet reached the rank of strangler: **soon,** from *sunu,* son, younger brother.

Thug, frightened or shy: **cheeha,** from *chick* + *a,* cry, scream.

Thug, expert: **chandoo,** from *chandu,* a hemp user or from *chand,* fraud, trick, con.

Thug initiated to the ritual knot: **goor ponch,** from *gur,* obscure, secret + *phams,* knot, or from *pamch,* assembly.

Thug, novice: **kuboola, kyboola,** from *kabul,* commitment; **beetos** (Hindustan), from *bit,* inferior, of low caste. In literature this word, which can also be spelled *vit,* also designates one who seduces with the charm of words, and, by extension, a great scoundrel; **kotuk,** from *kautuk,* trick, marvel, spectacle?; **margee** (Deccan), from *margi,* one who follows the road, sect member; **nowureea,** from *nav,* new + *var,* faith, one who joins his first expedition; **cheyla,** from *chela,* disciple. According to Sleeman, the Jumaldahee and Lodaha Thugs forced the novice to kick five times with his feet the back of his first victim to bring good luck to the expedition.

Thug of distinction: **baroo, burka,** from *bada,* big + *ka,* masculine gender, or from *barhkar,* superior.

Thug, River: **pungoo,** from *bamgal,* Bengal.

Thug, teacher: **gooroo,** *guru,* spiritual master.

Thug, weak: **jhoosa.**

Thug woman, old and venerable: **baronee,** from *bada,* feminine gender of big.

Thug Roles within Gangs

Chief: **mohil,** from *mukhi, mukhiya,* chief; **burka,** from *bara,* big.

Dismemberer: **kuthowa,** from the root of the verb *katna* + *wa,* to cut + agential; **katai,** the act of dismembering; the work or the trade of the dismemberer: **kuthae,** from *kat,* to cut + *ai,* abstract suffix.

Gang of twenty-five Thugs (or more): **bous,** from *bis,* twenty, or from *pacis,* twenty-five; **kharoo,** from *akhara,* assembly.

Gang or band of Thugs or of travelers: **taw,** from *tol,* group.

Gravedigger: **kurbakurree** (Deccan), from *kabr,* an Islamic word for grave (cf. *kabristhan,* cemetery); **lugha,** from *lupta,* out of sight, hidden, or from *lagna,* one who lays, that is, one who buries (the job of gravedigger is called **lughae**).

Holder of hands and feet while the strangler is doing his job: **oorwala,** from *aur,* on the side, toward + *vala,* agential; **shumseea, chumoseea,** from *chuna,* to touch, or from *chumna*, to embrace (his function is called **chumeeae**, and that of his assistant, **chumeea**).

Scout or spy: **kautgur**, from *kotval*, guardian?, or from *kat(na)*, to cut + *gur*, raw sugar, one who has cut the ritual sugar (his function is called **kautgurree**); **bykurreeae** (river Thugs, Lodaha, Motheea), from *bekar*, without work = one who seems idle; **tilha**, from *thilna*, to advance, to penetrate + *ai* (his function is called **thilae**).

Seducer: **sotha**, from *suthara*, pure, clean, elegant.

Servant of Thug (also a novice): **kuboola**, from *kabul*, contract, agreement, one who signed an agreement; **tyro**, from *thaharna*, to assist?; **kotuk** (Bengal, Bihar), from *kautuk*, trick, marvel, spectacle?; **ogaera** (Deccan), from *aghori (ya)*, disciple, servant.

Strangler: **kabita** (Lodaha and Jumaldahee Thugs), from *kabil*, capable, competent, adroit, adapted, sly, knowledgeable (his function is called **kabitae**); **bukote/bhurtote**, from *bhurkana*, to make one forget, to mislead (his function is called **bhurtotee**); **char** (Bungoo, Jumaldahee, Lodaha, Motheea), from *chor*, thief (his function is called **chareea**).

Strangler of a man on horseback: **pooturaet bhurtote**, from *put*, clog, or *boot*, boot + *rayyat*, peasant + **bhurtote**, strangler; **pootaraete**, to perform this action.

Thug in charge of making all traces of the crime disappear: **phurjhurowa**, from *pur*, house, body + *jharna*, to sweep.

Thug who brings back money to the families of the Thugs gone on an expedition: **maulee** (Lodhee and Korhareea), from *mal*, price, or from *mali*, that which has value, price; **phoola**, from *phal*, fruit, thus reward, or from *phul*, flower.

Thug who chooses the place for the murder: **maunkurreea**, from *maun*, silence or silent + *kari*, one who renders someone silent; **beyla**, from *bela* (feminine form), moment, or from *bil*, hole (his function is called **beylhae**).

Thug who drags the cadavers to the grave: **bojha**, from *bojha*, weight (his function is called **bhojae**).

Thug who pretends to be sick (Lodaha, Motheea, Jumaldahee): **ganoo**, from *ganam*, conspiracy?

Thugs in Danger

Bribe, ransom to free Thugs from prison: **kamp**, from *kapatna*, to cut, to take away?, or from *kamp*, earring (jewels very often make up the currency available to the people); **khat**, from *katna*, to cut, to take a sum (Deccan).

Handcuffs (also designates any iron implement): **bisendee**, from *bi*, two + *handi*, small iron pot; **thulee**, from *thali*, eating tray; **ghenae**, from *gherna*, to encircle, to surround.

Hunter of Thugs: **dhaundhoee**, from *dhumdhna*, to search; **karhoo** (also traitor, attacker, etc.), from *kaid*, capture, or from *kahar*, calamity, danger (*kahar karma*, to threaten, to attack, to put someone in a difficult position).

News (bad): **bunar**, from *benazar*, evil eye. Also a bad road for the Thugs.

News (good): **baee**, from *bai*, left (most good omens come from the left).

Object seen on someone that does not match that person's social status and consequently raises suspicions: **burg**, from *boz*, burden.

Person or place that is dangerous: **tikhur**, from *tikur*, forest, jungle.

Person who is watching the Thugs: **teel**, from *thiluha*, petty, bereft of value.

Person who unexpectedly arrives on the scene of the crime: **dantoun**, from *dhumdhna*, to search (see also policeman or guard, under "Trades, Castes, Classes" in the previous section).

Pursuit by villagers or others: **tukrar**, from *takrar*, complaint, inquiry; **tortunkur** (pursuit, arrest, molestation), from *tarna*, to punish, to beat; **geem**, from *gama*, movement, access, approach; **kahr, karhkurna,** from *kaid,* capture, or from *kahar,* calamity, danger.

Stockade to lock up Thugs and others: **doona,** from *dohna,* to accuse, to condemn.

Theft of loot by a Thug: **koot,** from *khot,* loss, or from *khota,* false, or again from *kut,* clever, mean, vicious; **bhons,** from *phams* (cf. the expression *lut-phams,* theft [Deccan]).

Thug hiding from his creditors: **khullee,** from *khali,* empty (cf. the expression *khali ho gaya,* he has become empty, he has nothing to give, thus he runs away).

Thug running away: **jhurowa,** from *jhad,* brush + *wa,* a pejorative suffix.

Thug stealing from Thugs: **kootha, koot,** from *khot,* loss, or from *khota,* false, or again from *kut,* clever, mean, vicious.

Thug who is a denouncer: **kuthowa,** from *katna* + *wa,* one who has cut himself; **koojaoo,** from *khoj,* research, the one who allows it + *(au),* sought; **kucha** (also a badly buried corpse), from *kacha,* unripe, imperfect.

Thugs' great enemy (also designates a forbidden victim, as the term is also applied to a leper, a person without nose or ears, or again a person emaciated by illness): **beelha,** from *bilona,* ugly, crippled, mutilated.

Traitor who knows the Thugs' secrets and who uses his knowledge to extort money from them: **mamoo,** from *mama,* mother's brother (favorable connotations are sometimes inverted, as for the godfather in the mafia; thus in the epic *Kamsh Mama,* the name given to Krishna's maternal uncle, designates a traitor).

3. VERBS DESCRIBING THUG ACTIONS

Affix specific to Punjab, at Multan: **nakhna,** to jump, to step over, to destroy = **karna,** to do, to accomplish.

Arresting, or seizing or to be arrested, or seized: **cham lena/chamoo jana,** from *cham,* skin + *lena,* take, or *jana,* lose, and, by extension, to lose one's life.

Assassinating travelers (= get rid of merchandise): **bunij ladhna,** from "*banij,* trade, merchandise, occupation."

Assembling, to give each other a rendezvous: **ektawohna,** from *ikahai,* together + *hona,* to become, or from *ikattha hona,* to assemble

Assessing a traveler's wealth: **sodhna, sodhlena,** from *sodh,* search, investigation, *sodhna,* to search.

Being arrested: **chamoo jana, chamlena,** from *cham,* skin + *lena,* to take, or from *jana,* to lose: to lose one's skin.

Being on one's guard (= to spy): **bykare dekhna,** from *bekari dekhna,* to appear to have no work.

Breaking clumps of dirt and spreading them on the graves: **kondul kurna/dalna,** from *kundal karna,* to make a circle.

Burying in a secure manner: **pucca kurna,** from *paka,* cooked, done, perfect.

Burying temporarily: **rhana kur dena,** from *rahna,* to store, to leave as is.

Camping, lodging: **khoturna,** from *khet, kshetr,* field, space?

Changing road or direction: **tupjana,** from *chhup jana,* to hide oneself; **khonchkahna** (Deccan).

Choosing the place for the murder (= "to wash the copper cup"): **bileea manjuna, kutoree manjna,** from *mamjna,* to be washed and *katori,* little cup, bowl. This might be linked to the Thug practice of often eating their meals at the very spot where they do their murders.

Consulting (each other): **kartee kurna,** from *katha,* discussion + *karna,* to make.

Consulting the omen: **jeelna, jeetjana, jeetae purjana,** from *jit,* victory + *pahcanna,* to recognize; the fact of consulting them: **rugnoutee,** from *akshan,* sign, omen, or raksha, protection?

Counting: **siharna,** from *siharna,* to accumulate, to collect.

Cutting up a corpse (to prevent it from swelling up): **kanthuna, kanth delna,** from *katna,* to cut.

Denouncing: **chourukna,** from *churana,* to steal?

Denouncing following a quarrel, becoming an enemy: **khutana, khutae, khutae dena,** from *khota,* false = turning one's vest inside out?

Detecting: **rumujna,** from *ramuj,* secret, enigmatic.

Digging graves to safely bury corpses: **kurbakurna,** from *kabr,* Muslim word for grave + *karna,* to make.

Dispersing at the approach of danger: **barana, barawnee kurna,** from *bahar,* outside + *na,* suffix or *ana,* to get out, to disperse; **kharoo phootna** (kharoo = a Thug gang), from *phatna,* to leave, to disperse, or from *phutna,* to burst.

Dividing the loot: **chatae lena, chutae lena,** from *chamtna,* to sort, to divide, to separate.

Dubbing someone with the *roomal,* solemnly installing someone into the function of strangler: **pulloo, pelhoo dena,** from *pala,* the side of a piece of clothing, or *pallu,* part of a sari + *dena,* to give.

Drawing lots to share the loot: **kouree/ghoughee phenkna, marna,** or **delna,** from *kaura,* cowrie, and from *phemkna,* to throw, or from *marna,* to beat, or from *dalna,* to throw.

Dying: **tookna, took jana,** from *tukna,* to die.

Eating: **oondana,** from *ann,* food + *dana,* grain, cereal; **gajna,** from *gachna,* to stuff; **taujna,** from *toshna,* to be satiated.

Escaping, to run away because of danger: **oogur jana,** from *ud jana,* or *udhar jana,* to fly away or to go to the other side; **jhurawun ho, jhurjana,** from *jharna,* to scatter (also means to escape from prison); **buhup, buhupna, buhapjana,** from *behad jana* or *bhag jana,* to run away; **dhons-jana, dhonsna** (also means to arrest Thugs in the Deccan), from *dhomsna,* to threaten, to terrorize, to attack + *jana,* to escape; **phosurna,** from *pasarna,* to spread (Deccan).

Excluding from a Thug group: **nuga kar dena,** from *namga,* naked + *kar dena,* to be. This as a punishment for having killed forbidden victims, which are: "sweeper, shoemaker (*chamar*), oil seller (*teli*), washerman (*dhobi*), jeweler (*sonar*), dancer, gypsy (*bhart,* is written *bhamd*), Nanak sect member (*nanukpuntee,* is written *nanakpamthi*), Shivaite ascetic (*jattadaree,* is written *jatavari*), elephant driver (*hatheewan,* is written *hathivan*)."

Expectorating: **khokhee karna,** from *khomkhi,* to cough.

Farting: 1. when the Thugs are gathered in a council: **mururee ka dhuneea,** from *murri,* to attach the two ends of a cord or to make a circle + *dhuni,* smoke; 2. on the place where the loot is shared out: **phurka dhuneea,** from *pur,* place + *ka* + *dhuni,* smoke.

Freed from prison: **chibilna.**

Gargling and spitting out sour milk: **duhee phuckana,** from *dahi,* milk + *phukna,* to spit.

Gathering information on travelers and reporting it: **dhaga le ana,** from *daga,* misleading (noun form), cheating (noun form), ruse + *le ana,* to report.

Giving the signal to strangle: **jirnee dena,** from *chirni,* the act of splitting, tearing, ripping (a piece of cloth) + *dena,* to permit, to authorize.

Guessing, to be aware of Thug projects, to be on one's guard: **bugjana,** from *bhagna,* to run away, to run; **chukjana, chuk ho jana,** from *chukna,* to miss + *jana,* to go, to stumble; **cheyt/cheek jana,** from *chet,* thought, awareness, to be on one's guard; **iter jana** (Deccan), the opposite of **gote hona** or of **chuk hona,** from *idhar,* here, or *udhar,* there + *jana.*

Helping the strangler: **gote purajana,** from the verb *ghomtna* whose participle is *gota,* the fact of strangling + *parajana,* to perform an action until its completion.

Hide/to be hidden: **lopee kurna/lopee hona,** from *lup* + *i*, hidden.

Hiding things from stranglers: **jhowar dena,** from *johan*, search + *dena* or *lena*, to give, to take; to hide oneself: **jhowar lena.**

Killing/being killed: **tubae dalna/tobae jana,** from *top, topi*, hat or turban + *dalna, jana;* **ludohur kurna,** from *lahu har karna*, to be covered in blood?

Killing between midnight and dawn: **khotub mem ladhna,** from *khotub*, which designates this time interval.

Killing forbidden victims: **naga lugna,** from *namga*, naked, exposed + *lagna*, to appear. This is the worst of crimes for Deccan Thugs.

Killing goats or other animals to eat: **lapna,** from *lap*, brandishing a sword.

Killing with a sword: **sutheea dalna, sutheeana, lumbhereeana,** see sword.

Looking at secretly: **choukana, choukna, chouklena,** from *chaukna*, to be on the alert, or from *cuk*, deceit, mistake.

Losing something, particularly one's way: **bunasna, bunas jana,** from *bhatakna*, to lose one's way?

Lying down to hide or to sleep: **lopna, lop ruhna,** from *lupna*, to hide.

Making signs of recognition on the road: **polakurna,** from *pola*, sign + *karna*, to make.

Making the traces of murder disappear: **phur jarna,** from *pur*, place, and *jharna*, to sweep, to clean.

Moving (oneself) slowly: **morna** (Deccan), from *mudhna*, to turn?

Observing, looking: **tippana,** from *tipna*, to notice.

Persuading a functionary or someone of the innocence of the Thugs: **dhaga kuranadena,** from *daga*, misleading (noun form).

Pillage, to be pillaged: **londh lena/londh hona,** from *luthana*, to loot, or *luthna*, pillage + *hona* (passive mode auxiliary).

Pretending to be sick: **gan karna,** from *ganam*, plot, calculation.

Pursuing the Thugs: **kharkuna (kharoo,** one who pursues), from *kaid*, capture, or *khoj*, search?

Ransoming: **thumonee dalna,** from *thamna*, to take in one's hand.

Rejecting a forbidden victim or one of no value: **phankdena,** from *phemkna*, to throw + *dena* (auxiliary).

Returning: **khonsana, khounsana,** from *khasna*, to run away, to run.

Rummaging: **tighunee kurna,** from *tighuna*, triple, to triple + *karna*, to make (to rummage into travelers' possessions is a promise of growing wealth).

Rushing in on the victims (without performing the rites): **khomusna,** from *khumasna*, same meaning in Gujarati.

Setting a date for a rendezvous: **maulee dena** (Deccan), from *mal*, price, or *mali*, that which has value, price + *dena*, to cause; **phool dena,** from *phal*, fruit or from *phul*, flower, or again from *pal*, time, and, by extension, speech + *dena*, to give (Hindustan) (cf. *Agra kee phool deea*: he set a rendezvous in Agra).

Setting out on a journey or resuming it: **ogalua** (Deccan), from *agal, age*, farther; before the start of day: **khotana,** from *katna*, to leave, to take off.

Shaking a piece of clothing to warn of danger: **phuruck dena,** from *phadak(na)*, to beat, to shake + *dena* (completive).

Sitting down, resting (for a traveler): **thibna,** from *thairana* or *thobana* (southern Raj.), make someone wait, or from *thwabal*, stop, stay; causal form: **thibana, thibae dena/chouka dena,** from *chaumka dena*, to be surprised, to be warned.

Sleeping, spending the night: **anjuna, anjruhna,** from *amjan*, night; **tooluk ruhna, toulukna,** from *talak*, until + *rahna*, to stay.

Snoring while asleep or while being strangled: **setna.**

Spitting: **thokee kurna,** from *thuk*, spittle, or from *thukna*, to spit, to damn. When the situation proves to be suddenly dangerous and the strangling has to be postponed, the gang leader spits after having given the signal for the murder.

Splitting into several groups when in danger: **putlee ho jana**, from *patla*, thin + *ho jana*, to become = to divide, to make oneself small; **barana, barawnee kurna**. See also "dispersing at the approach of danger," above.

Spying: **bykuree kurna/dekhna**, from *bekari*, to be without work + *karna*, to make.

Stabbing with a knife: **borkeeana, borkee marna, borkeeae dalna**, from *badki*, big, or *bharaki*, sharp + *marna*, to die, to hit.

Staining a piece of clothing or anything else with blood: **buneana**, from *pani*, liquid? + *ana*.

Stealing loot, looting other Thugs: **kootkurna, koot kur lena**, from *kut*, trick, falsehood, lie; **bhans lena** (Deccan), from *phams*, knot, trap, and *lena*, to take.

Strangling: **dhurdalna, dhurohurkurna**, from *dhur*, dust, and *dharna*, to hold (the fact of strangling: **dharohur**); **gorhna/gharna**, from *gharna*, to encircle; **ladhna** (a term common to all Thugs), from *ladna*, to load, to cover, to finish, to throw; **leepurna** (Thugs from Ujain), from *lipatna*, to encircle, to hook, to grasp; **tubae dalna/nakhna**, from *topi*, hat, turban + *nakhna*, to throw; **jheer dalna** (Thug from the west, Soosseea), from *chirna*, to split, to tear, to rip a piece of cloth (*chin*, cloth, rag, tear); **parnakhna** (Ujain and the west), from *pal*, piece of cloth + *nakhna* (Raj.), to throw (frequently affixed and corresponding to *karna*, to do); **ooharna/wahurna**, from *varna*, to dedicate, to encircle, to offer to a divinity; **gurkha mem dena**, from *gar*, neck + *mem*, on, in + *dena*, to give.

Strangling a victim in easy, favorable circumstances (**soosul, sosal**): **sosalladhna**, from *su* + *safal*, fruitful, efficacious + *ladna*, to throw.

Throwing the *roomal* clumsily around the victim's face or on top of the head: **bisul purna**, from *be*, bad, without + *safal*, efficacious, and *padna*, to fall.

Throwing the *roomal* skillfully around the victim's neck: **soosul purna**, from *su*, good, well + *safal*, efficacious + *padna*, to fall.

Trapping, to fall into a trap: **kartee kurna**, from *katha*, discussion; **bote hona**, from *bate hona*, to speak; **gote hona**, from *ghomtna*, to smother (Deccan).

Tying the loot into bundles or tying the victims' corpses: **choundhna**, from *chamdna*, to tie, to squeeze, to tie the hind legs of a horse; to tie someone's arms behind the back: **choundhee churana**, from *chunri*, a long fold in a sheet + *chamdna;* to tie one's turban: **agasee choundhna**, from *akash*, sky + *chamdna*.

Unveiling so as to be visible (particularly the traces of crime): **bae hojana**, from *bai*, left + *hojana*, to become; **purta purna** (to be recognized by wearing an object belonging to a victim), from *parda padna*, veil + *panda*, to fall, to be unveiled; **teekula parna**, from *tika*, an auspicious mark worn by women + *padna*, to fall.

Waking up sleeping travelers: **tankee dena**, from *tangi*, the fact of hanging = to hang (hanging being identified with strangling).

Washing oneself: **soosul karna**; this also means to gather the loot, to prepare the victim by persuading him to bare his neck.

Whispering, speaking softly: **katee must karna/must katee kurna**, from *katha*, discussion + *mast*, well, "happy" + *karna*, make.

Yelling for help: **doonrkurna, doonree lakarna, doonreeana**, from *dhuni*, sound + *lalkarna*, to call.

Yelling very loudly when being strangled: **lokharna**, from *lalkarna*, to call, to defy

4. NOUNS LINKED TO THESE ACTIONS

Accomplice who knows the secrets of the Thugs and is keeping them: **burgeela**, from *varg*, class, kind, species, group + *gilna*, to keep a secret, one who belongs to the same class and keeps the secret; **paoo**, from *bhau*, colleague in dialectical Hindi.

Honoraria of the initiate to the master: **nuzur,** from *nazrana* (Persian), a gaze, subsequently a gift, in particular to the king.

Money or other hidden possession: **sodh,** from *sodhna,* to search, to make inquiries (same word for the fact of looking for this money).

Negotiations with local chiefs to obtain protection or the freedom of a Thug: **dhaga,** from *daga,* ruse, trick.

Noise the pickaxe makes when digging into the ground: **khuruk,** from *kharak,* crack.

Omen, good or bad: **rugon,** from *lakshan,* sign, omen, protection, auspiciousness; bad omen: **khurtul, kotar** (Deccan), from *khatra,* danger.

Omen coming from the left: **dhilhaoo,** from *dhil,* that which unties, frees (usually a good omen).

Omen coming from the right: **thibaoo,** from *thobana,* to stop (usually a bad omen).

Rites: **tuponee,** from *tap,* fire, devotion, penance, austerity, or from *tapna,* to be warmed, to do penance; **kote** (Deccan), from *kot,* assembly, group; **panchayet kote,** from *panchayat,* assembly.

Ritual knot: **goor ghat/ghaunt,** from *gur,* ritual, secret + *gamth,* knot.

Sacred pickaxe: **kassee/kussee,** from *komchna,* to pierce; **mahee,** from *mahi,* earth (Deccan); **kodalee,** from *kudali,* a widespread agricultural digging tool.

Signal to murder: **jhirnee,** from *chirni,* strip of cloth that is being torn off; **sainee,** from *sai,* god, abbreviation of **Deoseyn,** "all is well," *dev* + *sami,* God + God's disciple.

Thug council: **mururee,** from *murri,* the fact of tying the two ends of a cord together to make a circle.

Thug idiom: **ramasee** from *ramna,* to wander, to bum around, or from *ramana,* to seduce, to charm, to fascinate; the lexicon of this idiom: **ramaseeana,** from *ramasee + ana,* collection.

Trick, falsehood, ruse, con: **seyp,** from *sap,* curse; **gunooa,** from *gunha,* crime; **townaree,** from *dhundri,* cry; **tona,** from *tona,* spell; **raba,** from *rab,* molasses; **chuck,** from *shak,* doubt, suspicion. We also find *ganam,* plot, in **gan karna,** pretending to be sick?; *daga,* ruse, in **dagha le ana,** to inquire about travelers and in **dagha kurana,** to persuade a functionary of the innocence of Thugs; *chamd,* fraud in **chandoo,** a thug expert.

Word to rendezvous: **bagh, baghdena** from *vak,* word; **phool** (Hindustan), from *phal,* fruit, or from *phul,* flower; **maulee** (Deccan), from *moli,* that which has value, price (*mal*); **syt** (Berar), from *chet,* thought.

5 . VICTIMS/TRAVELERS

Affix used to designate the number of persons killed in the course of an expedition: **rooh,** from *ruh,* soul; a victim: **eeloo,** from *ek,* one + *ruh,* soul; two victims: **bhitree;** three: **singhore;** four: **behra,** a word designating a toss of the dice coming up with four (one can speculate that this is also the case with **bhitree** and **singhore**); five victims: **puchrooh,** from *panch,* five + *ruh* (soul); six: **chehrooh,** from *chai,* six + *ruh.*

Auspicious object that belonged to a victim and that is dangerous to appropriate: **teekula,** from *tikla,* an auspicious mark worn by women.

Bad, badly: **bisul,** from *be,* without + *safal,* succeeded, efficacious. Is said of a difficult victim whose clothes protect the neck and of a Thug stained with blood that attracts suspicion; **bisul** is the opposite of **soosul** (*su* + *safal*).

Burial (temporary): **angjhap** (Deccan), from *amg,* body + *jhapna,* to fall, or from *jhap,* the fall (state or action of something that suddenly falls from a certain height); **rehna,** from *rahna,* to leave; temporary grave: **ruhna,** from *rahna,* or from *ruhna,* to be buried.

Elucidation of travelers' intentions: **dhaga,** from *daga,* trick, ruse.

Grave: **sancha,** from *samcha,* mold?

Grave, circular in shape and having a stake in the middle to keep animals from digging up the corpses: **gobba,** from *garbha,* matrix, fetus, saint of saints, central part of a temple.

Grave, oval or square in shape: **kurwa,** from *kahr,* a Muslim word for grave.

Murder (the first murder during an expedition): **sonoka/sonrka,** from *sona,* excellent thing, or *sona ka,* the one—murder—in gold.

Noise, confusion, clamor: **cheyns,** from *chimk,* scream.

Place badly chosen to bury victims: **chuckbele,** from *chuck,* mistake, or from *chak,* confused + *bil,* hole.

Place chosen to bury victims: **beyla,** from *bil,* hole; **kutoree,** from *katori,* bowl (cf. **kutoree mamjna,** to wash the bowl = to kill); **maun** (Deccan), from *maun,* silence, or from *maut,* death; the one who chooses the place: **maunkurreea,** from *maun* + *kari,* one who renders someone silent.

Place of rest where the loot is divided: **phur,** from *pur,* place.

Place where victims are killed: **phur,** from *pur,* place.

Stones, particularly on graves: **gota,** from *gomti,* small stone, or from *gomta,* stone fragment; **oorwala** (also the holder of hands in the Deccan): *aur,* on the side + *vala.*

Traveler: **kuj,** from *kuch,* departure, march.

Traveler in Thugs hands: **bunij/bunj,** from *banij,* trade, occupation; **neeamut,** from *niyat,* legal + *maut,* dead.

Traveler left for dead but who is found alive: **jywaloo,** from *jiva,* life.

Traveler, poor, without possessions (= useless thing): **phank,** from *phemkna,* to throw.

Traveler, wealthy, a blessing from heaven: **cheesa,** from *chiz,* object, and often object of value.

Traveler who discovers the Thugs' intentions: **cheyt,** from *chet,* awareness, thought.

Traveler who escapes: **buhup,** from *behad,* beyond limits; **ardal,** from *ardh,* one half; **adhoreea,** from *adhura,* incomplete (Hindustan); **tail,** from *tahal,* task, job, duty, from the root *tahalna,* to walk, or from *talna,* to escape from a difficulty (Varma dictionary); traveler who escapes at the moment of strangling: **saur,** from *suau,* one who has a long life.

Traveler who is suspect, who does not correspond to his appearances or caste: **komil,** from *kamil,* accomplished, in the know; **bydha,** from *vaidya,* one who knows.

Traveler without arms and/or legs, whom it is forbidden to kill: **awkhur** (Deccan), from *akhor,* thing without value, bad, rotten.

Travelers (a group of): **taw,** from *tol,* assembly.

Travelers too numerous to be killed: **tonkul/tonkal,** from *thok,* "wholesale," when referring to merchandise; **botoel,** from *bahut* too many + *tahal,* task.

Victim's cadaver: **gurtha,** from the verb *ghutna,* to strangle; **bhara,** from *bhar,* dead weight.

Victim's loud cries for help: **doonr,** from *dhuni,* sound; *senth,* from *siti,* whistle, piercing cry.

6. THE TERRAIN

Camping place for the night outside of the village: **thap/thapa,** from *thahr,* place of rest.

Direction taken for an expedition: **pusur,** from *pasarna,* length, area.

Ground, sandy: **rewaroo,** from *reti,* that which is cooked on the sand; **bhusmee,** from *bhesma,* ashes, or from *besna,* flour.

Jungle, large and uncultivated, very appropriate for murder: **bilgaree,** from *bil,* locale, hole + *gahra,* deep, thick, large.

Jungle or forest: **cheyhur,** from *chihur,* hair. In the enigmas, the jungle and the forest are often compared to hair. Inversely, in the *Mahabharata,* Draupadi's dirty, unkept hair is compared to a jungle with wandering wild animals.

Mountain landscape covered with jungles: **dhagsa,** from *dhakara* + *sa,* provokes terror (Deccan).

Ravine, small stream: **khureynja,** from *khodna,* to dig.

River: **dhurdo,** from *dhara,* river; **thapa,** from *thahr* (Bihar and Bengal). The Thugs often camp or rest on its banks.

Road: **daee,** from *dayam, dayi,* to the right (Deccan).

Road to avoid: **bunar,** from *bad* + *nazar,* evil eye?

Road with lots of traffic: **baee/dubaee,** from *bai,* to the left (from which usually the good omen comes; this expression evokes the sects of the left hand that behave in manners contrary to orthodox tradition).

Small path onto which the Thugs lead the travelers to kill them: **tuppul, tuppowal, tupole,** from *chupna,* to hide + *pag,* foot?

Town (large): **gote** (Deccan), from *goth,* an assembly.

Traces left on the road to let other Thugs know the gang passed there: **pola,** from *pol,* opening. In Hindi the expression *pol khulna* means unmasking an intrigue.

Village: **khubba,** from *kasha?*; **khuga; kaul** (Deccan); **khuleeta** (Koeleea Thugs), from *khula,* open space, or from the verb *khulana,* to be open, put aside, untied; **nudh,** from *nagar,* town; **jhoosa,** from *jaham,* place; **dharee,** from *dehra,* village (cf. *dehra delna,* to settle).

Well: **kiswara,** from *kisti,* boat?

7. THE WEATHER

Rain outside of the monsoon season, "tears": **ansootore,** from *amsu,* tears + *turra,* fragments, particulates. Bad omen, particularly during the first day of an expedition.

Thunder: **agasee birar** (Deccan), from *akash,* sky + *bahar,* rain?

8. UNITS OF TIME

First seven days of an expedition: **satha,** from *sat,* seven.

Interval of time between noon and sunset: **oturtee phoolkee,** from *utarti,* descending + *palki,* three-hour span.

Interval of time between sunrise and noon: **churtee phoolkee,** from *chadhti,* rising + *palki,* a three-hour span.

Interval of time between sunrise and sunset: **phoolkee,** from *palki,* a three-hour span of time.

Interval of time between sunset and midnight: **khotub,** from *katna,* to spend the time, passage of time.

Interval of time between sunset and nightfall: **chulub,** from *chalna,* to advance; killing during this time interval: **chulub mem ladhna.**

Moment of return from an expedition: **khous,** from *khush,* content.

Month: **khosur; khomur kosir** (Bihar).

Months and days during which Thugs do not go on expeditions: July (**savan,** from *shravan*), September (**koar,** from *kuar*), December (**poos,** from *paus*); Wednesdays and Thursdays.

Night: **kalee,** from *kali,* black.

9. ANIMALS/OMENS

Antelope, male: **kursaul**, from *kuramg*, antelope.

Apparition or sounds produced by animals taken as omens when they appear on the left: **pilhaoo**, from *pahalu*, side, direction, the aspect of a thing considered from the viewpoint of its positive and negative aspects; when the animals appear on the right: **thibhaoo**, from *thobawu* (Guj.), *thobana* (Raj.), *thaharna* (Hindi), to stop.

Ass: **khurkha**, from *khur*, horse hooves + *ka*, having hooves; **kanta**, from *khar*, ass, mule; **dhunteroo**, from *damd*, stick, punishment + *dheru*, the one who gives (and receives) blows.

Birds: blue jay: **tas**. Crow, croaking of the great mountain crow: **kogura**, from *kuhak, kuhuk*, call of the raven, *kauva*. Water Crow: **jalkagura**, from *jal*, water + *kauva*, raven. Grey shrike: **bhojunga/bhinjodoha**, from bhujamda, vulture?; its omen, **goma**; **muhoka** (*caculus castaneous*); its call or the bird itself: **chira**, from *chilla*. Bengal kite: **bhimjodha**, **ardhul** (Deccan), **kurtae** (Deccan). Grey wagtail: **roopareyl**. Kite (call of the): **agasee**, from *akash*, sky; its cry while in flight: **bhontee**. Owl: **rooparel**, from *ruruha*, owl; deep sound of the great owl: **korra**, or **kokatee**, from *gurgur, kurkur* (Deccan); or again **goorgoorooe**, from *ghughuana*, call of the owl, "sound (*gurgur*) similar to that of a water pipe"; call of two great owls responding to each other: **junejore baja**, from *jun*, time + *jod*, ensemble + *baja*, musical instrument. Owl (small): **khureyree**, from *ghughdi*, small owl (Doab, Bihar); its chirping: **chirreya**, from *chirana*, to cry; its muffled call repeated three or four times: **bees**; when it is in flight: **oorut putoree**, from *udna*, to fly + *patri*, bird. Raven, its call from a tree within sight of a river or lake: **julkagura**, from *jal*, water + *kauva*, raven. Sarus crane: its call, **konjul** (Bihar and Bengal); **julhar**, from *jal sar*, Indian cuckoo.

Braying of an ass: **dunda** (Deccan), from *daharna*, to roar, to scream; **kanta**, from *khar*, mule, ass.

Braying of ass that suddenly appears in front of a gang of Thugs: **mathaphore**, from *matha*, head + *phodna*, to shatter.

Cat: **bunjaree**, from *bamjari*, wife of the traveling grain merchant, *bamjara;* **manj/maunj** (Deccan), from *mamjar*, cat; **mudoreea** (Koeleea Thugs); bad omen during the day: **dhamonee kee manj**, from *dinman*, from morning till night + *ke* + *mamjar*, cat, or from *dhamki*, threat, intimidation +*manjar*, cat; bad omen during the night: **kalee kee manj**, from *kali*, night, etc.; cat fight, cats' screeches as they are fighting: **bhar**, from *barak*, battle.

Deer (young): **borkee**, from *badhna*, to grow; in a herd: **mirgmaul**, from *mriga*, deer + *mal*, precious.

Dog: **beetula** (Bihar and Bengal) (= **bheela**, enemy of the Thugs?, from *bit*, inferior, of low caste); **dhokne** (also used to refer to a Thug catcher), from *dhurt*, fox, or from *bhomkna*, to bark; **jokkur**, from *jakut*, dog; a dog seen excreting: **dhap**, from *dhappa*, noise, onomatopoeia; **chandanee-kee-dhap**, same but at night: from *chamdni*, moon light + *dhappa*, noise.

Fox: **sewalee** (Deccan), from *siyar, siyal*, fox or jackal.

Goat or sheep: **dheema**, from *dhimbha*, belly (also means stomach in Deccan).

Hare: **daheea**, from *dahad*, roaring (very bad omen); **dutooa**, from *damt*, tooth, the toothy one; its cry at night on the left: **roopauneea**, from *rup*, form + *ni*, having a form, beautiful, good (very good omen!); its passage on the road where the gang is traveling: **kharkuneea**, from *khargosh, kharha*, hare.

Horse: **phoorkana** (Deccan); mare: **phoorkanee**, from *puchkarna*, a whistling sound to please an animal, particularly horses and dogs; **potura/poturee**, from *put*, horse hoof; **khoruk/khorkanee**, from *khur* + *ak* (masculine gender) or from *ani* (feminine), having horse hoofs; **mawil/mawilee**, from *mal,* precious object, merchandise, capital.

Jackal: **munjwar,** from *mamjar,* cat; the lone cry of a jackal: **mahasutee** (Deccan), from *maha,* big, strong + *siti,* whistle; **bhalee/bharohee** (Hindustan), from *bura,* bad; short cry of the jackal: **ekareea,** from *ekda,* one time; omen linked to this cry: **buroee,** from *bura,* bad; lamentations of several jackals: **raul/raureen/rareyn,** from *rona,* to cry, or *raura,* big noise, clamor; two jackals crossing the road: **lohurburheya,** "from *lohar,* smith and *badhi,* carpenter"; the omen linked to this apparition: **kanta** and **mataphore,** see above, "braying of an ass."

Lizard: **matungee** (Deccan), from *mitti,* earth + *amga,* body, earth tone; cry of the lizard: **chirchera,** from *chirana,* chirping, or **bara muttee.**

Oxen: **lode, lodh,** from *ladna,* to load, a Hindustani word meaning "blood" in the Deccan; **lubba,** from *lappa,* that which carries, that which supports; **moeh** (Deccan), from *mahisi,* cow buffalo.

Snake: **lumpocha** (Berar), from *lambocha,* that which is long.

Wolf crossing the road: **burauk,** from *vakr* (Sanskrit), wolf; **walgee** (Deccan), from *valval* (Raj., Guj., Mar.), to waver; wolf cry: **chimmama,** from *chimkhna,* to scream.

10. PARTS OF THE BODY

Blood: **banee,** from *pani,* designating all that is liquid, including liquids emitted by the body, blood, water, etc.

Breaking wind, the fact of doing it (cf. discussion of omens in chapter 3): **dhuneea,** from *dhuni,* smoke; **oorut kawree,** from *ulat,* upside down + *kauri,* cowrie. (The Thugs use cowries to split up loot that is difficult to share equally; it is a bad omen when the shells come up upside down.)

Eye: **tighunee,** from *tikshan,* sight.

Hand: **gona,** from *gan,* number (also means number five in Deccan).

Head: **kudhooa,** *kaddu,* pumpkin; **nareal** (Deccan), from *nariyal,* coconut; **sirma,** from *sir,* head; **duller,** from *dulna,* to be agitated, to oscillate.

Neck: **gurkha,** from *gar,* neck; **gurkha mem dena,** to strangle.

Sneeze: **nakee/nukaree,** from *nak,* nose.

Stomach: **dheerna** (Deccan), **dheema,** from *dhimdha,* belly (see Goat, above); **kondoo** (Thugs from Koel), from *kotha,* stomach, gut, or from *tond,* belly; **jhuller/jheema** (Thugs from Multan), from *jhola,* bag, or from *jhaumd,* belly.

Throat: **lol** (Deccan), from *lol,* the tongue.

11. THE LOOT

Good of value set aside as a gift for the gang leader or village chief, or for any patron: **tome,** from *tumbe,* for you.

Hundred, one hundred of any sort of item: **ankura,** from *amkda,* number; **bheela, bheeta,** from *bitta,* riches.

Portion of loot: **beegha** (Bihar and Bengal), from *bagh,* part, division, from which comes *bigha,* land parcel; **chatae/chutaw,** from *chamtna,* to take away, to separate, to cut, to take; **gar, garbung,** from *kar,* tax, and also trick, fraud.

Portion of the loot reserved for the leader before it gets divided: **dhurae,** from *dahai,* one tenth (the traditional part of a leader and a king; cf. *Arthashastra* or *The Laws of Manu*).

Portion of the loot reserved for a leader of a band of at least twenty Thugs: **morka**, from *mukha*, mouth, chief.

Thing without value, throwaway: **phank** (also used to refer to a poor traveler lacking possessions), from *phemkna*, to throw away.

12. JEWELS, MONEY, PRECIOUS METALS AND STONES

Bracelet: **santa**, from *samth(a)*, ankle bracelet, or from *sampada*, gold, riches (Deccan).

Coin, copper: **khorae**, from *khodai*, that which is engraved.

Coin, eight *annas:* **khodeylee, khoreylee**, same meaning.

Coin, small: **ghoeela** (Oudh), from *goli*, round; **dhilbam**, from *diba*, the act of giving something and the price of something.

Coral: **rungeela**, from *ramgila*, colored; **gollee** (Deccan), from *garra*, having the color of red wax.

Earrings: **kaneelee**, from *kan*, ears.

Gold: **seea/situk** (Deccan), from *sikka*, money (see under mohur, below).

Gold coin: **sitkala**, from *satak*, 100?, or from *sikka* (Deccan).

Gold coin, small: **phangolee** (see Pearl, below—a gold coin is like the pearl of coins?); **chukura**, from *chakr*, round (Deccan).

Gold jewel: **boguma**, from *baghanaham, baghnakh*, jewel in the form of tiger claws and instrument with which to catch thieves (Somadeva Bhatta 1968, 7:216).

Knot in a turban or other piece of clothing (very often in a sari for women) to hide money, jewels, gold, etc.: **guthonie**, from *amth*, knot.

Mohur: **maurheea**, from *mohar*, seal; the mohur was the most important piece of gold at the beginning of the nineteenth century, equivalent to sixteen rupees in silver; **tareea**, from *tari*, ear ornament; **tarndee**, from *tarand*, bracelet; **cheek**, corruption, from *sikka*. See Money, next.

Money (and also strangling handkerchief): **sikka**, from *sikka*, money, coin; **entha, anchta, aentha**, from *aimt*, so much.

Pearl: **panderphulee** (Deccan), from *pandu + phul*, white flower; **puneeara**, from *pandu + har:* white necklace; **phangola**, from *pandu*, white + *goli*, gold ornament, round spheres.

Ring: **puloee**, from *payal*, toe ring, or from *puliya*, nose or ear ornament; or from *phulli*, jewel in the form of a flower worn in the ear or nose.

Ring, for finger, ear, or nose: **palwee** (Deccan), from *phulli*, jewel in the form of a flower worn in the ear or nose.

Rupees: **bhurka** (Deccan), from the verb *bharna*, to fill or to give money, or from *bhar*, transaction, business, work, or *bhar + ka*, anything belonging to, any physical or financial activity; **cheeota**, from *chitta*, white; twenty rupees: **sootlee**, from *sutli*, thread (allusion to the fact that the coins were put in a roll attached by a cord).

Silver: **sofedee**, from *safed*, white; **kourga** (Deccan), from *khurda*, small change.

Treasure: **gael**, from *golak*, a safe, collection; **sambhur**, from *samgraha*, collection; treasure made up of money: **pykee**, from *punji*, collection; **maunghee**, from *mahamga*, expensive, costly.

13. WEAPONS

Dagger: **dapnee** (Deccan), from *dhapna*, to charge, to thrust, to do harm.

Kerchief (strangling): **pulloo, pelhoo**, from *pallu*, a panel of a woman's clothing, veil; **roomal**, from *rumal*, kerchief; **sikka**, from *sikka*, that which is round, seal, coin, silver. The precious items contained here are used to designate the container that is the clothing in which money is hidden; **goputban**, from *gupt*, invisible + *bamdh*, belt.

Knife: **kanthun**, from *katna*, cutting; **borkee**, from *badki*, that which is big, or from *bhadak*, sharp.

Rifle: **baajunee**, from *pamjna*, pieces of metal soldered together; or from *bajna*, to make noise, to burst; **bharakee**, from *bhadakna*, to burst, to ring; **lokaree**, from *luki*, that which makes fire burn; **phutakee**, from *phataka*, firecracker, or from *phatna*, to burst, to explode.

Shield: **phutkee**, from *pat*, board, or from *pata*, having a half-circle shape.

Sword: **binderee**, from *bimdhna*, to pierce, or from *bind*, thousand, hitting one thousand [bull's eye], reaching its target; **cheeng** (Berar), from *chimja*, little boy; a term of affection that a woman might use to designate the male sexual organ; **eetha**, from *aimthna*, twist, turn: giving pain; **lumbheree**, from *lamba*, long; **luhtar**, from *loha*, iron + *tar*, wire: iron wire; **santh**, from *samt*, stick/sugar cane; **thenga**, from *tamga*, that which is hooked.

14. COMMON OBJECTS

Bag: **tirheea**, from *thaila*, bag, purse.

Copper cup: **bileea**, from *bela*, cup (also used to refer to *bil*, the place to kill or bury victims).

Copper pot: **dhungee**.

Door: **khom**, from *khom*, main door of a fort according to the Varma dictionary (1962).

Iron utensils (see Handcuffs): **bisendee**; **thulee**, from *thali*, tray.

Jug, small, empty: **bhurehur**. Strangely, the word designating an empty jug is almost the same as that for a full jug. Could Sleeman have made a mistake?

Jug, small, filled with water: **bhurahur**, from *bhara*, full + *har*, that which carries, jug.

Metal utensils: **dhamree** (Deccan), from *damri* (Guj.), copper money?, **dhara; anhur**, from *anna*, food + *har*, utensil?

Papers: **dhaga**, from *dhaga*, string, cord; valuable papers are usually rolled up and held together by a string; **puck**, from *parcha*, paper; **heyla**, from *hel*, pile.

Purse, money purse that is cut: **kanjoo** (Deccan), from *khamjar*, the dagger that cuts the purse?

Purse, the typical very small money purse of the thieves: **lutkuneea**, from *latakna*, to hang.

Water pipe: **dogga**, from *hukkah*, water pipe.

Weight: **dull**, from *sal*, piece.

15. ALIMENTS

Alcohol: **keyta**, from *chet*, awake, that which awakes.

Bread: **gorha**, from *gehum*, made of wheat or barley; **taup**, from *tapna*, to heat; **towree**, from *tava*, small convex half-moon-shaped plaque used to cook chapatis, or from *tauni*, small round plaque used to bake bread.

Flour: **bushmee**, from *besna*, flour, or from *bhesma*, ashes. Also used to refer to fine dirt and sand one finds when digging graves.

Food: **gorha**, from *gehum*, wheat, barley.

Liquor: **kaulkee**, from *khaulna*, that which is fermenting.

Meat, mutton or beef (Deccan): **khobba**, from *gadda*, fleshy, or from *go*, cow.

Rice, cooked: **kode** (Deccan), from *kaur,* mouthful.

Sugar, raw: **ladhka,** from *ladhka,* that which is preferred, or from *lata,* food made from molasses; **goor,** from *gur,* molasses.

Sweets: **kalunderee,** from *kalakamd,* a sweet in the shape of a ball.

Tobacco, dry: **dhooansa,** from *dhuam,* smoke.

Water: **neera,** from *nir,* water.

Wheat or corn just before harvest: **kapsee,** from *kapna* (Raj.), to cut, ready to be cut.

16. CLOTHING

Belt, hip: **potnee** (Thugs from the Koel district), from *pet,* stomach, and, by extension, something worn over the stomach; **surdhuneea,** from *dhuneea,* gas, that which surrounds the stomach; **dhotee,** from *dhoti,* material tied around the waist.

Blanket: **lewalee** (Deccan), from *loi,* blanket

Cloth bundle: **borcha,** see Clothes, new, below.

Clothing: **topka** (Deccan), corrupted version of *topa,* sowing; **chanda,** from *chadna,* that which covers.

Clothing, new (Deccan): **borcha,** from *burka,* coat; **seep** (Hindustan), from *khep,* cloth bundle; **seep** also means a bundle of clothes.

Clothing, not sown, in pieces: **leepra,** or **leep,** from *lugra,* a piece of material, rags?

Clothing, used: **oogaul,** from *ugal,* that which is obtained by stealing.

Jacket, vest: **tonga,** from *tamga,* that which is hung up; **anghura** (Doab), from *amgrakha,* jacket.

Shoes: **gonee,** from *gorari,* shoe, or from *god,* foot.

Turban: **agasee,** from *akash,* sky; **togree** (Berar, Deccan), from *topi,* hat + *pagri,* turban; **choundhee,** from *chunri,* dyeing technique, and, by extension, turban.

17. ADJECTIVES AND ADVERBS

Backward: **richee,** from *piche,* backwards.

Buried imperfectly: **kucha,** from *kacha,* imperfect.

Dangerous, uncertain: **nureehur,** from *nari,* woman; **tikkur,** from *takrar,* quarrel; its opposite is **bajeed,** from *bajit,* submitted, loser; **nissar,** from *nihsar,* powerless.

Forbidden, taboo: **eentab** (Deccan), from *inkar,* forbidden; **eetuk,** from *etraj,* obstacle, objection, opposition (contamination associated with the menstruation of a wife or daughter).

Forward: **pusur,** from *pas,* next to, near, toward; **khous,** from *khasna,* moving slowly.

Good, propitious: **sosul,** from *su,* good, excellent + *safal,* efficacious.

Heavy: **duldar,** from *dul,* weight.

Impure: **geeda,** from *gamdha,* dirty (also soiled, contaminated) because of that which is forbidden, taboo.

Low castes: **geeda,** from *gamdha,* dirty (also soiled, contaminated).

Suspicious: **chuck,** from *sak,* doubt, perplexity.

18. SAYINGS

Baean geedee sona leedee (*baem ghari, sona ladhi*): a jackal crossing the road from right to left is laden with gold.

Ratee bolee teetura, din ki bolee seear, ttuj chulee wa deysra, nuheen puree achanuk dhar (*rat bole titar, din ko bole siyar, tu chal is desh se, nahim pade* *achanak dhad*): If the partridge should call at night, or if the jackal/fox should call during the day, leave this country or you shall soon be captured.

19. CODED PHRASES

After having dispersed voluntarily or by accident: **bukh, bukh, bukh,** onomato-poeia.

Gang leader giving the order to chose the place for the murder: **jao, kutoree manj lao,** *jao katori mamj lao,* "Go clean up the cup!"

Gang leader giving the signal to strangle: **hukka bur lao** (Koeleea Thugs), from *hukka bhar lao,* "Bring your water pipe!"; **tombako kha lo, pee lo,** *tambhaku,* tobacco: "Eat or smoke your tobacco!"; **ae ho to ghyree chulo,** *aye ho to ghadi calo,* "If you're here, do come!"

Spies or scouts who signal that all is well, that the murder can be carry out: **bajeed** or **bajeed** or **Kahn Deo** or **Deomun** or **Deoseyn,** from *dev,* god + *manav,* man.

Spies or scouts who warn of a nearby danger (the gang then has to hide, speak softly, or walk slowly): **jhurwa** or **jhowar Khan** or **jhurwa Sing,** from *juhar,* greetings + *khan,* lord; **luchmun** or **luchmun sing** or **luchee ram,** from Laksh-man, Rama's young brother who followed him in his exile in the forest; **lopee** or **lopee khan** or **lopee sing?; nemee khan,** from *nama,* greetings; **gunga ram,** from the river Ganga + the god Rama; **sheikh jee, sheikh Mahummud,** from *sheikh,* Muslim leader.

To hide from sight: **taw must chowkaw,** from *tu mast chaumka,* "Be very careful."

To recognize a Thug from a non-Thug, the Thug must say: "Peace to you, friend!" The response must be, for a Muslim: **aulae khan salam,** from *aula,* holy man + *khan,* Muslim address for nobles; for a Hindu: **aulae bhae ram ram,** from *aula,* brother + *bhai,* Rama.

20. THUGS' CLAN AND SECT NAMES

Sleeman claims that there were seven original clans of Thugs and that they were all Muslim and all originary from Delhi. According to him they had the following names:

1. **Bharnt,** from *bhamdna,* to wander, or from *bhamdana,* to destroy, devastate, play tricks.
2. **Bursote,** of Barsoi in Bihar? Their sects: **Elabarkhanee,** from the Albaka hills in Madhya Pradesh? **Puchbheya,** from *pamch berar,* in Bihar?
3. **Bhys,** from the river Beas in Punjab; one of their sects: **Chireeapotee/Sireepotee** (**potee** = *putr,* son of).
4. **Huttar,** from Uttar in Bihar.
5. **Kachunee,** from Kachchh in Gujarat.
6. **Tundil/Tundul** from Tundla, in Uttar Pradesh. Sleeman writes that the Tundil and the Bahleems went directly to the Deccan at Multan without going through Agra.
7. **Bulheem/Bahleem,** from Balimila, in Andhra Pradesh. They are located rather south of the Narmada River.

These seven clans made up of different sects would have spread out over India under new names. These would be:

The **Agureea,** "from the town of Agra where they settled."

The **Bangureea,** from *vaghri,* itinerant.

The **Khokhureea,** from the Korhur district, between Etawah and Cawnpur? "Where they live after their expulsion from Delhi."

The **Soopurreea,** from Sheopur, near Gwalior, as Sleeman notes that "these three groups reside in the Gwalior area."

The **Bungoo,** from *banga,* Bengal, "the name given to the river Thugs." They number two to three hundred.

The **Gano,** from *gana,* Shiva's army, hired men.

The **Jumaldahee,** "a class of Thugs settled in Awadh and east of the Ganges. They are known as **Agureea** as they migrated from Delhi through Agra. They claim to be descendants from a man named **Jummad deen,** from *Jumma din,* from the Jumna river."

The **Lodhee/Lodaha,** "from *lodhna,* to charge, to cover; descendants of the Jumaldahee from the Awadh. Residing in Bengal and Bihar and, at the time of Sleeman's writing, mainly in the Terai. They number around three hundred," from *lodha, lodhee,* "a caste of Thugs common to all of India."

The **Motheea,** "from *muhti,* handful, *muthiya,* giving alms by the handful. They have the custom of giving a handful of rupees to their leader before sharing out the loot. They live in Rangpur, Dinapur, Purnea. They belong to the Tantooas caste."

The **Multaneea,** "from the city of Multan [present day Pakistan]. Like the **Chinguree,** they call themselves Naiks and travel with their yoke teams. One of their sects is the **Chinguree,** who are sometimes called Naicks, are all Muslims." Another of their sects, the **Qulundera** (from *qalandar,* dervish), "travel with monkeys and bears."

The **Sooseea,** from the caste Dhanuk (*dhanak,* carders, arrow and basket makers), one among the lowest castes. They "live in Rajasthan and Malwa. They work mainly in Gujarat, Khandesh and in Rajasthan. They are called Naicks and **tharee**" (from the Thar desert) "by the other classes of Thugs."

The **Dhoulanee,** from *Dhuliya,* a town of Maharashtra or of Dholpur.

The **Handeewul,** from *hamdi,* bowl + *wala,* "the men of the bowl. One of the Muslim Thug sects living in Telingana. They are angry that they are called this way as it implies they are eating from dirty and old clay pots."

The **Kathur,** "from *kathota,* great bowl. A sect of Thugs whose name is derived from a man who was partaking of the feasts of the seven clans in Delhi with a wooden dish, *kathur,* and who thus joined the fraternity."

21. FAMOUS THUGS

Balmeek: Valmiki, the author of the Sanskrit *Ramayana.* "The Thugs think he belonged to their profession and mention him with respect."

Dada Dheera: "A canonized Thug from the Bhurotse clan whom Thugs invoke while drinking alcohol in the course of certain ceremonies. His grave is visited by Thugs as a holy place, at Kumona in the Koel [Koelwar, in the Bihar]." *Dada* indicates that the person is canonized.

Jora Naek: "Famous **Moltanee** Thug chief from the **Hurta** clan. He was a Muslim; he and his woman servant Koduck Bunwaree killed a man who was traveling with 160,000 rupees. Upon returning home, they assembled all their fellow Thugs and distributed the loot. For this reason, Jora Naek is canonized along with his wife and woman servant. His disciple, from the Lodhee caste, is called **Koduck Bunwaree**" (from *kada Banjara* = austere Banjara, faithful to principles?) "and his wife is called **Kanee Ind**" (from *Rani Indu?,* the Hindu queen). "Invoked in the course of the **Tuponee,** during the **ghoor** (*gur*) (raw sugar) offering."

Nizam Oddeen Ouleea (Nizam-ud-din Awliya): a Sufi saint from the Chishti fraternity, "whose grave, in Delhi, is visited by numerous pilgrims from the whole of India, and in particular by the Thugs who claim him as one of their own." Sunnis and Shiites "have no trouble believing that he was a Thug who left the profession in his youth. His supernatural money purse, **dustul ghyb**" (from *dast*, hands + *ghaib*, invisible) "and his lavish spending with money he didn't have, led to this belief."

Rukut Beej Dana, from *rakta*, blood + *bij*, grain, seed + *danu*, demon. "The name of the demon the Goddess Kali killed with the **goputban**" (from *gupt*, invisible + *bamdh*, belt).

Notes

Abbreviations Used in the Notes
IOL: Indian Office Library (presently housed in the British Library)
NAI: National Archives of India
OIOC: Oriental and India Office Collections.

INTRODUCTION

1. *Calcutta Literary Gazette, Journal of Belles Lettres, Sciences and the Arts,* in Bruce 1968, 82–83 (emphasis added).

2. Report on the sessions of 1831–1832, letter no. 1356 from F. Curven Smith, Agent to the Governor General, to George Swinton, Chief Secretary to Government, Political Department, Fort William, 20 June 1832, in *Selected Records Collected from the Central Provinces and Berar Secretariat Relating to the Suppression of Thuggee, 1829–1832,* Nagpur: Government Printing, 1939. OIOC, V 19061, p. 107.

3. Moghul administrative territorial unit.

4. OIOC, V 19061, p. 105.

5. Hastings's exact title was "Governor General of Fort William in Calcutta." He occupied this position between 1774 and 1785.

6. *Pawn* is the English spelling of the Hindi word *pan,* which refers to a betel quid, a much appreciated treat made with areca nuts, lemon, honey, spices, and so on wrapped in a betel leaf.

7. OIOC, V 19061, p. 107.

8. Ibid., p. 105.

9. *Polygar:* "This term is peculiar to the Madras Presidency. The word is Tamil *palaiyakarran.* . . . The holder of a *palaiyam,* or feudal estate; *Zamindar,* from the Persian *zamin-dar,* landholder" (Yule and Burnell, 1968, 718–961).

10. OIOC, V 19061, p. 104.

11. See Benveniste 1973, 452–53, for the difference between *sacer* and *sanctum.*

12. One hundred forty devotees were supposed to have thus self-sacrificed in 1565 during the inauguration of the temple of Kamakhya. Their heads were offered on copper platters. See Gait 1967.

13. In English, these various practices are called respectively *hookswinging, ghat murders, jaganauth, sati.* On this rite see Weinberger-Thomas 1989.

CHAPTER ONE

1. Philips (1977, vol. II, letter 459), "Bentinck's minute on the defense of India, June 29, 1832," pp. 846–47.

2. *Sahib* is a word of Arabic origin very frequently used by the natives in referring to the Europeans, either as a term of address or attached to a title or a rank. It was to come to designate more specifically the British administrators who were to succeed the very exotic nabobs during Cornwallis's presidency (1786–1793).

3. From chapter 16 of Malcolm 1972: "Reflections on the condition of the British power in Central India—Its future administration," and so on.

4. Kipling's short story "The Man Who Would Be King" (1982b) draws a parallel with Western adventurers replicating the eighteenth-century pan-Indian phenomenon.

5. It still is so today in terms of the sometimes hostile relationships on the subcontinent with India's immediate large neighbors (Pakistan and China), with its smaller neighbors (Nepal, Bangladesh, Sri Lanka), and again with some of its regions, such as Kashmir.

6. This is Gordon's (1969) expression.

7. *Rajput* meaning literally "prince's son." At present it designates an ancient caste of warriors who are for the most part agriculturalists.

8. *Hakim* is a word of Arabic origin designating a judge, a chief, or a master.

9. According to Indian tradition, the *Arthashastra* is the work of the Brahman Kautiliya who is thought to have been a minister of King Chandragupta (last quarter of the fourth century B.C.). Charles Malamoud notes that "this tradition isn't backed by any sort of reliable evidence. It is more often thought at present that this text, in the form that has survived, dates from the first century A.D." (Malamoud 1994, 60).

10. In the Brahmanic tradition of the social-cosmic order, *dharma* implies the respect of the hierarchy of the four goals of human beings of which it is a part (deliverance, that is *moksha;* global order, that is *dharma;* material interests, that is *artha;* sexual desire and pleasure, that is *kama;* as well as respect for the social hierarchy of the four classes: priest, Brahman; warrior, Kshatriya; farmer, Vaishya; and servant, Shudra.

11. "The famous Talookdars of Oudh are large landowners possessing both villages of which Talookdar is only the superior proprietor" (Yule and Burnell 1968, 894).

12. See Pouchepadass 1979, 122–54, for this classification.

13. See, for instance, Roy 1973 and Malcolm 1972 (1832), 1:426–62. This name, according to Vincent Smith (1987, 494), comes from the Marathi word *pendhara,* designating the adventurers who were traditionally attached to the army of the *peshwa* of Pune.

14. See Roy 1973, 65–70, for this paragraph. The last sentence is from Sir John Malcolm 1972, 1:444.

15. Sleeman 1836, appendix, "Substance of Conversations held by Captain Sleeman with different Thug Approvers, while preparing the Vocabulary," hereafter referred to as "Substance of Conversations," 239–40.

16. This was, and still is, a major pilgrimage to the junction of the Ganges and the Jamuna held every 6 years.

17. This is the name of certain Tantric ascetics practicing the inversion of generally accepted orthodox Brahmanic values. See below, in chapter 3.

18. There are many stories of this type in the Kalhana history of the kings of Kashmir (see Lorenzen 1978, 66–67).

19. *Sannyasi,* from the Sanskrit *smnyasa,* designates the individual who has renounced the world and who is devoted to the pursuit of salvation; *gosain,* from the Sanskrit *gosvamin,* literally "the master of the cows," that is, of his emotions, designates the same sort of behavior. On this specific path to salvation, which has a lot of import in India, see chapter 3, below.

20. In the famous play *Matalimadhavan* by Bhavabuti, Matali, the heroine, is kidnapped by Kapalins who want to sacrifice her to Chamunda.

21. The term was first coined by Hobsbawm (1969).

22. "On a 1,500 km span from the Tapti valley to the area around Cape Comorin there is a series of enormous steps turned toward the west, each approximately 500 to 600 meters high; these are called the Western Ghats or the Sahyadri mountains" (Durand-Dastes 1968, 11–12)."

23. *Naik* comes from the Sanskrit *nayaka,* "chief." It is a form of address widespread in the Deccan and indicates high status among Hindus.

24. "They have neither the height, nor the lack of symmetry, nor the continuity" of the Western Ghats" (Durand-Dastes 1968, 14).

25. A subset includes the subdivisions of Ganjam, Vishakhapatnam, and Godavari, attached to the Madras presidency, while the west and the north of the territory are divided into Bastar, the Central Provinces, and Orissa. At present, these hills are still divided into the states of Orissa and of Andhra.

26. On the Gonds, see chapter 5, below.

27. Known as *meriah.* This term used by the British is thought to originate from a Gond word *mervi,* but the Gonds themselves use words such as *toki* or *kedi* to designate the victims (see Maltby 1818, 67).

28. From chapter 2, "View of the State of Society among the Hindoo Subjects of Great Britain, particularly with respects to Morals."

29. This chapter is titled "Imperial Britain: Personnel and Ideas."

CHAPTER TWO

1. They were to be attached to the Central Provinces in 1861.

2. In the *Skanda Purana* the river Narmada is supposed to have emerged in the form of a pretty young girl from the god Shiva's body after he completed a long spell of mortifications in the mountains of Vindhyachal (where the temple of Kali near Mirzapur is located). From whence the river's name, *narmada,* meaning "the one who gives pleasure" (Srivastav 1968, 7–8).

3. Sleeman's book *Ramaseeana* is made up of three parts, each with its own pagination in addition to that of the main body of the book. Consequently, abbreviated references to the "Introduction," to "Substance of Conversations," and to "Ramaseeana" had to be inserted within in-text references to clarify the page numbers. In-text references of Sleeman 1836 without such clarification refer to the main body of the book.

4. A *fatwa* is a judicial opinion passed by a Muslim judge.

5. Letter from G. Swinton to Major Stewart, Indore, 23 October 1829, in Sleeman 1836, Appendix X, 380–81.

6. In Philips 1977: 1, 426–27, Letter 191, "Court of Directors policy towards thagii, 6 April 1830."

7. Sleeman 1836: Regulation 17, Sections 2–4, 1817.

8. F. Curven Smith, Agent to the Governor General, Sagar and Narmada Territories, to W. H. Macnaghten, 26 June 1833, Home Department. Thug and Dacoity, NAI, Cons. B2, no. 4.

9. NAI, Home Dept., Thug and Dacoity, D2, no. 2, 1836, p. 514.

10. Deposition of Sheikh Sahabeen in the presence of Captain P. A. Reynolds, Hingolee, 27 October 1835, NAI, Thug and Dacoity, D2, no. 1.

11. F. Curven Smith to G. Swinton, letter no. 908 from 5 July 1830, OIOC, V 19061, p. 41.

12. W. Sleeman to Captain Reynolds, Superintendent, Hingolee, 9 June 1835, NAI, G2, p. 372.

13. W. Sleeman to Captain Reynolds, Superintendent, Mussoorie, 3 August 1836, NAI, A1, no. 1.

14. W. Sleeman to F. C. Smith, 4 October 1833, NAI, G2, copies of letters issued by W. Sleeman, 1833–1835, p. 78.

15. Letter no. 1866, from F. Curven Smith to H. P. Princep, Secretary to the Governor General in the Political Department, 19 November 1830, OIOC, V 19061, p. 52.

16. Ibid., p. 53.

17. It is true that the Hindu concept of political power is linked to the goddess: "all Hindu kings need a patron Goddess of his kingdom and of his dynasty." See A Vergati (1994, 125–46) on the kingdom of Marwar in Rajasthan.

18. Lieutenant H. W. Trevelyan, Assistant Agent General, Jodhpur, to Major N. Alves, Agent General, Jhaipur, October 1835, NAI, C1, no. 2. The same type of conflict erupted between Colonel Speirs and the *rana* of Udaipur, whose kingdom was populated by Bheels and Meenas "whose nature is that of a senseless brute and yet these are my merchants and husbandman. . . . If as in the territories of other chiefs or Rajasthan the arrest of Thugs should be commenced it would be followed by the desolation of my kingdom . . . and their flight from my dominions and taking up their residence in some other county." From Lieutenant Briggs to W. H. Sleeman, 5 August 1833, NAI, C1, no. 1, 1835, pp. 557–58.

19. Letter from G. T. Lushington to Lieutenant Colonel A. Lockett, Superintendent and Agent to the Governor General, Ajmer, 16 July 1832, OIOC, V 19061, p. 102.

20. Statement of Thug property sold by order of Lieutenant Lumley, Assistant General Superintendent at Solapur and Seroor from 14 May 1836 to 1 April 1838, NAI, E, no. 2, August 1838, p. 28.

21. Copies of letter issued by W. H. Sleeman, NAI, G2, 1833–1835.

22. Letter from the Deputy Secretary to the Government with an extract from the Honourable Court of Directors under the date 16 April 1834. To Francis Curven Smith, Agent GG in the Saugor and Nerbudda Territories, from C. E. Trevelyan. NAI, B2, no. 6, 1834, par. 10.

23. For more on this perspective, see Amin 1987.

24. NAI, H1, Section V, art. 2959.

25. Doorgha = Durga, one of the names of the goddess Kali. Confession made on 20 August 1833, NAI.

26. This is an approximate calculation based on the description of the roads taken and the destinations reached by Doorgha in his confession.

27. Deposition of Bheelam Barre Khan, jemadar of Thugs recently arrested, taken before Captain J. Hale, Assistant General to Superintendent, NAI, D2, pp. 497–515.

28. This was done by the grave diggers, *lugha* in Ramasee.

29. Deposition of Sayyid Amir Ali, to Captain Sleeman, 14 April 1832, NAI.

30. I have been inspired in this by Wiktor Stoczkowski (1992), who argues that the respective domains of science and of conjectural narrative make use of several types of explanation classified along three sets of binary oppositions: verifiable/non-verifiable, false/non-false, convincing/unconvincing.

31. This contrasts with the accused witch Chiara Signorini's statements when

interrogated by the Inquisition. Her deposition does show the link between the questions and the answers (see Ginzburg 1983).

32. James Paton, British Library, Addl Mss, 41300, p. 32.

33. Jubra Patun case, NAI, B1, no. 2.

34. According to the *Robert* French dictionary, *confession* comes from the Church Latin *confessare*. Its first meaning for the Catholic Church is to "tell one's sins to the priest within the sacrament of penance." The *aveu* [avowal, acknowledgment] first meant in European medieval feudal law "a written statement acknowledging the commitment of a vassal to his lord. It came to mean the act of acknowledgment [*aveu*] in the sense of "acknowledging certain facts painful to reveal," only in the seventeenth century.

35. Circular to the Magistrates and Joint-Magistrates. Instructions with reference to Acts XVIII and XIX of 1837 by the Right Honorable GG of India, NAI, A1, no. 2, 1837.

36. From Agent to GG to Captain W. H. Sleeman, Principal Assistant, Saugor, NAI, B1, no. 3, 3 December 1833.

37. Letter of W. H. Sleeman of 12 April 1832, cited by F. Curven Smith in his letter no. 1358 to G. Swinton, OIOC, V 19061, p. 113.

38. Letter no. 908 from F. Curven Smith to G. Swinton, 5 July 1830, OIOC, V 19061, pp. 48–49.

39. W. H. Sleeman to T. MacLeod, AAGG, 27 July 1833, NAI, G2 (letters issued by W. S., 1833–1835), pp. 57–58.

40. "Children often volunteer themselves to accompany parties sent after their parents or other near relations." NAI, G2, *op cit.*, p. 57.

41. Circular to the Magistrates and Joint Magistrates, NAI, A1 no. 2, 1837, *op cit.*

42. Letter no. 1866, F. Curven Smith to H. P. Princep, 19 November 1839, OIOC, V 19061, pp. 45–49.

43. Bundle of letters from 1838 "showing how the informers deliberately identified innocent persons," NAI, B2, no. 11.

44. W. H. Sleeman to Captain Reynolds, Superintendent, Hingolee, 9 June 1835, NAI, G2, p. 372.

45. Agent General to GG to Captain Sleeman, Principal Assistant, Saugor, NAI, B1, no. 3, 1833, par. 42.

46. C. Smith to Reynolds, NAI, H1, bundle 2, 1833/1834.

47. W. H. Sleeman to F. C. Smith, May 1833, NAI, G2, 1833–1835, pp. 5–6.

48. From W. H. Sleeman to F. C. Smith, Agent to the GG, Saugor. Jubra Patun trial of Thugs held at the Session of 1832/33 at Saugor, accused of murder by Thuggee, NAI, B1, no. 1.

49. From the word *chaprasi*, meaning "the bearer of a *chapra*," that is, an escutcheon that indicates the position of the bearer. In general it designates a messenger, a man of trust.

50. From the Arabic *munshi*, a secretary, writer, or interpreter. Applied to any respectable and well-educated native.

51. A question mark in this quote and subsequently indicates that a passage in the document was unreadable.

52. NAI, B1, no. 1, 1821, pp. 74–84.

53. NAI, B1, no. 1, p. 64.

54. W. H. Sleeman to Corbet, Assistant Surgeon, Political Agency, 19 February 1833; Corbet to Captain Sleeman, 28 February 1833, NAI, B1, no. 1, pp. 70–71.

55. Proceedings of a trial of a gang of Thugs, thirty in number, accused of the murder of seven men in Goolgunge about October 1829, held before F. C. Smith on the 1st of March 1833 and subsequent days in Saugor, NAI, B1, no. 2.

56. Depositions of Khuman zumeendar of Goolgunge, Jawra Khanlaul Suruk

Ameen and Gunesh Brahmin Jemadar, taken before J. C. Wilson, Assistant to the GG on deputation at Goolgunge, NAI, B1, pp. 71–76.

57. "Bunsee, 20 or 25 cases in which he only shared out the loot. Madaree, 3 or 4 cases, same M.O.; Pan Mohomod, see above; Kohman, 20 cases; Mahasook, 5 or 6 cases; . . . as a *jamadar*, Koolook, 2 or 3 cases."

58. "Rahmut Khan, 15 or 20 cases; Boodhoo, 20 cases; Kollok, 25 or 30 cases; Zalim, 8 cases; Peer Khan, 5 cases."

59. "Mankhan, 20 or 25 cases, *jamadar*, strangler at Lakheree; Dureea, 17 or 18 cases, hand holder at Patun; only shared out the loot at Lakheree; Luckmun, 20 cases; Shamshairah, 12 or 13 cases (also grave digger); Balkhishun, 50 cases."

60. Depositions of Khuman zumeendar of Goolgunge, Jawra Khanlaul Suruk Ameen and Gunesh Brahmin Jemadar, taken before J. C. Wilson, Assistant to the GG on Deputation at Goolgunge, NAI, B1 n. 2, pp. 71–76.

61. C. Smith to M. Amslie, Agent GG Humeerpore; McLeod, Junior Assistant on Deputation, Gwalior; H. Wilson, Principal Assistant, Etawah; Major Halves, Political Agent, NAI, B1, pp. 93–97.

62. The summary is found in NAI, B1, no. 1, pp. 114–50.

63. From the Hindi verb *gudna*, to pierce, penetrate, enter.

64. However, in 1834, "in the event of their running away or entering into conspiracy to convict innocent men, . . . his Lordship in Council considered preferable that they should be transported beyond sea for life." Macnaghten, Secretary to Government, Fort William, 3 January 1834, NAI, H1, no. 1, p. 427.

65. Letter no. 1356. F. Curven Smith to G. Swinton, 20 June 1832, OIOC, V 19061, p. 116.

66. C. Smith to G. Swinton, no. 888, 8 May 1832, IOL, Mss Eur D 1188, p. 127.

67. Letter 1356, 1832, OIOC, V 19061, p. 125.

68. The figures I found in the summary tables for the Thug trials vary; they are slightly lower than those in Tuker 1961.

69. Sir Thomas Munro, 28 July 1840, cited by R. C. Srivastava (1971, 5).

70. This in contrast to French law, which in principle is primarily based on law that is looked upon as a general and abstract norm.

71. GG to Lieutenant Colonel Steward, Resident, Hyderabad, NAI, T & D, 1833, p. 205.

72. W. H. Sleeman to Captain Reynolds, Hyderabad, 28 October 1833, NAI, G2 (1833–1835), p. 82.

73. J. C. Elwall, Officiating Superintendent at Bangalore, to the Commissioner for Affairs of His Highness the Rajah of Mysore, Bangalore, 1 January 1838, NAI, B2 n.11.

74. To F. Curven Smith, Agent to the Governor General, Saugor and Nerbudda Territories, from the Ho'ble the Court of Directors, 4 August 1830, OIOC, V 19061, p. 2.

75. W. H. Sleeman to J. Paton, 1 July 1835, NAI, G2, 1833–1835, p. 395.

76. J. Paton, London, British Museum, Add MS 41300.

77. W. H. Sleeman to C. Smith, 17 March 1834, NAI, G2 (1833–1835), p. 152.

78. W. H. Sleeman to C. Smith, 1835, NAI, G2 (1833–1835), pp. 323–24.

79. The Taxila gymnosophists' suicides had been described as exemplary since Alexander. See Schmidt 1988.

80. Curven Smith to the GG, 6 January 1833, NAI, H1, p. 417.

81. W. H. Sleeman to C. Smith, NAI, G1, copies of letters issued by W. H. Sleeman, 1832–May 1833, p. 96.

82. I will discuss in more detail in part 2 of the present work the currents of thought that had the most impact on Britain and India at the beginning of the nineteenth century.

83. W. H. Sleeman to W. H. Macnaghten, Secretary to the Government of India, 22 May 1835, NAI, G2 (1833–1835), p. 356.

84. W. H. Sleeman to H. M. Elliot, Secretary of Government of India, 2 February 1848, in Sleeman 1849, 345–46.

85. J. Paton to W. H. Sleeman, 5 January 1838, NAI, B2, no. 10, pp. 1–10.

86. Ibid.

87. Annual Reports of the School of Industry of Jabalpur, NAI, Thug and Dacoity, F9.

88. Another table describes the yearly amounts spent for new buildings, for wages for informers and their sons and teachers, and for the prisoners' food and clothing during the years 1857–1865. Entries for 1857 show the largest investment in buildings (4,978 rupees), an investment that goes down the following years. Expenses for food and clothing go slightly up (3,188 rupees for food, 230 rupees for clothes in 1857 and respectively 3,334 and 729 in 1865); wages for informers diminish slightly while those for their sons and daughters are augmented (1,034 in 1857, 1,568 in 1865), which indicates a rise in the young prison population (and thus evidence that the sexual control James Sleeman invoked was not efficacious). Finally, the wages paid to the craft teachers diminish (2,328 in 1857, 1,660 in 1865); their students, as William Sleeman notes, having become capable to be teachers in turn.

89. "One of good character and sober habits, who has served his full apprenticeship in that town at the trade of making carpets, known in the trade by the name of Brussel's Carpeting—that he shall be promised a salary of sixty pounds a year, or sixty rupees a month, with a prospect of increase after a period of good service—that he shall, like the Overseer, have a house built for him by the prisoners—that his passage shall be paid to India and to Jubbulpoor, and that his salary shall commence from the day he lands—that he have to bring with him two looms for the manufacture of the above named carpeting, with all the apparatus required for the same, so that he may be prepared to commence work immediately after his arrival—that the said two looms be made with all the latest improvements, and with wood that is likely to resist the effects of climate." W. H. Sleeman to H. M. Elliot, Secretary of Government of India, 2 February 1848, in Sleeman 1849, 346.

90. Major R. Ranken, Superintendent, Government School of Industry, to Colonel H. Hervey, General Superintendent, Thuggy and Dacoity Dept., Delhi, 28 March 1866, NAI, F9.

91. Flagellation was forbidden in 1860: the last ship for Australia left in 1867, and the last public hanging occurred in 1868.

92. W. H. Sleeman, 1849, "Acts passed by the Legislative Council of India for the Suppression of Thuggee and Dacoity," pp. 353–54. In her article cited earlier, "Providential Circumstances: The Thuggee Campaign of the 1830s and Legal Innovation," Radhika Singha (1993) studies rigorously and in detail the juridical aspects of the anti-Thug campaign. I am referring the reader to this invaluable work for more details.

93. J. R. Lumley to the Magistrate of Ahmednuggur, December 1837, Letters from the Assistant General Superintendent at Sholapur to the General Superintendent and others between October 1836 and December 1837, NAI, I1, pp. 262–63.

94. W. Sleeman to W. H. Macnaghten, Secretary General to the Government, 3 February 1838, NAI, Thug and Dacoity, G5, p. 107.

95. NAI, Thug and Dacoity, G4 and G5.

96. J. R. Lumley, op cit., NAI, I1 p. 261.

97. W. Sleeman to W. H. Macnaghten, Secretary General to the Government, 3 February 1838, NAI, Thug and Dacoity, G5, p. 107.

98. W. H. Sleeman to Lieutenant Burrows, 27 March 1838, to Captain Reynolds, 6 April 1838, NAI, G5, pp. 99 and 112.

99. The species *Datura alba* is consecrated to Shiva. It's a powerful narcotic that can kill at a large dose.

100. Parks 1850, 2:452–53, citing in part the *Agra Messenger* of 2 December 1848.

101. G. Lyall, Resident Jenkins, etc., "Reply to Political letter dated 27 March 1839 on the subject of the operations for the suppression of Thuggee." London, 15 July 1840, NAI, B2, no. 20.

102. J. Currie, officiating Secretary to the GG. Government of India's reply to W. H. Sleeman's request to have special legislation for dacoits, especially the Budhuks, NAI, B2, no. 18, 1839.

103. Report of the United Provinces Criminal Tribes Enquiry Committee, Allahabad, 1948, par. 9. Cited in Pouchepadass 1979, 137.

104. Blackburn 1978, 48–49. The criminal tribe of the Kallars at the beginning of the twentieth century is a modified version of the 150-year-old representation of the "savage Collerie." The relationship between these two constructions is made clear in an inspector's writing in 1879 that theft is in their blood. Still, according to Blackburn, in 1892 another inspector, F. Mullaly, claimed on the basis of secondary and tertiary sources that "crime is a natural stimulant to the Kallars."

105. Zauberman 1989, *Caste criminelle* (Criminal caste), black-and-white documentary film (Paris: Les Films du Paradoxe/La Sept).

CHAPTER THREE

1. In Watters (n.d., 160), we read something very similar: "When the Thugs saw that this pilgrim was a remarkably handsome man, they decided to sacrifice him to their cruel goddess Durga."

2. English translation from Trevelyan 1837, 369–70.

3. J. Fryer 1873, Letter III, "A Description of Surat and Journey into Ducan," 286–87.

4. Deposition of Bheelam Bhare Khan jemadar of Thugs, recently arrested, taken before Captain J. Hale, Assistant General to Superintendent, NAI, B2, no. 2, pp. 497–515.

5. *Patel* is a word of Marathi origin designating hereditary nobles put in charge of villages by the government and serving as middlemen between villagers and government officials.

6. Though almost all the Ramasee words (in bold) described in this chapter were part of the lexicon compiled by Sleeman, there are a few exceptions. These exceptions, which often are variants of words in Sleeman's lexicon, are part of his vocabulary that he used in his writing: **bora** (*bara*), a Thug of distinction; **subehdar** (*subedar*), an army captain's title; **katee karna** (from *katha*, story, tale, discussion + *karna*, to make), whispering; **jemadar** (variant of **jamadar**), title of a leader of a group of warriors; **deo**, as well as **deonum** and **deoseyn**, which are capitalized in Sleeman's lexicon (from *deva*), god; **bisul** or **bisul parta** (in this volume's lexicon: **bisul purna**), a botched strangling; **bele**, the term Sleeman often uses as the name for mass burial sites of Thugs' victims (**beyla** in this volume's lexicon). *Trans.*

7. S. P. Sangar (1967, 84–85) in his work on crime during the Moghul period also describes Thugs as counterfeiters.

8. *Ari* is possibly a corrupted form of *aru*, to cut; *tulucar*, the corrupted form of *turrukan*, *turuska*, originating in Turkey.

9. These are military terms: *jamadar*, leader of a squad, and *subadar*, leader of a company.

10. *Shikha* in Sanskrit and Hindi stands for the tuft of hair Brahmans have on

the top of their heads and, by extension, for any sharp point (for example, as that of a sword), the top of a mountain, or a crest (as that of a peacock). I translate it here by "flame," a flag with two thin points, to conform to Sleeman's translation. *Nishan* means a mark, a sign, a flag, a coat of arms.

11. One of them remembers that a victim had time to say just before dying: "I die by mistake!" (*Hum se check ho gya.*)

12. J. Paton, British Library, Addl Ms 41300, p. 81.

13. Ibid., pp. 16 and 18.

14. NAI, Thug and Dacoity, K1, 1829–1836, pp. 1–15.

15. Ibid, pp. 16–22.

16. NAI, Thug and Dacoity, K1, 1829–1836.

17. Deposition of Takoordass, twenty-five years old, in front of Lieutenant Burrows at Dharwar, 11 December 1837, NAI, Thug and Dacoity, D23, pp. 218–21.

18. In Sanskrit *tulsi* or *tulasi,* the Hindus' very odoriferous sacred balsam. It is particularly revered by the Vishnuites, though not by only them. It can be seen next to temples, to the front doors of houses, and so on.

19. R. V. Russell, 1969: part II, vol. II, "Kanjar," p. 331; part II, vol. II, "Banjara," pp. 162; part II, vol. IV, "Thug," pp. 561.

20. Jubra Patun trial of Thugs held at the Session of 1832–33 at Saugor, accused of murder by Thuggee, NAI, B1, no. 1, pp. 43–44.

21. In English in French text. *Trans.*

22. Deposition of Gureeb Daas, NAI, Thug and Dacoity, 1838, D 2.3. (This file could not be found again at the Delhi archives. The date is correct but the exact page numbers are missing.)

23. Deposition of Punna in front of Captain Sleeman, 29 May 1832, NAI, Thug and Dacoity, A 1.1. (This file could not be found again at the Delhi archives. The date is correct but the exact page numbers are missing.)

24. Deposition of Sayyid Amir Ali in front of Captain Sleeman, 14 April 1832, NAI, Thug and Dacoity, D1, pp. 50 and 71. (This file could not be found again at the Delhi archives. The date is correct but the exact page numbers are missing, so page numbers are approximate.)

25. Deposition of Sayyid Amir Ali.

26. Meadows Taylor retells this story in his novel.

27. *Purana,* which means "old," designates here a large ensemble of post-Vedic texts, the oldest ones dating from approximately the fifth and sixth centuries. They deal with a variety of themes, including royal genealogies and the incarnations of the gods and goddesses passing through the infinite cycles of creation, preservation, and destruction of the world.

28. *The Markandeya Purana* (1969), Canto 87, "The Slaying of Chanda and Munda," p. 499.

29. Ibid., Canto 88, "The Slaying of the Asura Rakta-Vija," p. 505.

30. "Oh Kali, the Man Eating One, Oh Kali, Great Kali, Kali of Calcutta!"

31. J. Paton, British Library, Addl Mss 41300, p. 27.

32. I owe this clear definition of a sect to Catherine Clémentin-Ojha.

33. J. Paton, British Library, Addl Mss 41300, p. 41.

34. Ibid., Addl Mss 41300, pp. 73–74.

35. Laws of Manu II, 48: "Some wicked men suffer a change of their (natural) appearance in consequence of crimes committed in this life, and some in consequence of those committed in a former (existence)" (*Laws of Manu* 1964, 439–440).

36. *Aitareya-Brahmana,* 3, 2, 29, cited in Lévi 1966, 87.

37. Cited in Biardeau 1976, 79. The English text used here is from S. Radhakrishnan, ed. and trans., *The Principal Upanishads,* London: Allen & Unwin, 1953.

38. J. Paton, British Library, Addl Mss 41300, pp. 41 and 53.

39. Ibid., pp. 27–30.
40. Ibid., pp. 54 and 41.
41. Ibid., p. 59.
42. Chapter 13, "Thugs and Poisoners."
43. The root *do-* is in the French word *donner*, that is, "to give" in English. *Trans.*
44. They belong to four distinct, hierarchized categories based on their ancestors, their personal status, the kind of work they do, and their professional abilities. Each of these categories has a different name, but pilgrims refer to them as a whole as Pandas.

CHAPTER FOUR

1. It was common for several generations of one family to serve in India, and marriages between the families of employees of the Company were frequent (Cohn 1987a, 433).
2. This expression and concept is from Touraine 1974.

CHAPTER FIVE

1. "Sir John Tackeray, Acting Principal Collector in the Carnatic, Collector in the Southern Maratha Country, issued a general order to his mamlatdars" in Guha 1985, 25.
2. "Communities made up of villages are small republics having at their disposal all they need and do not depend on others. They seem to last while everything else passes; dynasties collapse one after another and revolutions succeed each other. Hindus, Pathans, Moghuls, Marathas, Sikhs, and British can each be masters in turn, but the communities of villages remain unchanged" (C. T. Metcalf, 17 November 1830, cited in Stokes 1986, 128).
3. See also Mill 1826 and Halévi 1928.
4. Sleeman writes:

> In England machinery does more than three-fourths of the collective work of society in the production, preparation, and distribution of man's physical enjoyments, and it stands in no need of this daily food to sustain its powers; they are independent of the seasons; the water, fire, air, and other elemental powers which they require to render them subservient to our use are always available in abundance. . . . wanting no food itself, it can always provide its proprietors with the means of purchasing what they require from other countries, when the harvests of their own fail. When calamities of season deprive men from of employment for a time in tillage, they can, in England, commonly find it in other branches of industry, because agricultural industry forms so small a portion of the collective industry of the nation; and because every man can, without prejudice to his status in society, take to what branch of industry he pleases. (Sleeman 1915, 159)

5. Sleeman in *Rambles:* chapter 19, "Marriage of a Stone with a Shrub"; chapter 22, "Interview with the Raja who marries a Stone with a Shrub."
6. The Gonds were a tribal society speaking the same Dravidian language, Kui, and sharing the same culture. They lived in a mountainous territory extending from the *zamindari* of Angul to the river Godavari in the south and to the *zamindaris* of Patna and Kalahandi in the west. The British decided to eliminate their "rituals" but without exterminating the individuals in charge of them. They adopted a policy of persuasion (though the British did threaten reprisals if they should be disobeyed). It was to take ten years, and using the Thugs' repression

explicitly as a model, for a special agent to be appointed. He was to administer the repression of the *meriah* sacrifice (the Oriya word for sacrifice). See Brandstadter 1985.

7. Sleeman 1915, 117, note 1: Sleeman cites Bolingbroke, *Letters on the Study and Use of History,* London: T. Cadell, 1770.

8. Sleeman titles his chapter 10 "Veracity."

9. See Murr 1987 on the work of the famous Father Dubois, *Hindu Manners, Customs, and Ceremonies.*

10. In a series of lectures titled "British Ethnologies of India," given in Paris at the *Centre d'étude de l'Inde,* in May 1992.

11. As Clifford Geertz (1983, 10) notes,

> "Translation" . . . is not a simple recasting of others' ways of putting things in terms of our own ways of putting them . . . but displaying the logic of their ways of putting them in the locutions of ours; a conception which again brings it rather closer to what a critic does to illuminate a poem than what an astronomer does to account for a star.

12. This analysis has been inspired by Sperber 1982, 49–85.

13. This discipline was first called organology, a name given to it by its inventor, Franz Joseph Gall (1758–1828).

14. I am grateful to Francis Schmidt for this reference.

15. On this passage in Grant, see Clive 1973, 345.

16. In the Hobson-Johnson lexicon, *babu* was first a term of respect, similar to *mister,* then a term of contempt as it came to designate westernized native employees of the British (Yule and Burnell 1968, 44).

17. D. Maurer, *Whiz Mob: a Correlation of the Technical Argot of Pickpockets with Their Behaviour Pattern* (Gainesville, Fla.: The American Dialect Society, 1955), 4, cited in Mehrotra 1977.

18. This is T. Trautmann's expression. See note 10 above.

19. In *Rambles* Sleeman devotes a part of chapter 53 to the "Inability of Europeans to speak Eastern languages" and admits his own weakness in this domain. This is an embarrassing admission when we think of the "Conversations" he held with the Thugs and his description of their vocabulary!

20. I am borrowing this expression from Paul Veyne (1983).

CHAPTER SIX

1. It is eighty-three pages long.

2. The author calls upon the French distinction between *confession,* "confession," and *aveux,* "avowal, acknowledgment," that is, an act of acknowledging certain facts or states of being painful to reveal (see chapter 2, note 34). *Trans.*

3. These are songs of unhappy love.

4. Fanny Parks, the fearless traveler, recounts her visit to the region of Kutchowra for a leopard hunt. She found herself next to a well in the woods that had belonged to one Heera Singh, the father of the present owner. Heera Singh had been a Thug and had amassed an immense fortune by attracting travelers to the well and having his people strangle them and throw their bodies in it. Eventually Heera Singh repented and forbade any killing on his property, even that of antelopes.

5. They have a lot of traits in common. The framework and the various narratives of *One Thousand and One Nights* hint at borrowings from an Indian source, possibly from the famous *Ocean of Stories.* For a study of the avatars of a tale through its Indian, Iranian, Arab, and European versions, see Claude Bremond 1984.

6. *Peri* is a word of Persian origin (*pari*, feather, wing) designating a winged being, a spirit, a fairy.

7. This passage on Amir Ali's loves is a shorter version of an article I published in *Rêver l'Asie*, 1992.

8. This deposition is part of documents the author consulted in archival repositories in India and Great Britain. Unfortunately, the file has been lost, so the exact reference is no longer available (van Woerkens, personal communication). *Trans.*

9. The English renders poorly the French play on *"sauvagerie"* which in French can refer to being wild, or shy, as well as savage. *Trans.*

10. See Stocking 1987, where he writes about the "infamous activities of Burke and Hare, unwittingly accepting sixteen murdered bodies as the 'legitimate' merchandise of the grave-robbing traffic that regularly supplied the needs of anatomical demonstrators" (64).

11. See note 2 above. *Trans.*

12. *The Gothic Flame* is the title of a book by D. P. Varma (1966), cited by Mario Praz in his introduction to *Three Gothic Novels* (1978).

13. Mario Praz (1978, 10) cites Burke's *Philosophical Enquiry* (1757) and two essays by J. and A. L. Aikin, "On the Pleasure Derived from the Objects of Terror" and the "Enquiry into Those Kinds of Distress Which Excite Agreeable Sensations," published in *Miscellaneous Pieces in Prose* (London, 1773).

14. "C'est l'Ennui! —L'oeil chargé d'un pleur involontaire / Il rêve d'échafauds en fumant son houka." These lines were translated by Praz (1978, 9). *Trans.*

15. The first film on the "myth," *Frankenstein*, by J. Searle Dawley, came out in 1910 in the United States. The second one was James Whale's famous *Frankenstein* (1931), starring Boris Karloff.

CHAPTER SEVEN

1. "Du meurtre religieux et philosophique dans l'Inde," File no. 2486, Bibliothèque des langues orientales de l'INALCO. The file indicated that the article came from the journal *Anthropologie*, pp. 95–128, and was translated from an article in the *Edinburgh Review*. Neither the original English title of the article nor any additional information about the French and English publications is available.

2. "Du meurtre religieux et philosophique dans l'Inde," File no. 2486, Bibliothèque des langues orientales de l'INALCO.

3. Pont-Jest was famous at the time, though he has fallen into oblivion today. He was a prolific writer who published more than thirty books, in which he drew from his travels in India and China and his participation in the Crimean War. He set upon a literary career at age twenty-six. He became a journalist and then a novelist and was entrusted in 1868 with the judicial section of the *Figaro*. During the whole of his career he remained interested in crime as well as in distant countries. His real name was René Delmas, and he was born in Reims in 1830 and died in Paris in 1904, and we do not know to what literary current his literary choices were linked. His biographical entries contain little information except that he was antirepublican. His affection for the emperor and the nobility—as evidenced by his pen name of Pont-Jest—might have made of him a *mamelouk*, as the "unconditional supporters of imperial dictatorship" (Plessis 1979) were called at the time. What dangers did he run during the Commune, dangers that might have led him to go into exile in England? From exile he directed the *Fronde*, possibly aimed at attacking the Commune. On the other hand we might wonder whether he was a "colonialist," that is, a partisan of colonial expansion, a stance more likely to be found among republicans in this Third Republic, impatient to restore the moral order (Girardet 1972).

4. This theme repeats an article I published in *Rêver l'Asie* in 1993.

5. This 560-page-long serial was published with numerous illustrations in *Le Petit Journal,* a republican and conservative newspaper. It had a run of 475,000 that was sold at 5 centimes per small page.

6. From the Hindi *karavala,* sword, scimitar.

7. I have analyzed this film in *Les Temps Modernes* (1992). I am following here the main lines of my argument.

8. In color, 1990, three hours and thirty-five minutes.

9. This story is a well-known episode of Shankara's legend, which I have evoked in chapter 1. He traveled preaching several times throughout the whole of India. The stages of his journey, punctuated by miracles and extraordinary word fights with his adversaries, led him to the Himalayas and to the mount Kailash, the residence of Shiva and his spouse Parvati. From there he brought back five crystal phalluses (*sphatika linga*) that he later on consecrated in five Shivaite temples scattered across India, but three of which are located in the north of India.

10. The lingam, Shiva's phallus, has always been for Westerners an object of surprise and misunderstanding. In India Shiva is the sole god having a double representation, anthropomorphic and phallic, the proof of his superiority over the other gods as claimed in *Shivapurana,* which gives an account of its origins: the supreme god Parameshvara, wanting to stop Brahma's and Vishnu's arrogance, appeared to them in the disembodied form of a column and showed them his phallic emblem coming out of the column in his desire to bless the world (*Shivapurana,* vol. 1, vv. 28–29).

11. Henry James, who admires Kipling's varied talents, his extraordinary familiarity with India, his imperial fiber, and his love of the lowly and enlisted men, sees "photographic vignettes" in *Soldiers Three.* Robert Buchanan, as soon as the book came out in 1899, also admired "his photographic images that have an unmatched freshness and newness." Sir Walter Besant, in 1900, made the same compliment and added to it the qualities of the newly born cinema: "There is so much truth in this story, there is such a feel for the real in the way he presents it, that we can see it as we see the animated pictures that the new photography projects on a cloth." The fate of these soldiers was indeed to be embodied one day by Gary Grant and Douglas Fairbank Jr.!

12. See Mitter 1977, in particular his first chapter, for the Christian-inspired demonic masquerades that Hindu gods were put through until "Europe learned Sanskrit" at the end of the eighteenth century, as described by Raymond Schwab.

13. This she-devil the height of three stories fills the public's expectations, a public that wants to be frightened: a small idol would be disappointing, as evidenced by Fanny Parks's comment after visiting the temple said to be of the Thugs, near Mirzapur, where she was terribly disappointed by Kali, "squat, with two small black feet resting on black rats," and whose size was that of a "child's toy!" (1850, 1, 203).

CONCLUSION

1. One of the most important religious celebrations of northern India. It is devoted to the Goddess and marks the end of the rainy season (first two weeks of October). Traditionally it marks the start of military campaigns.

2. From the Arabic *muharram,* which designates the first month of the lunar year and by extension a great Shiite celebration. The Shiites, or "Ali's party," believe that Mohamed's position after his death should have gone to Ali, his son-in-law, his daughter Fatima's husband. In 680 his sons Ḥusayn and Ḥasan attempted to overthrow the ruling caliphate and were killed on the tenth day of the month of *muharram.* In Iraq, the celebration of *muharram* commemorates the martyrdom of the Prophet's family.

3. In the eighth century some Shiite extremist groups looked upon "strangling with a cord as a religious duty!" (Lewis 1982, 61).

4. This line of thinking is inspired by Duclos (1994).

LEXICON

1. Rather than citing literally from Sleeman's original text, I have translated the author's glosses, as they are more specific and are linked to etymologies and other linguistic information. *Trans.*

References

Ahmed, A. F. S. 1965. *Social Ideas and Social Change in Bengal, 1818–1835*. Leiden, Germany: Brill.

Amin, Shahid. 1987 "Approver's Testimony, Judicial Discourse: The Case of Chauri Chaura." *Subaltern Studies* 5:166–202

Archer, Major. 1833. *Tours in Upper India*. 2 vols. London: Bentley.

Arnold, D. 1986. "Rebellious Hillmen: The Gudem-Rampa Risings, 1839–1924." *Subaltern Studies* 1:89–142.

Balfour, Edward. 1968. *Encyclopaedia Asiatica and of Eastern and Southern Asia*. 9 vols. 1858. Reprint, Graaz, Austria: Akademishe Druck-u-Verlagsanstalt.

Bandit Queen. 1994. India: Channel Four Films.

Banerjee, T. K. n.d. *History of Indian Criminal Law*. Calcutta: RDDHI.

Barret-Ducrocq, F. 1991. *Pauvreté, charité et morale à Londres au XIXème siècle*. Recherches Politiques. Paris: Presses Universitaires de France.

Bates, Ch. 1992. "The Invention of Perdition: Human Sacrifices and British Relations with the Indian Kingdom of Bastar in the 19th century." Lecture given at Centre d'Études de l'Inde, Paris.

Bathnagar, O. P. 1966. Introduction to *The Administration of the East India Company: A History of Indian Progress*, by J. W. Kaye, edited by O. P. Bathnagar. 1853. Reprint, Allahabad: Kitab Mahal.

Baudelaire, Charles. 1868. *Les Fleurs du Mal*. Paris: Calmann-Lévy.

———. 1964. *L'Art romantique*. Edited by Hervé Falcou. Paris: Julliard.

Bayly, Christopher A. 1983. *Rulers, Townsmen, and Bazaars, 1770–1870: North Indian Society in the Age of British Expansion*. Cambridge: Cambridge University Press.

———. 1990a. *Indian Society and the Making of the British Empire*. The New Cambridge History of India. Cambridge: Cambridge University Press.

———. 1990b. *Imperial Meridian: The British Empire and the World, 1780–1830*. New York: Longman.

———, ed. 1990c. *The Raj: India and the British, 1600–1947*. London: National Portrait Gallery Publications.

Beane, W. Charles. 1977. *Myth, Cult, and Symbols in Sakta Hinduism*. Leiden: Brill.

331

Belaval, Yvon. 1976. Preface to *La philosophie dans le boudoir,* by Marquis de Sade, ed. Yvon Beleval. Paris: Gallimard.

Benveniste, Émile. 1973. *Indo-European Language and Society.* London: Faber and Faber.

Bhagavad Gita. 1976. Translated from the Sanskrit into French by Sylvain Lévi and J.-T. Stickney. Paris: Librairie Maisonneuve. (English version used for quotes is the *Bhagavad Gita,* translated from the Sanskrit by Ramanada Prasad [Fremont, Cal.: American Gita Society, 1999]. *Trans.*)

Bhargava's Standard Illustrated Dictionary, Hindi-English, 6th ed. 1946. Compiled and edited by R. C. Pathak. Banaras: Shree Ganga Pustakalaya.

Bhavabuti. 1981. *Malati-Madhava: Three Sanskrit Plays.* Harmondsworth, Great Britain: Penguin.

Biardeau, Madeleine. 1976. "Le sacrifice dans l'hindouisme." Pp. 7–154 in *Le sacrifice dans l'Inde ancienne.* Paris: Presses Universitaires de France.

————. 1981. Entries "Avatara," "Cosmogonie védique," and "Devi, La déesse en Inde." In *Dictionnaire des Mythologies,* vol. 1. Director Yves Bonnefoy. Paris: Flammarion.

Blackburn, Stuart H. 1978. "The Kallars: A Tamil "Criminal Tribe" Reconsidered." *South Asia* 1:38–51.

Blanckaert, C. 1992. "L'ethnographie de la décadence: Culture morale et mort des races (XVIIème-XIXème siècles)." *Gradhiva* 11:47–65.

Bloomfield, M. 1923. "The Art of Stealing in Hindu Fiction." *American Journal of Philology* 44:97–133.

————. 1924. "On False Ascetics and Nuns in Hindu Fiction." *Journal of the American Oriental Society* 45:202–42.

Borges, Jorge Luis. 1923. *Oeuvres complètes.* La Pléiade. Paris: Gallimard.

Bouillier, Véronique. 1992. "Deux castes sectaires sivaïtes: les Jangam et les Kusle (vallée de Kathmandou)." Pp 117–36 in *Ascèse et renoncement en Inde, ou la solitude bien ordonnée,* ed. Serge Bouez. Paris: L'Harmattan.

————. 1994. "La violence des non-violents ou les ascètes au combat." Pp. 213–43 in *Violences et non-violences en Inde,* ed. Denis Vidal, Gilles Tarabout, and Eric Meyer. Purusartha 16. Paris: EHESS.

Brandstadter, E. S. 1985. "Human Sacrifice and the British-Kond Relations, 1759–1862." Pp. 89–107 in *Crime and Criminality in British India,* ed. A. A. Yang. Tucson: University of Arizona Press.

Bremond, Claude, ed. 1884. "La famille séparée." In *Les avatars d'un conte,* ed. Claude Bremond. *Communications* 39:4–45.

Bruce, George. 1968. *The Stranglers: The Cult of Thuggee and Its Overthrow in British India.* London: Longman.

Bruce, R. F. 1985. "Bandits and Rebellion in 19th Century Western India." Pp. 48–61 in *Crime and Criminality in British India,* ed. A. A. Yang. Tucson: University of Arizona Press.

Brunner, Hélène. 1974. "Un tantra du Nord: le netra tantra," *Bulletin de l'École Française d'Extrême Orient* 61:125–197.

Buchanan, C. 1813a. *Colonial Ecclesiastic Establishments: Being a Brief View of the States of the Colonies of Great Britain and of Her Asiatic Empire in Respect to Religious Institutions.* London: Cadell and Davies.

————. 1813b. *An Apology for Promoting Christianity in India.* London: n.p.

Campbell, J. 1864. *A Personal Narrative of Thirteen Years Service amongst the Wild Tribes of Khondistan.* London: n.p.

Carman, J. B., and F. A. Marglin. 1985. *Purity and Auspiciousness in Indian Society.* Leiden: Brill.

Caunter, H. 1836. *The Oriental Annual, or Scenes in India, Comprising Twenty-Two Engravings from Original Drawings by William Daniel*. London: Edward Churton.

Champion, C. 1993. "L'image de l'Inde dans la fiction populaire française aux XIXème et XXème siècles." Pp. 43–68 in *Rêver l'Asie, Exotisme et littérature coloniale aux Indes, en Indochine et en Insulinde*. Paris: EHESS.

————. 1995. "Entre la caste et la secte: un quissa du répertoire des Bhartrhari Jogi musulmans de la région de Gorakhpur (Uttar Pradesh)." Pp. 25–41 in *Les ruses du salut*, ed. Marie-Louise Reiniche and H. Stern. Purusartha 17. Paris: EHESS.

Clémentin-Ojha Catherine. 1992. "Qu'est-ce qu'être orthodoxe? Le cas des ascètes vishnouites du *catuh sampradayah*." In *Ascèse et renoncement en Inde, ou la solitude bien ordonnée*, ed. Serge Bouez. Paris: L'Harmattan.

————. 1994. "L'initiation de la Devi, violence et non-violence dans un récit vishnouite." Pp. 141–54 in *Violences et non-violences en Inde*, ed. Denis Vidal, Gilles Tarabout, and Eric Meyer. Purusartha 16. Paris: EHESS.

Clive, John. 1987. *Macaulay: The Shaping of the Historian*. Cambridge: Harvard University Press.

Coburn, T. B. 1988. *Devi-Mahatmya, The Crystallization of the Goddess Tradition*. Delhi: Motilal Banarsidass.

Cohn, B. S. 1964. "The role of the Gosains in the Economy of 18th and 19th Century Upper India." *The Indian Economic and Social History Review* 1 (4): 175–82

————. 1987a. "The British in Benares: A Nineteenth Century Society." In *An Anthropologist among the Historians and Other Essays*. Delhi: Oxford University Press.

————. 1987b. "Notes on the History of the Study of Indian Society and Culture." In *An Anthropologist among the Historians and Other Essays*. Delhi: Oxford University Press.

————. 1987c. "The Recruitment and Training of British Civil Service Servants in India, 1600–1860." In *An Anthropologist among the Historians and Other Essays*. Delhi: Oxford University Press.

————. 1987d. "The Census, Social Structure, and Objectification in South Asia." In *An Anthropologist among the Historians and Other Essays*. Delhi: Oxford University Press.

Cooter, R. 1984. *The Cultural Meaning of Popular Science: Phrenology and the Organization of Consent in Nineteenth-Century Britain*. Cambridge History of Medicine. Cambridge: Cambridge University Press.

Crooke, W. 1907. *Natives of Northern India*. The Natives Races of the British Empire. London: Constable.

————. 1968. *The Popular Religion and Folklore of Northern India*. 2 vols. Delhi: Munshiram Manoharlal.

————. 1974. *The Tribes and Castes of the North Western India*. 4 vols. 1896. Reprint, Delhi: Cosmo.

Cunningham, A. 1882. *Report of a Tour in Bihar and Bengal in 1879–1880, from Patna to Sunargaon*. Archaeological Survey of India, vol. 15. Calcutta: Office of the Superintendent of Government Printing.

Das, Veena, 1985. "The Goddess and the Demon, An Analysis of the Devi Mahatmya." *Manushi* 30:28–32.

The Deceivers. 1988. United States: Merchant Ivory Productions. Film.

Delamare, Georges. 1938. *Désordres à Pondichéry*. Paris: Les Éditions de la France.

Deleury, G. 1991. *Les Indes florissantes.* Paris: Laffont.

De Quincey, Thomas. 1925. *The Arts of Cheating, Swindling, and Murder.* New York: Arnold.

————. 1963. *De l'assassinat considéré comme un des Beaux Arts.* Translated by Charles Baudelaire. Paris: Nouvel Office d'Édition.

Digby, S. 1986. "The Sufi Shaikh in Medieval India." Pp. 57–78 in *Islam en Asie du Sud,* ed. M. Gaborieau. Purusartha 9. Paris: EHESS.

Dirks, N. 1986. *The Hollow Crown: Ethnohistory of a Little Kingdom in South Asia.* Cambridge South Asian Studies. Cambridge: Cambridge University Press.

Dodwell, H. H., ed. 1968. *The Cambridge History of India.* Vol 5, *1497–1858.* Delhi: Chand and Company.

Drummond, R. 1808. *Illustrations of the Grammatical Parts of the Guzerattee, Mahratta, and English Languages.* Bombay: Courier.

Dubois, Abbé J. A. 1906. *Hindu Manners, Customs, and Ceremonies.* 1825. Reprint, Oxford: Clarendon.

Duclos, Denis. 1994. "Pourquoi tant de tueurs en série aux États-Unis?" *Le Monde Diplomatique* 26 (August): 26–27.

Dumont, Louis. 1966. *Homo hierarchicus.* Paris: Gallimard [This version is longer than the English language one. *Trans.*]

————. 1970. *Homo Hierarchicus: the Caste System and Its Implications.* Translated by Mark Sainsbury. Chicago: The University of Chicago Press.

————. 1986. *Essays on Individualism: Modern Ideology in Anthropological Perspective.* Chicago: The University of Chicago Press.

Durand-Dastes, François. 1968. *Géographie de l'Inde: Que sais-je?* Paris: Presses Universitaires de France.

Eck, D. L. 1993. *Banaras, City of Light.* 1983. Reprint, Harmondsworth, Great Britain: Penguin.

Edwardes, Michael. 1969. *Glorious sahibs. The Romantic as Empire-Builder, 1799–1838.* New York: Taplinger.

————. 1988. *The Sahibs and the Lotus.* London: Constable.

Embree, A.T. 1962. *Charles Grant and British Rule in India.* London.

Farquhar, J. N. 1908–1926. Entry "Thags." Pp. 259–60 in *Encyclopaedia of Religion and Ethics,* vol. 12, ed. J. Hastings. New York: Charles Scribner and Sons.

————. 1925. "The Fighting Ascetics of India." *Bulletin of the Rylands Library* (Manchester) 9:431–52.

Farrère, Claude. 1935. *L'Inde perdue.* Paris: E. Flammarion.

Favret-Saada, J. 1977. *Les mots, la mort, les sorts.* Paris: Gallimard.

Finley, M. I. 1990. *The Use and Abuse of History.* Harmondsworth, Great Britain: Penguin.

Fisher, M. H. 1981. "British Expansion in North India: The Role of the Resident in Awadh." *The Indian Economic and Social History Review* 18 (1): 69–82.

Foucault, Michel. 1966. *Les mots et les choses.* Paris, Gallimard.

————. 1979. *Discipline and Punish: The Birth of the Prison.* Translated by Alan Sheridan. New York: Vintage.

————. 1999. *Les Anormaux: Cours au Collège de France, 1974–1975.* Collection Hautes Études. Paris: Gallimard/Le Seuil.

Fourcade, Marie. 1994. "Les dénommées 'tribus criminelles.'" Pp. 187–212 in *Violences et non-violences en Inde.* Purusartha 16. Paris: EHESS.

Frankenstein. 1910. United States: Edison Films.

Frankenstein. 1931. United States: Universal.

Freitag, Sandria B. 1985. "Collective Crime and Authority in North India." Pp. 140–63 in *Crime and Criminality in British India,* ed. A. A. Yang. Tucson: The University of Arizona Press.

Fryer, John. 1873. *A New Account of East India and Persia, in Eight Letters, Being Nine Years Travels, Begun 1672, and Finished 1681.* 1698. Reprint, London: Trübner and Company.

Frykenberg, R. E. 1969. *Land Control and Social Structure in Indian History.* Madison: University of Wisconsin Press.

Gaborieau, Marc, ed. 1986. Introduction to *Islam en Asie du Sud.* Purusartha 9. Paris: EHESS.

Gait, Edward A. 1967. *A History of Assam.* 1907. Reprint, Calcutta: Thacker, Spink and Company.

Garbe, Richard Karl von. 1903. "Über die Thugs." *Beiträge zur indischen Kulturgeschichte,* 185–98.

Geertz, Clifford. 1983. *Local Knowledge.* New York: Basic Books.

Ghosh, J. M.. 1923. *The Sannyasis in Mymensingh.* Dacca: P. B. Chakrabarty.

Girardet, Raoul. 1972. *L'idée coloniale en France de 1871 à 1962.* Paris: La Table Ronde.

Ginzburg, Carlo. 1989. *Clues, Myths, and the Historical Method.* Translated by John and Anne C. Tedeschi. Baltimore, Md.: Johns Hopkins University Press.

————. 1983. *The Night Battles: Witchcraft and Agrarian Cults in the Sixteenth and Seventeenth Centuries.* Translated by John and Anne Tedeschi. Baltimore, Md.: The Johns Hopkins University Press.

Gonda, J. 1965. *Les religions de l'Inde.* Vol. 2, *L'hindouisme récent.* Paris: Payot.

————. 1976. *Visnuism and Sivaism.* 1970. Reprint, Delhi: Munshiram Manoharlal.

Goody, Jack. 1977. *The Domestication of the Savage Mind.* Cambridge: Cambridge University Press.

Gordon, Stewart N. 1969. "Scarf and Sword: Thugs, Marauders and State Formation in 18th Century Malwa." *The Indian Economic and Social History Review* 6 (4): 403–29.

Goudriaan, Teun and Gupta, Sanjukta. 1981. *Hindu Tantric and Sakta Literature.* History of Indian Literature, vol. 2, fasc. 2. Wiesbaden: Harrassowitz.

Grant, Charles. 1812–1813 and 1831–1832. *Observations on the State of Society among the Asiatic Subjects of Great-Britain, Particularly with Respect to Morals; and on the Means of Improving It* (written chiefly in the year 1792). London: Parliamentary Papers 282, 734, and General Appendix no. 1, pp. 3–92.

Grierson, G. A. 1926. *Bihar Peasant Life.* Patan: Superintendent Government Printing, Bihar and Orissa.

————, ed. 1973. *Linguistic Survey of India.* Vol. 1, part 1. 1927. Reprint, Delhi: Motilal Banarsidass.

Grousset, R. 1929. *Sur les traces du Bouddha.* Paris.

Guha, Ranajit., ed. 1982. "On some Aspects of the Historiography of Colonial India." *Subaltern Studies* 1:1–7.

Guha, Sumit. 1985. *The Agrarian Economy of the Bombay Deccan, 1818–1941.* Delhi: Oxford University Press.

Gunga Din. 1939. United States: RKO Pictures.

Halbfass, Wilhelm. 1983. "Kumarila on Ahimsa and Dharma." In *Studies in Kumarila and Sanakra.* Studien zur Indologie und Iranistic. Monographie 9. Reinbeck: Wezler.

————. 1984. "Indian Philosophers on the Plurality of Indian Traditions." Pp. 58–64 in *Identity and Divisions in Cults and Sects in South Asia,* ed. P. Gaeffke and D. A. Utz. Philadelphia: Department of South Asia Regional Studies.

————. 1991. "Vedic Apologetics, Ritual Killing, and the Foundation of Ethics." Pp. 88–129 in *Tradition and Reflection: Explorations in Indian Thought.* New York: State University of New York.

Halévi, Elie. 1928. *The Growth of Philosophic Radicalism.* Translated by Mary Morris. London: Faber & Gwyer.

Hartman, C. G. 1969. *Aspects de la déesse Kali dans son culte et dans la littérature indienne ancienne.* Helsinki: Helsingfors.

Hawley, J. S. and D. M. Wulff. 1984. *The Divine Consort.* Delhi: Motilal Banarsidass.

Heber, Reginald. 1983. *Narrative of a Journey through the Upper Provinces of India, from Calcutta to Bombay, 1924–1925.* London: n.p.

Hervey, General C. 1892. *Some Records of Crime.* 2 vols. London: Sampson, Low, Marston, and Company.

Hilberg, Raoul. 1988. *La destruction des Juifs d'Europe.* Paris: Fayard.

Hiltebeitel, A., ed. 1989. *Criminal Gods and Demon Devotees.* Albany: State University of New York Press.

Hjejle, Benedict. 1979. *The Social Legislation of the East India Company: A Study in British Administration.* Ph.D. dissertation. University of Copenhagen.

Hobbes, Thomas. 1991. *Leviathan.* Edited by Richard Tuck. Cambridge, U.K.: Cambridge University Press.

Hobsbawm, E. J. 1969. *Bandits.* London: Weindenfeld and Nicolson.

Hughes, R. 1988. *The Fatal Shore: A History of the Transplantation of Convicts to Australia, 1787–1868.* London: Pan.

Hulin, M. 1992. "*Dharma des renonçants et renoncement au dharma.*" Pp. 25–39 in *Ascèse et renoncement en Inde,* ed. S. Bouez. Paris: L'Harmattan.

Hutton, James. 1857. *A Popular Account of the Thugs and Dacoits, the Hereditary Garroters and Gang-Robbers of India.* London: W. M. H. Allen.

I Misteri della giungla nera (The mysteries of the black jungle). Italy: Republic Pictures. Made-for-television miniseries.

Indiana Jones and the Last Crusade. 1989. United States: Paramount.

Indiana Jones and the Temple of Doom. 1984. United States: Paramount.

Ingham, K. 1956. *Reformers in India, 1793–1833: An Account of the Work of Christian Missionaries on Behalf of Social Reformers.* Cambridge: Cambridge University Press.

Joi Baba Felunath (The elephant god). 1978. India: RDB Productions. Film.

Kane, P. V. 1968–1975. *History of Dharmasastra (Ancient and Mediaeval Religious and Civil Law),* 2nd rev. ed. Vol. 1–5. 1930–1962. Reprint, Poona: Bhandarkar Oriental Research Institute.

Kaye, J. W. 1966. *The Administration of the East India Company: A History of Indian Progress.* Edited and with an introduction by O. P. Bathnagar. 1853. Reprint, Allahabad: Kitab Mahal.

Kincaid, Dennis. 1973. *British Social Life in India, 1608–1937.* 1938. Reprint, London: Routledge and Kegan Paul.

Kinsley, D. 1987. *Hindu Goddesses, Visions of the Divine Feminine in the Hindu Religious Tradition.* Delhi: Motilal Banarsidass.

Kipling, R. 1930. *Soldiers Three and Other Stories.* London: Standard Book Company.

———. 1982a. "Gunga Din." Pp. 615–18 in *The Portable Kipling,* ed. Irving Howe. Harmondsworth: Penguin.

———. 1982b. "The Man Who Would Be King." Pp. 28–67 in *The Portable Kipling,* ed. Irving Howe. Harmondsworth, Great Britain: Penguin.

Kolff, Dirk H. A. 1971. "Sannyasi Trader-Soldiers." *The Indian Economic and Social History Review* 8 (2): 213–18.

———. 1990. *Naukar, Rajput, and Sepoy: The Ethno-History of the Military Labour Market in Hindustan, 1450–1850.* Cambridge: Cambridge University Press.

Lacassin, F. 1983. "Préface." In *Le Juif errant,* by Eugène Suë. Bouquins. Paris: Laffont.

Laws of Manu. 1964. Edited and translated by G. Bühler. 1886. Reprint, Delhi: Motilal Banarsidass.

Lecercle, Jean-Jacques. 1988. *Frankenstein: mythe et philosophie.* Paris: Presses Universitaires de France.

Lévi, Sylvain. 1966. *La doctrine du sacrifice dans les Brahmanas.* 1898. Reprint, Paris: Presses Universitaires de France.

Lewis, B. 1982. *Les Assassins.* 1967. Reprint, Paris: Berger-Levrault.

Lingat, R. 1967. *Les sources du droit dans le système traditionnel de l'Inde.* Paris: Mouton.

Lombard, Denys. 1993. *Rêver l'Inde: Exotisme et littérature coloniale aux Indes, en Indochine et en Insulinde.* Edited by C. Champion and H. Chambert-Loir. Paris: EHESS.

Lorenzen, David N. 1978. "Warrior Ascetics in Indian History." *Journal of the American Oriental Society* 98 (1): 61–75.

———. 1991. *The Kapalikas and the Kalamukhas: Two Lost Shivaite Sects,* rev. ed. 1972. Reprint, Delhi: Motilal Banarsidass.

MacMunn, G. 1936. *Tempête sur l'Inde, Les activités secrètes et l'Intelligence Service aux Indes depuis la guerre mondiale.* Paris: Payot.

Madhava-Vidyaranya. n.d. *Sankara-dig-vijaya.* Madras: Shri Ramakrishna Math.

Mahapurush (The holy man). 1965. Second film of a double bill titled *Kapurush-O-Marapurush* (The coward and the holy man). India: RDB Productions.

Malamoud, Charles. 1972. "Observations sur la notion de reste dans le brahmanisme." *Wiener Zeitschrift für die Kunde Südasiens* 17:6–26.

———. 1976a. "Terminer le sacrifice." Pp. 155–204 in *Le sacrifice dans l'Inde ancienne.* Paris: Presses Universitaires de France.

———. 1976b. "Village et forêt dans l'idéologie de l'Inde brâhmanique." *Archives européennes de sociologie* 17 (1): 3–20.

———, ed. 1980. *La Dette.* Purusartha 4. Paris: EHESS.

———. 1986. "Les morts sans visage. Remarques sur l'idéologie funéraire dans le brahmanisme." Pp. 441–53 in *La mort, les morts dans les sociétés anciennes,* ed. J.-P. Vernant. Cambridge: Cambridge University Press, and Paris: MSH.

———. 1987. "Spéculations indiennes sur le sexe du sacrifice." *L'Écrit du temps* 18:7–28.

———. 1994. "La dissuasion dans l'Inde ancienne." Pp. 53–60 in *Violences et non-violences en Inde.* Purusartha 16. Paris: EHESS.

Malcolm, John. 1972. *A Memoir of Central India Including Malwa and Adjoining Provinces.* 2 vols. 1832. Reprint, Shannon, Ireland: Irish University Press.

Mallisson, F. 1992. "La secte ismaélienne des Nisari ou Satpanthi en Inde: hétérodoxie hindoue ou musulmane?" Pp. 105–13 in *Ascèse et renoncement en Inde,* ed. S. Bouez. Paris: L'Harmattan.

Maltby, T. J. 1882. *The Ganjam Manual.* Madras: n.p.

Marglin, Frédérique. A. 1985. *Wives of the God-King.* Delhi: Oxford University Press.

Markandeya Purana, The. 1969. Translated and with notes by F. E. Pargiter. 1904. Reprint, Varanasi: Indological Book House.

Markovitz, Claude. 1991. "L'État colonial vu par les historiens." Pp. 193–206 in *De la royauté à l'État dans le monde indien.* Purusartha 13. Paris: EHESS.

Marshall, P. J. 1981. "A free Though Conquering People: Britain and Asia in the Eighteenth Century." Inaugural lecture, King's College, London.

Masters, John. 1952. *The Deceivers.* London: Sphere.

———. 1954. *Bhowani Junction.* New York: Viking.

Matringe, D., ed. 1988. *Hir Varis Sah, Poème pendjabi du XVIIIème siècle.* Vol 1.

Introduction, transliteration, translation, and commentaries by D. Matringe. Pondichéry: Institut Français d'Indologie.

Mayhew, H. 1867. *Criminal Prisons of London.* London: Griffin, Bohn and Company.

Mays, J. B. 1967. *Crime and the Social Structure.* London: Faber and Faber.

Mehrotra, R. R. 1977. *Sociology of Secret Languages.* Simla: Indian Institute of Advanced Studies.

Méry. 1859. *Les Étrangleurs de l'Inde.* Paris: Louis Chappe, Librairie Éditeur.

Metcalf, T. R. 1964. *The Aftermath of Revolt: India 1857–1870.* Princeton: Princeton University Press.

————. 1995. *Ideologies of the Raj.* Cambridge: Cambridge University Press.

Miles, A. 1937. *The Land of the Lingam.* London: The Paternoster Library.

Mill, James. 1826. *The History of British India.* 6 vols. London: Baldwin, Cradock and Joy.

Mill, John Stewart, and Bentham, Jeremy. 1987. *Utilitarianism and Other Essays.* London: Penguin Books.

Mirabeau, Octave. 1957. *Le jardin des supplices.* 1899. Reprint, Paris: Fasquelles.

Mirsky, N. 1986. Preface to *Confessions of a Thug,* by Meadows Taylor. Oxford: Oxford University Press.

Mitter, Partha. 1977. *Much Maligned Monsters: History of European Reactions to Indian Art.* Oxford: Clarendon.

Mookerjee, Ajit. 1988. *Kali, the Feminine Force.* London: Thames and Hudson.

Murr, Sylvia. 1987. *L'Indologie du Père Coeuedoux, stratégies, apologétique et scientificité.* Vol. 2 of *L'Inde philosophique entre Bossuet et Voltaire.* Paris: École Française d'Extrême-Orient.

Muthiah, S., and R. Ramachandran. 1990. *An Atlas of India.* Delhi: Oxford University Press.

Nandy, A. 1983. *The Intimate Enemy: Loss and Recovery of Self under Colonialism.* Delhi: Oxford University Press.

Nigam, Sanjay. "A Social History of a Colonial Stereotype: The Criminal Tribes and Castes, 1871–1930." Ph.D. dissertation, School of Oriental and African Studies, London.

————. 1990. "Disciplining and Policing the 'Criminal Tribes' by Birth." *Indian Economic and Social History Review* 27 (1): 131–164.

Oddie, G. A. 1986. "Hook-Swinging and Popular Religion in South Asia during the Nineteenth Century." *The Indian Economic and Social History Review* 23 (1): 93–106.

O'Flaherty, W. D. 1973. *Asceticism and Eroticism in the Mythology of Siva.* London: Oxford University Press.

————. 1988. *The Origin of Evil in Hindu Mythology.* Delhi: Motilal Banarsidass.

Padoux, A. 1992. "Sivaïsme et hétérodoxie. A propos des 'sectes sivaïtes hétérodoxes.'" Pp. 59–69 in *Ascèse et renoncement en Inde,* ed. S. Bouez. Paris: l'Harmattan.

Parks, Fanny. 1850. *Wanderings of a Pilgrim in Search of the Picturesque During Four and Twenty Years in the East with Revelations of Life in the Zenana.* 2 vols. London: Pelham Richardson.

Paz, Octavio. 1983. *Rire et Pénitence.* Paris: Gallimard.

Peggs, J. 1828. *India's Cries to British Humanity, Relative to Suttee, etc.* London: n.p.

Pennant, T. 1798. *The View of Hindoostan.* 2 vols. London: n.p.

Perrot, M., ed. 1980. *L'impossible prison, Recherches sur le système pénitenciaire au XIXème siècle.* Paris: Seuil.

Pfirrmann, Gustav. 1970. Religiöser Charakter und Organisation der Thag-Brûderschaften. Ph.D. dissertation, Universität zu Tübingen.

Philips, C. H. 1977. *The Correspondence of Lord William Cavendish Bentinck, Governor-General of India, 1828–1835.* Edited and with an introduction by C. H. Philips. Vol. 1, 1828–1831; vol. 2, 1832–1835. Oxford: Oxford University Press.

Plessis, Gérard. 1979. *De la Fête impériale au Mur des Fédérés 1852–1871.* Paris: Seuil.

Pont-Jest, René de. 1879. *Le procès des Thugs.* Paris: Paul Dupont.

Potts, E. D. 1967. *British Baptist Missionaries in India, 1793–1837. A History of Serampore and His Missions.* Cambridge: Cambridge University Press.

Pouchepadass, Jacques. 1979. "Délinquance de fonction et normalisation coloniale: les tribus criminelles dans l'Inde britannique." Pp. 122–54 in *Les marginaux et les exclus de l'histoire.* Cahiers Jussieu 5. Paris: 10/18.

——. 1991. "L'État et la structuration de l'espace politique dans l'Inde coloniale." Pp. 25–53 in *De la royauté à l'État dans le monde indien,* ed. J. Pouchepadass and H. Stern. Purusartha 13. Paris: EHESS.

Praz, Mario. 1978. Introductory essay. Pp. 7–34 in *Three Gothic Novels, ed.* P. Fairclough. Harmondsworth, Great Britain: Penguin.

Raiders of the Lost Ark. 1981. United States: Paramount.

Ramsdell, D. B. 1983. "Asia Askew: U.S. Best-Sellers on Asia, 1931–1980." *Bulletin of Concerned Asian Scholars* 15 (4): 2–25.

Rawson, P. 1973. *Tantra: The Indian Cult of Ecstasy.* London: Thames and Hudson.

Reeves, P. D. 1971. Introduction to *Sleeman in Oudh,* ed. P. D. Reeves. Cambridge: Cambridge University Press.

Reiniche, Marie-Louise 1995a. Introduction to *Les ruses du salut,* ed. M.-L. Reiniche and H. Stern. Purusartha 17. Paris: EHESS.

——. 1995b. "Le sel de la caste, Dévotion sivaïte dans le sud tamoul." Pp. 157–81 in *Les ruses du salut,* ed. M.-L. Reiniche and H. Stern. Purusartha 17. Paris: EHESS.

Renou, Louis. 1950. *La civilisation de l'Inde ancienne.* Paris: Flammarion.

——, ed. 1963. *Contes du vampire.* Translated from the Sanskrit and annotated by Louis Renou. Paris: Gallimard.

Renou, Louis, and Filliozat, J. 1953. *L'Inde classique.* Vol. 1. Paris, Jean Maisonneuve.

——. 1985. *L'Inde classique.* Vol. 2. Paris: Imprimerie Nationale.

Reynolds. 1837. "Notes on the T'hags." *The Journal of the Royal Asiatic Society* 4:200–13.

Ricoeur, Paul. 1985. *Temps et récit.* 3 vols. Paris: Seuil.

Rosselli, J. 1974. *Lord W. Bentinck: The Making of a Liberal Imperialist, 1774–1839.* London: Sussex University Press.

Roy, M. P. 1973. *Origin, Growth, and Suppression of the Pindaris.* New Delhi: Sterling.

Russell, R. V. 1969. *The Tribes and Castes of the Central Provinces of India,* 4 vols. 1915. Reprint, Oosterhout, Holland: Anthropological Publications.

Salgari, Emilio. 1985a. *I Misteri della giungla nera.* 1895. Reprint, Milan: Arnoldi Mondadori.

——. 1985b. *Le Avventure di Sandokan.* 1901–1907. Reprint, Milan: Arnoldi Mondadori.

Sangar, S. P. 1967. *Crime and Punishment in Mughal India.* Delhi: Sterling.

Sanskrit-English Dictionary, A. 1979. Edited by Sir Monier Williams. 1899. Reprint, Delhi: Motilal Banarsidass.

Sapir, E. 1963. *Selected Writings of Edward Sapir.* Berkeley: University of California Press.

Schmidt, F. 1988. "Entre Juifs et Grecs: Le modèle indien." Pp. 33–47 in *L'Inde et l'imaginaire*. Purusartha 11. Paris: EHESS.

Schwab, R. 1950. *La Renaissance orientale*. Paris: Payot.

Sen, S. P. 1979. *Social and Religious Movements in the Nineteenth and Twentieth Centuries*. Calcutta: Institute of Historical Studies.

Sharma, C. R. 1976. "Aspects of Public Administration in Northern India in the First Half of the 17th Century." *Journal of Indian History* 54:107–15.

Shelley, Mary W. 1969. *Frankenstein; or, The Modern Prometheus*. Edited by M. K. Joseph. 1818. Reprint, London: Oxford University Press.

Sherwood, R. 1820. Reprint. "Of the murderers called Phansigars." *Asiatic Research* 13. Original article, "Of the Murderers Called Phansigars." *Madras Literary Gazette*, 1819.

The Shivapurana, 1981. Translated by a board of scholars, edited by J. L. Shastri. Ancient Indian Tradition and Mythology. Delhi: Motilal Banarsidass.

Shulman, D. 1981. "On South Indian Bandits and Kings." *Indian Economic and Social History Review* 17 (3): 283–306.

Siegel, Lee. 1991. *The Net of Magic, Wonders, and Deceptions in India*. Chicago: The University of Chicago Press.

Singha, Radhika. 1993. "'Providential' Circumstances: The Thuggee Campaign of the 1830s and Legal Innovation." *Modern Asian Studies* 27 (1): 83–146.

———. 1998. *A Despotism of Law. Crime and Justice in Early colonial India*. Delhi: Oxford University Press.

Sleeman, James L. 1933. *Thug, or a Million Murders*. London: Sampson, Low, Marston, and Company.

———. 1934. *La Secte secrète des Thugs, Le culte de l'assassinat aux Indes*. Paris: Payot.

Sleeman, William H. 1830. Anonymous letter "to the Editor of the *Calcutta Literary Gazette*." *Calcutta Literary Gazette*, 16 October.

———. 1836. *Ramaseeana, or a Vocabulary of the Peculiar language Used by the Thugs with an Introduction and an Appendix Descriptive of the System Pursued by That Fraternity and of the Measures Which Have Been Adopted by the Supreme Government for Its Suppression*. Calcutta: Military Orphan Press.

———. 1839. *A Report on the System of Megpunnaism, or the Murder of Indigent Parents for Their Young Children Who Are Sold as Slaves*. N.p.: Serampore Press.

———. 1840. *Report on the Depredations Committed by the Thug Gangs of Upper and Central India from the Cold Season of 1836–37 down to Their Gradual Suppression, under the Operations of the Measures Adopted against Them by the Supreme Government in the Year 1839*. Calcutta: Bengal Military Orphan Press.

———. 1849. *Report on Budhuk Alias Bagree Dacoits and Other Gang Robbers by Hereditary Profession*. Calcutta: Bengal Military Orphan Press.

———. 1858. *A Journey through the Kingdom of Oude in 1849–1850*. 2 vols. London: Richard Bentley.

———. 1889. *Wolves Nurturing Children in Their Dens*. Oxford: Bodley Library, Per 18933 c. 395, 3rd series, XII, pp. 87–97.

———. 1915. *Rambles and Recollections of an Indian Official*. Edited and annotated by V. A. Smith. 1915. Reprint, Oxford: Oxford University Press.

Sleeman in Oudh. 1971. An abridgement of W. H. Sleeman's *A Journey through the Kingdom of Oude in 1849–1850*. Edited and with an introduction and notes by P. D. Reeves. Cambridge: Cambridge University Press.

Smith, K. J. M. 1988. *James Fitzjames Stephen, Portrait of a Victorian Rationalist*. Cambridge: Cambridge University Press.

Smith, Vincent A. 1987. *The Oxford History of India*, 4th ed. Edited by Percival Spear. 1919. Reprint, New Delhi: Oxford University Press.

Soltykoff , Alexis de. 1851. *Voyage dans l'Inde*. 2 vols. Paris: Curmer and Lecou.

Somadeva Bhatta. 1968. *The Ocean of Story, Being C. H. Tawney's Translation of Somadeva's Katha Sarit Sagara (or Ocean of Streams of Stories)*. 10 vols. 1924–1928. Reprint, Delhi: Motilal Banarsidass.

Sperber, Dan. 1982. *Le savoir des anthropologues. Trois essais*. Paris: Hermann.

Spry, H. H. 1832–1834. "Some Accounts of the Gang-Murderers of Central India Commonly Called Thugs." *The Phrenological Journal and Miscellany* 8:511–30.

————. 1837. *Modern India with Illustrations of the Resources and Capabilities of Hindoustan*. 2 vols. London: Whittaker and Company.

Srivastav, P. N. 1968. *Gazetteer of India, Madhya Pradesh, Jubbulpur*. Bhopal: Gazetteer Department.

Srivastava, R. C. 1971. *Development of the Judicial System in India under the East India Company, 1833–1858*. Lucknow, India: Lucknow Publishing House.

Stein, B. 1980. *Peasant State and Society in Medieval South India*. New Delhi: Oxford University Press.

————. 1985. "State Formation and Economy Reconsidered." *Modern Asian Studies* 19 (3): 387–413.

Stietencron, H. von. 1989. "Hinduism: On the Proper Use of a Deceptive Term." In *Hinduism reconsidered*, ed. G. D. Sontheimer and H. Kulke. New Delhi: Manohar.

Stocking, G. W. Jr. 1987. *Victorian Anthropology*. New York: The Free Press.

Stoczkowski, Wiktor. 1992. "Les origines de l'homme, entre l'imaginaire commun et savant. Épistémologie, narration et banalités collectives." *Gradhiva* 11:67–80.

Stokes, Eric. 1959. *English Utilitarians and India*. Oxford: Clarendon.

————. 1986. *The Peasant Armed: The Indian Revolt of 1857*. Oxford: Clarendon.

Suë, Eugène. 1983. *Le Juif errant*. 1844–1845. Reprint, Paris: Laffont.

Tadié, A. 1994. Introduction to *Le livre de la jungle*, by Rudyard Kipling. Paris: Garnier-Flammarion.

Taguieff, P.-A. 1999. *La force du préjugé, Éssai sur le racisme et ses doubles*. Collection Tel. Paris: Gallimard.

Tartakov, G. M. 1979. "Who Calls the Snake Charmer's Tune?" *Bulletin of Concerned American Scholars* 2 (2): 26–39.

Taylor, Meadows. 1986a. *Confessions of a Thug*. With a preface by Nick Mirsky. 1839. Reprint, Oxford: University Press.

————. 1986b. *The Story of My Life*. Edited by his daughter. 1882. Reprint, New Delhi: Asian Educational Service.

————. 1995. *Mémoires d'un Thug*. Translated by Lucienne Escoube. 1942. Reprint, Paris: Phébus.

Tessier, H. n.d. *Les Étrangleurs de l'Inde*. Paris: L. Boulanger.

Thakur, U. 1978. *Homicide in India, Ancient and Medieval Period*. New Delhi: Abhinav.

Thapar, R. 1989. "Imagined Religious Communities, Ancient History and the Search for a Hindu Identity." *Modern Asian Studies* 23 (2): 209–31.

Thévenot, Jean de. 1684. *Voyages de Mr de Thévenot, contenant la relation de l'Indostan, des nouveaux Mogols et des autres Peuples et Pays des Indes*. Paris: Biestkins.

Thomas, P. 1988. *Secrets of Sorcery Spells and Pleasure Cults of India*. 1966. Reprint, Bombay: D. B. Taraporevala Sons and Company.

Thornton, E. 1837. *Illustration of the History and Practices of the Thugs and Notices of Some of the Proceedings of the Government of India for the Suppression of the Crime of Thuggee*. London: W. H. Allen.

Thurston, E. 1965. *Castes and Tribes of Southern India*. 7 vols. 1909. Reprint, New York: Johnson Reprints.

Tod, J. 1971. *Annals and Antiquities of Rajasthan*. 3 vols. 1825. Reprint, Delhi: Motilal Banarsidass.

Touraine, A. 1974. *Pour la sociologie*. Points. Paris: Seuil.

Trautmann, T. R. 1992. "British Ethnologies of India." Lecture given at the Centre d'Études de l'Inde.

Trevelyan, C. E. 1837. "The Thugs or Secret Murderers of India." *The Edinburgh Review* 64:357–395.

Tuker, Francis. 1961. *The Yellow Scarf: An Account of Thuggee and Its Suppression*. London: J. M. Dent.

van der Veer, Peter. 1994. *Religious Nationalisms*. Berkeley: University of California Press.

van Woerkens, Martine. 1992. "Le cinéma des Thugs." *Les Temps modernes*, nos. 552–553:287–303.

———. 1993. "Un procès des Thugs en 1887 et Les Confessions d'un Thug ou les trois femmes de Amir Ali." In *Rêver l'Asie*, ed. Denys Lombard. Paris: EHESS.

van Woerkens-Todorov, Martine. 1988. "Trois barbares en Asie: une énième histoire de Thugs. Pp. 257–79 in *L'Inde et l'imaginaire*. Purusartha 11. Paris: EHESS.

Varady, Robert G. 1979. "North Indian Banjaras: their Evolution as Transporters." *South Asia* 2 (1 and 2): 1–18.

Varma, D. P. 1966. *The Gothic Flame, Being a History of the Gothic Novel in England*. New York: Russell and Russell.

Varma, R. 1962. *Manak Hindi Kosh (Hindi-Hindi Dictionary)*. 5 vols. Allahabad: Hindi Sahitya Sammelan.

Vergati, A. 1994. "Le roi et les déesses: la fête de Navaratri et Dasahra au Rajasthan." *Journal Asiatique* 282 (1): 125–146.

Vernes, Henri. 1950. *La marque de Kali*. Paris: Marabout Junior.

———. 1962. *La couronne de Golconde*. Paris: Marabout Junior.

———. 1964. *Les joyaux du maharajah*. Paris: Marabout Junior.

Veyne, Paul. 1971. *Comment on écrit l'histoire*. Paris: Seuil.

———. 1983. *Les Grecs croient-ils en leurs mythes?* Paris: Seuil.

Ward, W. 1811. *An Account of the Writings, Religions and Manners of the Hindus*. London: n.p.

Watters, T. n.d. *On Yuan Chwang's Travels in India (A.D. 629–645)*. Delhi: Munshiram Manoharlal.

Weber, J. 1988. *Les Établissements français en Inde au XIXe siècle (1816–1914)*. Paris: Librairie de l'Inde.

———. 1993. "La société franco-indienne en péril." Pp. 381–401 in *Rêver l'Asie*. Paris, EHESS.

Weber, M. 1959. *Le savant et le politique*. With a preface by Raymond Aron. Paris: Union Générale d'Éditions.

Weinberger-Thomas, C. 1989. "Cendres d'immortalité: la crémation des veuves en Inde." *Archives des Sciences Sociales de Religions*, no. 67:9–51.

———. 1999. *Ashes of Immortality: Widow-Burning in India*. Translated by Jeffrey Melman and D. Gordon White. Chicago: University of Chicago Press.

Wiener, M. J. 1990. *Reconstructing the Criminal: Culture, Law, and Policy in England, 1830–1914*. Cambridge: Cambridge University Press.

Wilson, H. H. 1977. *Religious Sects of the Hindus*. 1861. Reprint, New Delhi: Cosmo.

Woodruff, J. G. 1929. *Shakti and shakta: Essays and Addresses on the Shakta Rantrashastra*. Madras: Ganesh and Company.

Woodruff, J. G. (Arthur Avallon). 1982. *Hymns to the Goddess and Hymn to Kali.* 1913. Reprint, Madras: Ganesh and Cy.

Wright, C. 1854. *Life in India.* Boston: C. Wright.

Yang, Anand A. 1985. *Crime and Criminality in British India.* Tucson: University of Arizona Press.

Yule, Henry, and Burnell, A. C. 1968. *Hobson-Jobson; A Glossary of Colloquial Anglo-Indian Words and Phrases, and of Kindred Terms, Etymological, Historical, Geographical, and Discursive,* 2nd ed. Edited by William Crooke. Delhi: Munshiram Manoharlal.

Zauberman, Yolande. 1989. *Caste criminelle* (Criminal caste). Paris: Les Films du Paradoxe/La Sept. Black-and-white documentary.

Zimmer, H. 1953. *Les philosophies de l'Inde.* Paris: Payot.

INDEX